D0984710

What is it that troubles and preoccupies us about the anxieties and anguishes of social and private life? Have advances in the disciplines of psychoanalysis, psychology or the social sciences in general ministered to our needs in these areas? In this forcefully argued collection of essays, Frank Cioffi examines Wittgenstein's reflections on the comparative claims of clarification and empirical enquiry. Though writing from a position of admiration and indebtedness, he expresses reservations as to the limits Wittgenstein places on the relevance and desirability of empirical knowledge. His discussions extend from Wittgenstein's reflections on human sacrifice and other ritual practices dealt with by Frazer to Freud's account of the sources of anxiety, depression, dreams and laughter. He asks both whether it is empirical investigation or more lucid reflection that these phenomena demand, and what kind of question this itself is.

WITTGENSTEIN ON FREUD AND FRAZER

WITTGENSTEIN ON FREUD AND FRAZER

FRANK CIOFFI

University of Kent at Canterbury

CAMBRIDGE
UNIVERSITY PRESS

PUBLISHED BY THE PRESS SYNDICATE OF THE UNIVERSITY OF CAMBRIDGE
The Pitt Building, Trumpington Street, Cambridge CB2 1RP

CAMBRIDGE UNIVERSITY PRESS
The Edinburgh Building, Cambridge CB2 2RU, United Kingdom
40 West 20th Street, New York, NY 10011-4211, USA
10 Stamford Road, Oakleigh, Melbourne 3166, Australia

First published 1998

Printed in the United Kingdom at the University Press, Cambridge

Typeset in 11/12½ pt New Baskerville   [SE]

A catalogue record for this book is available from the British Library

Library of Congress cataloguing in publication data

Cioffi, Frank
Wittgenstein on Freud and Frazer / Frank Cioffi
p.   cm.
Includes bibliographical references and index.
ISBN 0 521 59307 7 (hardback). – ISBN 0 521 62624 2 (paperback)
1. Wittgenstein, Ludwig 1889–1951.   2. Explanation – Controversial
literature.   I. Title.
B3376.W654C56   1998
192 – dc21   97-29411   CIP

ISBN 0 521 59307 7 hardback
ISBN 0 521 62624 2 paperback

To Edward Greenwood for three decades of
instruction and hilarity

Contents

Acknowledgements

I want to thank for their help and support my wife, Nalini, my nephew Sagar Nair, and my colleagues David Ellis and Nick Bunin.

'Information, contemplation and social life' is reprinted by permission of Macmillan Press Ltd. 'Wittgenstein and the Fire-festivals' is reprinted by permission of Blackwell Publishers. 'Explanation, self-clarification and solace' is reprinted by permission of the Johns Hopkins University Press. 'Wittgenstein on making homeopathic magic clear' is reprinted by permission of Routledge. 'Wittgenstein and obscurantism' is reprinted by permission of the Editor of the Aristotelian Society, © 1998.

Introduction

The question which runs throughout these essays is: when is it a mistake to take our interest in a phenomenon in the direction of an enquiry into its causes and conditions rather than towards an enhanced grasp of the impression it produces, or the ruminations it incites? How pervasive is the tendency to proceed as if a phenomenon called for empirical enquiry when what is really wanted with respect to it is clarity as to the sources of our preoccupation and, where appropriate, untroubled contemplation of it? Wittgenstein thought that Frazer's accounts of human sacrifice and other ritual practices, and Freud's dealings with dreams, jokes and mental life in general, provided examples of this error. How are such criticisms to be assessed?

There are complexities and ambiguities in Wittgenstein's denial of the appropriateness of empirical enquiry that arise whatever substantive topic he is dealing with, whether psychoanalytic, aesthetic or anthropological. These complexities and ambiguities emerge clearly in his objections to Frazer's manner of dealing with the enigmatic method of choosing the successor to the priest of the temple of Diana at Nemi in classical times by mortal combat with a runaway slave seeking asylum.

One class of grounds for declaring empirical considerations irrelevant is conceptual. The questions, explicitly posed, make an answer which depends on further information logically anomalous. In his remarks on Frazer's account of the ritual of succession at Nemi Wittgenstein says, 'The very idea of wanting to explain . . . the killing of the priest-king seems wrong . . .', and that one reason why the attempt to find an explanation is wrong is that we have only to put together in the right way what we know without adding anything, and the satisfaction we are trying to get from the explanation comes of itself.[1]

---

[1] 'Remarks on Frazer's *Golden Bough*' in *Wittgenstein: Sources and Perspectives* ed. C. G. Luckhardt, Sussex: Harvester, 1979, p. 61.

This remark combines both of Wittgenstein's conceptual objections to Frazer's dealings with ritual practices – that the phenomena dealt with are beyond empirical explanation *and* that understanding them does not require it. Both these grounds fail. But Wittgenstein has additional non-conceptual grounds for denying the pertinence of empirical enquiry. These are that whatever relevance empirical method may have to the question of the nature and origin of ritual practices this is not the central question which Frazer raises and is not, in any case, the question which arises for us when we contemplate human sacrifice and the ritual life of mankind.

An example of a conceptual unexplainability thesis – what I call a 'limits' thesis in 'Wittgenstein and obscurantism' – is to be found in Wittgenstein's discussions with Schlick and Waismann on the explanation of aesthetic value where Wittgenstein says 'whatever I was told I would reject . . . not because the explanation was false but because it was an *explanation*'.[2] This is a familiar view in contexts where value is under discussion. What is odd is to find it expressed where the question is ostensibly empirical: whether particular, like 'Why must the priest at the temple of Diana be slain?' or general like 'Why did people engage in human sacrifice?'

Frazer asks of the ritual of succession at Nemi, in which the incumbent priest is replaced by a runaway slave who has killed him in combat, what this unique method of recruitment to the priesthood means and how it came into being. It is difficult to see how Frazer's answer to this question, which is that the rite represents a survival from a time when the belief was held that the replacement of the aging priest by a more vigorous successor, as evidenced by his victory in combat, would enhance the agricultural welfare of the community, is *conceptually* inappropriate as we are told by Johnston, Hacker, Rhees, Bell and others that it is.[3] But these commentators also follow Wittgenstein in producing additional and epistemically distinct grounds for thinking Frazer mistaken in advancing empirical explanations of human sacrifice (as of ritual generally): he is failing to rise to the occasion.

---

[2] B. F. McGuinness, *Wittgenstein and the Vienna Circle*, Oxford: Blackwell, 1979, p. 116.
[3] (P. Johnston, *Wittgenstein and Moral Philosophy*, London: Routledge, 1989; Peter Hacker 'Developmental hypotheses and perspicuous representations', *IYYUN The Jerusalem Philosophical Quarterly*, July 1992; Rush Rhees, 'Introduction to remarks on Frazer's *Golden Bough*', *The Human World*, no. 3, May 1981; Richard Bell, 'Understanding the Fire-festivals', *Rel. Stud.* 14, 1978.

Similar considerations arise in connection with Wittgenstein's objections to psychoanalytic explanation. The objection that Freud confounds causes with reasons or, as Wittgenstein also, more specifically, puts it, hypotheses with 'further descriptions', is entangled with the quite distinct objection that Freud advances explanations when the matters he deals with demand clarification, that is, they call for an elucidation of the relation in which we stand to the phenomena rather than an explanation of them. And the same ambiguity characterises Wittgenstein's objections to causal explanation in aesthetics where he once again alternates between the objection that causal hypotheses are conceptually inappropriate responses to requests for the explanation of aesthetic experiences and that they are not what we really want.

This non-conceptual construal of Wittgenstein's objections supplies a solution to G. E. Moore's perplexity as to why remarks on Frazer, Freud and aesthetics should figure in the same lectures ('mingled in a curious way' as Moore puts it).[4] The mistake shared by Frazer and Freud and those who conceive of aesthetic explanations as requiring empirical validation is not that of raising explicitly a-causal questions to which they confusedly and incongruously give causal answers but their failure to address the a-hypothetical, clarificatory, resolvable-by-reflection-and-apposite-description questions which, in Wittgenstein's view, the occasion called for.

There are two distinct grounds for holding that a discourse, even though conceptually appropriate to the questions raised, mistakes what the context calls for. One is that it betrays signs of interests more central than that of the only information-resolvable question addressed, but which, nevertheless, make their presence felt. This is how it is put by Paul Redding. '(Frazer's) response to his own questions in which he ignores its tone and responding merely to its syntactic form, offers an explanation, is, given what we can grasp about his needs from his tone, inappropriate.'[5] But Redding also expressed another, distinct, non-conceptual thesis, one which does not depend on any individual peculiarities of Frazer's text, when he writes, 'The response which Wittgenstein thinks appropriate . . .

---

[4] G. E. Moore, 'Wittgenstein's lectures 1930–33', *Philosophical Papers*, New York: Colliers, 1959, p. 305.
[5] Paul Redding, 'Anthropology and ritual: Wittgenstein's reading of Frazer's *The Golden Bough*', *Metaphilosophy*, vol. 18, nos. 3 and 4, July 1987, p. 263.

rather than constituting an act of discovery of something new' is more like 'the identification and acknowledgement of something known but misconstrued or denied' (ibid. p. 263). This transcends Frazer, so who is being referred to?

How is a claim of this kind – one as to the appropriateness of a response – to be assessed? P. Johnston appears to be advancing the same genre of claim when he writes, 'Frazer and Freud seek to offer explanations in contexts where Wittgenstein holds that what is required is not an explanation but that clarification embodied in the attainment of an *Übersicht*' (i.e. a survey or snyopsis of the already known) (Paul Johnston, 1989, p. 50). How is it to be determined that what a context requires is not explanation but '*Übersicht*'? In what does inappropriateness consist? What makes the proffering of explanation in such contexts like handing a bereaved person a copy of the coroner's report, as Redding graphically puts it?

Though it is correct to maintain that the question why the Beltane Fire-festival or the Nemi rite affect us as they do is not to be resolved by discovering how they originated, there are no substantial textual grounds for holding that Frazer was subliminally preoccupied with this question. But this need not absolve Frazer from error. On this view the question Frazer does not raise nevertheless arises and it was remiss of him not to address it. And the problem this sets us is how a claim of this nature is to be dealt with. When a particular text gives us no grounds for the judgement that empirical aims have been erroneously pursued when what was called for was something else, where are these grounds to be sought? What kind of fact is it that empirical explanation has been erroneously pursued when the grounds proffered for the error are neither conceptual confusion nor that a division of purpose is manifested in a particular text?

Rush Rhees writes of the Beltane Fire-festival: 'What is important is . . . the evidence which makes its connection with an actual practice of human sacrifice overwhelmingly probable prior to any historical research and independently of anything the research may bring to light . . .'[6] The question this raises is for whom are Rhees's judgements of relative importance coercive? Just after saying that 'even the attempt to seek an explanation (of the Nemi rite) is a mistake,' Wittgenstein remarks – 'For someone troubled

---

[6] 'Language and ritual' in *Wittgenstein and his Times*, Bryan McGuinness (ed.), Oxford: Blackwell, 1982, p. 99.

by love an explanation will not help much. It will not bring peace.'[7] In 'When do problems and methods bypass one another by?' I quote an instance of someone 'troubled by love' who appears to ask the very kind of question Wittgenstein holds impertinent to the occasion – Chaucer's Medea, abandoned by Jason, and plaintively asking – 'Why liked me thy yellow hair to see / more than the boundes of mine honesty'? I held this to illustrate Wittgenstein's view of how the form of a question may mislead us as to its character since Medea's question is not to be taken as the manifestation of the kind of straightforward epistemic demand, which psychoanalysis and socio-biology both claim to address. Though, of course, questions of this form may often be manifestations of just such a demand there are occasions when, as Wittgenstein says, what is really wanted is not an hypothesis. The problem this sets is, 'When?' How do we identify such occasions?

EXPLANATION VERSUS CLARIFICATION

This arraignment of the relevance of empirical enquiry on the grounds that its success will not meet our needs is not peculiar to Wittgenstein. In a commentary on Proust I find the following remark: '(Those) who occupy themselves with outer social activities – the Dreyfus case, the World War – are attempting to escape the primary obligation to interpret the inner significance of their own impressions.'[8] Proust himself, in the preface to his translation of Ruskin's *Sesame and Lilies*, writes: 'What happiness for a mind tired of seeking the truth within itself to tell itself that it is located outside . . . and that in order to reach it one has to go to some trouble; this trouble will be entirely material and will, for one's mind, be a relaxation.'[9]

The striking thing about Wittgenstein's remarks on Frazer is not just how often, in commenting on what is ostensibly an hermeneutic enterprise, Wittgenstein turns away from interpreting the phenomena to relating them 'to our own feelings and thoughts' but that these much outnumber his straightforwardly interpretative efforts. Wittgenstein has more to say about how we feel

[7] L. Wittgenstein, 'Remarks on Frazer's *Golden Bough*' in *Sources and Perspectives*, Luckhardt, 1979, p. 63.
[8] Milton Hindus, *Marcel Proust*, London: Thames and Hudson, 1962, p. 174.
[9] Marcel Proust, *On Reading*, Ontario: Souvenir Press, p. 43.

about Nemi, Beltane, *et al.* than how their practitioners felt about
them. He tells us that Frazer was wrong to imply that what
impresses us about the Beltane festival, in which a pretence is
made of burning a man, is its roots in the practice of human sacrifice rather than its relation to 'our own feelings and thoughts'.
He sometimes explicitly urges the priority of this concern with self-
clarification. He says, for example, of the practice of treating an
illness as if it could be washed away like dirt and is apparently based
on 'childish' theories, 'The correct and interesting thing to say is
not that it has come from (the childish theories) but rather that it
could have come from them.' In other words, a survey of our relation to ritual practices – which of them we can make sense of and
how and which not and why – is what is called for by the phenomena Frazer records rather than the rationale and genesis of the
practices themselves. That this judgement of Wittgenstein's
belongs to we/us/our discourse rather than to that of conceptual
analysis proper also emerges from the commentaries. Rush Rhees
writes: 'Wittgenstein questions the dependence of *our* impression
on the hypothesis and asks why *we* are moved to say they are deep
and terrible and what it means to say this about them.' (My italics.)

The philosopher/sociologist Georg Simmel attempted a characterisation of what I have referred to as 'we/us/our' discourse
when he spoke of 'a mental category . . . which is deep rooted
and not easily described by traditional concepts . . . a third something in man beyond his individual subjectivity and the logical
objective thinking which is universally convincing . . .' In distinguishing his 'third something' from both 'particular real individuality' and 'an objectivity beyond men and their lives . . .',
Simmel writes:

A feeling in us distinguishes, often with instinctive sureness, between those
convictions and dispositions which we modestly recognize as purely personal and subjective and those which we believe to be shared by some –
perhaps all – other men . . . it seems as if something universal spoke in us'[10]

These 'convictions and dispositions' that are not 'purely personal'
but may, nevertheless, be shared by only some rather than all men
are reminiscent of the phenomenon Husserl describes in his fifth
Cartesian Meditation as an 'experiential sense of thereness for

---

[10] Georg Simmel, 'The nature of philosophy' in *Essays on Sociology, Philosophy and Aesthetics*,
edited by Kurt Wolf, Harper Torchbooks, 1965, p. 296.

everyone' but then immediately qualifies parenthetically ('that is, everyone belonging to the corresponding cultural community ...'[11]. That is, not 'thereness' for all others but only 'thereness' for relevant others. It is this kind of communitarian truth which Wittgenstein aspires to in most of his judgements as to the relative importance of clarificatory and explanatory interests but they fail to attain it unless the pertinent community is more narrowly circumscribed. How shall this be done?

WHEN HAVE PROBLEMS 'THERENESS'?

In his discussion of the natural, though misleading, associations which surround the phenomenon of fire Gaston Bachelard tells us that fire is among those objects whose contemplation 'can release reveries whose development is as regular and inevitable as sense experience'.[12] An example of the kind of sense experience which manifests the regularity in development which Bachelard claims for certain reveries is provided by Joyce in his account of the childhood of the hero of *Portrait of the Artist*: 'When you wet the bed first it is warm then it gets cold.' Not many ruminations and reveries have a sequence as regular and inevitable as this. And certainly not many of those imputed by Wittgenstein to readers of Frazer have. But even when they do not this does not make utterances concerning such reveries and ruminations false or pointless. To determine the extent to which they are true we have to make explicit the unstated restrictions on the scope of the utterance.

Consider Wittgenstein's remark about the 'depth' of the impression made by Frazer's account of Nemi and Beltane. It is obviously figurative, so in what sense could it be true? This can be illuminated by a comparison with the less figurative use of the term 'depth' in some remarks on the aesthetics of painting, where we are told that the distance of the rear plane from the picture plane determines the depth of the picture and so if a picture is not flat it has either shallow space or deep space. This is then illustrated by a comparison between Matisse's *Odalisque* and Tintoretto's *Christ at the Sea of Galilee*.

[11] Edmund Husserl, *Cartesian Meditations*, The Hague: Martinus Nijhoff, 1960, p. 92.
[12] Gaston Bachelard, *The Psychoanalysis of Fire*, London: Routledge and Kegan Paul, 1964, p. 88.

The rear plane of the Matisse is close to the picture plane, that of the Tintoretto is far back. Fra Angelico's *Madonna* is deeper than the Matisse, Renoir's *Mme. Charpentier* deeper than the Fra Angelico, and Cezanne's *Maison Maria* is deeper than the Renoir. But the Tintoretto is deeper still.[13]

Consider how picture 'depth' differs from literal three-dimensional depth, e.g., the depth to which the parsley sank in the butter on a hot summer's day, from which Sherlock Holmes was able to infer something or other. This belongs with Simmel's 'logically objective thinking which is universally convincing . . .' Does Pepper's concept of picture depth? I am not sure. But it does not belong with Simmel's 'individual subjectivity' either. It belongs with his 'third something' which is neither 'particular individuality' nor 'the logical objective thinking which is universally convincing'. And yet though I don't know how general the perception of relative depth in Western painting is I do know that Matisse is shallower than Tintoretto. This means that I must be placing an implicit limitation of scope on judgements of picture depth.

A communitarian judgement can be straightforwardly false. A simple example is provided by the psychiatrist Anthony Clare who, writing one Christmas on the appeal of Santa Claus, imputed it to the fact that his love is unconditional. This is quite wrong. It is an integral part of our conception of Santa Claus that his love (or anyway his gift-giving) is not unconditional but is restricted to children who have been 'good'. (The popular song captures this essential ingredient: ('You better be good, you better not cry / You better not pout / I'm telling you why / Santa Claus is coming to town.') Although there are many for whom the practices described by Frazer do not have depth there are nevertheless those whom Wittgenstein's remarks will incite to an awareness that they were seeking from explanation a satisfaction it cannot give and that their interest in the phenomena described by Frazer and others had sources other than those they had explicitly acknowledged.

If we are not to treat Wittgenstein's remarks as mere *Flaschenpost* – messages in a bottle – how shall we circumscribe the community of whom Wittgenstein's remarks might be true? We can designate it with the aid of an analogy used in *The Brown Book* at a point at which Wittgenstein wants to evoke the ineffable char-

[13] Stephen C. Pepper, *The Principles of Art Appreciation*, New York: Harcourt Brace, 1949, p. 216.

acter of a certain kind of aesthetic experience, and says that it seems to be saying something and 'it is as though I had to find out what it says'.[14] The community for which Nemi and human sacrifice in general raise self-clarificatory rather than explanatory/hermeneutic issues are those to whom the phenomenon of human sacrifice seems to be saying something and imposed on them an obligation to discover what it was that it was saying, but they misrepresent the position if they give this perceived demand for self-clarification the same status as that of picture depth.

In his remarks on colour Wittgenstein writes: 'This much I know. A physical theory cannot solve the problems that motivated Goethe.'[15] Can we equally say, 'An empirical theory cannot solve the problems that motivated Frazer'? We are told by several commentators that, though Frazer may have thought he was engaged in an explanatory enterprise, he inadvertently reveals that what he really sought was clarification via the attainment of a perspicuous view. Wittgenstein says of 'the conception of a perspicuous view (*Übersicht*)' that it makes possible that understanding which consists just in the fact that we 'see the connections'. I do not think that Frazer shows that under the guise of seeking and advancing explanation of the practices he discusses he was really concerned with the attainment of a perspicuous view. But the category of a perspicuous view is indispensable if we are to understand our reflective lives better.

Recent attempts to deal scientifically with social life provide several candidates for texts which appear to straddle obliviously the line between empirical explanation and that special mode of understanding which 'consists just in the fact that we see the connections'. In 'Information, contemplation and social life' (pp. 19–46) I treated Goffman's work on stigma – 'abominations of the body . . . blemishes of individual character . . . the tribal stigma of race, nation, and religion . . .' etc . . .,[16] as an example of discourse whose scientific rationale is at odds with several features of his procedure and, in particular, his provision of synoptic views of our involvement in social life while ostensibly laying the foundations for a science of it. But this must be distinguished from the more general thesis that certain topics incite us to seek self-clarification

[14] L. Wittgenstein, *The Blue and Brown Books*, Oxford: Blackwell, 1958, p. 56.
[15] L. Wittgenstein, *Remarks on Colour*, Oxford: Blackwell, 1980, p. 206.
[16] Erving Goffman, *Stigma*, Englewood Cliffs, New Jersey: Prentice-Hall, 1964, p. 4.

with respect to them whether any particular text manifests a striving after synopticality or not. An example may make this antithesis, between explanatory and synoptic, self-clarificatory interests, and the way in which the latter may obtrude themselves, clearer. At one point in *Stigma*, where Goffman discusses the 'moral career' of the pimp, he expresses regret that the 'passing dodges' of pimps have not been more fully documented. But the conflict of feeling provoked in men of a certain upbringing by what Goffman calls the 'moral career' of the pimp doesn't find its natural consummation in a more fully documented account of the pimp's 'daily round'. Contrast Goffman's discursive, sociological, dealings with the pimp with the impression conveyed by Frans Masereel's woodcut, *The Pimp* (1922). Masereel's pimp – a 'Mac-the-Knife' figure – stands at the centre of a swirl of women evincing varying manners and degrees of thraldom. As pertinent to the concerns of ethnomethodology as it might be to learn of the techniques mastery of which enables a pimp to run his girls and keep them all happy without coming to the attention of the police there is a competing interest with which we tend to confound it. Not only is Masreel's 'Pimp' of more pertinence to some of us than Goffman's object of ethnomethodological enquiry but if it wasn't for the non-theoretical, personal, fantasy-driven interest expressed by Masereel's pimp we would take little interest in Goffman's. For this rival interest the fact that we think of the pimp as like the owner of a sweetshop is of central relevance, however infelicitous a real pimp might find the analogy (or a real sweetshop proprietor).

Another image whose interest transcends its historicity is that depicted by David in his painting of Count Belisarius, blind and soliciting alms from a soldier formerly under his command. The story of Count Belisarius, reduced to blindness and beggary, does not sacrifice its interest as an image of 'fallen greatness and blighted fame' because it is a legend; it just loses one kind of interest and gains another'.[17]

Neither in the case of the pimp, nor of Count Belisarius, nor of the priest at Nemi must the demand for articulation of the hinter-

---

[17] Gibbon has an apposite comment on this story: 'That he was deprived of his eyes, and reduced by envy to beg his bread, "Give a penny to Belisarius, the general!", is a fiction of later times, which has obtained credit, or rather favour, as a strange example of the vicissitudes of fortune.' The distinction between credit and favour is a nice one. (Edward Gibbon, *The Decline and Fall of the Roman Empire*, abridgement by D. M. Low, London: Penguin, 1960, p. 579.)

land of thought they incite be asked to meet criteria of universality. But nor are they just messages in a bottle. Their incitement to non-explanatory, *Übersicht*-pacified reflection has 'an experiential sense of thereness for others'. Nevertheless, it is an error to dismiss them as delusory because their self-clarificatory, non-explanatory interest does not have 'thereness-for-everyone'. I have said that though in the case of Goffman there are grounds for feeling that a synoptic/contemplative demand was being exploited and disguised as an explanatory one I doubted that the same was true of Frazer. No commentator before Wittgenstein had noticed that there was anything other to be done with Frazer's account of human sacrifice than applaud it, like Jane Harrison and the Cambridge School of classicists, or demonstrate its implausibility like Andrew Lang. We ought to resist the temptation of maintaining that those who make explanatory demands but not clarificatory ones are in error.

THE COMPARATIVE VALUE OF CLARIFICATION

If we insist on the priority of clarificatory interests what are we giving up explanation for? What more can be said of this wrongly foregone alternative to empirical enquiry that is clarificatory rather than explanatory? I think it closely akin to this account of the rationale for aesthetic discussion by a literary critic in the Leavisian tradition: 'when I start talking with a friend about a film, a painting or a poem . . . the ideal hope is that what I have enjoyed will become clearer to me . . . as my friend and I exchange our impressions . . . We want to bring the experience into fuller consciousness . . .'[18] But what seems perfectly natural in the case of aesthetic experiences may seem forced when it is the impression made by empirical phenomena which are treated of. Can these, too, be matters of bringing our experience 'to fuller consciousness' rather than determining the history or causal conditions of that which occasions it? This is just what is maintained by Rush Rhees, an associate and disciple of Wittgenstein's, who, after saying of his experience of Mozart's *Requiem* that the desire it leaves him with is for 'help in formulating better what is in my mind', extends this to an array of non-aesthetic issues, including

[18] J. M. Newton, 'Literary criticism, universities, murder', *Cambridge Quarterly*, Summer/Autumn, 1971, p. 335.

the predicament of 'A man . . . bewildered by the sort of person he
finds himself to be . . .'[19] Bewilderment at the sort of person one
'finds oneself to be' involves an internal relation between ourselves and our thwarted characterological aspirations and so is not
to be dissipated by learning the causal conditions of this discrepancy. Rhees, unlike Wittgenstein on Frazer, is not criticising a
particular text and so cannot appeal in vindication to its ambiguities and ambivalences. But even when there is such a text issues
which transcend it can arise. When Wittgenstein says of Goethe's
work on colour that what Goethe was really seeking was a phenomenology and not a physics of colour this might appear to
depend on Goethe himself manifesting this confusion of purpose
in his reflections on colour. But it is clear from what Wittgenstein
says elsewhere that he holds that a phenomenology of colour is not
only what Goethe was 'really seeking' but what our colour experience 'really' demands. Similarly with his objections to Frazer on
Nemi. It would not settle the matter in Frazer's favour merely that
his text was unambiguously empirical. The matters addressed,
Wittgenstein holds, demand what Frazer fails to provide – answers
to questions such as, 'What makes human sacrifice deep and sinister?' 'What is it about the Beltane festival that impresses us?'
'What is it that is particularly terrible about the burning of a man?'
etc. Questions which can only be resolved by uncovering the
connection between the phenomena and 'our own feelings and
thoughts'.

When we come to Freud the case is the same. Even if Freud did
not provide as much textual warrant for Wittgenstein's charge of
confusion between explanatory and clarificatory enterprises as he
in fact does, this would not necessarily absolve him from having
addressed the wrong question. Wittgenstein's objections to Freud
compel us to distinguish and address individually the same two
epistemically distinct issues as his objections to Frazer: the conceptual question, 'What issues can reflection, rather than
investigation, resolve?', and the non-conceptual 'When should
questions which demand investigation give way to those that
respond to reflection?' In an entry on dream interpretation, in his
notebooks for 1947, Wittgenstein illustrates the slide from one to
the other, 'It's like searching for a word when you are writing and

---

[19] Rush Rhees, 'The tree of Nebuchadnezzar', *The Human World*, no. 4, 1971, p. 25.

then saying: "That's it; that expresses what I intended!". Your acceptance certifies the word as having been . . . the one you were looking for . . .' Though this is an apt description of a certain kind of interpretative craving which commonly arises in connection with dreams, what Wittgenstein goes on to say raises a distinct issue: 'What is intriguing about a dream is not its causal connection with events in my life, etc., . . . but rather the impression it gives of being a fragment of a story.'[20] For a psychoanalyst or a scientific student of dreams this is like saying, 'What is intriguing about bird flight is not the problems in aerodynamics it sets us but its evocation of a mode of existence less constrained than our earth-bound one.' Wittgenstein is pitting explanatory against self-clarificatory interests and resolving the conflict in favour of the latter. We are in the realm of we/us/our, 'thereness for others' discourse with the pertinent 'we' unspecified. Rather than treat Wittgenstein's objection to Freud as a claim that the problems Freud addresses demand self-clarification and not explanation, it would be better to construe it as an attempt to alert us to the fact that there are occasions on which the 'self' we are attempting to fathom – or its products, like dreams – does not figure as merely a datum for causal explanation but as a complex intentional object whose multiple aspects we are striving to discriminate, articulate and arrange and towards which we are trying to clarify our feelings.

In 'Explanation, self-clarification, and solace' (pp. 128–154), in connection with Chaim Kaplan's expression of bewilderment at an atrocity he had witnessed in the Warsaw Ghetto, I question whether we have a clear enough conception of what an explanation of the holocaust would look like for a demand for such an explanation to make sense. But there is more than the obscurity of the question, 'Why the holocaust?' to suggest that demands for empirical explanation do not adequately express the feelings it arouses in us. A review of some holocaust memoirs describes them as raising the question of 'how one may describe the indescribable and explain the inexplicable' and yet concludes that 'historians should wait until their testimony is complete' before attempting 'an objective assessment'.[21] This gives us more than just our own feeling that the explanatory question has usurped the place which

---

[20] *Culture and Value*, London: Blackwell, 1980, p. 68.
[21] *The Observer*, 27 November 1988.

properly belongs to the self-clarificatory one. The text itself illustrates this confusion. For how would it facilitate the task of 'describing the indescribable and explaining the inexplicable' to solicit further testimony? Redding's comparison of Frazer's attempts at an explanation of human sacrifice to someone giving a person, demoralised by bereavement a copy of the coroner's report could equally well apply to attempts at an explanatory treatment of the holocaust. We may feel that it is not what the occasion calls for. But how do we identify occasions? Particularly when we are dealing with printed texts which, unlike letters and conversations, say, have anonymous addressees.

The non-conceptual sense of the limits of empirical explanation was expressed by Peter Winch with specific reference to the holocaust. While conceding that it raises questions which may yield to empirical enquiry, Winch nevertheless maintained that the bewilderment provoked 'is not to be removed by any sort of explanation'.[22] Winch's comment transcends commentary on a particular text and implies that there is something problematic about the holocaust itself which isn't the sort of problematicality to be dissipated by any advances in empirical understanding. What kind of problematicality is this then, and what kind of mistake is someone making who nevertheless procedes toward empirical enquiry? What is it which further empirical data on the holocaust fails to articulate with? It is, in part at least, a firmer grasp of those aspects of the holocaust which move us to speak of them as 'inexplicable' and 'indescribable'. But why should those who are unaware of any mental hinterland requiring more adequate expression than they have hitherto been able to give it be held in error? Is to lack a need to be in error? We need not impugn holocaust research because there are others of us for whom the most salient feature of the holocaust is its unarticulated implications – to whom it 'seems to be saying' something – and what it seems to be saying to us is not just 'Explain me!'

One of Wittgenstein's most striking applications of his judgement of the irrelevance of historicity was his reply to Drury's remark that the New Testament, unlike the Old, lost its significance if it was not an account of what really happened. Wittgenstein disagreed,

[22] Peter Winch, *Simone Weil: The Just Balance*, Cambridge: Cambridge University Press, 1989, p. 155.

maintaining that 'it would make no difference if there had never been an historical person such as Jesus is portrayed in the gospels'.[23] It might at first appear that this statement is irredeemably false. But it can be given the same construal as his remarks on the Beltane fires. There is in our response to the Gospel stories, as in our response to accounts of the origins of the Fire-festivals, something which is independent of the historicity of these accounts. No one would deny that what we can infer about the authorship of Luke's gospel, say, from its characteristic double vocatives ('Martha! Martha!', 'Simon! Simon!') has a very different kind of interest from that of the peculiar resonance of The Sermon on the Mount.

Nevertheless, there are many to whom to give putatively historical accounts an interest independent of the historicity of that of which they purport to be accounts will seem epistemically perverse. Now, must it follow from the fact that the great majority of those familiar with the gospel accounts of the life of Jesus would agree with Drury rather than Wittgenstein show that Wittgenstein was wrong? Wittgenstein himself seems to have changed his mind about the importance of the veridicality of the gospel story because a few years later he was conceding that enormous importance might hinge on the historicity of Christ's resurrection – 'if . . . he is dead and decomposed . . . he is a teacher like any other and can no longer help'.[24]

We can absolve Wittgenstein of inconsistency if we pose the historicity issue in a manner which strips it of soteriological implications and give it the same character as disputes about the historicity of Homer's account of the Trojan war: salvation is not annexed to the historicity of Achilles' encounter with Hector, or Priam, and so the irrelevance of historicity in our response to *The Iliad* can be discussed without distraction. Similarly, we can best see what Wittgenstein was getting at in his dismissal of historicity if we retell the gospel story thus: 'A long time ago there was a Jew who believed he had been sent by God to preach a gospel of human brotherhood, and to suffer the terrible ordeal of crucifixion, that all men might be saved and enjoy eternal life. But there are people who say there was no such man and that the story is a garbled

[23] Maurice Drury, 'Conversation with Wittgenstein' in Rush Rhees, ed. *Recollections Of Wittgenstein*, Oxford, 1984, p. 116.
[24] *Culture and Value*, Oxford: Blackwell, 1980, p. 33.

amalgam of diverse persons and events.' Put in this way would we still think it perverse to find the reverberations of this story more arresting than its problematic historicity? Georg Simmel remarked this peculiar direction of interest. 'Emotional reactions are associated with our ideas even though they are conceived purely from the standpoint of their qualitative content and without regard to the question of their reality . . . We associate the mere idea of a very noble or very abhorrent deed, a uniquely complex personality, or a remarkable turn of fate with certain feelings. These feelings are independent of our knowledge that those men and events really existed, persisting even if we discover that they did not exist.'[25]

The torment that beset Nathaniel West's Jesus-obsessed 'Miss Lonely Hearts', in striving to take what he called 'a rational view of this Christ business', would not have been facilitated by a mastery of the synoptic problem. Why should there not be others who stand in a similar relation to 'this Christ business' and why should the illuminating effect on them of Wittgenstein's remark to Drury, on the irrelevance of historicity, be invalidated because others do not share it? I have suggested that Wittgenstein's judgement as to the irrelevance of empirical enquiry need not be treated as indiscriminately universal. He addresses an imagined audience (whose membership is not explicitly circumscribed) to the effect that reflection will persuade its members that they have misunderstood themselves; that their primary need is not for an empirically adequate account of the phenomena which impress them – explanation – but for an account of the source of its power to trouble, delight or preoccupy them – self-clarification.

On the view I wish to recommend only those addressed are the proper arbiters of the truth of the thesis and thus only they can say whether the perplexities which matter most to them are out of reach of empirical discourse. This suggests that Wittgenstein's remarks as to the relative interest of clarificatory and explanatory questions are not invalidated because they fail to achieve unanimous assent in those addressed.

This failure of unanimity is common with respect to the kind of 'explanation' of aesthetic impressions that Wittgenstein says we 'long for' and which he compared to the 'making of a gesture'.

[25] Georg Simmel, *The Problems of the Philosophy of History*, Free Press, 1977, pp. 160–2.

However, many listener's to Mozart's *Requiem* will experience no strong need, such as Rush Rhees did, for help in formulating what was at the back of their minds. The pianist Alfred Brendel is said to possess a 'stunning gift for metaphoric translation of sound into sight . . .': An A-minor chord in Schumann's Kinderszenen is compared to 'a mouth opened by sleep . . .'; one of Beethoven's Diabelli variations is described as 'a tamed goblin', another as a 'maniac and moaner' and a third as 'a jumping jack in a bad temper'.[26] What strikes some music lovers as wondrously illuminating or felicitous will strike others as synaesthetic maundering. When I put Wittgenstein's remark that Brahms' themes were reminiscent of the prose of Gottfried Keller to a professor of German literature he said 'Oh no! Theodor Storm, surely.' Now *he* had entered into the spirit of the thing. On the other hand, E. M. Forster's Margaret Schlegel reflects dismissively on her sister's tendency to make comparisons across the arts: 'Helen's one aim is to translate tunes into the language of painting and pictures into the language of music . . . what's gained I would like to know?' Thus the appetite for what Wittgenstein describes as 'putting things side by side' is not universal. But it is only when we leave aesthetics for other matters that we find strong objection taken to the desertion of explanation proper for clarification/evocation. For example, the psychoanalyst Charles Hanly's accusation that in objecting to Freud's interpretation of a certain dream because it advanced explanations which were incongruous with the feelings of the dreamer Wittgenstein was like someone who obstructed a diagnosis of cancer to the detriment of the patient. But although what Wittgenstein assumes about the *generality* of the demand for clarification is sometimes false it is not therefore stripped of illuminating power.

G. E. Moore tells us that

In answer to the question why the new subject he had created should be called 'philosophy' Wittgenstein said that though what he was doing was different from what Plato or Berkeley had done yet people might feel that it takes the place of what they had done – might be inclined to say, 'This is what I really wanted . . .'[27]

---

[26] Peter Conrad, *The Observer*, 14 March 1993.
[27] G. E. Moore, 'Wittgenstein's lectures 1930–3', *Philosophical Papers*, New York: Colliers, 1959, pp. 228–9.

This rationale for our communications can be generalised beyond philosophy to those judgements of relative epistemic priority I have been discussing. If we are to engage in such discourse without needless acrimony and confusion we must have the courage of our parochialism, recognise that only those with whom we share our preoccupations and epistemic temperament will see the point of our communications and relinquish any claim on the attention of those who do not.

In his discussion of the meaning of life at the end of the *Tractatus* Wittgenstein offers a pungent demonstration that the prospect of immortality 'will not do for us what we always try to make it do': 'Is the riddle solved by the fact that I survive for ever? Is this eternal life not as enigmatic as our present one?'[28] The response to these remarks is often, but not invariably, appreciative. It is not appreciative when those to whose attention it is called never felt the temptation to link the solution of the riddle of life to their own eternal continuance. But does the fact that this response occurs impugn the value of Wittgenstein's observation to those who had in some confused but implicit manner conferred a riddle-solving potency on eternal life? In the same way, the value of Wittgenstein's remarks on the limits of the problem-solving potential of science, and of knowledge in general, depends on whether those who come to them are startled into an awareness that the consummation of the project of knowledge cannot do for them 'what they always try to make it do'. This is the way it is with Wittgenstein's dismissal of the epistemic projects of Freud, Frazer and others: we must mentally prefix them with the salutation, 'To whom it may concern'.

[28] L. Wittgenstein, *Tractatus Logico-Philosophicus*, London: Routledge and Kegan Paul, 1931, p. 185.

CHAPTER ONE

Information, contemplation and social life

I

Wittgenstein has a remark in which he admonishes us to remember that not everything which is expressed in the language of information belongs to the language game of giving information.

In this paper I want to illustrate how the language of information may be used to disguise the character of the interest we take in social life, an interest whose candid and undisguised manifestations are to be found in literature.

When rivalry between sociology and literature has been discussed, it has usually been rivalry with respect to information value.

In Lionel Trilling's review of *The Lonely Crowd*, for example, he says of *Middletown*, a famous sociological work of the late 1920s, that all it had done was to confirm Sinclair Lewis's *Babbitt* by statistics. Trilling's remark stands in a tradition of such utterances. Labriola said that Balzac was a better sociologist than Comte, and Ranke that Scott's *Quentin Durward* was better history than that of most historians. D. W. Harding once observed how little social psychology had added to 'the understanding of national differences shown by Henry James in his novels'. And there is no dearth of cases in which a novelist has been proved right about some corner of reality in just the way in which an acute and sensitive journalist might be proved right. For example, a character in a novel by Christopher Hollis, torn between becoming a minister of the Church of England or playing cricket for Berkshire, finally decides on ordination because, as Hollis puts it, Berkshire is only a second-class county. But however felicitously Hollis may have dramatised what many have felt about the condition of the Church of England, and however strongly subsequent sociological enquiry may have confirmed this, it would be a mistake to see in this kind of palpable hit the basis of the rivalry between literature and sociology. For it is not this kind of particular exterior fact about social reality which literature is under an obligation to get right, and the kind of thing it is under an obligation to get right social research proper can neither confirm nor disconfirm.

The rivalry I want to call attention to is of a different kind. It arises not when literature, like sociology, participates in the language game of giving information but when sociology, like literature, traffics in objects of contemplation. For we sometimes communicate facts in the same spirit in which we tell stories or paint pictures.

A trivial but clear example of how a claim to characterise social reality may raise issues indistinguishable from those raised by literature is afforded by Peter Berger's account of how the activities of courtship and marriage illustrate that even where 'society apparently allows us some choice the powerful hand of the past narrows down this choice even further'.

This is Berger's description of the progress of his proto-typical couple, caught up in the trammels of society, towards a destiny of 'shared bed, bathroom, and the boredom of a thousand bleary-eyed breakfasts'. Under the influence of the idea that 'sexual attraction can be translated into romantic emotion', they begin holding hands in moonlight, from whence they advance to 'tentative explorations' and from thence to the enjoyment of 'what they originally planned to save for afterwards' (no doubt leaving behind them 'silk handkerchiefs, cigarette ends or other testimony of summer nights'), eventually arriving at the stage where they go through a ceremony in which 'she gives up her name and he his solvency'.

Anyone who wished to dispute this account of courtship and marriage would have to do so in the same terms, in the same tone and with the same doubts and inconclusiveness as he would the necessity of the young house agent's clerk in *The Waste Land* being vain as well as carbuncular, and the typist to whom he made love bored and indifferent. What is true of this example is also true of the specimens of sociological discourse which I shall be discussing. The issues they raise do not find their natural consummation in judgements which could be corroborated or overthrown by empirical research.

The examples I shall discuss are Thorsten Veblen's analysis of conspicuous consumption, a specimen of Everett Hughes's studies of the drama of work, David Riesman's ostensible documentation of a growth in other-directed modes of behaviour, and Erving Goffman's work on the analysis of performances. I have brought these authors together because they all seem to me to be story-tellers posing as theorists.[1]

The most prominent feature of these works is also the most misleading. It is that they all contain a great deal of information and this inclines us to think of their authors as informing and their readers as being informed. Whereas we have recourse to them for the same reasons for which we have recourse to fiction, drama and the wider activity of non-utilitarian communication of which these are only specialised developments and of which a primitive specimen is afforded by the institution of gossip. The feature of gossip which provides the connecting link between literature and the specimens of sociology I shall be discussing was clearly described by D. W. Harding:

the essential fact in gossip as in entertainment is that the speaker who raises a topic is presenting what he takes to be an interesting situation – actual or possible – in what he regards as an appropriate light. He expects his hearers to agree on the interest of the situation and the fittingness of his attitude . . . The playwright, the novelist, the song-writer and the film-producing team are all doing the same thing as the gossip . . . Each invites his audience to agree that the experience he portrays is possible and interesting, and that his attitude to it, implicit in his portrayal, is fitting.[2]

The difference between the mode of interest which the gossip and his audience display in any facts communicated, and that which a scientist might take in the same facts, is akin to one once noted by Santayana between two distinct kinds of interest which we might take in a communication independently of its own factual or fabulous status.

We must ask ourselves, says Santayana, whether we are tracing a sequence of events and attempting to infer their probable course, or formulating an interest and defining a policy 'which definition

[1] Thorsten Veblen, *The Theory of the Leisure Class* (London, 1925); Everett C. Hughes, *Men and their Work* (Glencoe, Ill., 1958); David Riesman, *The Lonely Crowd* (New York, 1953); Erving Goffman, *The Presentation of Self in Everyday Life* (New York, 1959); Erving Goffman, *Stigma* (New York, 1963).
[2] D. W. Harding, 'The role of the onlooker', *Scrutiny* (December 1937).

is really knowledge of nothing but (our) own hearts'. He continues:

When La Rochefoucauld says, for instance, that there is something about
our friends' troubles that secretly pleases us, many circumstances in our
own lives or in other people's suddenly recur to us to illustrate that *aperçu*;
and we may be tempted to say, there is a truth. But is it a scientific truth
or is it merely a bit of satire, a ray from a literary flashlight, giving a partial
clearness for a moment to certain jumbled memories . . . The whole
cogency of such psychology lies in the ease with which the hearer on listening to the analysis recasts something in his own past after that fashion
. . . it appeals to the interlocutor to think in a certain dynamic fashion
inciting him . . . to give shape to his own sentiments. Knowledge of the
soul, insight into human nature . . . is in these cases a vehicle only . . .
while the result aimed at is agreement on some further matter, conviction and enthusiasm, rather than psychological information.

II

An example of the mistaking of an exercise in the manipulation of
our sentiments towards certain facts for their discovery or explanation is provided by Robert Merton's discussion of Veblen's thesis
that consumption is often to be explained as a 'symbolisation of
"pecuniary strength and so of gaining a good name"'. Merton
writes:

The exercise of 'punctilious discrimination' in the excellence of 'food,
drink, shelter, service, ornaments, apparel, amusements' results not
merely in direct gratification derived from the consumption of 'superior'
to 'inferior' articles, but . . . more importantly, in a *heightening or reaffirma-
tion of* social status. The Veblenian paradox is that people buy expensive
goods not so much because they are superior but because they are expensive.[3]

   This was never a paradox and whoever calls our attention to it is
actuated by other motives than that of passing on a discovery.
   Consider the Chinese sociologist Fei Hsiao-tung's idyllic reminiscence of the way of life of the gentry in his home town of Soo
Chow at the turn of the century:

Tea houses, big gardens, and magnificent residences are the paraphernalia of the gentry. From morning until nightfall, the leisured gentlemen
gather in the tea houses to amuse themselves in sipping tea, in listening

[3] Robert K. Merton, *Social Theory and Social Structure* (Glencoe, Ill., 1957).

to the story-tellers, in talking nonsense, in gambling, and in smoking opium. It would appear to a New Englander that such a town is no better than a concentration camp of voluntary deserters from life. But, to them, leisure means prestige as well as privilege. By displaying the leisure at their disposal, they stand high in the eyes of the lower classes.

I can't find any implication in this passage that the gentry of Soo Chow were not perfectly aware that by 'displaying the leisure at their disposal they (stood) high in the eyes of the lower classes'. But Fei was no doubt familiar with Veblen and it could be argued that his reminiscence was tinted by this knowledge.

Let us therefore consider a statement of Veblen's supposedly novel thesis where this possibility is ruled out. In the *Pensées* Pascal says:

To be smartly turned out is not undue vanity; for it shows that a great number of persons work for you. Your hair is proof that you have a valet, etc., etc. Now it is no mere superficiality, no mere outward show to have several arms. The more numerous your arms are the more powerful you are. Similarly to be well turned out is to reveal your strength.

It might be argued that even this does not establish the truistic character of Veblen's notion of conspicuous consumption as a means of status affirmation, since Pascal was after all a genius. But was it also a genius who said of Alexandre Dumas, whose Negro ancestry was apparent in his features, that he was capable of wearing livery and riding on the outside of his own carriage so as to create the impression that he had an African footman in his service?

Nor was this notion ever the property of a few extraordinarily perceptive observers of social life. For has anyone ever been puzzled as to why M. de Renal in Stendhal's *The Red and the Black* hires Julian Sorel to tutor his children? When Stendhal tells us that it was to cut a better figure than his rival, M. Valenod, he is not augmenting our knowledge of social life, he is exploiting an existing paradigm of intelligibility; invoking one of the familiar motives for which people do things.

Though I believe I have said enough to establish the truistic status of the notion of 'pecuniary emulation', these considerations are insufficient to overthrow the conventional classification of Veblen's writing on conspicuous waste as a contribution to social science. To see why, consider the related sociological notions of reference groups and relative deprivation. A reference group is a class of persons with which someone compares himself in respect of his success, personality, good fortune, etc. The concept of relative deprivation directs attention to the fact that his estimate of himself in these respects will depend on what this group is, and that it may not coincide with the group of which he may seem to an outsider to be a member. Now there are so many remarks in literature which imply or presuppose that any individual's sense of grievance will depend on with whom he compares himself that there is as much reason for regarding it as common knowledge as there was in the case of conspicuous consumption. Perhaps the most well known is Carlyle's apostrophe to the reader on the subject of happiness in *Sartor Resartus*: 'I tell you, blockhead, it all comes of what you fancy your deserts to be. Fancy that you deserve to be hanged you will feel happiness to be only shot; fancy that you deserve to be hanged in a hair halter it will be a luxury to die in hemp.'

Merton rightly rejects this sort of argument as an adequate ground for denying the explanatory value of the notion of relative deprivation:

> though the specific fact that self-appraisals are relative to 'the' group framework was often remarked, it was not conceptualised in terms general enough to lead to systematic research on the implications of the fact. Such a term as 'reference group' is useful, not because the term itself helps explain behaviour, but because it does not easily allow us to overlook this component in self-appraisals. The very generality of the term leads to the perception of similarities beneath apparent dissimilarities of behaviour.

And it is true that an investigator who bore the notion of reference group in mind would have been spared certain surprises. For example, he would have been less perplexed at the fact that there was greater dissatisfaction with promotion prospects in the US Air Force where promotion prospects were comparatively good than in the Military Police where they were poorer. And he would have had an idea as to where to look for the explanation. For, sensitised by the concept of relative deprivation, it would have occurred to him that an Air Force private, say, would number among those acquaintances with whom he entered the Air Force many more who had since received promotion than a private in the Military Police, and that this might account for his greater dissatisfaction.

So the invitation to remember that an individual's self-appraisals will depend on what standard of comparison he employs is not a mere contemplative exercise, in spite of its truistic character, since we are expected to recall it on suitable occasions in order 'to interpret otherwise anomalous or inconsistent findings'. It seems, then, that there will be occasions when the decision as to whether we are confronted with a contemplative exercise or an adjuvant to explanation will require judgements of a rather delicate order. However, Veblen's transactions with 'pecuniary emulation' is not one of these. And this in spite of the attention he devotes to apparently 'inconsistent and anomalous findings'.

Consider Veblen's observations on pecuniary emulation as it is manifested in dress, of which he says that 'no line of consumption affords a more apt illustration':

Dress . . . should . . . make plain to all observers that the wearer is not engaged in any kind of productive labour . . . it is contrived at every point to convey the impression that the wearer does not habitually put forth any useful effort.

Much of the charm that invests the patent leather shoe, stainless linen, the lustrous cylindrical hat and the walking stick comes of their pointedly suggesting that the wearer cannot when so attired bear a hand in any employment that is directly and immediately of any use.

The general disregard of the wearer's comfort which is an obvious feature of all civilised women's apparel, is evidence to the effect that . . . women . . . are servants to whom has been delegated the office of putting in evidence their masters' ability to pay.

The corset is a mutilation undergone for the purpose of lowering the subject's vitality and rendering her permanently and obviously unfit for work.

Classical studies are described as 'habitual contemplation of the ideals, speculations and methods of consuming time and goods, in vogue among the leisure classes of antiquity' and as 'familiarity with the animistic superstitions and the exuberant truculence of the Homeric heroes'.

Their cultivation is to be attributed to the fact that 'it is necessary that the scholar should be able to put in evidence some learning which is conventionally recognised as evidence of wasted time; it is their utility as evidence of wasted time and effort . . . that has secured to the classics their position of prerogative in the scheme of the higher learning'.

As a final example, consider Veblen's explanation of why 'the ideal of priestly decorum' precludes productive effort. He points

out that there is a 'striking parallelism' between the 'devout consumption' which goes on in the service of an anthropomorphic
deity and that which goes to the service of a gentleman of leisure
in that both are characterised by a large element of conspicuous
waste. 'The priest is expected to refrain from useful effort and,
when before the public eye, to present an impassively disconsolate
countenance very much after the manner of well-trained domestic
servants.' The abstention of the priestly class from any labour
which may contribute to the well-being of mankind is thus
accounted for in terms of the necessity for vicariously putting into
evidence their deity's exemption from productive effort; it is just
their way of impressing on the congregation that God, having
rested on the seventh day, is still resting. So that, thanks to Veblen,
we now see the similarity between the vestments of the priest and
the livery of a flunkey, sharply creased trousers and a taste for
Sophocles, a high gloss on shoes and the *Odyssey*, neat and spotless
garments and familiarity with the social organisation of the Greek
polis, the custom of mutilating the body with corsets and the mind
with the study of Greek grammar. I can't resist remarking, though,
that the function of facilitating the 'perception of similarities
beneath the apparent dissimilarities' which Merton assigns to such
notions is reminiscent of the traditional definition of wit. Might
not this, rather than any explanatory use to which it can be put, be
the real source of the memorableness of Veblen's account of
conspicuous consumption?

III

Everett Hughes's essay *Work and the Self* consists largely of an invitation to take note of the following predicaments: dealing routinely
with the crisis of others; making mistakes which are fateful, if not
fatal, for them; having one's own crises routinely dealt with; having
to suffer the fateful consequences of the routine mistakes of
others; having to clear away the dirt made by others; making dirt
for others to clear away.

And these are the terms in which Hughes describes his programme: 'Our aim is to *penetrate more deeply* into the personal and
social drama of work, to understand the social and psychological
devices by which men make their work tolerable or even make it
glorious to themselves and others.' The expression 'penetrate

more deeply', which Hughes italicises, is metaphorical, and he does not explain what sort of understanding is at issue here. Hughes confesses that initially he thought of the work of his students on boxers, jazz musicians, pharmacists, prostitutes, etc., as 'merely informative, an American ethnology', but that later he came to value them for their systematic implications: 'We may be here dealing with a fundamental matter in social science, the matter of finding the best laboratory animal for the study of a given series of mechanisms.'

This statement illustrates the operation of the tendency to which Hughes himself calls attention in his paper – that of describing one's work in the most prestige-laden manner. By using expressions like 'laboratory animals', 'social science', 'mechanisms', he attempts to assimilate his investigations to those of the exact sciences. Of course Hughes is also aware of the great discrepancy between his investigations and scientific ones, and tries to bridge this gap in the usual manner by describing his work as a 'prelude to a full and systematic treatment'. But he does not say what this 'full and systematic treatment' could possibly consist in, or what more he and his students could do than enlarge the number of his anecdotes and extend the range of social life from which they are drawn.

Consider Hughes's account of the problem of dirty work as it impinges on janitors:

Janitors turned out to be bitterly frank about their physically dirty work. When asked, 'What is the toughest part of your job?', they answered almost to a man in the spirit of this quotation: 'Garbage. Often the stuff is sloppy and smelly. You know some fellows can't look at garbage if it's sloppy. I'm getting used to it now, but it almost killed me when I started', or as another put it, 'The toughest part? It's the messing up in front of the garbage incinerator. That's the most miserable thing there is on this job. The tenants don't co-operate. You tell them today, and tomorrow there is the same mess over again by the incinerator.'

At the conclusion of his evocation of the janitor's work drama Hughes says: 'Let your mind dwell on what one might hear from people in certain other occupations if they were to answer as frankly and bitterly as did the janitors.' By all means; let us let our minds dwell on these things. 'Attention must be paid', as Mrs Willy Loman says in *Death of a Salesman*. But for Hughes the point of the mind-dwelling he exhorts us to is that it should persuade us of the necessity for conceptual revision of our assumptions about work, or for further empirical investigation. I want to say, rather, that the contemplation which Hughes's paper involves us in has no systematic implications and is not a prelude to anything except that, perhaps, we may from time to time think of the janitor and his status pain and of what it implies about social life, as Hughes, whether he was aware of it or not, intended that we should.

He proceeds as if by simply describing some recurrent human situation and placing the expression 'the problem of' before it, he is demonstrating the existence of a subject for investigation. Indeed 'problem' is one of the most frequently used words in Hughes's paper, and he seems to oscillate between two senses without being aware of how it deprives his arguments in favour of the necessity for scientific investigation of the 'social drama of work' of their cogency, while at the same time providing them with their plausibility. He speaks of the *problem* of dirty work, or the *problem* of mistakes, or the *problem* of routine versus emergency, to refer to the problems which confront the participants in these situations. And of course there are such problems; and it is a criticism of Hughes's paper as a contribution to social science, though not as a piece of sensitive social observation and vivid reporting, that the existence of these problems is a truism. But Hughes also speaks as if the problem in question is a problem *for* the social scientist; as if its existence in some way disappointed his theoretical expectations and had therefore to be explained or accounted for.

Contrast Hughes's talk of the problem of dirty work, etc., with talk of the problem of increasing industrial output, or decreasing absenteeism, or of reducing crime, where the problem is the practical one of bringing about or preventing certain conditions; or with talk of the problem of accounting for a surprising event like Truman's defeat of Dewey in the presidential elections of 1948, say, where the task is the theoretical one of explaining how certain incorrect expectations came to be entertained or certain unexpected occurrences came to pass, and the difference between the two uses becomes blatant. The situations described by Hughes may be problems, but they are not problematic.

IV

David Riesman's *The Lonely Crowd* is ostensibly an account of a change in the nature of the vicissitudes undergone and the satisfactions pursued by those members of American society whose characters are optimally adapted to its requirements and of why this change should have come about.

The change in question was from a character-type relatively impervious to the needs and wishes of his peers, and able to steel himself against their indifference or hostility, whom Riesman designates as inner-directed, to an other-directed type whose main characteristic is 'a heightened self-consciousness about relations with people, to whose expectations and preferences he is sensitised'. But as with the other works we have discussed, the adoption of a rationale which appears to demand documentation is merely a device for proffering accounts of contingencies which people entertain and circulate and feel have an intimate bearing on their prospects of felicity; for speaking to them of their lives, but under the auspices of science.

A clue to his real as opposed to his explicit aim is provided by Riesman's language, which is a literary language, a language of evocation, not of reference.

Riesman has been characterised by one critic as a 'master of ambiguity'; another has spoken of 'the spirited unconnectedness' of his observations, and still another has complained of the looseness of the link between 'the conceptual imagery and the copious exemplifications'. I suggest that these faults are due not to a deficiency of methodological or conceptual rigour but to the strength of the synoptic compulsion under which Riesman laboured.

A well-founded criticism of Riesman is easily explained on this assumption. The criticism is that he alternates between two radically different notions of social character. One is of behaviour in conformity with dispositions produced by early socialisation, and the other of behaviour which is in conformity with the ideology or ethos of the social establishment in which it occurs. On the view here propounded this equivocation, which wrecks the arguments in which it occurs, is not due to conceptual confusion but to Riesman's adherence to his real but unacknowledged programme which is to evoke the entire range of social vicissitudes which beset us, whether in coping with the characterological demands produced by our early socialisation or with the requirements of the social establishments in which we function.

In *The Lonely Crowd* Riesman had maintained that 'the decreased number of progeny requires a profound change in values – a change so deep that it has to be rooted in character structure'. Since we now know that the belief in a long-term decrease in the number of progeny was mistaken, and since a stage of incipient population decline was said to exert its influence on character structure in multifarious but intuitively intelligible ways, we are naturally interested to see what Riesman has to say about this. It is that 'the option for children rather than more saving, or consumer goods, could be regarded as itself a demonstration of the change . . . towards a high value on personal relations'.

The manner in which the presence of a novel attitude towards social relations is just as well attested to by the desire to limit as to increase the number of offspring is typical of the argumentative texture of the book, and confirms Santayana's dictum that we are in 'a region of speculation where any man with a genius for quick generalisation can swim at ease'. More striking still is the fact that even before *The Lonely Crowd* went to press, Riesman and his colleagues already knew, through the work of Joseph E. Davis, that demographers no longer believed that the population of the United States was in a state of incipient decline.

In the course of his book Riesman observes of the comedian W. C. Fields that 'his wild fantastic suspicions . . . may have served many in his audience as a support to their own doubts concerning the unquestioned value of smooth amiability and friendliness'. Isn't the service performed by Riesman of a kindred sort? Doesn't it consist in the relief and delight he causes us to feel in the recognition of our community in what Lionel Trilling called 'the exacerbated sense of others'?

This applies even more strongly to the section of the book in which Riesman deals with the topic of autonomy. Once again the apparent form of his remarks is that of a succession of hypotheses, this time of recipes for facilitating the achievement of autonomy, and once again they illustrate how remote from questions empirical investigation can be called on to decide are the issues they raise.

As a result of his 'heightened self-consciousness about his relations to people', the other-directed person finds himself in these characteristic predicaments:

In his social relations: hemmed about by subtle but none the less constricting interpersonal expectations.

At work: exhausted at having to satisfy an almost limitless demand for personalisation.

At play: feeling responsible for the mood of the group and guilt at not contributing to its fun.

In his love life: anxiously speculating as to whether to assume the sexual initiative towards some woman who may turn out to be a more knowing consumer than he is a marginally differentiated product.

And at odd moments: indulging nostalgic reveries of a time when there were still comforting possibilities of escape to the frontier; when a Huck Finn could light out for the territory and a Karl Marx for the British Museum.[4]

One of Riesman's proposals for ameliorating other-directedness and expediting the achievement of a state in which we all live autonomously ever after is the creation of 'a new type of engineer whose job it is to remove psychic hazards springing from false personalisation' by 'the elimination of locales that coerce the emotions'. To this end Riesman suggests the automating of filling stations so that we can help ourselves to petrol without the necessity of coming into any contact with the attendant. Though it is not clear how freedom to choose whether or not to personalise one's relation to a filling-station manager is served by replacing him with an automatic pump, this prospect is, none the less, intensely agreeable, borrowing some of its charm from submerged memories of the childhood fantasy of wandering through a deserted city, its shops chock-full of goodies to be had for the taking.

Another of Riesman's proposals for 'depersonalising work and making it less strenuous emotionally' is to construct 'indices of personalisation and then set ceilings beyond which they would not be permitted to go'. The notion of devising 'indices of personalisation' has a scientistic flavour and conjures up pictures of sociostats being installed in all service establishments and wired up like pinball machines to read 'tilt' if the staff are too insistently personalised. Otherwise we are in the world of the Diogenes Club.[5]

Consider Riesman's equivocation with the notion of personalisation. Sometimes the sense demanded by the context is one in

---

[4] All the distinctive phraseology in this passage is that of Riesman and his collaborators.

[5] The Diogenes Club was started for the convenience of the many men in London who, 'some from shyness, some from misanthropy, have no wish for the company of their fellows yet are not averse to comfortable chairs and the latest periodicals . . . contains the most unsociable and unclubable men in town. No member is permitted to take the least notice of any other one . . . no talking is, under any circumstances, permitted, and three offences, if brought to the notice of the committee, render the talker liable to expulsion . . . a very soothing atmosphere.' Sherlock Holmes's brother, Mycroft, was a founder-member.

which to refuse to personalise is to eschew effusiveness for whatever degree of civility the occasion seems to call for, whereas at other times personalisation can only be avoided by keeping out of social encounters in which, though civility is all that is called for, we will coercively engage in effusiveness. Riesman's conception of autonomy-enhancing conditions thus applies both to states of insulation from the pressures exerted by others in face-to-face interactions and to states conducive to the development of the capacity to engage in face-to-face contacts without excessive compliance.

I suggest that this incoherence is too blatant to be due to intellectual confusion and has its source in the intensity of Riesman's wish to regale us with two agreeable prospects – on the one hand, a vision of being protected from the coercive expectations of others, and on the other, of having successfully effected a characterological mutation in which we would have no need to be.

The mild euphoria produced by this section of the book has one source in Riesman's conception of character as something which, if not so easily altered as a hair style, ought nevertheless to prove no more intractable to determined effort than learning to write in italic script. For example, other-directedness is expected to yield to the reminder that 'Loneliness can no more be assuaged in a crowd of peers than thirst by drinking sea water'. 'If other-directed people should discover . . . that their own thoughts and their own lives are quite as interesting as other people's . . . we might expect them to become more attentive to their own feelings and aspirations.' What is this but Dale Carnegie on how to do without friends or influence?

Riesman writes of the problem of achieving autonomy as if we were not confronted by genuine ambiguities in our relations to others, as if we were in possession of an unequivocal conception of ourselves, our rights and our talents, and only lacked the means to enforce it.

This comes out clearly if we contrast Riesman's account with D. W. Harding's discussion of the 'predicament of those who are isolated without being self-sufficient' in his famous essay *A Note on Nostalgia.* Harding speaks there of the need for 'discrimination in resisting social coercion' and 'of the knife-edge balancing between humility and servility' which genuine independence involves. He has written elsewhere of the difficulty of distinguishing 'between a

valuable persistence in individual development and the worthlessness of self-conceit'.

A poignant illustration of this dilemma is to be found in the
reply which the nineteenth-century poet George Darley made to a
well-intentioned correspondent's suggestion that he should
attempt 'to sustain himself on the strength of his own approba-
tion': 'But it might be only my vanity, not my genius that was strong
. . .' To the exhortation to solace himself by thinking of his admirers he replies: 'Their chorus in my praise was as small as the voice
of my conscience and like it served for little else than to keep me
uneasy.' This has a tang of reality missing from Riesman's remarks
on the subject.

In the light of these features is it too bold to suggest that what
we are being presented with in Riesman's reflections on autonomy
is just another consolatory fantasy ultimately no different from the
lighthouse-keeper fantasies, Haroun-al-Rashid fantasies, Diogenes
Club fantasies and other reveries produced by 'the exacerbated
sense of others'?

V

The hero of Goffman's book on the presentation of self is a 'performer', a harried fabricator of impressions with a capacity for
deeply felt shame, whose acute awareness that there is no interaction in which the participants do not take an appreciable chance
of being slightly embarrassed, or a slight chance of being deeply
humiliated, leads him to minimise the risks he takes of exposure.
He is given to having fantasies and dreams, some that pleasurably
unfold a triumphant performance, others full of anxiety and
dread that nervously deal with vital discreditings in public.[6] The
book is an inventory of the hazards which befall him in the course
of what Goffman variously describes as 'fostering an impression,
staging a character, sponsoring a reality, projecting an image, presenting an appearance, engaging in a routine, putting on a show,
defining a situation'.

Goffman's procedure is to state, in an abstract-sounding way,
either the main truism or some corollary of it and then to produce
a succession of examples from memoirs, biographies, fiction, or

---

[6] This passage is an amalgam of phrases from Goffman's book.

what he refers to in his preface as 'respectable researches where
qualified generalisations are given concerning reliably recorded
regularities'. These are some of the facts with which Goffman illustrates the ubiquity of impression-fostering: that in communities in
which accent is an index of social status many people when talking
over the telephone will adopt a more cultured accent than that
which they would use in face-to-face communication; that there is
often a striking difference between the quality of the curtain
material used for the windows at the front of the house and that
used for those at the back; that people have been known to paste
on their luggage exotic labels of countries which they have never
visited; that in the United States people who cannot afford television sets may nevertheless have masts installed on their roofs so
that they will seem to own television sets; that girls who live in communal hostels and know that the number of telephone calls they
receive will be taken as evidence of their popularity will arrange to
receive telephone calls and when paged will delay replying so that
as many other residents as possible will know that they are being
called to the telephone.

The point about these facts is that even those we were previously
ignorant of are immediately intelligible because we are familiar
with the motives of which they are a manifestation. Their role
cannot, therefore, be one of dissipating scepticism as to the principles they illustrate. For what particular purpose, then, have these
reminders been assembled?

We have seen in connection with relative deprivation that a
statement which is a truism may nevertheless yield explanatory
fruit if assiduously borne in mind. If we give the notion of self-
presentation a similar point, Goffman can be construed as implicitly proferring advice to those engaged in explanatory enterprises
to the effect that when confronted by a practice, or custom,
characterising interaction between persons, which seems puzzling
or inexplicable, they should look for some impression which it is
in the interests of the practitioner to produce or maintain, and it
may then become intelligible. For example, if you are puzzled as
to why a girl with perfect hearing and in range of the voice of
someone who is paging her to come to the telephone, nevertheless does not reply until the fact that she is being paged has been
forced on the notice of a large number of persons whom it would
not seem to concern, ask yourself what interest might be served by

such a practice. It may then occur to you that the circumstances are such that the number of calls will be construed as an index of her popularity, and her behaviour will then become intelligible. Perhaps Goffman might be of use to someone in this way. His observation that if a baseball umpire is to give the impression that he is sure of his judgement he must give an instantaneous decision rather than a considered one, so that the audience will be sure that he is sure, reminded me that Bernard Berenson was notorious for the rapidity with which he sometimes arrived at his attributions and suggested an agreeably discreditable reason for it. But there seems to me to be a discrepancy of sufficient proportions between this meagre heuristic harvest and Goffman's expository effort to justify looking further for the motives behind it.[7]

Though the range of Goffman's examples sometimes does us a service by enhancing our sense of solidarity in absurdity, thus relieving us of excessive apprehension as to our own impression-creating activities, it is not unusual for Goffman to be determined in his choice of illustrative material and, ultimately, of the categories which the material illustrates, by motives less admirable than sheer gusto at the variety of human impression-management. Goffman repeatedly calls attention to the 'staging contingencies' which impostors and liars share with ordinary people. One of the reasons he gives for the necessity of this is instructively feeble. It is that we might not otherwise credit the fact that apparently instrumental objects, or activities, like television sets, motor-cars and ocean voyages, have 'in many cases' a predominantly impressive function. But neither is Goffman's constant citation of quasi-criminal activities due to a simple desire to empty his notebooks. An unconscious compulsion to give a predatory cast to social

---

[7] It may be Goffman's awareness of the truistic character of his central thesis which intermittently goads him into a display of paradox on the subject of the self and its performances, so that while conceding that 'the general notion that we make a presentation of ourselves to others is hardly novel', he nevertheless insists that 'the very structure of the self can be seen in terms of how we arrange for such performances'. For example, 'when we observe a young American middle-class girl playing dumb for the benefit of her boy friend, we are ready to point to items of guile and contrivance in her behaviour. But like herself and her boy friend, we accept as an unperformed fact that this performer *is* a young American middle-class girl. But surely here we neglect the greater part of the performance' (*The Presentation of Self*, p. 74). Goffman's feints at elucidating this remark are as recalcitrant to intelligible paraphrase as the Duchess's counsel to Alice to be what she would seem to be: 'Never imagine yourself not to be otherwise than what it might appear to others that what you were or might have been was not otherwise than what you had been would have appeared to them to be otherwise.'

encounters seems to be at work. For example, in his discussion of team collusion he points out that whispering as a means of disguised communication between team members suffers from the drawback that, though secrets can be kept in this way, the fact that secrets are being kept cannot itself be kept secret. This typically unnecessary observation gives him the opportunity to acquaint us with less obtrusive means of deception. And so we are told that, for example, American shoe salesmen, when they are dealing with a customer who needs a shoe of a size larger than is available, will hand the shoe over to an assistant with the instruction to 'stretch them on the thirty-four last'. This phrase tells the assistant not, as it might seem, to stretch the shoes, but to wrap them and hold them under the counter for a short time. If it is a question of the width of the shoe and the customer insists on a B width the salesman will ask another, 'Say, Benny, what width is this shoe?' By addressing his colleague as 'Benny' he has indicated that the correct answer is width B.

The piquancy of these examples is enhanced by their being juxtaposed with instances of what Goffman insists is structurally identical behaviour on the part of Cabinet Ministers, civil servants and business executives.

Goffman's apparent reason for this procedure is the necessity for documenting his observations that 'there is hardly a legitimate everyday vocation or relationship whose performers do not engage in concealed practices which are incompatible with fostered impressions . . . individuals with widely different social roles live in the same climate of dramaturgical experience'.

But the real function of Goffman's gratuitous exemplifications is the familiar literary one of deflationary juxtaposition. For example, he writes: 'The talks that comedians and scholars give are quite different but their talk about their talk is quite similar.' In this respect Goffman's procedure is quite in the spirit of the incident in Proust in which Marcel's grandmother comments on the striking similarity between the attitude of the woman who looks after the toilet conveniences on the Champs-Elysées and that of the hostesses of the Faubourg St Germain: 'I heard the whole of her conversation . . . could anything have been more typical of the Guermantes, or the Verdurins and their little circle?' Were it not for the presence of so many citations we might suspect Goffman of trying to teach Marcel's grandmother to suck eggs. But thanks to his command of 'respectable researches where qualified general-isations are given concerning reliably reported regularities', we now know what formerly we had only suspected – that a touch of impression-fostering makes the whole world kin. The colonel's lady and Rosy O'Grady 'live in the same climate of dramaturgical experience'.

It is not merely in his selection of examples that this particular bent of Goffman's displays itself, but also in his manner of describing them. Consider the phenomenon he calls 'ritual profanation of the front region'. He tells us that when those of a higher status have temporarily vacated a region which they normally occupy, those of lower status may take advantage of the opportunity to 'ritually profane it'. This has an arrestingly obscene ring about it. But in Goffman's examples it involves nothing more sinister than mimicking absent superiors and generally larking about in their office space. In other words, when the cat's away the mice will practise ritual profanation of the front region.

Again, in connection with what he calls the problem of controlling access to the back region, Goffman writes: 'If the bereaved are to be given the illusion that the loved one is really in a deep and tranquil sleep then the undertaker must be able to keep the bereaved from the work-room where the corpses are drained, stuffed and painted in preparation for their final performance.' So even the natural reluctance to see a loved face in the initial stages of putrefaction is turned against us and made to seem contemptible. Life being what it is, one dreams of revenge and sociology.

The continuous flow of citations from specialist books, journals and unpublished researches which Goffman indulges in are, when scrutinised, seen to be idle wheels, merely part of his own 'symbolic sign equipment'. For example, to demonstrate the necessity of 'adapting one's performance to the information conditions under which it must be staged', Mayhew's *London Labour and the London Poor* is drawn on for the information that the ageing prostitute of Victorian days would frequent the darker parks; and Sleeman's book on thugs, the Indian stranglers, for the fact that they ascertained whether their victims knew anyone in the vicinity and were therefore likely to be missed before striking; and an unpublished study for the fact that the claims advanced by clothing salesmen, which can be immediately checked, are more moderate than those of furniture salesmen, which can't.

The underlying rationale can't be that we understand the tendency of the ageing prostitute to confine herself to the less well-lit areas better when we see it as a special case, and only one of many, of 'adapting one's performance to the information conditions under which it must be staged'; for how could we understand it better than we already do?

It might help to enforce this point if I remind you what a genuinely problematic issue concerning performances is like. In any encounter there are those who are more and those who are less able to maintain a performance in the face of disruptive threats, and there are those who are more and those who are less demoralised by the discrediting of appearances which failure entails. We may all be poor fellow performers but some of us are poorer than others.

It might be argued that Goffman's achievement lies not in any particular aspect of impression-management which he has documented or illustrated but in his demonstration that the phenomena have a ubiquity which necessitates and justifies a generic title to comprise them and to sensitise us to their occurrence. Even this is doubtful.

At the close of Shakespeare's *Henry IV, Part II*, we have an excellent illustration of that species of impression-management which Goffman calls 'exaggerating the uniqueness of a transaction'. A bedraggled Falstaff is waiting for Prince Hal, now King, to pass through a London street and at first regrets that the haste with which he had returned from Gloucestershire had not allowed him time to spend Shallow's thousand pounds 'on new liveries'. But Goffmanesque considerations obtrude themselves and comfort him:

FALSTAFF . . . But 'tis no matter; this poor show doth better; this doth
    infer the zeal I had to see him.
SHALLOW It doth so.
FALSTAFF It shows my earnestness of affection.
SHALLOW It doth so.
FALSTAFF My devotion –
SHALLOW It doth, it doth, it doth.
FALSTAFF As it were, to ride day and night; and not to deliberate, not
    to remember, not to have patience to shift me –
SHALLOW It is best, certain.
FALSTAFF But to stand stained with travel, and sweating with desire to
    see him; thinking of nothing else, putting all affairs else in
    oblivion, as if there were nothing else to be done but to see him.
SHALLOW 'Tis so, indeed.

I do not quote this to show that Shakespeare anticipated Goffman, but to show that the presence of such things in literature argues a confident dependence on quickness of uptake in an audience that shows that we are already hair-trigger fine to the phenomenon of impression-management and do not require sensitising. If we require anything, it is to be made more comfortable with the innocuous presentational requirements of a great deal of social interaction rather than more self-conscious than we already are by having them assimilated to the tactics of confidence men, unscrupulous salesmen and Indian stranglers.

Consider the rapidity with which anecdotes of aplomb or discomfiture circulate in our lives and the role that they play there. I should like to instance one from my own sub-culture which is nevertheless, I think, self-explanatory. It concerns a very popular American radio broadcaster of the late 1930s, known as Uncle Don, who had a daily programme for children and on Sundays read them the so-called funny papers. On one occasion, on concluding one of his Sunday readings with his usual chortly-chuckly farewell to his child audience, Uncle Don turned to the studio engineer and, under the mistaken impression that he was off the air, remarked in the hearing of a million of the nation's children and their parents, 'That ought to hold the little bastards till next week.' It might seem at first that the phenomenon illustrated by the enormous number of occasions on which this anecdote has been related, giving it the status of a legend, and the position it, and others like it, occupy in the background of our imaginative lives is precisely what Goffman illuminates. I am concerned rather to call attention to the degree to which Goffman's own work on impression-management has the same status and function as these anecdotes, and illustrates rather than illuminates our preoccupation with the contingencies of pretence and exposure.

Goffman has an ironic reflection in one of his papers on 'the touching tendency to keep part of the world safe from sociology'. But nowhere does he seem to be aware of the discrepancy between his own account of the point of his activities and that which would strike a sociologically oriented observer. Goffman's role analysis, like some theologians' hell, seems to be for other people.

I have suggested that the reason Goffman insists on illustrating his truisms is often that he enjoys dwelling on specimens of humbug or fatuity and shrewdly suspects that some of his readers will too. But often there is a purer and more universal motive at work as well. For example, we are told that a circumspect, prudential performer will choose his audience so as to economise the effort he has to expend on putting over his act and minimise the possibility of its disruption. This near-tautology provides Goffman with the opportunity of reporting that in America it sometimes happens that after the patient is unconscious another surgeon will be introduced into the theatre to perform the operation for which the patient's physician will later be credited.

This last item is a soberer version of the secret surgeon legend, a tall variant of which was retailed by Yeats who overheard it in a barber shop. In Yeats's version, one surgeon, who emerges from a trap-door after the patient is well under, performs all the operations in London, the other London surgeons being really his agents.

I wish to maintain that it is inessential that of these two anecdotes one is a tall story which Yeats passed on because, as he said, he 'loved what is bizarre in life', whereas the other was adduced in support of a sociological thesis that an audience which is unconscious provides optimal conditions for the management of an impression. In retailing these stories Goffman and Yeats are both participating in the same institution, the same communal rite or, if you like, the same form of life.

VI

Goffman's book on stigma is largely devoted to bringing out what is common to the predicaments and moral careers of different kinds of stigmatised persons.

For those of us who have a stigma, the world of normal persons is divided between those who know about our stigma and to whom we are therefore 'discredited' persons, and those who do not and to whom we are therefore only 'discreditable', i.e. potentially discredited persons. Our problem with regard to the first group is the 'management of tension', with regard to the second 'the control of information'. In other words, if people know about our stigma we have to try to keep them from thinking about it; and if they don't know, we have to try to keep them from finding out, unless, that is, we have decided to tell them. Those who, though themselves nonstigmatised persons, share in our opprobrium because of their relation to us, are the 'courtesy sigmatised'. Normals are further subdivided into those who can only recognise a stigma if it is blatant and those who, though specially gifted at spotting the unobtrusively stigmatised, are nevertheless comparatively un-censorious or even sympathetic. These Goffman designates as 'the wise'. And so on.

In the course of the book we learn, if that is the word, that:

Instead of cowering the stigmatised individual may attempt to approach mixed contacts with hostile bravado.

An individual's intimates can be just the persons from whom he is most concerned to conceal something shameful.

Ex-mental patients are sometimes afraid to engage in sharp exchanges with a spouse or employer because of what a show of emotion might be taken as a sign of.

When an individual acquires a stigmatised self late in life, the uneasi-ness he feels about new associates may slowly give way to uneasiness felt concerning old ones.

It is clear that Goffman's theses concerning the problems involved in stigma management are as truistic and as insusceptible of an information-rationale as those concerning impression-fostering in *The Presentation of Self.*

Merton's case for the point of giving truisms handy labels and bearing them in mind seems inapplicable here. There are no anomalies to be accounted for. It is one thing to bring the notion of relative deprivation and reference-group theory to the under-standing of behaviour apparently incongruent with its circum-stances, such as that the morale of Southern-based American Negro soldiers was superior to that of Northern-based ones. It is quite another to bring the notion of tension management and informa-tion control to the fact that persons with hidden stigmas are posed the problem of whether or not to disclose them, or that stigmatised persons who are attempting to pass will devote much thought to the development of a routine which segregates those who know from those who don't, or that people with facial disfigurements will expe-rience trepidation about meeting strangers and may therefore attempt to restrict their appearances to a familiar round. These latter instances of behaviour are non-problematic; there is nothing here which needs explaining. So we have to seek elsewhere for Goffman's reasons for so persistently calling our attention to them.

The aim of affording 'meditative spleen a grateful feast' is much less in evidence in *Stigma* than in *The Presentation of Self.* Though we suspect that someone of Goffman's marvellous expressive powers could have found a less loaded way of marking the distinctions between those with a stigma of which we are aware, and those with a stigma of which we are not aware, than by designating them as the discredited and the discreditable.

He tells us, too, that 'we normals' regard the stigmatised as 'less than human'. In consequence when he observes that 'the stigmatised individual exhibits a tendency to stratify [so that] he can take up, in regard to those who are more evidently stigmatised than himself, the attitudes the normals take towards him', we have stronger grounds for refusing to credit this than our natural reluctance to do so. Similar considerations apply to Goffman's characteristically conspiratorial view that 'cautionary tales concerning the risks of passing form part of the morality we employ to keep people in their places'. Such tales are no more part of the morality we employ to keep people in their places than the even more popular anecdotes of lovers surprised by inopportunely returned spouses are part of the morality we employ to keep them out of other people's beds.

The situations which attract Goffman and which he tends to document are just those whose dramatic nature and poignancy arouse the interest of gossips, novelists and story-tellers, and whose standardised affective values make them dependable ways of controlling an audience's responses.

When he produces half-a-dozen examples to illustrate that, even in the case of an apparently blatant stigma, occasions may arise in which concealment may, for a short period, be successfully practised we think of Gerty MacDowell's flirtation with Bloom on Sandymount Strand. Similarly the statement that 'the tendency of a stigma to spread from the stigmatised individual to his close connections provides a reason why such relations tend either to be avoided or terminated' prompts the reflection that anybody who didn't know this wouldn't have been able to follow the denouement of the Sherlock Holmes story *The Yellow Face.* And what the readers of the *Strand Magazine* had no diffiulty in following, it cannot require sociological penetration to discern.

In *Daniel Deronda,* George Eliot briefly touches on the predicament of the possessor of a hidden stigma who, having decided on a policy of candour, encounters the dilemma that while it would be unseemly to disclose his secret in a company in which it has no immediate relevance, it may become relevant before he has had an opportunity to disclose it. Daniel Deronda replies to Joseph Kalonymos's suggestion that he has actively concealed the possibility of his Jewishness with the statement: 'You can understand that I shrank from saying to a stranger "I know nothing of my mother".' Of course he can understand it and so can we. Why then does Goffman feel it necessary to call our attention to the fact that 'the individual's stigma may relate to matters which cannot be appropriately divulged to strangers'? Might it not be for the same reason that George Eliot did? Simply because it is arresting.

Take the pre-Jamesian novel's authorial intrusion and generalising commentary, substitute for dramatised episodes in the lives of invented characters quotation or paraphrase from memoirs, autobiographies, field studies, etc., replace character and plot as principles of organisation with the 'shared contingencies of a social category', and you have something which looks very like Goffman's essays on stigma and impression-management. Considered in the light of this analogy, Goffman's habit of quotation from primary sources (which are otiose in terms of his official purpose), viz., 'a polio patient states . . .', 'similarly an amputee . . .', 'a cripple adds . . .', 'a blind person's statement may be cited . . .', can be seen as a device for producing a succession of inside views; and this is to be explained not in terms of the requirements of the argument but for the reason which Wayne Booth gives in *The Rhetoric of Fiction* – that inside views enhance our sense of identification with the characters.[8]

What do we gain from playing Don Cleophas to Goffman's Asmodeus? In Goffman's hands the documentation of the moral careers of the halt, the deaf, the black and the queer, with which his book is crowded, function like parables. Their interest resides in the fact that the predicaments presented, though exotic, have

---

[8] This may explain, too, why inside views are rarely resorted to in *The Presentation of Self*, where a satirical 'distance' is the effect aimed at. The necessity for this precaution can be seen if we consider what can happen when it is neglected, as in the case of the redrafted suicide note which Goffman cites to illustrate the ubiquity of impression-fostering. Goffman uses the discrepancy between 'By the time you read this nothing you can do will be able to hurt' and 'By the time you get this I will be where nothing you can do will hurt me' to show 'that the final feelings of a desperately uncompromising person were somewhat rehearsed in order to strike just the right note'. The effect of Goffman's resort to direct quotation here is that instead of relishing the irony of Goffman's reflections we find ourselves reflecting, without much relish, on Goffman.

striking affinities with those in which we, who are apparently
normal, find ourselves. Goffman himself is aware of this. On one
occasion he observes that '. . . the problems people face who make
a concerted and well-organised effort to pass are problems that
wide ranges of persons face at some time or other', and on another
that 'the most fortunate of mortals is likely to have his half-hidden
failing, and for every little failing there is a social occasion when it
will loom large creating a shameful gap between virtual and social
identity . . . the occasionally precarious and the constantly precarious form a single continuum'.

And yet, in spite of this, Goffman is able to persuade himself that
when he relates incidents like that of 'the epileptic, subject to
grand mal seizures [who] may regain consciousness to find that he
has been lying on a public street, incontinent, moaning, and
jerking convulsively', it is to illustrate a hazard of passing, presumably for the purpose of demonstrating the adequacy of his conceptual schema. Whereas it, and stories like it, are in part
Mithridatic rehearsal, as Goffman himself implies in his allusion to
ageing as the universal stigma, and in part fee-grief, a way of dis-
charging the obligation to mourn.

VII

But the value of Goffman's reflections on stigma is far from
exhausted by the interest of the anecdotes he retails taken individually. For even if we were familiar with the primary sources on
which he draws – Chevigny's account of his blindness; Mrs
Linduwska on her adjustment to polio; the American war veteran,
Russell, on life with hooks instead of hands; Vascardi on what it is
like to be under four feet tall; Peter Wildeblood on the life of a pre-
Wolfenden homosexual, etc. – Goffman's treatment of the subject
would still be of value to us.

Wherein does its value and interest lie? I suggest that this value
is a function of Goffman's synoptic mode of presentation and a
tribute to its exorcistic power. Carlyle is said to have remarked of
the appeal of history that the past is attractive because it is drained
of fear. Something of the same effect seems to attach to the aura
of timelessness which the implication of being law-governed casts
over phenomena. The production of these synoptic views, like
their enjoyment, is not a prolegomenon to any scientific advance.

It is an end in itself. The layout is itself the achievement and is neither a prelude to discovery nor a facilitant of discovery.

These writers mistake their synoptic compulsion for an explanatory one and we abet them in this because, though surveys are not theories, the mind craves them.

But this way of putting it doesn't seem to me to do justice to the extent of the discrepancy between the apparent interest of this discourse and its real function. For it is not merely in mistaking a taxonomic exercise for an explanatory one that we are deceived – what is being rendered surveyable is not what we think. For order is being introduced not into the facts about stigma, compliance or dirty work but into our sentiments about these.

There are investigative activities whose prosecution demands an extremely hazy and indefinite expectation as to what their successful consummation would involve. If the question of what precisely the activity is preparatory for, and what its successful issue would amount to, is strongly pressed, either its value is dissipated or its presumed nature is called into doubt. The specimens of sociological discourse which I have been discussing seem to me to be examples of this. The failure of empirical investigations to relieve the craving which impels us to pursue or to frequent them may produce the illusion that our disquietude is due to ignorance, to a residue of undiscovered facts. We are left feeling that a super-Balzac could tell us what we need to know. So, pending the Namierisation of human life, we suspend judgement.

But it is not the kind of knowledge which results from empirical enquiry that we really need. It is not our state of information which requires altering. What we need is to sort out our thoughts, feelings, reminiscences, sentiments on the topic in question. But this expectant posture towards as yet uncompleted programmes of research affords us a pretext for avoiding the effort of introducing some coherence and stability into our attitudes, or for postponing such efforts without pretext and without deluded notions as to the sources of our indecision.

A critic of *The Lonely Crowd* looks forward to a sequel in which 'its diffuse insights are replaced by tested empirical propositions and coherent theory'. But would a sequel which answered to such a description belong to the same genre? Mr Darling's epitaph, which Riesman puts to such good use, retains its illuminating power irrespective of its typicality or veridicality, because this power comes from our noticing the reverberations on our feelings of the idea of 'a man who knew no master but his God'. It is our stereotypes of frontier America and the relation in which we stand to these which matter and not the historical reality.

It is true that Riesman takes his own pretensions to historical accuracy quite seriously. But when he expresses regret at the impossibility of having the men and women of the nineteenth century fill out questionnaires, or submit themselves to the 'Witkin tilting-room/tilting chair experiment', an effect of incongruity is produced. These considerations seem discontinuous with those that we spontaneously bring to bear on the stories he tells us.

So we have to distinguish between the bits that are there to sustain the illusion that we are following the unfolding of an empirical investigation and those bits for whose sake the illusion must be sustained. And how are we to safeguard ourselves from arbitrariness in such a matter? How can I lose if I am allowed to say of those features of a discourse which are incongruous with my characterisation of it that thoughts are being forced out of their natural paths? I lose if you say that I have lost.

Wittgenstein has an apposite analogy in the *Investigations*: '. . . one may say of certain objects that they have this or that purpose. The essential thing is that this is a lamp, that it serves to give light: – that it is an ornament to the room, fills an empty space, etc., is not essential. But there is not always a sharp distinction between the essential and the inessential.'[9]

Nevertheless, I have tried to show that many statements and statement-sequences which are presented and discussed in the idioms appropriate to informative-explanatory enterprises really stand to us as do stories and pictures, play a role in our lives more akin to that of stories and pictures.

---

[9] *Philosophical Investigations*, p. 62.

CHAPTER TWO

Aesthetic explanation and aesthetic perplexity

I

Most of us have had addressed to us at one time or another remarks
which purported to account for the impression made on us by a work,
or a portion of a work of art. We have also a rough idea of what we
mean by an hypothesis. How are these two things – advancing hypotheses and analysing or explaining impressions – related? Before
expounding what I take to be Wittgenstein's answer to this question
I want to provide some specimen aesthetic problems and solutions in
the light of which the adequacy of his answer might be assessed.

Here are some examples of what it seems natural to call
manifestations of aesthetic perplexity;[1]

From my boyish days I had always felt a great perplexity on one point in
Macbeth: it was this: the knocking at the gate, which succeeds to the murder
of Duncan, produced on my feelings an effect for which I never could
account: the effect was – that it reflected back upon the murder of a peculiar awfulness and depth of solemnity . . . yet I never could see why it should
produce such an effect . . . and I . . . set myself to study the problem.

(why was it that) in responding to Coleridge's line ('It was an
Abyssinian maid,/ And on her dulcimer she play'd,/ Singing of Mount
Abora.') I could not think of Abora as a paradisal mount . . .?

When I opened (Dali's Autobiography) for the first time and looked at
its innumerable marginal illustrations I was haunted by a resemblance I
could not immediately pin down. I fetched up at (an) ornamental candle-
stick. What did this remind me of?

What is the secret of the strange effect produced by the Mona Lisa, of
'its subdued and graceful mystery'? Why does she seem to look at us, to
have a mind of her own, to change before our eyes, to seem at one time
mocking, and at another sad, etc., etc?

---

[1] De Quincey, Maude Bodkin, George Orwell, pastiche (the phrase in quotes is Pater),
Freud, Herbert Spencer, Marcel Proust.

47

One is curious to know what the peculiar quality is which enables us to distinguish as 'uncanny' certain things within the boundary of what is 'fearful'.

We do not ascribe gracefulness to cart-horses, tortoises and hippopotami . . . but we ascribe it to greyhounds, antelopes, racehorses. What then is this distinctive peculiarity of structure and action which we call grace?

At a bend in the road I experienced, suddenly, that special pleasure, which bore no resemblance to any other, when I caught sight of the twin steeples of Martinville . . . In ascertaining and noting the shape of their spires, the changes of aspect, the sunny warmth of their surfaces, I felt that I was not penetrating to the full depth of my impression, that something more lay behind that mobility, that luminosity, something which they seemed at once to contain and to conceal.

These are the attempts at their resolution:[2]

My solution is this . . . We were made to feel . . . that love and mercy (were) gone, vanished, extinct, and that the fiendish nature had taken (their) place . . . this effect is finally consummated by the (knocking at the gate) which (signifies) that ordinary life is resuming its sway . . . the human has made its reflux upon the fiendish; the pulses of life are beginning to beat again; and the re-establishment of the goings-on of the world in which we live first makes us profoundly sensible of the awful parenthesis that had suspended them.

When I questioned my own experience, why it was that in responding to Coleridge's line, I could not think of Abora as a paradisal mount the answer came in form of a dim memory of some mountain named by Milton.

Take away (from Dali's pictures) the skulls, ants, lobsters, telephones and other paraphernalia and every now and again you are back in the world of Barrie, Rackham, Dunsany and 'Where the Rainbow Ends.'

Everyone who has ever tried to draw or scribble a face knows that what we call its expression rests mainly in two features: the corners of the mouth and the corners of the eyes. Now it is precisely those parts which Leonardo has left deliberately indistinct by letting them merge into soft shadow. That is why we are never quite certain in what mood Mona Lisa is really looking at us.

The essential feature in the production of the feelings of uncanniness is intellectual uncertainty. For example, whether an apparently animate being is really alive or whether a lifeless object might not be in fact animate.

One night while watching a dancer . . . I remarked that the truly graceful motions were those performed with comparatively little effort. After

---

[2] De Quincey, Bodkin, Orwell, Ernest Gombrich, Freud's paraphrase of Jaentsch, Spencer, Proust.

calling to mind sundry confirmatory facts, I presently concluded that grace, as applied to motion, describes motion that is effected with economy of force; grace as applied to animal forms describes forms capable of this economy; grace as applied to posture describes postures which may be maintained with this economy; and grace as applied to inanimate objects describes such as exhibit certain analogies to these attitudes and forms.

Presently their outlines and their sunlit surface, as though they had been a sort of rind, were stripped apart; a little of what they had concealed from me became apparent; an idea came into my mind which had not existed for me a moment earlier, framed itself in words in my head . . . what lay buried within the steeples of Martinville must be analogous to a charming phrase since it was in the form of words which gave me pleasure that it had appeared to me

What account shall we give of the transition from the questions of the first list to the answers of the second? Can we give the same account of all of them?

A thesis which runs like a refrain through Wittgenstein's remarks on aesthetics is what I shall call the sufficiency-of-reflection thesis but which Wittgenstein sometimes states negatively as 'aesthetic explanations are not causal hypotheses'.[3]

There is a 'why' to aesthetic discomfort, not a cause to it. (p. 14)

The answer in these cases is the one that satisifed you . . . (p. 18)

The criterion for its being the one that was in your mind is that . . . you agree. (p. 18)

An entirely new account of correct explanation . . . You have to give the explanation that is accepted. That is the whole point of the explanation. (p. 18)

Here explanation is on the same level as utterance – where utterance is the only criterion. (p. 18)

. . . an aesthetic explanation is not a causal explanation. (p. 12)

The sort of explanation one is looking for when one is puzzled by an aesthetic impression is not a causal explanation. (p. 20)

The puzzles arising from the effects the arts have are not puzzles about how these things are caused. (p. 28)

In aesthetic investigations 'the one thing we are not interested in is causal connections'. (Moore, p. 301)[4]

---

[3] All page references not otherwise attributed are to *Lectures and Conversations*, Blackwell, 1970.   [4] G. E. Moore, *Philosophical Papers*, New York, 1966.

'To ask "Why is this beautiful?" is not to ask for a causal explanation.'
(Moore, p. 301)

There are two natural but mistaken interpretations to put on
Wittgenstein's remarks on aesthetic explanation. One does
Wittgenstein less than justice, the other more. Both are to be
found in David Pears' condensed account:[5]

'If someone complains that a door is too low (on aesthetic
grounds, not practical grounds), he does not mean that he has a
feeling of discomfort which will be removed if the door were made
higher. It may be true that his feeling of discomfort could be cured
in this way, but it is one thing to describe the feeling prognostically
by its cure, and quite another thing to describe it diagnostically by
saying that at the time it was directed at a certain object, the
lowness of the door. The success of the cure may suggest that the
feeling was directed at the object, but it does not prove it. The
connection between the feeling and its object is an inner logical
connection but it is only a contingent inference that, if the feeling
vanishes when the door is made higher, it must have been directed
at the lowness of the door. It might still have had a different object.
This example, which is Wittgenstein's, is characteristic of him. The
case is a simple one, and nobody could suppose it likely that in
such a case the cure would indicate the wrong object. But the
example illustrates a feature of aesthetic judgements which
according to him is essential to them, and which according to him
cannot be given a causal analysis – they are directed at objects, or,
to be more specific, at aspects of objects.'

What does Wittgenstein less than justice is to see cases like the
lowness of the door as the major source of his conviction of the
inadequacy of a causal analysis of aesthetic explanation. He has
much more interesting and cogent reasons for this conviction. But
Pears does Wittgenstein more than justice in the first and last sen-
tencies of the paragraph – in the last sentence by allowing a
construction on his denial that statements which give the objects of
feelings are susceptible of causal analysis more defensible than
Wittgenstein's own, for Wittgenstein doesn't only mean that
someone who believes his impression to have such and such a
source is not merely entertaining a causal hypothesis, he also means

---

[5] David Pears, 'The development of Wittgenstein's philosophy', *New York Review of Books*,
January 16, 1969.

that such a belief has no causal implications; and in the first sentence, by stating Wittgenstein's strong a-causal thesis in a manner which enhances its plausibility by speaking of complaints rather than explanations and by equivocating on the word 'feeling.'

The arguments and examples with which Wittgenstein supports the claim that aesthetic explanations are not causal hypotheses suggest that it is a mnemonic for two distinct theses. One, that aesthetic explanations take the form of similes or of further descriptions, of finding the words that sum the experience up; the other, that aesthetic explanations name objects of feelings or sources of impressions rather than causes and are thus immune from experimental revision.

When Wittgenstein denies that aesthetic explanations are hypotheses he is sometimes contrasting causal hypotheses with statements which give the object of a feeling, but at others with statements which attempt to convey the character of an experience by simile, gesture, counterpart or mnemonic, though he may be unaware – at least he never explicitly acknowledges – that he is working with two distinct notions of aesthetic explanation.

When Wittgenstein is contrasting causal hypotheses with remarks which give the object of a feeling he has three kinds of failed candidate for explanatory status in mind – those in which the explanandum is inappropriate because it is an ulterior effect and not constitutive of the work (for example, that the general effect of the Toreador Song was an increase in the functions of the cardiovascular system, or that Tchaikovsky's *Sixth Symphony* ought not to be played to mental patients who are depressed, fatigued or convalescent, but may be employed to subdue hilarity);[6] those in which the explanans is inappropriate (for example, 'particular kinds of mechanism in the brain', p. 20); those in which their relation is inappropriate (experiences incapable of being felt determinants of the effect, for example, the asymmetry of the horizon behind the Mona Lisa's head in relation to the mysteriousness of her smile, or the convexity of the sides of Doric columns which is a condition of their appearing parallel). The question is whether these exhaust the ways in which causal knowledge can bear on aesthetic judgements as to the sources of impressions.

---

[6] Ida M. Hyde, 'The effects of music upon cardiograms and blood-pressure' in *The Effects of Music* by Max Schon, London, 1927.

At other times Wittgenstein conceives of an aesthetic explanation in such a way that not even giving the object of directed feeling would be an example of one. When Wittgenstein speaks of 'the sort of explanation one longs for when one talks about an aesthetic impression' (p. 19) or the 'sort of thing we would call an explanation of an aesthetic judgement' there are suggestions that it is not the door being too low or high, or a bass too loud or soft of which he is thinking and which are behind his conviction that aesthetic explanations are not hypotheses.

If we want to understand why Wittgenstein denies that a hypothesis can explain an aesthetic impression we must take note of the kind of thing which he elsewhere calls explaining an aesthetic effect. In *Philosophical Investigations* (p. 527) he says: 'In order to explain a theme in music I could only compare it with something else which has the same rhythm pattern. One says, "This is as if a conclusion were being drawn," or "this is, as it were, a parenthesis", etc.' In the *Brown Book*[7] (p. 166) he says of someone who justifies the way he plays a tune by comparing bits of it to an answer to a question: 'This shows what an explanation in aesthetics is like.' And in the next paragraph he says that 'suddenly understanding a musical theme may consist in finding a form of verbal expression which I conceive as the verbal counterpart[8] of the theme', and that understanding the expression on a face may consist in finding 'the word which seemed to sum it up'. In Moore's notes he says that an appropriate way of getting someone to see what Brahms was driving at might be to compare him to a contemporary author.

'What word would sum this up?' and 'What sentence (or contemporary author) does this musical phrase remind me of?' are more representative examples of what Wittgenstein thinks of as aesthetic questions and which prompts his remarks about their a-causality than 'What is wrong with this door?' On this view the main point of Wittgenstein's remarks on aesthetic explanation is not to call attention to the difference between the hypothesis that, for example, the mysteriousness of the expression on the face of La Gioconda is due to the shading of the areas round the eyes and mouth, and the remark that the 'object' of our feeling is the eyes and mouth, but between either or both of these and the remark

---

[7] *The Blue and Brown Books*, Blackwell, 1958.
[8] The text has 'counterpoint' which I take to be an error in transcription.

that the Mona Lisa impresses us as she does because her beauty is the deposit 'of strange thoughts, fantastic passions and exquisite reveries into which the soul with all its maladies has passed . . . and the eyelids are a little weary' etc., etc., etc. If Pater's is an acceptable account of the effect of La Gioconda this is not because he provides anything comparable to the lowness of the door but because his were 'the words that seemed to sum it up'.

II

I shall argue that where an object remark is clear it will have causal implications which can't be suspended. And I mean this as a piece of natural history which follows from accepting Wittgenstein's invitation to look at the use made of such sentences, the conversations they are part of and of what is said before and after them. The conversation could eschew topics such as the neurophysiological substrate, or the ulterior psychological effects, or even psychological causes not capable of being felt determinants, and still discuss issues only experimentally resolvable.

Consider the implications of the following story (which I have abbreviated)[9] for Wittgenstein's a-causal thesis: When Michelangelo showed Soderini the completed *David*, Soderini said that he was dissatisfied with the shape of David's nose which was too thick. Vasari, who relates the story, continues: 'Michelangelo . . . to satisfy him climbed on the scaffolding by the shoulders, seized hold of a chisel in his left hand, together with some of the marble dust lying on the planks, and as he tapped lightly with the chisel let the dust

---

[9] The story as Vasari tells it doesn't make much sense. My abbreviation consists in leaving out the remark that Michelangelo noticed Soderini was badly placed for seeing the nose. If this were the case, what was the point of the experiment? Why did Michelangelo not merely tell Soderini to move and why is the story felt to be discreditable to Soderini? I have an additional reason for suspecting the story is apocryphal. There are several similar ones in circulation. Pope claims to have played the same trick on Lord Halifax, who had objected to four or five phrases in Pope's translation of the *Iliad* that they were not as well turned as they might be. Pope was advised by a friend to leave the lines unaltered and re-read them to Halifax at a later time. 'I followed his advice, waited on Lord Halifax some time after, said "I hoped he would find his objections to those passages removed", read them to him exactly as they were at first, and his lordship was extremely pleased with them and cried out: "Ay, now they are perfectly right! Nothing could be better."' (Joseph Spence, *Observations, Anecdotes and Characters of Books and Men, Collected from Conversations*, ed. James M. Osdborne, vol. I, Oxford University Press, 1996, pp. 87–8). The moral of this anecdote is the same as that of the Soderini one, assuming that Halifax believed what he was saying.

fall little by little, without altering anything. Then he looked down at (Soderini), who had stopped to watch, and said: "Now look at it." "Ah, that's much better", replied Soderini, "Now you've really brought it to life".' Does this anecdote not demonstrate the propriety of experimental checks on object claims? How does Wittgenstein evade this conclusion? His account of this episode would run either that Soderini was (absurdly) complaining of a non-directed and thus non-aesthetic feeling of displeasure of which he conjectured the thickness of the nose to be the cause (and which complaint Michelangelo's experiment showed to be unfounded), or that Soderini's complaint pertained to a directed feeling of displeasure which Michelangelo's experiment left untouched.

The plausibility of this dilemma depends on an equivocation which Pears carries over into the first sentence of his paraphrase – an equivocation which Wittgenstein intermittently attempts to avoid – in one place by making the distinction between discomfort and discontent, and in another between directed discomfort and undirected discomfort. 'The expression of discontent is not the same as the expression of discomfort. Not an expression of discomfort plus knowing the cause. "I feel discomfort and know the cause" makes it sound as if there were two things going on in my soul – discomfort and knowing the cause – We have here a kind of discomfort which you may call directed, e.g., if I am afraid of you my discomfort is directed.' (p. 14)

This equivocation produces the impression that in asking for empirical confirmation of an aesthetic explanation we are committed to the absurdity that the phenomenon we want explained could be described without mentioning the aesthetic object which produced it – that if the judgement or feeling to be explained is contingently and not internally related to the object proffered by the explanation it is an ulterior effect and thus of no aesthetic interest, like the somnolence produced by a lullaby, or the ataractic effect David's playing had on Saul, or the disinclination to hilarity produced by Tchaikovsky's *Symphonie Pathétique*.

Making the distinction between ulterior and directed feeling simultaneously one between diagnostic and prognostic judgement confuses the issue and conceals the fact that Wittgenstein is working two distinctions, not one – a distinction between directed and non-directed feelings and between experimentally corrigible (prognostic) and non-corrigible (diagnostic) judgements. Once we see this we can entertain the possibility that aesthetic explanations may proffer experimentally corrigible judgements about the objects of directed feelings and can reject the dilemma – either experimentally corrigible (prognostic) and ulterior and thus not aesthetic, or directed and thus such that assent is the only criterion.

We can get a better grasp of the distinction between directed and non-directed feelings by considering William James' failure to draw it properly, or at any rate clearly, in the following remarks:

Nature has many methods of producing the same effect. She may . . . fill us with terror at certain surroundings by making them really dangerous, or by a blow which produces a pathological alteration of our brain. It is obvious that we need two words to designate these two modes of operating. In the one case the natural agents produce perceptions which take cognisance of the agents themselves; in the other case, they produce perceptions which take cognisance of something else. What is taught to the mind by the 'experience', in the first case, is the order of the experience itself – the 'inner relation' corresponds to the 'outer relation' which produced it, by remembering and knowing the latter. But in the case of the other sort of natural agency, what is taught to the mind has nothing to do with the agency itself, but with some different outer relation altogether . . . the tinnitos aurium discloses no properties of the quinine; the morbid dread (of solitude, perhaps) no brain pathology; but the way in which a dirty sunset and a rainy morrow hang together in the mind copies and teaches the sequences of sunsets and rainfall in the outer world.

In this passage James doesn't make it clear enough that the fact that certain perceptions 'take cognisance of the agents themselves' isn't sufficient to relate the perceptions 'internally' to their effects, and treats the morbid dread of solitude, or the terror of dangerous surroundings as if the dread were related to the solitude and the terror to the surroundings as dirty sunsets are to rainy morrows. But the quinine and the ringing in the ears might come to hang together in the mind as the dirty sunset and the rainy morrows already do without their standing to each other as the dread or the terror to their respective objects, the solitude and the danger. It would still be only a matter of having a feeling *plus* knowing the cause.

Ortega makes the relevant distinction in the following passage:[10] 'An aesthetic pleasure must be a seeing pleasure. For pleasures

---

[10] Ortega Y Gasset, *The Dehumanization of Art*, New York, 1956, p. 25.

may be blind or seeing. The drunken man's happiness is blind. Like everything in the world it has a cause, the alcohol; but it has no motive. A man who has won a sweepstake is happy, too, but in a different manner; he is happy "about" something. The drunken man's merriment is enclosed in itself, he does not know why he is happy. Whereas the joy of the winner consists precisely in his being conscious of a definite fact that motivates and justifies his content-ment . . . his is a happiness with eyes.' When Wittgenstein says 'There is a why to aesthetic discomfort not a cause to it' he is calling attention to the same phenomenon as Ortega, the differ-ence between a blind pleasure and a seeing one – between the drunkard's euphoria and the gambler's, between so many ccs of alcohol in the blood and a royal flush.

But the distinction between having a directed feeling, of aes-thetic discomfort for example, and merely having a feeling and knowing its cause does not coincide with that between explanations for which assent is the only criterion and those for which it is not. Columbus, in order to keep up the spirits of his crew, increased their ration of wine and made false entries in his log book, thus pro-ducing not just a psychophysical cocktail but a causal-intentional one. Both factors were causes; one was an object as well.

A clearer grasp of the distinction between directed and non-directed feelings seems to me to have done nothing to enhance the plausibility of Wittgenstein's argument for the sufficiency of assent. It is still not clear why it should be thought that because a judgement is vulnerable to empirical overthrow it must pertain to ulterior effects, i.e. non-directed feelings – why someone who thinks that a door is too low must either be complaining of a non-directed feeling of discomfort which he thinks due to the height of the door or, alternatively, not be speaking prognostically. The feeling that the door is too low isn't just the feeling that goes away when the door is raised. These are not related as a headache to the aspirin that relieves it. The question is whether they need to be in order for an experiment to be a natural way of determining the correctness of the claim that the object of the feeling is, for ex-ample, the lowness of the door – whether an explanation couldn't possess both features which Wittgenstein thinks mutually repug-nant – that of pertaining to the object of a directed feeling and of being vulnerable to empirical refutation, i.e. *not* such that 'assent is the only criterion'.

Consider what is at issue between Darwin and Duchenne when Duchenne attributes the difference between a natural smile and one produced by galvanising the great zygomatic muscle to the fact that in the latter case the orbicular muscles of the lower eyelids were not as contracted as usual whereas Darwin, though he concedes a role to the lower orbiculars, asserts that it is predominantly the failure of the normal drawing up of the upper lip, which would have altered the look of the naso-labial furrow, that gives the electrically induced smile distinctiveness. This is certainly an experimental issue. Why is it not an aesthetic one? The causal terms in this example are not differently related than the dissatisfaction with the door and its lowness, i.e. as feeling and object. It is not a case of *inferring* the artificiality of the smile from the contours of the face but of *seeing* it there. We might mark this distinction by adapting a remark of Merleau-Ponty's about bodily gestures in general and say that the smile does not merely convey its meaning, but is 'filled' with it.[11] This involves 'directedness' and yet the natural sequel to the disagreement between Darwin and Duchenne is, nonetheless, an experiment. Wittgenstein doesn't dispose of this with his remark that 'the expression is not an *effect* of the face. You could not say that if anything else had this effect it would have the expression on this face.' (p. 30)

We can draw on Wittgenstein himself for an example of an impression which is both directed and not internally related to the object preferred in the explanation of it – that of the faces whose similarity is held to be due to the shape of the eyes (*Brown Book*, p. 136). The similarity of the faces is not an ulterior effect like the headache produced by the colours in a flower bed, or the mood of sadness produced by a picture (Wittgenstein's examples). Though it is directed towards the faces it can be described without mentioning the shape of the eyes which play the role of explanans in the object remark. Yet if the similarity of the faces survived a perceptible dissimilarity in the shape of the eyes would not the object

---

[11] I am not sure what makes it appropriate to speak of perceiving qualities rather than of inferring them. Helen Keller said she could feel Shaw's egotism in his hands. Was she speaking figuratively? If someone were blindfolded and had to distinguish galvanic smiles from real ones by running his hands over the surface of faces, would he ever come to the point where he *felt* the falseness of the eyes? What fine shades of behaviour would tempt us to say of someone that he now felt the falseness in the eyes as formerly he had seen it there? In *Zettel* 506 Wittgenstein discusses what it might mean to call hair colour friendly.

remark have been empirically refuted? This is the consequence of being able to individuate the object on a different basis from the feeling which it explained. But the relevance of causal considerations is not confined to such causes.

It might seem that a more restricted version of Wittgenstein's a-causal thesis is nevertheless tenable – remarks that give the objects of directed feelings which, unlike the similarity of the faces or the naturalness of the smile, cannot be identified independently of the objects proffered in explanations of them are bereft of prognostic implications and thus settlable by assent. This is not so.

Goethe's Mephistopheles tells Faust: 'Having imbibed this potion you will soon see Helen in every female.' The potion that Mephistopheles offers Faust is not related to his subsequently seeing Helen in every female as an aphrodisiac to the excitation it induces. The object of Faust's feeling would be internally related to it, yet the relation of the potion to hyper-susceptibility to feminine charms is a causal one. Bottom's 'sleek, smooth ass's head and fair large ears' were the object of Titania's infatuation. That the fairness of the ears was in the nature of 'a further description' of Bottom's charms doesn't preclude its cause from having been the love juice which Puck placed on Titania's sleeping eyes, nor the appropriateness of a conversation dealing with her condition from calling her attention to this occurrence. William James observed that 'the joyous animal spirits of the Three Musketeers awaken dismal and woeful consciousness of cruelty and carnage in a reader depressed with seasickness'. The 'dismal and woeful consciousness of cruelty and carnage' is as internally related to the activities of the Three Musketeers as the expression of sadness to the face, but it is, nonetheless, eligible for causal explanation which calling attention to the seasickness provides.

I don't mean to suggest by these examples that abnormal physical conditions play an appreciable role in aesthetic discussions. I am only making the theoretical point that even where a feeling is identified via its object the relevance of causal enquiry is not excluded. The following example is more typical of the way causal questions enter aesthetic discussion. Dr Johnson is criticising the diction of a passage in *Macbeth*:[12] 'When Macbeth is confirming

---

[12] *Rambler*, p. 68. Johnson is in error as to the speaker. It is Lady Macbeth.

himself in his horrid purpose he breaks, in the violence of his emotions, into a wish natural to a murderer:

> Come, thick night
> and pall thee in the dunnest smoke of Hell
> that my keen knife see not the wound it makes.

. . . we cannot but sympathise with the horror of the wretch about to murder his master, his friend, his benefactor, who suspects that the weapon will refuse its office and start back from the breast which he is preparing to violate. Yet this sentiment is weakened by the name of an instrument used by butchers and by cooks in the meanest employments: we do not immediately believe that any crime of importance is to be committed with a *knife* and from long habit of connecting a knife with sordid offices feel aversion rather than terror.'

Isn't it appropriate to protest that no one without an a priori notion of what constitutes permissible poetic diction could have suffered the 'Disturbance of his Attention from the Counteraction of the Words to the Ideas' of which Johnson complained and to support this claim by appealing to the fact that those without such preconceptions, though as familiar as Johnson with the domestic associations of the word knife, and just as capable of picking out the 'low' words, do not undergo such disturbances of the attention? And isn't this an inductive procedure?

Wittgenstein sometimes suggests that aesthetic judgements are a-causal because they are like interjections. In *Zettel* 551 he says of the remark 'the smell is marvellous!!': 'There might, however, be a language in which the people merely shut their eyes and say "Oh this smell!" and there is no subject–predicate sentence equivalent to it.' The question is whether 'The door is too low' can shed the subject-predicate form as readily as 'The smell is marvellous', whether it is always equivalent to 'This ugly low door'. But the a-causality of 'the door is too low' need not depend on its interjectional status. Wittgenstein invites us to place still another construction on his claim that dissatisfaction with the lowness of the door won't lend itself to a causal analysis. The man who says the door is too low just doesn't like low doors. There can be no cause because there is no effect. That the door be raised is 'an end in itself, not a means to another end'. (Moore, p. 301) But then there can be no question of explanation either.

Wittgenstein succeeds in showing that aesthetic remarks like 'the door is too low', 'the bass is too loud or moves too much' need not be causal remarks. But it doesn't follow from this that answers to the questions 'What is wrong with the door, the bass, the flower bed' might not be causal answers. 'What is wrong with the door' might be a-causal if it were addressed to someone else and meant 'Let us see if your taste is as good as it ought to be, i.e. how well you have assimilated the rules of good construction, etc.' but not if the question 'What is wrong with the door, statue, music, verse, etc.' is asked by the same person who later decides that it is the height of the door, the loudness of the bass, the thickness of the nose, the profusion of dark colours in the flower bed, etc., etc., which is responsible for his impression. Wittgenstein's example in the footnote on p. 15, which pertains to someone asking what is wrong with a picture, not in a pedagogic spirit, but from genuine ignorance as to the source of his conviction, illustrates the kind of issue to which his analysis fails to apply.

We don't have to treat Johnson's objection to low words as a categorical demand any more than Johnson himself treated the demand for observance of the unities as categorical. He argued that the causal consequences attributed to their violation were absurd. That is, he treated them as causal claims. And this is how on many occasions aesthetic judgements ask to be treated.

One of the reasons for Wittgenstein's mistake here is that he doesn't distinguish clearly between aesthetic judgements as to the source of an impression or object of a feeling, and another class of remark which *is* a-causal. These are cases where, though the source of our feeling, 'discomfort', impression of similarity, etc. is unknown to us, when it is discovered it is held to characterise the feeling internally – for example 'That's the peculiar rhythm I meant – the three against the four.' As James remarks apropos the related phenomenon of trying to recall a forgotten name: 'We can only designate the difference (between the efforts involved in recalling different names) by borrowing the names of objects not yet in mind.'

Wittgenstein confounds the relation in which we stand to a percept, an object of sensory inspection, with that in which we stand to 'a thought at the back of our minds' (perhaps because a perceptual situation might provoke a peripheral nagging aware-

ness which refuses for a time to come to verbal expression).
Nevertheless, there are two distinct situations:
(1) What is it that I am wanting to say about the similarity of the
     faces? O yes! that it is the shape of the eyes which makes them
     similar.
(2) It is the shape of the eyes which makes the faces look similar.
In the first case assent is, as Wittgenstein says, the only criterion but
not in the second. Just as, though assent is the only criterion for
the name at the back of my mind when I was trying to remember
the Prime Minister who succeeded Salisbury, it is nevertheless *not*
the only criterion for its actually being the name of the Prime
Minister who succeeded Salisbury.

Pears illustrates this assimilation in the paragraph after the one
I quoted: 'If, instead of considering a simple example (like complaining of the door's height) we took a case in which the person
who was making the aesthetic judgement found it difficult to formulate it precisely, the situation would be more problematical,
but essentially the same'; and Pears goes on to speak of 'a vague
and hesitant answer' giving way to a 'firmer and more precise'
one. But the situation would not be 'essentially the same'. Causal
considerations don't enter into the assessment of such remarks
not because we are dealing with objects of feelings but because we
are dealing with what James describes as the task of 'bringing
certain qualities which were blurred and marginal into distinct
consciousness'. The class of remarks that Pears refers to here
don't owe their immunity to experimental revision to the a-causal
relation in which a feeling stands to its object but to the relation
in which the vague formulation of an answer stands to a more
precise one, or a clearer and more confident explanation to 'a
vague and hesitant' one.

Even though I individuate, identify my impression via my
delayed recognition of its source I would still feel that I was under
an illusion if I discovered that it was causally dependent on conditions of a certain kind. If Johnson had not been immediately aware
as to what it was that troubled him about the phrase 'that my knife
see not the wound it makes' and it then dawned on him that it was
the word 'knife', so that he had no other way of referring to his
misgiving except as that produced by 'knife', so that there was
something non-hypothetical about his judgement, he might, nevertheless, still be persuaded to withdraw it if he were convinced

that his displeasure was a function of his preconceptions about poetic diction. We can easily imagine Soderini standing before the *David* and wondering what it is that he feels to be wrong with it and then realizing that it was the thickness of the nose in the same spirit that one finds the word that was at the back of one's mind. There is certainly something here which experiment can't over-throw but it is not that Soderini's 'aesthetic discomfort' was due to the *David*'s nose being too thick.

What I say when I enlarge on what I felt is part of what I felt, not the cause of what I felt, but describing the source of one's impres-sion isn't always just a matter of enlarging on what one felt. Spencer's analysis of grace and Jaentsch's account of the uncanny are both a-causal, a-hypothetical, but not because of their object-feeling or source-impression structure but because they are illustrations of an activity which has been generically characterised by Mill as 'bringing before people's minds as a distinct principle that which as vague feeling has already guided them in their employment of a term'.

Perhaps we miss the causal-hypothetical component in aesthetic judgements of the lowness-of-the-door, shape-of-the-eyes, kind because of the ease with which perception passes into rumination – as in Gombrich's account of the Mona Lisa smile – where, because the viewer can't say where the boundary of the mouth and eye corners are, he is therefore unsure of the meaning of the smile – and so his experience goes from indeterminacy of outline to tantalising ambiguity of expression. He could be wrong about the role of the shading round the eyes of the Mona Lisa in a way in which he could not be wrong about the role played in his impres-sion by his sense of the ambiguity of the face.

Another source of the impression that such remarks are a-causal may be that they are so often certain. If I have a schematic face made up of a circle with two dots for eyes and a line for a mouth there is a gross oddity about asking whether I am sure that my judgement as to its smiling or lugubrious character is directed at the mouth corners. There is something spuriously experimental about reasssuring myself by erasing the downward projection of the lines and replacing them with upturned ones to see what I then will think about it.[13]

---

[13] And yet, 'It is in the inner angle of the eyebrow and the corners of the mouth that expression in the human countenance principally resides: according to the direction in which these parts are drawn, is the character of the face entirely changed. "To

It is so difficult to give a sense to our being wrong on such occasions that we may be tempted to conclude that the remarks are not merely certain but 'apodictic'. (p. 22) And cases like this do occur in criticism. When Orwell says 'one can often improve Kipling's poems, make them less facetious and less blatant, by simply . . . transplanting them from Cockney into standard speech', or when Kenneth Clark says of Michaelangelo's *David* 'cut out the head and the hands and you have one of the most classical works of the renaissance. Put them back and you put back the rough Tuscan accent', we seem competent to assess their correctness without accepting the invitation to experiment. Perhaps it was with cases like this in mind that Wittgenstein said 'it is a causal explanation of this sort – the person agreeing with you sees the cause at once'. (p. 18)

But even if we can say 'at once' that a rose by any other name would smell as sweet (an apparently counterfactual thesis) couldn't there be more complex cases where our conviction might be undermined experimentally? For example, 'no man could have fancied that he read "Lycidas" with pleasure had he not known its author' (Johnson). Wasn't it the implications of this remark or remarks like it that Richards was experimentally investigating when he distributed to his Cambridge classes for comment poems of which the spelling had been modernised and the author withheld? Those roses didn't smell as sweet. And this limitation of Wittgenstein's sufficiency-of-reflection thesis is a serious one because of the ubiquity of suggestibility in influencing our acceptance of the class of aesthetic judgements under discussion, a tendency which can only be held in check by demonstrations of how often they prove unfounded. Proust states the problem in its most general form in an essay: 'Is it really my mind which is so delighted by this book, or just my taste for what is in fashion, the copy-cat instinct which makes for so much unanimity in the tastes of a generation, or some other contemptible preference?' It is at least plausible to suggest that

demonstrate the importance of these features Pietro di Cortona performed the following experiment before Francis the first of France: he drew a countenance unmoved by passion, and then touching lightly with his pencil these parts he showed that monarch that according as he gave them a direction upwards or downwards, he produced the expression of laughter or grief."' (R.E. Wright-St. Clair, 'David Monro's lecture on the expression of passion', 1840, *Bulletin of the History of Medicine*, Volume 30, November–December, 1956).

the resolution of issues like these involves us in causal judge-ments.[14]

III

The difference between aesthetic explanations and causal hypo-theses does not lie in the directed-to-objects character of aesthetic explanations conferring immunity to empirical refutation on them but on certain other features – the indeterminacy of the causal relations they proffer and the indeterminacy of the effects they explain. It is the indefiniteness of the relations into which the cause-object enters and not in its being the target of a directed feeling that its unsuitability for experimental assessment lies.

These are the last six lines of Keats' sonnet 'On first looking into Chapman's Homer', followed by a literary critic's elucidation of their effect.[15]

> Then felt I like some watcher of the skies
> When a new planet swims into his ken;
> Or like stout Cortez, when with eagle eyes
> He stared at the Pacific – and all his men
> Look'd at each other with a wild surmise –
> Silent, upon a peak in Darien.

'The effect of breathless, awe-struck silence is obtained through Keats' resourceful use of verse-structure . . . The secret is in the dra-matic pause after "wild surmise". Three factors contribute to this: the drama of the imagined situation itself; the position of the words at the end of the line; and the fact that "surmise" rhymes

---

[14] 'There is nothing in the art of verifying so much exposed to the power of imagination as the accommodation of the sound to the sense. It is scarcely to be doubted that on many occasions we make the music that we imagine ourselves to hear, that we modulate the poem by our own disposition, and ascribe to the numbers the effects of the sense.' (Johnson, *Rambler*, p. 92).

'In literature we can easily convince ourselves of the emotional significance . . . of par-ticular consonant and vowel sounds and still more easily of the effects of rhythms. Always the difficulty is to discover how far the sounds and rhythms alone, without the sense of the words they go with, are responsible for the emotional effects; they provide projective material in which the willing are tempted to hear expressive qualities that have quite other sources.' (D.W. Harding).

Of course I can't allay the more profound doubt as to whether the kind of self-knowledge involved in cases like this demands an objectivist methodology or whether it can be achieved by a particular kind of reflection which is not to be assimilated to any species of inductive reasoning. It is this problem which is the major link with Wittgenstein's remarks on Freud and accounts for their interpolation in a lecture on Aesthetics. [15] Robin Mayhead, *John Keats*, Cambridge University Press, 1967, p. 61.

heavily with two previous words. The resulting impression is that of a wide-eyed catch of the breath, after which the isolated "Silent" comes out with superb appropriateness.' What is the right thing to say about remarks like this? Is it that in them the role of explanans is played by objects of feelings and not causes? And thus that assent, not experiment, is the appropriate criterion of correctness?

Let me try to make good my assertion that if an aesthetic explanation makes a simple and determinate claim with respect to the object, or the source of an impression, then it is amenable to experimental assessment. Here is an example – John Canaday, an art critic, says of Holbein's portrait of Queen Christina, 'If the figure were truly centred it would convey to us the impression of a much more four-square, more obvious, more everyday woman.' Theodore L. Shaw thought this statement 'so flagrantly untrue' that he submitted a modified version of Holbein's portrait, in which the figure was truly centred, to one hundred and ninety-eight persons, none of whom, Shaw exultantly reports, found the figure of Queen Christina more four-square, more obvious, or more everyday. Let us put aside the question of the generality of Canaday's claim and restrict ourselves to asking whether had Canaday himself felt that Shaw's modified, truly centred figure was no more four-square, more obvious, more everyday a woman than the original he would have had any choice but to withdraw his original claim as to the source of his impression. Wouldn't Shaw's employment of what Wittgenstein calls 'an if-then technique' have settled the question? If this is so, then the empirical undecidability of other examples can't be a function of their feeling-object structure, which it shares with the Queen Christina example, but of their complexity and indeterminacy.

What is striking about Shaw's experiment is that so many people were able to say whether Queen Christina became more everyday as she was moved to the centre of the canvas. Normally the difficulty in cases of this kind is not that we are unsure about how the outcome of the experiment bears on the original claim, but that we are unsure of how to characterise the outcome. Here is a simple example of what I mean by this from Herbert Spencer's essay on style.[16] Spencer is arguing for the superiority of the order of noun and adjective in English to that in French: '. . . it is better to say "a

[16] Herbert Spencer, 'The philosophy of style' in *Literary Style and Music*, London, 1950. p. 9.

black horse" as we do in English, than a "horse black" as do the
French, because if "a horse black" be the sequence, immediately
on the utterance of the word horse, there arises a picture answering to that word and as there has been nothing to indicate what
kind of horse, the image may be that of a brown horse, brown
horses being the most familiar. The result is that when the word
black is added a check is given to the process of thought. Either
the picture of a brown horse has to be suppressed and the picture
of a black one summoned in its place, or else, if the picture of a
brown horse be yet unformed, the tendency to form it has to be
stopped. But if on the other hand, "a black horse" be the expression used no such mistake can be made. The word black, indicating an abstract quality, arouses no definite idea. It simply prepares
the mind for conceiving some object of that colour and the attention is kept suspended until that object is known. It follows that the
one sequence gives the mind less trouble than the other and is,
therefore, more forcible.'

I am at a loss to decide by introspection whether there is anything in it. No doubt Spencer had persuaded himself that he had
experienced the effect he speaks of. I think my difficulty is a
general one and is one of the sources of the persuasiveness of
Wittgenstein's view that such remarks are a-causal. It is only with
much grosser effects, such as those Bradley attributes to the
double plot in the last act of *King Lear,* that I can feel some confidence. ('The number of essential characters is so large, their
actions and movements are so complicated, and events towards
the close crowd on one another so thickly that the reader's attention, rapidly transferred from one centre of interest to another, is
overstrained. He becomes, if not intellectually confused, at least
emotionally fatigued.') I am also sure that I experience no jolting
at the violation of the unities in *Antony and Cleopatra.* But if the
argument takes a subtler turn and invokes the loss of intensity, I
am always afraid that what I take for recognition may be complais-
ance. The effect is so fine that any one already persuaded of the
efficacy of the cause will think he is experiencing it.

Here is an example from painting: 'Pieter de Hooch has an
extremely clever expedient for making us aware of the solemn
silence of interiors and courtyards: through a perspective of
rooms, or a lateral passage more luminous than the rest of the
picture, a figure retires or approaches: we imagine the sound of a

footstep echoing in a magical void. The sound, like that of a stone falling into a quiet pool, is a comment upon the immense surrounding silence.' (Mario Praz)

Is it idiosyncratic incapacity which renders me unable to say in such cases whether the paintings in which Pieter de Hooch, or others, employ this device is characterised by a more solemn silence than those in which they do not? No one in the Arnolfini is walking. Is it less solemnly silent? Yet I am happy not to raise such questions and to relish Praz's comment and others like it and I think my practice quite general and not to be explained in terms of the conceptual inappropriateness of having recourse to causal enquiry to settle object claims.

Whether a woman is more everyday and four-square, whether identification with Dick Diver (of *Tender is the Night*) is more intense in the chronologically told version of the novel, whether the effect of silent awe at the end of 'Chapman's Homer' is enhanced by the line division, may well be questions which it is inappropriate to treat as experimental, but not for the reason Wittgenstein gives – that they are a-causal. Though Wittgenstein is right about the recalcitrance to empirical assessment of much aesthetic explanation of the object-proferring, lowness-of-the-door, loudness-of-the-bass, too-smiling-face, shape-of-the-eyes kind, he is wrong about its sources. These are its causal complexity and indeterminacy. Confronted with specimens of this degree of complexity we are no wiser as to the object than as to the cause.

Rather than say that such aesthetic explanations are not hypotheses let us say that they are not put to the uses to which hypotheses are normally put. There is a moral to the resistance that they offer to causal paraphrase, i.e. paraphrase which puts them in a shape such that experiment could bear on them; but this moral is not their conceptual distinctiveness but their functional distinctiveness. They have features which compel us to admit that their point is not to advance our causal knowledge of the matters with which they deal. This is to be distinguished from Wittgenstein's stronger thesis that aesthetic explanations are not hypotheses because aesthetic explanations must mention objects and object remarks don't have causal implications.

The critic expresses himself in a causal mode because his aim is to evince and enhance aspects, and this is one way of doing it. He chooses features of the work (or of its history) congruent with his impression and ascribes a causal influence to them. The impression made by a first reading, determined perhaps by the dramatic situation, feeds back into subsequent readings, seizing on whatever is consonant with the original impression and pressing it in the service of an intensified expressiveness.

Here are some examples of what I mean by pressing features into the service of an enhanced expressiveness: – Robert Graves says of a line from the description of the banquet in 'St Agnes' Eve' – 'And lucent syrups tinct with cinnamon' – that the absence of variation in the vowel sounds was deliberate: 'Keats was surely intending to suggest here a gourmet's fastidious pursing of the lips.' Leigh Hunt reports that Keats defended Shakespeare's line about bees – 'the singing masons building roofs of gold' – against Wordsworth's complaint about the repeated *g* sound by pointing out 'that it was in harmony with the continued note of the singers'.

We could treat remarks of this kind as proto-experimental. Perhaps with sufficient ingenuity we might excogitate an experiment which we agreed was continuous with or implicit in our original judgement; but is this what we generally want? It is this class of cases, more typical than those which clearly, determinately, name the object of a feeling, which Wittgenstein's claim that 'you have to give the explanation that is accepted. That is the whole point of the explanation' illuminates and for which it holds.[17]

IV

I now pass to Wittgenstein's second thesis: in aesthetics explanations are not hypotheses because hypotheses are not what we want

---

[17] Whereas it would be characteristic of aesthetic discussions for someone who didn't share Canaday's impression of Queen Christina to contradict him and support this by an appeal to consensus, there is something unnatural about disputing his account of the sources of this impression by an experimental procedure. Canaday may have been wrong, as we often are in such cases, as to where the thought that Queen Christina was not an everyday woman had come from. Maybe being dressed like a queen had something to do with it. And this is not a question as to the character of a rumination but as to what incited it – a causal question. But when we are given an acceptable account of the nature of a rumination we are not too fussy about the literal correctness of any implication as to what set it off. Consider de Quincey and the knocking at the gate. How can we be reasonably sure that his rumination would not have taken the same course even had there been no knocking at the gate? The drunken porter business would still have been there to mark the reflux of the human on the fiendish. But has anyone, in the century and a half that essay has enjoyed currency, raised this sort of issue with respect to it? And yet it has been praised for its empirical, psychological, non-impressionistic character.

when we ask for the explanation of an impression. What then do we want?

In attempting to explain what it is that 'one longs for when one talks about an aesthetic impression' Wittgenstein occasionally expresses a view as to what is wanted which, though it is illuminating – one had forgotten or overlooked how much critical talk answers to it – is nevertheless too limiting – a synaesthesic demand. What this amounts to is the attempt to provide an equivalent in a different modality for the experience we wish to characterise or elucidate. In Lecture Two, Wittgenstein speaks of 'gestures' as a means of elucidating impressions. And in his lecture on descriptions he says '. . . with some people, me especially, the expression of an emotion in music, say, is a gesture'. Wittgenstein may have been one of those persons referred to by Havelock Ellis in whom 'the motor imagery suggested by music is profuse . . . and may be regarded as an anomaly comparable to synaesthesia'. Ellis says that for him the gesture made 'by some melodies of Handel was that of a giant painting frescoes on a vast wall space'. Heine expresses related sentiments in *Florentine Nights*. He tells of a deaf painter who '. . . was enthusiastically fond of music and . . . knew how, when near enough to the orchestra, to read the music on the musicians' faces, and to judge the more or less skilful execution by the movements of their fingers; indeed, he wrote critiques on the opera for an excellent journal at Hamburg. And is that peculiarly wonderful? In the visible symbols of the performance the deaf painter could see the sounds. There are men to whom the sounds themselves are invisible symbols in which they hear colours and forms.'

There is another way in which Wittgenstein thinks one might convey the character of an impression. In his lecture on description he says that whereas one person might describe the impression made on him by a piece of music by making a certain gesture another, a painter perhaps, might describe his impression by drawing an appropriate face. Orwell provides an instance of this in his essay on Dickens: 'When one reads any strongly individual piece of writing one has the impression of a face behind the page. It is not necessarily the actual face of the writer . . . what one sees is the face the writer ought to have.' And Orwell goes on to describe the face he sees behind Dickens' writing. Orwell's imagining a face behind the page is like Wittgenstein's painter drawing an appropriate face to go with the music that had impressed him.

   In the same lecture Wittgenstein says of the experience of 'being
intrigued and wanting to describe': 'You may one day find a *word*
or you find a verse that fits it. It is as though (the composer) said
". . ." and you have a verse. And now perhaps you say: "And now I
understand it."' An example of what Wittgenstein means is provided by his own experience of finding certain themes of Brahms
extremely Kellerian, that is, of finding that a comparison with
Keller illuminated the impression made by Brahms' music.
Sometimes this works the other way round and an effort to
understand finds its consummation in a musical experience.
Wittgenstein found that a piano piece of Schumann's ('Wie aus
der Weiter Ferne') expressed for him the essence of pastness – 'of
the experience of long, long ago'. One thinks of Ezra Pound's
notion that the best criticism of a poem is a musical setting of it
and of his setting Catullus and Villon to music because he found
them untranslatable, and of Schumann reporting that when he
played Schubert he felt as if he were reading a novel scored by
Jean-Paul Richter.
   If, as Wittgenstein says, to understand aesthetic discourse we
have to describe a culture, then the culture we have to describe in
order to understand this conception of aesthetic explanation is
that in which Caruso's voice was described as violet and Melba's as
pink, and which produced aphorisms like 'hearing is an inward
seeing' and 'music is an audible dance', the idea of a colour clavi-
chord, Rimbaud's sonnet *Vowels*, Baudelaire's poem *Correspon-
dances* and the passage in Hoffmann's *Kreisleriana* which suggested
it, Mörike's synaesthesic description of the trombone sounds in
the graveyard scene in *Don Giovanni,* and Heine's anecdote about
the deaf painter who criticised performances on the basis of movements made by the musicians.[18]
   But aesthetic explanation encompasses activities more discursive than the provision of good similes and more akin to what

---

[18] An example of Wittgenstein's relish in aesthetic explanations which employs synaesthesic description is provided by Engelmann in his *Memoir.* 'Wittgenstein was enraptured
by Mörike's immortal story, *Mozart's Journey to Prague* . . . especially by the passages
describing musical effects in words: "Coming as from remotest starry worlds, the sounds
fall from the mouth of silver trombones, icy cold, cutting through marrow and soul; fall
through the blueness of the night," he would recite with a shudder of awe.' (Paul
Engelmann, *Letters from Ludwig Wittgenstein,* Blackwell, 1967, p. 86.) Since Engelmann
describes Mörike's lines as 'one of the great passages in literature' they are no doubt
more impressive in the original German. 'Through marrow and cucumber', as Thomas
Mann's Hofrat Behrens might have said.

Lionel Trilling once called 'recapitulating the moral history of the race'. We could say that Orwell was recapitulating a bit of the moral history of the race when, in attempting to account for 'the undefinable familiarity' of the postcards of Donald McGill ('What do these remind you of? What are they so like?'), he invoked the Sancho Panza view of life ('extracting as much fun as possible from smacking behinds in basement kitchens'), working class reconciliation to the passing of youth, 'the celebration of the unheroic', and went on to speak of 'the sub-world of smacked bottoms and scrawny mothers-in-law which is a part of Western European consciousness'. Remarks like these are only figuratively 'gestures' or 'similes' but they are more often what we want when we ask for analyses of our impressions than are synaesthetic resonances or counterparts.

It is this kind of thing and not low doors, loud basses, etc., etc., of which Wittgenstein is thinking when he speaks of aesthetic explanations often taking the form of answers to questions like 'What is at the back of my mind?', 'What does this remind me of?', or 'What is in our minds when we say so and so?' (for example, in Wittgenstein's mind when he had the 'queer idea' and there was a 'tremendous philosophy behind' Michelangelo's *Creation of Adam*).

When Wittgenstein says that aesthetic analyses are not hypotheses he is not merely thinking of causal hypotheses. He is sometimes addressing himself to questions like: How could the name of Guermantes contain, as it did for Marcel, the essence of the feudal age? What makes McGill's postcards an epitome of what Orwell found in them – how, in what manner, are the proverbial thousand words contained in the picture? Not like beads in a box; for it would make no difference if we imagined these beads to come into existence as they emerged from a hole in the lid (*Brown Book*, p. 40). And so 'utterance is the only criterion' and 'All we can say is that if it is presented to you, you say "yes, that's what happened".'

In remarks like these Wittgenstein is calling attention to explanans that fail to stand to impressions as causes to effects, not because they stand to them rather as objects to feelings but because they stand to them as further descriptions to original experience; for example, as allusions to flowingness and continuity stand to the impression of gracefulness, or as uncertainty as to whether an apparently animate object is inanimate, or an inanimate one animate, stands to the impression of uncanniness. And it is to this feature and not to their feeling-object structure that they owe their settlability by reflection.

This comes out in Wittgenstein's remark on Freud's explanations of jokes at the end of Lecture Two: 'You might call the explanation Freud gives a causal explanation. If it is not causal how do you know it is correct? You say: "yes, that's right".' (p. 18) I am not sure that the temptation to describe Freud's joke-reductions as causal explanations is very strong. But Wittgenstein is arguing for a more interesting thesis than their a-causality. They are not only unlike accounts of the substrate processes of which conscious events may be an epiphenomenon, like for example, those underlying an attack of migraine, they are also unlike a literal description of the migraine attack itself ('first I get this pain behind my eyes, then what I see goes funny, then I feel sick . . .'). In Moore's notes Wittgenstein says that the person who agrees with Freud's account of why he laughed 'is not agreeing to a hypothesis' and, further, that his agreement 'tells you nothing as to what was happening at the moment when he laughed' and in the lectures that 'Freud transforms the joke into a different form which is recognized by us as an expression of the chain of ideas which led us from one end to another of a joke.' By parity we can say that the critic transforms an experience, of a poem say, into a different form which is recognised by us as an expression of the chain of ideas which led us from one end of the poem etc. Here is an example of Freud leading us from one end of a joke to another: 'There is a witty and pugnacious journalist in Vienna, whose biting invective has repeatedly led to his being physically maltreated by the subjects of his attacks. On one occasion, when a fresh misdeed on the part of one of his habitual opponents was being discussed, somebody exclaimed: "If X hears of this, he'll get his ears boxed again." The technique of this joke includes, in the first place, bewilderment at its apparent nonsense, since we cannot see how getting one's ears boxed can be an immediate consequence of having heard something. The absurdity of the remark disappears if we insert in the gap: "he'll write such a scathing article upon the man that . . . etc."'[19]

Freud's reconstruction of the chain of ideas which led from one end to the other of the Kraus joke isn't like Sherlock Holmes'

[19] Sigmund Freud, *Jokes and their Relation to the Unconscious*, Routledge and Kegan Paul, 1960, pp. 77–8.

reconstruction of the reveries which led Watson from the portrait of Henry Ward Beecher to his Jezail-inflicted wound. If the thoughts that figure in Freud's account had actually occurred to us as we listened there would have been no joke. Yet this does not preclude the correctness of Freud's account. It is in these cases that 'all we can say is that if it is presented to you, you say, "Yes, that's what happened".'

Consider Empson's account of a line from Herbert's poem *The Pilgrimage*:

> That led me to the wild of Passion, which
> Some call the wold:
> A wasted place, but sometimes rich.

'. . . in wondering what the occasional riches of a wold can be like, you find yourself, after reviewing deserts and oases, Spain's vine-yards and barren rock, and Horace Walpole's remark about Blenheim that it was like the castle of an ogre who had desolated the surrounding country, in the knightly fairyland of Spenser among vast and inhuman wildernesses and the portentous luxury of enchanted castles.' This (and the same is true of Empson's other analyses) is not a description of what went on in our minds as we read the words, 'a wasted place, but sometimes rich'. There is nothing here analogous to an account of what went on in our stomachs during an attack of indigestion, or even to Dupin-like reconstructions of the course of a brown study. Otherwise the poem would just stop while the associations trooped by. (We may even owe our acquaintance with Walpole's remark about Blenheim Castle to Empson's analysis without this imperilling the adequacy of the analysis.)

Consider Maude Bodkin's attempt to account for the fact that she could not think of Abora in *Kubla Khan* as a paradisal mount but instead found herself associating the name with caverns, sub-terranean winds and tumult. 'The answer came in the form of a dim memory of some mountains named by Milton and associated with fierce winds.' She discovered the relevant lines in a passage in *Paradise Lost* describing the soil of hell that 'such appeared in hue, as when the force / of subterranean wind transports a hill / torn from Pelorus, or the shattered side / of thundering Aetna . . .' Bodkin comments: 'The "or" sound was the link that led to the recall of Milton's wind-vexed Pelorus . . . the name of Boreas, the north-wind, and the words "to bore" were also, I think, associated with the sound "Abora" and helped to determine the image it awakened.' If we treat Bodkin's remarks as hypotheses the thought strikes us that since each of the items mentioned, for example Boreas, might well be a sufficient condition of her impression of Mount Abora she is in no position to state that the other factors she mentions – 'pelorus' and 'bore' – played any role in determining 'the image it awakened'.

More fatal still to the plausibility of her account, if construed as a causal explanation, is that she herself says that the lines preceding 'Abora' were a factor in the production of her associations to the name ('the associations which the name gathered from the description preceding it were rather of caverns of subterranean winds and of tumult . . .'). It follows that its non-paradisical character might have been entirely independent of the clang association with Milton's 'Pelorus'. And yet this seems not to matter and so suggests that in spite of their formally causal–hypothetical character they don't function as empirical explanations. Bodkin's putative causal factors seem to operate more like John Wisdom's 'psychological fixed stars', evincing her impression and perhaps clarifying, intensifying, or even transforming ours rather than causally explaining either of them.

In the case of Orwell's explanation of the impression produced by the Dali illustrations, the psychological fixed stars are Rackham, Dunsany, Barrie and 'Where the Rainbow Ends'. We need not construe Orwell as reporting the successful result of his search for the conditions of his response to Dali's marginal illustrations, but, as in the case of Bodkin's associations to the name Mount Abora, rather of evincing his response in publicly communicable terms. What is important in this context is that the aspects of Dali to which Orwell calls attention, be products of the same spirit as Barrie, Rackham, etc., and not that Barrie, Rackham, etc., actually entered Orwell's mind in some subliminal form as he inspected Dali. It is that in virtue of which they might have come to mind rather than their actually coming to mind that 'explains' Orwell's (and our) response. So that we can say here what Wittgenstein says of Frazer's account of the origin of the Beltane Festival: 'What is important is not that there was this connection, but that there could have been such a connection.'

There is a striking bit of evidence that in this remark

Wittgenstein has hit upon a highly characteristic but little noted feature of the analysis of impressions. In *Seven Types of Ambiguity* William Empson observes:

Continually, in order to paraphrase a piece of verse, it is necessary to drag in some quite irrelevant conceptions; thus I have often been puzzled by finding it necessary to go and look things up in order to find machinery to express distinctions that were already in my mind; indeed, this is involved in the very notion of that activity, for how else would one know what to look up? So that many of my explanations may be demonstrably wrong and yet efficient for their purpose and vice-versa.

Whereas Wittgenstein gives object remarks the same epistemic status as similes and further descriptions I have argued that they are epistemically like causal hypotheses, and like similes only with respect to the use to which they may be, and often are, put. This separation of function from epistemic status is best illustrated with examples whose epistemic status is not in dispute. If our indifference to the indeterminacy and empirical warrantability, or even falsehood, of a putative explanation may co-exist with its undoubted empirical character, that ought to do something to undermine the argument that object remarks are not causal because their value, point, interest, doesn't generally depend on their causal warrantability. The role of genetic explanations in aesthetics provides us with an analogy to the role of causal ones.

The conventional view of the role of genetic remarks in aesthetics is expressed by Monroe Beardsley in his paper 'The classification of critical reasons'. Beardsley says there that 'a statement about the relation of the work to its antecedent conditions . . . may help explain why the work has a particular feature which in turn helps explain why the work is good (as one might say that something in Munch's childhood experience explains the "cry of terror" in so much of his work, while the presence of that cry of terror, as an intense regional quality, helps explain why the works are good). But the genetic reason itself does not explain directly why the work is good, and is therefore not a relevant reason . . .' But someone who, in the course of a discussion of Munch's paintings of screaming heads, referred to his childhood experience of terror need do so for the reasons which Beardsley mentions, in order to 'explain why the work is good' and therefore it need not be, in Beardsley's sense, an irrelevant reason. How much interest would the invocation of the biographical facts of Munch's

childhood, in a discussion of the 'regional quality' of his portray-
als of a cry of terror, have for someone who felt, like one critic, that
Munch's screamer 'looks more like a man overtaken by seasickness than a poet mastered by cosmic emotion'? The facts of
Munch's childhood would be just as explanatory, and perhaps
even more so, if the 'intense regional quality' did not contribute
to making the painting good, but I don't think we would then have
heard of them. It is to a presumed shared quality that they owe
their presence in discussions of Munch. I mean to illustrate by this
that we often invoke biographical facts to convey our impression
of the work rather than to explain the presence of those features
of it which produced that impression. Though it must be admitted
that we are not often clear-headed about this it is, nevertheless, a
characteristic critical use of biographical data. This comes out in
the remark of a practising biographer which refers to his finding
Melville's letters to Hawthorne a help 'in putting a name to' a distinctive feature of *Moby Dick*. It is the way they help us to 'put names
to' aspects of a work that often gives genetic facts their critical
interest. When Kenneth Clark says that Freud's account of the
genesis of Leonardo's paintings of St Anne and the Virgin Mary in
Leonardo's childhood feelings of having two mother figures,
'whether or not true in fact seems to express the mood of the
picture' he is illustrating this independence of illuminating power
from historicity. The same moral emerges from another remark of
Kenneth Clark's. He says he threw away a plaster bust of Mozart on
first hearing the *G Minor Quartet* because he felt that the man the
bust portrayed couldn't have written it. This illustrates our propensity to express ourselves in a genetic mode. Clark really threw
it away because it was an absurd counterpart, it didn't make the
right gesture. It wasn't the face he felt behind the music. It didn't
stand to it as the face Orwell imagined behind Dickens' novels
stood to them.

    Though it is difficult to give a rational justification of Clark's
behaviour, we nevertheless understand it perfectly, just as we
understand Auden's wish that all of Beethoven's correspondence
had been destroyed, Swann's refusal to credit that the music that
had so moved him was composed by the feeble old music master,
Vinteuil, Marcel's shock at the discovery that the painter Elstir and
the ridiculous M. Biche were one and the same, and that the same
people who go to the trouble of making journeys to Stratford,

Abbotsford, or Gad's Hill, nevertheless, do not wish to hear of the second-best bed, Scott's financial debacle, or of the Ellen Ternan affair and Dickens' mistreatment of his wife.

The American poet, William Cullen Bryant, is said to have grown up within view of a rural graveyard – 'a circumstance that can alone explain', says Max Eastman, his writing a great poem on death (*Thanatopsis*) at the age of eighteen. No one would accept a claim so feeble if there weren't a ready made mould for it. I am even inclined to suspect that the story of Bryant's having lived by a graveyard is due to the poem rather than the reverse. We can apply, or at least adapt, to this situation what Wittgenstein said of conjectural reconstructions of the history of ritual practices: 'What we are really concerned with is not descent of one from the other but with a common spirit.'

I hope these examples have done something to incline you to the view that though remarks which are formally genetic, and thus hypotheses, figure in critical discourse the criteria by which their suitability is assessed is the contribution they can make to expressiveness. And that just as this does not impugn their empirical, conjectural character neither does our tolerance of the unamenability to empirical assessment of those aesthetic explanations that proffer indeterminate objects as explanans impugn theirs.

CONCLUSION

I have distinguished two questions to which Wittgenstein addresses himself when he discusses aesthetic explanation. One question deals with the character of the explanations given when someone attempts to explain an impression by pointing out that a bass is too loud or moves too much, or that eyes have such and such a shape, or that a word is archaic, or a door too low. At other times, when Wittgenstein speaks of aesthetic explanation he is thinking of explanation in the sense in which 'Tintern Abbey makes articulate what one feels before a Constable landscape' might be considered one and is using the term in the same sense as Lionel Trilling's remark that 'one understands very easily why many readers of *Pride and Prejudice* are moved to explain their pleasure in the book by reference to Mozart, especially *The Marriage of Figaro*'. It is this kind of explaining of which one can say 'assent is the only criterion'.

It is true that I don't stand to the source of my impression as to a cause, but not for the reason that an aesthetic judgement as to the source of my impression is not vulnerable to empirical overthrow, but for another reason – that such a judgement, unlike a hypothesis, necessarily designates an object of directed feeling.

Wittgenstein confuses the thesis that the analysis of an impression is not reducible to, or the equivalent of, a causal claim with the thesis that it does not imply a causal claim. However, there are many cases where unless the corresponding causal remark is true, the object claim must be withdrawn. Though an object claim is not necessarily true simply because the corresponding causal claim is true, an object claim is not true unless a causal claim is true. It says more but does not say less.

The illusion of the non-prognostic character of object remarks is generated in two main ways – one is by making it appear that the alternative to a non-prognostic account is that non-directed, ulterior feelings are being explained; the other is by making it appear that where a feeling is identified via its object (or as Pears puts it, is logically connected with it), the object remark has no prognostic implications and so no empirically corrigible ones. Neither of these is true. Aesthetic impressions are sometimes identifiable independently of their putative sources and, even when they are not, causal enquiry has a bearing on their explanation.

Wittgenstein assimilates answers to the question, 'What's wrong with it?', to a variety of a-causal neighbours – interjection, categorical demand, saying what thoughts an aesthetic object provokes ('What is at the back of our mind') – but this still leaves answers to such questions which are both causal and appropriate to the assessment of aesthetic explanation.

What is true is that many ostensibly causal claims defeat attempts to put them in a shape in which causal reasoning could be brought to bear on them. Wittgenstein incites us to notice how often when this happens we are happy to take the 'simile' and let the hypothesis go. Nevertheless, there are occasions when the appropriate form of an aesthetic enquiry is empirical. The pertinent answer to the question why Titania was enthralled by the metamorphosed Bottom is that she was drugged. The history of taste is full of donkey's ears rendered fair by ideological potions.

The value of Wittgenstein's remarks is in the light they throw on those cases in which our perplexity does not take the form of wanting something which stood to our experience as low doors or hyperkinetic basses but of 'being intrigued and wanting to describe'. Gombrich did not stand to the impression made by the Mona Lisa as Marcel stood to his impression of the steeples of Martinville. These were different problems and called for different kinds of resolution. It is primarily the second of these problems to which Wittgenstein is addressing himself when he denies that aesthetic explanations are hypotheses. In maintaining that assent is the only criterion of correctness Wittgenstein is rejecting the view that the later account which dissipates our perplexity as to the character of our impression is either a literal recapitulation of our experiences at the time or an account of the processes of which they were epiphenomena. Aesthetic explanations of this kind are no more descriptions of a temporal process than was the ecphrastic exercise with which Marcel relieved the torment of the spires.

Wittgenstein says many true and illuminating things about aesthetic explanations but from none of them does it follow that causal judgement plays no role, or a nugatory one, in the analysis of aesthetic impressions. What he has shown is that there are aesthetic perplexities which don't find their natural consummation in the discovery of causal connection, and there are aesthetic explanations which don't call for, although they may initially seem to invite, the empirical assessment we normally extend to hypotheses.

CHAPTER THREE

Wittgenstein and the Fire-festivals

I

In his notes on 'Wittgenstein's lectures (1930–33)' G. E. Moore reports that one of the chief points which Wittgenstein wished to make in connection with Frazer's *Golden Bough*[1] was that 'it was a mistake to suppose that . . . the account of the Beltane Festival "impresses us so much" . . . because it has "developed from a festival in which a real man was burnt".'[2]

The following remarks will give an idea of the sort of thing Frazer says about Fire-festivals:

All over Europe the peasants have been accustomed from time immemorial to kindle bonfires on certain days of the year, and to dance round or leap over them. Not uncommonly effigies are burned in these fires, or a pretence is made of burning a living person in them. And there are grounds for believing that anciently human beings were actually burned on these occasions.[3]

In another chapter he writes:

The pretence of throwing the victim chosen by lot into the Beltane fire, and the similar treatment of the man at the Midsummer bonfire in Normandy, may naturally be interpreted as traces of an older custom of actually burning human beings on these occasions.[4]

In another, he says:

In the popular customs connected with the Fire-festivals of Europe there are certain features which appear to point to a form of practice of human sacrifice . . . the pretence of burning people is sometimes carried so far

---

[1] Wittgenstein was using the one-volume abridged edition published in 1925 and it is to this edition that the page references in *Synthese* correspond. My quotations are also from the abridged edition.   [2] G. E. Moore, *Philosophical Papers* (London, 1962), p. 309.

[3] *Ibid.*, first paragraph of chapter 62, 'The Fire-festivals of Europe'.

[4] *Ibid.*, chapter 65, 'Balder and the mistletoe'.

that it seems reasonable to regard it as a mitigated survival of an older custom of actually burning them. Thus in Aachen, as we saw, the man clad in pea-straw acts so cleverly that the children really believe he is being burned. At Jumieges in Normandy, the man clad all in green . . . was pursued by his comrades, and when they caught him they feigned to fling him upon the midsummer bonfire. Similarly, at the Beltane fires in Scotland the pretended victim was seized, and a show made of throwing him into the flames, and for some time afterwards the people affected to speak of him as dead.[5]

Frazer then goes on to describe human sacrifice by fire as practised by the Celts in ancient times and concludes that

it seems reasonable to suppose that . . . from these annual festivals are lineally descended some at least of the Fire-festivals which, with their traces of human sacrifices, are still celebrated year by year in many parts of Europe.[6]

What is there to object to in all this? For example, what is objectionable about invoking an ancient practice in which a man was burnt to explain a contemporary practice in which an effigy is burnt?

In the light of the 'Remarks on Frazer's *Golden Bough*'[7] Wittgenstein seems to mean two (at least) distinct things by his claim that it was a mistake for Frazer to see the phenomenon of the Fire-festivals as calling for an historical reconstruction of the original sacrificial rituals of which they were mitigated survivals. He means that many of the Fire-festivals are intelligible as they stand, that in their details, or in the demeanour of their participants, they directly manifest their 'inner character', their relation to the idea of the sacrificial burning of a man. They strike us as commemorations or dramatisations of this idea independently of any empirical evidence that they originated in such an event. But Wittgenstein has another more radical objection to Frazer's dealings with the

[5] *Ibid.*, chapter 64, 'The burning of human beings in the fires'.   [6] *Ibid.*
[7] 'Bermerkungen über Frazer's *The Golden Bough*', *Synthese*, XVII (1967), 223–53.
   All page references unless otherwise indicated are to *Synthese*. I have made use of three translations: an unpublished one by A. C. Miles; that by A. C. Miles and Rush Rhees published in *The Human World*, no. 3, May 1971, but with the omission of some twenty remarks which Rhees came to feel did not belong with the others; and an unpublished version by Professor A. E. Manser of the University of Southampton.
   The bulk of Wittgenstein's remarks are not addressed to Fire-festivals or to human sacrifice, but to the general character of ritual.
   The Fire-festivals are discussed in a sequence of remarks which begins on page 246 and ends on page 252.

Fire-festivals than his failure to see that the festivals themselves evince a sacrificial significance independently of empirical evidence as to their origins. It is his failure to see that what was called for by the 'deep and sinister' character of the festivals was an account of 'the experience in ourselves from which we impute' this 'deep and sinister character' and of 'what it is which brings this picture into connection with our own feelings and thoughts'.

This view emerges unmistakably in the following:

> But why should it not really be (partly, anyway) just the *thought* (of the Festival's sacrificial origin) that makes the impression on me? Aren't ideas frightening? . . . Hasn't the *thought* something terrible? – Yes, but that which I see in those stories is something they acquire, after all, from the evidence, including such evidence as does not seem directly connected with them – from the thought of man and his past, from the strangeness of what I see and what I have seen and heard in myself and others. (p. 251)

Here the antithesis to our thoughts of the sacrificial origin of the ritual is not our thoughts as to 'its inner character' but 'our thoughts of man and his past and the strangeness of what we have (noticed) in ourselves and in others'.

I am not sure how aware Wittgenstein is of the distinctiveness of these theses, for he does not signal the transition from one to the other. (But these are notes meant for his own use.) The following remarks on the rule of succession to the priesthood of the Temple of Diana at Nemi, according to which the priest succeeded to office by slaying his predecessor and retained it till he himself was slain, also illustrate the duality of Wittgenstein's objections to Frazer:

> When Frazer begins by telling the story of the King of the Wood at Nemi, he does this in a tone which shows that something strange and terrible is happening here. And that is the answer to the question 'Why is this happening?': Because it is terrible. In other words, what strikes us in this course of events as terrible, impressive, horrible, tragic, etc., anything but trivial and insignificant, *that* is what gave birth to them.
> Here we can only *describe* and say, human life is like that.
> Compared with the impression that what is described makes on us, the explanation is too uncertain.
> Every explanation is an hypothesis.
> But for someone worried by love an explanatory hypothesis will not help much – it will not bring peace.
> The crush of thoughts that do not get out because they all try to push forward and are wedged in the door. (pp. 235–6)

The last three remarks do more than merely claim that the rule of succession does not require to be traced to its origins for us to see its point. They suggest the inappropriateness of *any* hypothesising for enlightening us as to our relation to the Fire-festivals, and that it is rather our 'crush of thoughts' with respect to them which need clarification. But that 'what strikes us . . . as terrible, impressive, horrible, tragic, etc., . . . is what gave birth to them' is no less an explanatory hypothesis than Frazer's account of their remote origins. And so knowledge of the inner character of the eighteenth-century festival, what it meant to its celebrants, can no more resolve 'our puzzlement as to why they impress us' than can knowledge of its origins. But I will postpone discussion of this issue until I have dealt with Wittgenstein's first objection to Frazer – that Frazer gives an historical reconstruction of the origin of the festival when what is called for is an account of its 'inner character'.

II

According to Wittgenstein Frazer was mistaken in thinking that the impression produced on us by the Beltane Festival called for an effort of historical reconstruction which would trace it to its beginnings. The speculative wonder which colours our impression of the festival is not concerned with the origin of the festival, but with its expressive significance. And though the idea of the burning of a man enters into these speculations it is not as a causal antecedent of the festival but as its meaning. The ritual is *about* the burning of a man.

The question is: Is what we may call the sinister character of the Beltane Fire Festival as it was practised a hundred years ago – is this a character of the practice in itself, or only if the hypothesis regarding its origin is confirmed? I think it is clear that what gives us a sinister impression is the inner nature of the practice as performed in recent times. (p. 247)

The authors of a paper on 'Wittgenstein's implied anthropology' (Rudich and Stassen) seem to have misunderstood Wittgenstein's point on this issue: 'Wittgenstein's attack on Frazer's work is really an attack on the very idea of historical understanding, or more exactly on any causal account of history.'[8] This

---

[8] N. Rudich and M. Stassen, 'Wittgenstein's implied anthropology' in *History and Theory*, vol. x, no. 1 (1971), pp. 84–9.

is a mistake. What Wittgenstein denies is not the possibility of historical explanation but its appropriateness where what is at issue is 'the inner nature of the practice' – the expressive significance a people's ritual practices have for them.

Rudich and Stassen say that Wittgenstein is denying that 'a given set of practices can be explained by uncovering their origins and causes in the earlier experiences of a society'. But what Wittgenstein says is: 'even if its ancient origins and its descent from an earlier practice is established by history it is still possible that there is nothing sinister at all about the practice today . . .' And if it *is* sinister today we don't require the historical account to confirm that this is so. The historicity of the hypothetical explanation is of no account in such cases, not because Wittgenstein thinks there can be no knowledge of historical causation, as Rudich and Stassen say, but because the practice need not have the significance for those whose behaviour impressed us and for which the historical explanation purports to account that it had for its originators, and can have this significance irrespective of how it originated.

If the impression that the practice is deep, sinister and age-old does not arise out of independent knowledge of its antiquity, etc., how then does it arise? Wittgenstein thinks the impression arises directly from the details of the ritual and the demeanour of the celebrants, who behave as if they were commemorating a remote, long past, horrific event. This may create the illusion that 'it is the hypothesis (of antiquity) that gives the matter depth', whereas this springs from the aspect presented by the eighteenth-century ritual itself. Wittgenstein not only holds that what gives the Beltane Festivals their distinctiveness is our sense of their meaning rather than their origins, he also has a subsidiary thesis as to how genetic hypotheses contribute to our sense of this significance. Remarks on p. 241 and p. 251, together with allusions to 'the spirit of the Festival' and to its 'infusion' with a mood or atmosphere which mere play or a theatrical performance does not have (p. 242), constitute a subsidiary thesis as to how Frazer's stories of sacrificial origins (and genetic accounts in general) may contribute to clarifying our sense of the character of a phenomenon even when there is no genetic connection between them and what they purport to explain. On p. 241 he speaks of cases where an hypothetical link is not meant to do anything 'except to draw attention to the similarity, the connexion, between the *facts*. As one might illustrate the internal relation of a circle to an ellipse by gradually transforming an ellipse into a circle but not in order to assert that a given ellipse, in fact, historically, originated from a circle (Theory of Development) but only to sharpen our eye to a formal connexion.' And on p. 252 he says, 'What is correct and interesting is not to say: this proceeded from that, but: it could have thus proceeded.'

After remarking that it only 'seems as if it is the hypothesis (of its origins) that gives the Festival depth' Wittgenstein says, 'And we may remember the explanation of the strange relationship between Siegfried and Brunhilde in our Niebelungenlied. Namely that Siegfried seems to have seen Brunhilde before. It is now clear that what gives this practice depth is its *connexion* with the burning of a man . . .'

Wittgenstein's remark reminds us how often we express ourselves in a genetic-historical mode to evince our sense of the distinctiveness of an experience. Michelangelo describes his love for Vittoria Colonna (*La dove io t'amai prima*) and Goethe his for Frau von Stein (*Ach! du warst in abgelebten Zeiten/Meine Schwester oder meine Frau* – In time long past and in another life / You must have been my sister or my wife) in terms similar to Siegfried's. This is how Theophile Gautier accounts for the deep impression made by the smiling faces of Leonardo's portraits: 'We have seen these faces before, but not upon this earth; in some previous existence, perhaps, which they recall vaguely to us. How else explain the strange, almost magic charm which the portrait of the Mona Lisa has?' Henry Adams was so struck by his first sight of Chartres Cathedral that he had the absurd fancy that he had participated in its construction.

Frazer conjectures the 'the King of the Wood was formerly burned, dead or alive, at the midsummer fire festival which was annually celebrated in the Arician grove'. This fact (assuming it to be one) stands in quite a different relation to the rule of succession and the way of life it enforced on the Nemi priest than the original sacrificial burnings do to the Beltane Fire-festival. In spite of the causal warrantability of the connection it could not be said of the life of the Nemi priest, as Wittgenstein says of the Beltane Festival, 'what gives this practice depth is its connection with the burning of a man'. For it is not by way of historical evidence that the burning of a man enters into our impression of the Beltane Festival.

The Beltane Festival as it has come down to us is the performance of a play, something like children playing at robbers. But then again it is not like this. For even though it is prearranged so that the side which saves the victim wins, there is still the infusion of a mood or state of mind in what is happening which a theatrical production does not have. (p. 250)

We see more readily the work that Frazer's human sacrifice story does in the case of the Beltane Fire by looking at the Baldur Bale Fires, which he also traces to a defunct tradition of human sacrifice, this time Scandinavian rather than Druidical. In the Baldur Bale Fires no effigy is burned, and the theme of human sacrifice is entirely a product of Frazer's reconstructive ingenuity ('the burning of an effigy is a feature which might easily drop out after its meaning was forgotten'). It has been said that the Baldur Bale Fires 'have as much to do with the Midsummer Fires as the crematorium at Golders Green'.[9] But even if we put aside all doubts of this kind Frazer's account does not illuminate the Baldur Bale Fires as it does the Beltane Fires, for the idea of a burning man, even if historical, is not expressed in the demeanour of the celebrants. The Baldur Bale Fires are not *about* the burning of a man, even if they are causally related to ancient burnings in a way that makes it correct to speak of them as mitigated survivals of such burnings.

This point can be further illustrated by these remarks from an essay on 'Mythological forms of bakers' cakes':

The various shapes of bakers' cakes, handed down to us by former generations, are quite worthy of a little consideration. What is the real significance of these queer, mysterious forms, and why are they so time-honoured and so unchangeable? . . .

The gingerbread man can be traced back to the sacrifice of prisoners, knights and footsoldiers. Human sacrifices, however, even in the most ancient times, were sacred to the gods alone, and were not eaten by the worshippers themselves, but only their baked and painted effigies. These figures were originally painted with the blood of the victims. It is for this reason that these gingerbread figures are still ornamented with red . . .

In still more remote times according to the Edda, men not only drank the blood of their enemies slain in battle, but also ate their hearts. This

---

[9] Sir William Ridgeway, 'The methods of Mannhardt and Frazer as illustrated by the writings of the Mistress of Girton', Cambridge Philosophical Society, 1923.

was also done at the execution of prisoners of war. Later on, heart shaped cakes took the place of these hearts, and our gingerbread hearts are the lineal descendants of these hearts once offered in sacrifice.[10]

The effect on our thoughts of the knowledge, for example, that the red colouring on the gingerbread man once stood for the victim's blood tells us nothing about the place of gingerbread men in our lives. The sacrifice story gets no purchase. It has nothing to latch on to. 'No trace of that ancient horror is left on it . . . the depth lies merely in the thought of its descent.' This is not the case with the Beltane Festival. The account of the different forms of bakers' cakes illustrates the difference between a practice possessing a physiognomy of terror, or depth, and these lying 'merely in the thought of its descent'.

('Madam Homais was very fond of those small, heavy loaves, shaped like a turban, which are eaten with salt butter during Lent: a last survival of Gothic fare, perhaps going back to the time of the Crusades, with which the sturdy Normans used once to gorge themselves, fancying that they saw in the yellow torchlight on the table, between the jugs of mead and the huge joints of pork, Saracens' heads to devour.' I have seen those loaves again since being struck by this passage in *Madame Bovary* but they remained just loaves.)

Wittgenstein's objection to Frazer's supposing that 'the Beltane Festival impresses us so much because it developed from a festival in which a real man was burnt' has a parallel in the criticism Santayana makes of a certain kind of explanation of the impression made by the night sky. Paul Valéry speaks of 'the mysterious effect that a clear night and the presence of stars has on men'. Santayana once addressed himself to the question why the sight of a starry sky should have this mysterious effect:

To most people I fancy, the stars are beautiful; but if you ask why, they would be at a loss to reply, until they remembered what they had heard about astronomy and the great size and distance and possible habitation of those orbs. The vague and allusive ideas thus aroused fall in so well with the dumb emotion we were already feeling, that we attribute this emotion to those ideas, and persuade ourselves that the power of the starry heavens lies in the suggestion of astronomical facts.

Santayana argues against this view:

---

[10] 'Mythological forms of bakers' cakes', *Current Literature*, 1898.

Before the days of Kepler, the heavens declared the glory of the Lord; and
we needed no calculation of stellar distances, no fancies about a plurality of worlds, no image of infinite space, to make the stars sublime.[11]

Santayana's 'dumb emotion we were already feeling' is akin to
Wittgenstein's 'crush of thoughts that could not get out'. The
sinister aspect of the Fire-festivals is to the prehistoric burning
of a real man as the power of the starry heavens to the
suggestion of astronomical facts. In both cases the enlightening,
perplexity-dissipating power of a hypothesis has been misattrib-
uted.

Wittgenstein's remark that a 'hypothesis of development' may
be 'a disguise for a formal connection' alerts us to the ubiquity of
ostensibly genetic explanations (*Entwicklungshypothese*) whose
point lies in evincing a sense of the character of a phenomenon.
What attention to the strictly formal features of genetic remarks
overlooks is how often we implicitly translate them into a form
other than that which they reveal to simple inspection. Genetic
accounts are, on many occasions, taken as claims as to the 'inner
nature' of the practice of which they purport to give the genealogy
or as evocations or elucidations of the impression these make on
us.

The view once found in rationalist polemic that the institution
of female religious celibacy is the end product of a development
which began with temple prostitution is not relished or resented
as a hypothesis but as an articulation either of our own suspicions
or of a vaguely familiar presumption as to the relation of religiosity to sexuality. It is taken as a claim as to its inner character rather
than merely as a hypothesis as to its temporal development. The
hypothesis puts the practice against a background which may alter
its aspect for us. Similar considerations apply to the theory that the
sacrament of the Eucharist was evolved from the totem feast. The
real objection to the development hypothesis is not that it is empirically false but that it draws the terms sexuality and religiosity, or
sacrament and primitive ritual (e.g. Holy Communion and ritual
cannibalism) unjustifiably close together. Our rejection of the
'formal connection' may take a misleading form as scepticism
about the genetic hypothesis when it is really what Wittgenstein
refers to as 'the similarity between the facts' to which 'one's eyes

[11] George Santayana, *The Sense of Beauty* (New York, 1961), p. 80.

have been sharpened' by the 'hypothetical connecting link' that one wishes to contest.[12]

The proposal of a genealogical relation between dynamically inert items, though it may invite scepticism, arouses no vehement repudiation because it involves no aspect change and thus no claim as to the 'inner character' of a phenomenon. An effect similar to that of the developmental hypothesis may be produced by juxtaposition, arrangements of the data, which make no historical claims as to the unfolding of one practice from another or of both from a common prototype – for example, by introducing Bernini's *St Theresa* as an intermediate term between overtly orgiastic religiosity and the mystical transports of the female celibate, or the southern Italian practice of swallowing boluses on which the pictures of sacred personages have been pasted as a term between ritual cannibalism and the sacrament of the Eucharist.[13]

If one person assigns a genetic origin to a phenomenon, another person (or even the same person) is likely to find it redolent of that from which it supposedly originates. If someone says that a phenomenon has a sexual origin, someone else is likely to feel that it is redolent of sexuality. That is, it is those who bring mysticism and sex together for other reasons for whom there will seem point in bringing sexuality into phylo- or onto-genetic relationship with mysticism. The evolution of the genital apparatus from the cloaca is particularly striking for those whom the thought that love has pitched his mansion in the place of excrement has already struck. If the impulse to bite did not play a role in our erotic lives the hunger-into-sexuality theory would have a different kind of interest for us (if it retained any at all).

---

[12] The phrases in quotes are from p. 241. On this page Wittgenstein says: '"And so the Chorus hints at a hidden law" is what we feel like saying of Frazer's collection of facts.' The quotation ('*Und so deutet das Chor auf ein geheimes Gesetz*') is from Goethe's poem to Christine Vulpius on the metamorphosis of plants. The reference to the schema of a plant which follows is an allusion to Goethe's notion of primal phenomena. Here is a gloss on Goethe's views which brings out their affinity to those I find in Wittgenstein. The expositor (Owen Barfield) says Goethe wants to distinguish 'an arbitrary surmise not based on anything inherent in the phenomena but brought to them from outside from Goethe's *Ur-phänomen* which was more in the nature of a thought to be found in the phenomena themselves'.

The capacity of practices to illuminate each other does not depend on the lineal descent of one from another or of both from a common ancestry. The 'hidden law' proclaimed by Frazer's 'collection of facts' is that of their association, not of their generation. [13] Frazer, chapter 50, 'Eating the God'.

III

I have said that Wittgenstein has a more radical thesis according to which even the 'inner nature of the practice as performed in recent times' is irrelevant to the question why the Beltane Festival impresses us. On this view the task set us by our impression of the Fire-festivals was rather to elicit, articulate and lay open to view 'the crush of thoughts that do not get out because they all try to push forward and are wedged in the door.'

The following remarks seem to support this construction:

Above all: whence the certainty that a practice of this kind must be age-old (what are the data, what is the verification)? But *have* we any certainty, may we not have been led into a mistake because we were over-impressed by historical considerations? Certainly, but that still leaves something of which we are sure . . . It is our *evidence* for it, that holds what is deep in this assumption. And this evidence is again non-hypothetical, psychological . . . What I want to say is. What is sinister, deep, does not lie in the fact that that is how the history of this practice went, for perhaps it did not go that way . . . but in what it is that gives me reason to assume it. (p. 248)

What makes human sacrifice deep and sinister anyway? . . . this deep and sinister aspect is not obvious just from learning the history of the external action, but we impute it from an experience in ourselves. (p. 249)

But it is not just the idea of the possible origin of the Beltane Festival that makes it impressive, but what we may call the overwhelming probability of this idea. What we get from the material. (p. 250)

. . . that which I see in those stories is something they acquire, after all, from the evidence, including such evidence as does not seem directly connected with them – from the thought of man and his past, from the strangeness of what I see and what I have seen and have heard in myself and others. (p. 251)

Moreover one element of (Frazer's) account is lacking and that is the one which brings this picture into connexion with our own feelings and thoughts. This element gives the account its depth. (p. 246)

These remarks seem to me to commit Wittgenstein to a stronger thesis than merely that the question to be asked concerning the Fire-festivals is not of what primitive practices they are 'mitigated survivals'.

Preoccupation with the origins of the Fire-festivals is mistaken, not because it is impertinent to 'the inner character of the ritual' but because it is impertinent to the impressions it engenders.

The following remark implies that the impression of depth produced by a practice may be a function not of the mien of the performers, or of any of its details but of the background we bring to it.

If it were the custom at some festival for men to ride on one another (as in horse-and-rider games), we would see nothing more in this than a way of carrying someone which reminds us of men riding horses. But if we know that among many peoples it had been the custom, say, to use slaves as mounts and to celebrate certain festivals mounted in this way, we should then see in the harmless practice of our time something deeper and less harmless. (p. 247)

But it now seems that, given 'our thoughts of man and his past and the strangeness of what we have noticed in ourselves and in others', the fact that men pretend to burn men is sufficient to account for our impression that the practice is deep and sinister irrespective of the celebrants' conception of it.

'What makes human sacrifice something deep and sinister' is not to be determined by historical investigation into either the origin *or* the contemporary significance of the Fire-festivals. That men should pretend to burn men gets its 'depth' from our prior knowledge that men have burned men, not from our conviction that in this particular ritual men were once burned. The worries provoked by accounts of the Fire-festivals are not historicity worries. The natural direction of enquiry in a case like this is towards 'my thoughts of man and his past and the strangeness of what I have (noticed) in myself and in others'. It is these which 'make what is so uncertain into something to worry about'.

If it is 'the overwhelming probability of the idea' that men were once burned that makes the Beltane Festival impressive, then it is to an understanding of the source of this overwhelming probability that we must look for 'the satisfaction that comes from explaining'. If 'it is what connects this picture with our feelings and thoughts that gives the contemplation of its depth', then 'it is what connects this picture with our feelings and thoughts' that is the proper subject of our enquiries and reflections. If 'it is our evidence for it that holds what is deep in this assumption' then 'it is our evidence for it' that requires investigation. (And, says Wittgenstein, 'this evidence is non-hypothetical, psychological'.) If '. . . what we see in these stories is something they acquire from the evidence, even from such evidence as does not seem directly connected with them', then what is called for is a garnering of this evidence. Facts like Pip's readiness (in *Great Expectations*) to credit Orlick's story that it was necessary to stoke the forge fire with a live boy every seven years ought to find a place in such an account.

The inner character of the festival (by which Wittgenstein says he means 'All those circumstances in which it is carried out that are not included in the accounts of the festival') is just as conjectural as its origins and cannot be determined, as the question 'Why does this impress us?' can, by merely bethinking ourselves. All that can be so determined is the relation in which we ourselves stand to the idea of the ceremonial burning of a man. And it is Frazer's failure to address himself to *this* question which is finally the basis of Wittgenstein's criticism of his dealing with the Fire-festivals.

Although whether any particular practice does symbolise what it seems to is a hypothetical question, i.e. an historical one, the relation between what it seems to mean and those features in virtue of which it seems to mean it is not hypothetical and so is not to be determined by historical research – for example, why the use of a cake for the drawing of lots seems especially terrible. On p. 249 Wittgenstein says: 'The fact that for the lots they use a cake has something especially terrible to us is of central importance in our investigation of practices like these.' Our response, our impression of the inner character of the festival, rests on the assumption that cakes play the same role in their lives as in ours. If we learned that the only purpose to which they put cakes was for choosing the Beltane victim and that they were considered inedible for normal purposes, this detail of the ritual would look very different to us. And to this extent historicity plays a role in our enquiries. But, historicity apart, 'there is still something of which we are sure'. The use of the cakes for drawing lots is just the kind of thing which Wittgenstein says we could invent for ourselves (pp. 238, 251). What Wittgenstein may be calling attention to here is the way in which the eruption of the demonic into the quotidian, or reminders of the domestic in the midst of the tragic and terrifying, confers a distinctive cast on phenomena. The principle is the same as that of the knocking at the gate in *Macbeth*, or Auden's lines about 'the dreadful martyrdom' running its course while 'the torturer's horse scratches its innocent behind on a tree', or the drowning boy and the oblivious ploughman in Brueghel's *Fall of Icarus* which inspired them, or 'the terrible blood sacrifice' in

Hans Castorp's dream and the sunny Mediterranean seascape and tokens of 'man's courteous and enlightened social state' against which it is consummated. It is as if the use of the cakes for picking victims was a deliberate attempt to make the ritual emblematic of this feature of life. But even if this were not the allusion intended the cakes would nevertheless be no less appropriate a means of making it. It is this which is 'non-hypothetical, psychological' and 'of which we are sure'.

That this is happening 'because it is terrible', that 'what strikes us in this course of events as terrible, impressive, horrible, tragic, etc., . . . is what gave birth to them' is *not* 'something of which we can be sure'. What we can be sure of is that if *we* wished to give expression to the sentiments we feel to lie behind these practices then these practices would serve.

Wittgenstein says of Frazer's theory of sacrificial origins:

. . . this ancestry may be very uncertain and one feels like saying: 'Why make what is so uncertain into something to worry about?' (like a back-ward-looking Clever Elsa). But worries of that kind are not involved here. (p. 248)

If ritual slaughter on the scale the Aztecs practised it strikes us as an appropriate way of dramatising how things are, then even if Frazer is right, and they only did it from 'a mistaken theory of the solar system', 'there is still something of which we are sure', and it is this 'which makes what is so uncertain into something to worry about'.

In these remarks Wittgenstein seems to be approaching a conception of the kind of interest the stories of human sacrifice have for us which has been noted by the sociologist Simmel.

For Simmel, our interest in histories is a product of two different kinds of interest. Certain 'events' – a very noble or very horrible deed, a peculiarly complicated personality, a strange fate of an individual or group – we find *interesting*, whether the events in question are known to have occurred or whether they are frankly fictional . . . (Simmel) is concerned with affirming that . . . 'the feelings attached to pure contents constitute a domain for itself, that they come to the fore and persist after the disappearance of those feelings produced by the existence (Sein) of the contents . . .'[14]

Jorge Luis Borges illustrates the distinction Simmel had in mind. 'Among Paul Valéry's jottings, André Maurois observed the follow-

---

[14] R. Weingartner, *Experience and Culture* (Middletown, 1962), pp. 136–7.

ing: Ideas for a frightening story: it is discovered that the only remedy for cancer is living human flesh. Consequences.'[15] Imagine someone momentarily taken in by Borges's anecdote, then realising it was invention. The difference this would fail to make is the difference Simmel and Wittgenstein are calling attention to.

A phrase comes to mind from a discussion of poetry by the critic Hazlitt – 'unravelling the web of associations wound round a subject by nature and the unavoidable conditions of humanity'. I take Wittgenstein to be saying that our perplexity with respect to certain phenomena calls for this effort at unravelling rather than any search for further empirical knowledge.[16]

IV

The most interesting question to arise out of Wittgenstein's remarks on the Fire-festivals is why Frazer should be criticised for failing to answer a question he never posed. Wittgenstein makes it an objection to Frazer's empirical method that someone troubled by love will not be helped by a hypothesis. 'It will not bring peace.' (It other words – 'Someone troubled by the thought of human sacrifice will not be helped by a hypothesis. It will not bring peace.') But Frazer never promised to bring peace, never even said he was addressing himself to 'why human sacrifice impresses us'. So Wittgenstein's objection must be that he ought to have. Now what kind of claim is this?

Why should accounts of the Fire-festivals be made the occasion of reflection on 'what makes human sacrifice deep and sinister' rather than of enquiry into the origin and development of the Fire-festivals? The issue is one of deciding when an interest, or a

---

[15] As quoted by William Gass.

[16] An illustration of 'the web of associations wound round a subject by nature and the unavoidable conditions of humanity' is given by Wittgenstein on p. 251 where he objects to Frazer's speaking of the primitive view that fire is purificatory or that it has some intimate connection with the sun, as theories.

That fire was used for purification is clear. But nothing can be more probable than that the cleansing ceremonies of thinking people . . . were brought into connection with the sun. If one thought (fire-cleansing) is forced on one person, and another (Fire-sun) on another people, what can be more probable than both thoughts being forced on a people . . .

The *complete* destruction through fire, or else through smashing to pieces, tearing apart, etc. must have struck man.

But even if one knew nothing of such a connection in thought between purification and the sun, one could accept that it would appear in some place.

felt perplexity with respect to a topic (in Wittgenstein's words 'Why does this impress me?') calls for further empirical information for its resolution, and when this is an illusion.

There are two different kinds of situation in which this question arises. In one the problem is already sufficiently defined for us to be able to point out the error in expecting an empirical resolution of it. This is so with some of the aesthetic questions which Wittgenstein discusses in the lectures on Aesthetics – e.g. 'Why do these bars give me such a peculiar impression?'[17] But there is another kind of situation, one in which the questions raised are empirical as formulated, and there is no lack of fit between them and the answers proposed, and where criticism takes the form of claiming that the wrong question has been posed. This is the case with respect to Wittgenstein's criticism of Frazer's account of the Fire-festivals. Unwedging our crush of thoughts with respect to a subject and allowing them to file through singly is an activity which can profitably be distinguished from empirical research, but how is it to be determined when it is to be pursued in its stead?

In 1906 William James was visiting Stanford University and found himself caught up in the San Francisco earthquake, of which experience he has left us an account.

I personified the earthquake as a permanent individual entity . . . It came moreover, directly to *me*. It stole in behind my back, and once inside the room, had me all to itself, and could manifest itself convincingly. Animus and intent were never more present in any human action, nor did any human activity ever more definitely point back to a living agent as its source and origin.

All whom I consulted on the point agreed as to this feature in their experience, 'It expressed intention', 'It was vicious', 'It was bent on destruction', 'It wanted to show its power', or what not . . . For science when the tensions in the earth's crust reach the breaking-point, and strata fall into an altered equilibrium, earthquake is simply the collective name of all the cracks and shakings and disturbances that happen. They *are* the earthquake. But for me *the* earthquake was the *cause* of the disturbances, and the perception of it as a living agent was irresistible. It had an overpowering dramatic convincingness.[18]

---

[17] Cf. Wittgenstein, *Lectures on Aesthetics, Psychology and Religious Belief* (Oxford, 1966), p. 20.
   In the lectures Moore attended, the example Wittgenstein gave of aesthetic questions which he thought like 'Why does the Beltane festival impress us?' were 'Why is this beautiful?' and 'Why will this bass not do?'
[18] William James, 'On some mental effects of the earthquake', *Memories and Studies* (New York, 1911), pp. 212–13.

The sort of mistake Wittgenstein is charging Frazer with is the mistake James would have made had he felt that what his experienceof the San Francisco earthquake called for was an account of the San Andreas Fault. For there would have been no 'formal' relation between the San Andreas Fault and James's 'crush of thoughts'.

But it is one thing to say that talk of the San Andreas Fault would not tell us anything as to James's experience of the San Francisco earthquake, and quite another to say that someone who undertakes a seismological study of the San Andreas Fault ought rather to address himself, in the manner of James, to the question of what it is like to get caught up in an earthquake. Though it is possible that someone whose interest in seismology was the sequel to his experience of an earthquake might come to agree that he had misunderstood himself, if he did not agree we would have to withdraw (failing behavioural tokens that he was mistaken). Whereas in the other kind of case we have hard philosophical arguments that his problems and his methods pass one another by. Someone who wants to know what is going on in his brain when he listens to Brahms may be making a mistake, but it is not the same kind of mistake as that of someone who thinks his research into the brain is going to resolve his aesthetic puzzlement as why he finds Brahms 'extremely Kellerian' or, generally, why certain bars make such a peculiar impression on him; what the 'tremendous philosophy' is which he senses behind *The Creation of Adam*; why Beethoven reminds him of Michelangelo.

The sight of a decaying carcass might provoke us to an investigation of the chemistry of putrefaction or it might take us to reflections of the kind which Rilke expressed apropos Baudelaire's poem 'Une Charogne': 'What was he to do when this presented itself to him? . . . It was his task to perceive, in this horrible, this apparently only repulsive, thing that existence which is valid throughout all existence. Selection and rejection are not possible.'[19] It is as plain that the chemistry of putrefaction would be irrelevant to someone on whom the task that the sight of a decaying carcass imposed was to 'perceive that existence which is valid throughout all existence' as that this achievement would be of no interest to someone whom the same sight provoked to biochem-

---

[19] R. M. Rilke, *Malte Laurids Brigge*.

ical speculation. What isn't plain is what it would be to show that one of these enterprises was undertaken in mistake for the other.

Argument on such an issue can only take the form of reminders that our perplexity with respect to certain topics is not always a matter of factual ignorance, and that the interest certain phenomena have for us does not invariably find its natural consummation in further empirical knowledge ('the stupid superstition of our time', p. 239), and of citing occasions on which we mistakenly overlooked this.

In an essay, 'Hymns in a man's life', D. H. Lawrence says '. . . the miracle of the loaves and fishes is just as good to me now as when I was a child. I don't care whether it is historically a fact or not. What does it matter?' He quotes:

> O Galilee, sweet Galilee,
> Come sing thy songs again to me!

and comments 'to me the word Galilee has a wonderful sound. The Lake of Galilee! I don't need to know where it is. I never want to go to Palestine.'[20] No one would quarrel with Lawrence's feeling that a geographical or historical enquiry would not be an appropriate response to the wonder produced in him by the hymns of his childhood.

But are there general criteria for determining when such enquiries are inappropriate?

If someone searches for further information to relieve him of the oppression of his perplexity with respect to some impression, we cannot prove that this is a mistake. But if such a one were later to tell us that he had been under an illusion as to what more information could do for him we would understand him.[21]

---

[20] D. H. Lawrence, 'Hymns in a man's life', *Phoenix II* (London, 1968), p. 597.

[21] Someone who mistakenly thinks that astronomical investigation is the appropriate response to the feelings produced in him by the stars at night might nevertheless fail to discover that he has moved off in the wrong direction because the empirical enquiry prolongs his trafficking with the objects of his impression and so is the occasion of experiences continuous with those that initiated his interest. Suppose that Bradley, the eighteenth-century astronomer who discovered 3,000 new stars, owed his sense of vocation to the experience described by Valéry – the mysterious impression made on him by the night sky. Though he would be no wiser as to this mystery at the end of his professional life than he was at its beginning, he would at least have spent a considerable part of it looking at stars. And this might cause him to overlook the discrepancy between the questions with which he began and the answers with which he emerged.

If a modern star-fancier decided to make astronomy his vocation and, after arduous study, found himself indoors monitoring bleeps he might come to feel that he had

An analogous kind of disillusionment is expressed by the Irish playwright John Millington Synge over aspects of his sojourn on the Island of Aran. His enthusiasm for Gaelic culture led him to live, from time to time, among the Aran islanders, about whom he complained that it was 'only in the intonation of a few sentences or some old fragments of melody' that he caught 'the real spirit of the island . . . For in general the men sit together and talk with endless iteration of the tides and fish and the price of kelp in Connemara.'[22] There are impressions which call for enquiry with respect to them to be undertaken in the spirit in which Synge visited Aran – to sit by a turf fire listening to Irish songs, poems and stories, avoiding, as he could, the talk of tides and fish and the price of kelp in Connemara.

What Synge was after were further manifestations of 'the real spirit of the island' and perhaps a clearer sense of the unity of these manifestations. The contemplation of such cases may help us to avert a misunderstanding of the role which further experience plays in such enquiries. It is the formal relation in which it stands to the original impression ('the crush of thoughts') that gives new information its point.[23]

The same distinction can be illustrated by the predicament of someone infatuated with the idea of China, which he pictures as 'A land of poetry and graciousness . . . where the most serious business of life is to drink tea in a latticed pavilion, beside a silent lake, beneath a weeping willow' (Hugh Honour, *Chinoiserie*), and who

---

misunderstood himself. John Cowper Powys said of the stars, 'My tendency has been . . . to accept them with what Spengler calls the "physiognomic eye"; in other words, to wonder at them *in their precise visible appearance*, eliminating from my consciousness all those bewildering astronomical and mathematical calculations with regard to their size and distance, their origin and destination. What has always arrested me are the usual configurations of the stars; so many astounding twists and twirls and spirals up there in the Boundless.' (*Autobiography* (London, 1934), p. 171). If Powys had been less clear-headed as to the source of the fascination the night sky held for him and gone in for radio-astronomy we would have an example of the kind of disillusionment I am talking about.

[22] John Millington Synge, *The Aran Islands* (Dublin, 1911), pp. 49–50.

[23] William Empson illustrates the operation of this principle in the practice of criticism:

Continually, in order to paraphrase a piece of verse, it is necessary to drag in some quite irrelevant conceptions; thus I have often been puzzled by finding it necessary to go and look things up in order to find machinery to express distinctions that were already in my mind; indeed, this is involved in the very notion of the activity, for how else would one know what to look up? So that many of my explanations may be demonstrably wrong and yet efficient for their purpose and vice-versa. (*Seven Types of Ambiguity*, 2nd edn (London, 1949), p. 253)

feels a lack of closure, a compulsion to find out or do something with respect to his picture. One conception of his problem would take him to Granet, Needham or Wittvogel, to hydraulic civilisations, patrimonial bureaucracy and the asiatic mode of production; the other to reminiscences of Arthur Waley's *Hundred and Seventy Chinese Poems*, willow-pattern plates, snatches of gnomic wisdom from *Explaining Conjunctions* or *King Mu of Chou*, even, perhaps, to *The Wallet of Kai Lung* and *Terry and the Pirates*, with all their multitudinous reverberations and interrelations, in search of the secret of their power over him. What such a Sinophile really wants is not further knowledge but something like Spengler's prime symbol or Goethe's '*Urphänomen*'. Reflecting on the source and character of his infatuation with China is quite another enterprise from attempting to explain the sources and conditions of the distinctiveness of Chinese culture. We overlook the difference between these two enquiries because one so often contributes to the other. Proust says of his account of Chardin's life, 'I have shown what the work of a great artist could mean to us by showing all that it meant to him.' It is somewhat in this way that our Sinophile might profit from his Sinological researches.

A correct historical reconstruction of the role of human sacrifice in the development of culture, up to and including the survivals themselves, might well be as irrelevant and unilluminating as to the impression made on us by the Fire-festivals as Sinology to Chinoiserie, optics to the beauty of the rainbow, the topography of Palestine to 'Galilee, sweet Galilee' or sidereal astronomy to 'the frosty glories of Orion'. But why is this an objection to Frazer? Why should he not ignore the question 'Why does this impress us?' for the question 'How did this originate?'

It may sharpen our sense of the distinctiveness of the relation in which we stand to the theme of human sacrifice if we contrast this with the explanatory problem posed us by the outrigger canoe, say. A reconstruction of the origins of the outrigger canoe, tracing it to a raft, the centre log of which was hollowed out while the outer planks were retained as floats, may put me in mind that the sight of an outrigger canoe always makes me obscurely aware of its likeness to a raft, the central log of which had been hollowed out. But this reconstruction would diminish greatly in interest should it prove that the outrigger had evolved rather from a double canoe, the smaller of which had dwindled to a float. The fact that the mistaken reconstruction successfully evoked the impression made on me by the sight of an outrigger canoe would not redeem it. We do not stand to the accounts of human sacrifice as to the outrigger canoe. The impression produced by an outrigger canoe has no 'depth'.

There is a suggestion as to what Wittgenstein means by depth on p. 249:

What makes human sacrifice something deep and sinister anyway? Is it only the suffering of the victim that impresses us in this way? All manner of diseases bring just as much suffering and do *not* make this impression.

The contrast between the suffering of disease and that of sacrifice is not quite the contrast Wittgenstein means to make. He doesn't mean to contrast our impression of inflicted with that of non-inflicted suffering (though this too raises questions worth pondering). He means to contrast *ritually* inflicted suffering with suffering inflicted for some other purpose. We see what Wittgenstein is getting at if we compare any of the burnings Foxe recounts in his *Book of Martyrs* (which also make an impression in their way) with the impression made by the Beltane Festival. There is no 'queer pointlessness' about the burnings Foxe describes, i.e. no rituality and thus, on Wittgenstein's anti-utilitarian view of rituality, no symbolic purport.

The remark continues: 'No, this deep and sinister aspect is not obvious just from learning the history of the external action, but we impute it from an experience in ourselves.' It is not just our conviction that 'the festival is connected with the burning of a man' that confers depth on the practice, but our obscure sense of that in virtue of which he was burnt.

Rituality is often employed to mark the special relation in which we stand to a contingency. Therefore, contemplating such rituals differs from direct meditation on the contingency itself; e.g. the difference between thinking of those who fell in the world wars, say, and reflecting on, rather than joining in, the two minute silence. Ritual death and suffering may have natural death and suffering for its subject. So reflection on the Fire-festivals has features which distinguish it from the straightforward contemplation of atrocity. That to which it stands in some trophic, figurative relation is what gives the ritual its depth. And the task it sets us is to articulate this.

V

What then would be the kind of thing it would be appropriate to produce for the purpose of unperplexing someone who asked why an account of men celebrating a festival by pretending to throw one of their number into a fire should make such a deep impression on him? Something like this:

At all times and in all places men have been fascinated and appalled by the notion of divinity . . . This violent and deleterious aspect of divinity was generally manifested in sacrificial rites. Often moreover the rites were extravagantly cruel: children were offered to monsters of red-hot metal, gigantic wicker figures crammed with human beings were set alight, priests flayed living women and clad themselves in the streaming bloody spoils. Acts as horrifying as these were rare; they were not essential to the sacrifice but they underlined its significance . . . the frightfulness of the divine, (which) will only protect us once its basic need to consume and ruin has been satisfied.[24]

What makes Bataille's account more appropriate than Frazer's is that Bataille's is less likely to encourage the illusion that its assessment requires an effort of historical scholarship. It is more patent that what we are called on to do is to seek for what makes human sacrifice 'deep and sinister' among our crush of thoughts about man and his past, to see whether 'the frightfulness of the divine' is among the 'experiences in ourselves from which we impute' this deep and sinister character. Someone who found Bataille's account acceptable would stand to it, not as he stands to a hypothesis, but as Wittgenstein says someone who was impressed by Frazer's account of the life of the King of the Wood at Nemi stood to the phrase 'the majesty of death' (p. 236).

A common temptation with respect to troubling accounts like those of human sacrifice is the sceptical question 'Did this really happen?'; but your troubled response need be no less appropriate if it had not really happened. It is the failure to see this which earns Wittgenstein's reproof 'like a backward-looking Clever Elsa' (p. 248). (Clever Elsa, the eponymous heroine of a Grimm *Märchen*, was sent to the cellar to fetch some beer with which to toast her betrothal, but having spied an axe on the wall above the barrel fell to brooding about the possibility that it might fall on her as yet

---

[24] Georges Bataille, *Death and Sensuality* (New York, 1969), pp. 176–7.

unconceived child's head when in the course of time he was sent
to the cellar to fetch beer.)

Suppose that on learning that in Africa, in times past, men were
used as mounts you were caused to think, in a troubled way, of
Marlowe's Tamburlaine harnessing his defeated enemies to his
carriage, or of the Old Man of the Sea in Sinbad's fifth voyage, and
other similar episodes. You might then experience relief on discovering that this African practice was due to the prevalence of the
Tsetse fly, which precluded the use of animals as burden beasts,
and thus sprang from a utilitarian motive and not any relish for
degrading their fellows. But there are occasions on which the
relief afforded you by this kind of discovery would be an illusory
one. You would have failed to penetrate to the root of the matter,
as Wittgenstein thinks Frazer did.

Dr Johnson observed that confronted with accounts of horror
the mind takes refuge in incredulity. Sometimes it takes refuge in
empirical research. I understand that there is an institute pursuing an enquiry into the history of the persecution and extermina-
tion of racial and religious minorities in Europe. Whatever the
value of such an enquiry, it often generates illusions as to what its
successful prosecution could achieve (and is in part fed from such
illusions). There is an ingredient in the dismay occasioned by
reminders of the theme of *homo homini daemon* with which even the
most lucid narrative is incommensurate.[25]

There are several ways in which empirical enquiry, though
fundamentally irrelevant, nevertheless ministers to the disturbance occasioned by certain phenomena. One of these is suggested by Proust in his dealings with jealousy. Swann tells Odette
that providing him with details of her Lesbian affairs would relieve
his torment: 'If I were able to form an idea of the person that
would prevent me from ever thinking of her again . . . It's so soothing to be able to form a clear picture of things in one's mind. What
is really terrible is what one cannot imagine.' What Proust says of
Swann – 'He was seeking information to dispel suffering' – has a
more general application and helps explain our behaviour in
these matters.[26]

---

[25] Rush Rhees has discussed this sort of incommensurability in another area of our lives,
that of sexuality, in 'The tree of Nebuchadnezzar', *The Human World*, August 1971.

[26] Edmund Leach, raising the question of 'How is it that some thousands of people will
spend their ten shillings on a paperback version of *The Golden Bough*?', answered in terms

Sometimes a different principle is at work – the psychic distance which certain modes of presentation are able to introduce between the facts and our troubled response to them. For example, this appreciation of a Frazerian scholar's treatment of cannibalism: 'It is a welcome relief to pass sometimes from factual reports of head-hunting expeditions and the various grizzly practices that follow such expeditions . . . to the deliberate and measured commentary of a man of E. O. James's calibre.'[27] The relief afforded to some minds by 'deliberate and measured' commentaries is derived by others from scientistic dealings with the 'tragic' and the 'terrible'. There are people for whom an account which allows them to translate concentration camp guards herding men, women and children towards gas ovens into Lewinian topological vectors is as consoling as Sophocles or Job.

I am saying: we sometimes fail to see the irrelevance of our epistemic activities with respect to a certain phenomenon because we are more anxious to alter its aspect in a congenial direction than to understand that aspect in its relation to us. We are less likely to see fear in a handful of dust of which we know the chemical formula.

Nevertheless someone who has been moved by human sacrifice to devote himself to an historical reconstruction of the development and atrophy of the institution might find his conclusions, however warranted, disappointing in some obscure way. And if he chanced to read Hans Castorp's rhapsodising on the lesson of his dream of the blood sacrifice – two hags in a temple dismembering and eating a child – ('Well and truly dreamt. I have taken stock. I will remember.') might feel, 'that is what I really wanted'.[28]

of the 'fascination with the brute sadism of primitive sacrifice', and added 'it is an odd thought but I can find no other' ('Golden Bough or Gilded Twig?', *Daedalus* 90 (Spring 1961), pp. 383–4). I don't know about the sales of *The Golden Bough* but I suggest that pursuits which seem to manifest 'a fascination with brute sadism' are often undertaken not from relish but in the hope of making it less disturbing.

'What is gained by the journey which Dante forced his reader to make amid hideous detail, through depth beyond depth of horror? . . . The contemplation of all this scenery of torment has for its purpose the conquest of pain.' (Maude Bodkin, *Archetypal Patterns in Poetry*, London, 1934)

27 Garry Hogg, *Cannibalism and Human Sacrifice* (London, 1958), pp. 135–6.
28 Hans Castorp's epiphany on 'the horrible blood sacrifice' (in the chapter 'Snow', *The Magic Mountain*) may seem to go further than Wittgenstein's desideratum – the provision of 'a perspicuous presentation' which will leave us clearer as to the source of our impression ('arranging the factual material so that we can easily pass from one part to

As an illustration of the ubiquity of the error with which Wittgenstein taxes Frazer, consider the following account of the state of Napoleon's Grand Army after crossing the Berezina in its retreat:

the temperature sank to $-13°$. To warm themselves for a few minutes, the soldiers would set whole houses on fire. Some of the details given by Segur seem scarcely credible: 'The light of these conflagrations', he writes, 'attracted some poor wretches whom the intensity of the cold and suffering had made delirious. They dashed forward in a fury, and with gnashing teeth and demoniacal laughter threw themselves into these raging furnaces, where they perished in dreadful convulsions. Their starving companions watched them die without apparent horror. There were even some who laid hold of the bodies disfigured and roasted by the flames, and – incredible as it may seem – ventured to carry this loathsome food to their mouths.' (One hopes that here Segur's sense of drama carried him somewhat beyond the literal truth.)[29]

Why should we find comfort in the thought that Segur may have been exaggerating? Is this not reacting like a backward-looking Clever Elsa? The dismay Segur's story occasions us is not to be assuaged by casting doubts on its historicity. 'Worries of that kind are not involved here.' 'There is still something of which we are sure.' Segur's anecdote takes us to thoughts of human demoralisation and the collapse of solidarity; and the question of what makes these virtualities so disturbing, what gives them their depth, remains to be dealt with even if Segur was exaggerating. We can extend to these enormities what Wittgenstein says about ritual

another and have a clear view of it. – Showing it in a perspicuous way,' p. 241.) But this account may over-intellectualise Wittgenstein's view as to the problem set us by the phenomenon of human sacrifice. Someone 'troubled by love' is not likely to be untroubled by statements which address themselves to his condition just because they are non-hypothetical and confine themselves to sorting out his crush of thoughts.

Wittgenstein's analogy with someone troubled by love is better adapted to bring out the irrelevance of empirical hypotheses than to illustrate that what is wanted is 'an arrangement of factual material', 'putting together what we already know'. What would this come to in such a case? A synoptic view of thraldom which took in Catullus, the Chevalier des Grieux, Quasimodo, King Kong and the love-troubled one among others? Would this bring peace?

The crush of thoughts formula may fail to do justice to what is at issue here, unless we construe it to encompass recognition of the need for some satisfactory mental attitude towards that which makes us uneasy as well as the purely intellectual relief of discovering what it is. (Rilke's turn of phrase can serve us here. The predicament of someone troubled by the Fire-festivals is better rendered: 'What was he to do when this thing presented itself to him? What was it his task to see in it?' than as 'what makes human sacrifice deep and sinister?').

[29] Christopher Herold, *The Age of Napoleon* (New York, 1964), p. 323.

practices: 'We could invent them for ourselves and it would only be an accident if they were not found somewhere or other.'[30]

It is the space which the story finds already prepared for it that has to be scrutinised and understood, and not the space which the events themselves may occupy. If I am right about this, perhaps Wittgenstein's oft-quoted remark as to the existence of experimental psychology making us 'think we have the means of solving the problems which trouble us; though problem and method pass one another by', is open to a supplementary construction. We begin in envious wonder at the blue-eyed ones, Yeats' 'completed arcs', and this wonder takes the form of speculation as to how they got that way, but in time we come to understand that we really want something other than, or at least more than, what differential psychology can tell us. What we really need is to understand how we stand to those images of daily beauty that make us ugly, how they enter our lives and our feelings about ourselves.

We must construe Wittgenstein's remarks not as attacks on historical or empirical enquiry, but as attempts to make us more clear-headed as to our purposes in undertaking such enquiries and as to the kind of satisfaction they can and cannot yield.

There is such a thing as disinterested curiosity about the past and it can be successfully prosecuted, but it sometimes happens that historical research presents itself as the appropriate response to the impression made by certain objects or events when this is as much an illusion, though one more insidious and less easily exposed, than the comparable illusion of thinking that learning what goes on in the brain when we listen to music is going to illuminate our feelings for music.

The main burden of my argument has been that on many occasions we mistake the nature of the problem involved in accounting for the impressions which perplex, preoccupy or trouble us, or in assessing the discourse in which this is attempted, thinking that what we want with respect to them are historical reconstructions or causal explanations, and that it is a merit of Wittgenstein's reflections on Fire-festivals to have forced this fact on our attention. Wittgenstein's most fundamental objection to Frazer is one which Frazer could not have met, either by attempting to do justice to the expressive–cathartic aspect of ritual, or by addressing

---

[30] Wittgenstein, *Philosophical Investigations*, p. 232.

himself to the 'inner nature' of survivals themselves rather than to their origins. He would have had to concede that his entire programme had been misconceived; that what was called for by the notion of human sacrifice was neither an historical nor a causal enquiry, but rather an attempt to unravel the web of associations wound round the subject by nature and the unavoidable conditions of humanity.

CHAPTER FOUR

When do empirical methods by-pass 'the problems which trouble us'?

His discussion of aesthetics was mingled in a curious way with criticism of assumptions which he said were made by Frazer in *The Golden Bough* and also with criticisms of Freud.

(G. E. Moore, '*Wittgenstein's Lectures, 1930–3*')

Every explanation is an hypothesis . . . But for someone worried by love, an explanatory hypothesis will not help much. It will not bring peace . . . The crush of thoughts that do not get out because they all press forward and are wedged in the door.

('Remarks on Frazer's *Golden Bough*')

For us, the concept of a perspicuous presentation is funda-mental . . . This perspicuous presentation makes possible that understanding which consists in seeing the connections.

('Remarks on Frazer's *Golden Bough*')

An entirely new account of correct explanation. Not one agreeing with experience, but one accepted. You have to give the explanation which is accepted. This is the whole point of the explanation.

(*Lectures and Conversations in Aesthetics*)

I

Wittgenstein thinks it was wrong of Frazer to respond to the Fire-festivals by launching an investigation into their origins, and of Freud to respond to dreams by looking for causal relations between them and other aspects of our lives. What kind of mistake is this? Is it the same mistake? Is it really a mistake?

Wittgenstein's criticisms of Freud and Frazer have an interest which extends beyond Wittgensteinian exegesis because they raise

107

a much broader problem, which one might formulate as follows:

There are questions which present themselves as empirical, i.e. such that they require further information for their resolution, but with respect to which we are told, or come to feel obscurely ourselves, that this is an illusion, that the consummation we are seeking is not to be found in more empirical knowledge, or via scientific explanation, but elsewhere and otherwise. What is the character of this 'elsewhere and otherwise'? Is it such that we may, nevertheless, speak of knowledge and understanding, of ignorance relieved by further reflection? And if the error is not to be characterised in these terms, that is in terms of mistaking one kind of epistemic need for another, how is it to be characterised?

Wittgenstein implies that his criticisms of Freud and Frazer are of a piece with his objections to a scientific or experimental aesthetics. This sets us the exegetic puzzle, which Moore expresses in his phrase 'mingled in a curious way', of finding the common element in these criticisms.

I will say straightaway, dogmatically, without any attempt at exegetical justification, what common feature it was that Wittgenstein was recording, or thought he was recording, using Wittgenstein's own idioms. They (Freud, Frazer and also I. A. Richards and Frank Ramsey in their dealings with aesthetic questions) all confounded formal, internal relations with external, causal ones; hypotheses with similes and 'further descriptions'; the notion of truth with that of truthfulness; explaining with 'explaining' or making clear; directed with non-directed feelings or states of mind; scientific speculation with the provision of synoptic views.

There are two possible constructions to be placed on the confusion of which Wittgenstein speaks. Both have exegetical warrant. Both presuppose that there are certain phenomena which induce in us a desire for a clearer grasp of the relation in which we stand to them, or, to use Wittgenstein's own expression, a sorting out of our 'crush of thoughts' with respect to them. (Some other expressions he uses in this connection are 'being intrigued and wanting to describe', 'the sort of explanation one longs for', the thought 'at the back of one's mind', the impression – particularly with music – that an experience seems to be 'saying something, and it is as if one had to discover what it was saying'.)

The first of the two confusions I referred to is to think of the situations described above as requiring empirical investigation for their resolution; of thinking that when I ask why I am impressed, I am asking the same kind of question as when I ask why I am bilious, only about my mind instead of my body; of failing to see the difference between 'What is it that I am feeling?' and 'What is it that I am sitting on?'

There is reason to think that Freud does sometimes make this mistake, particularly in his joke book. I don't think that Frazer does, or that Freud invariably does. The alternative construction that can be placed on 'confusion' raises issues that are both more profound and more intractable. The confusion consists not in employing an empirical method on problems for which it is inappropriate, but in ignoring the problems for which it is not appropriate for problems for which it is. On this view, Frazer's mistake was not that having raised the question 'Why do the Beltane fires impress us?' he then foolishly (and incomprehensibly) began investigating their origins in hopes of an answer, but that having come to hear of Fire-festivals he pursued empirical investigations with respect to them instead of reflecting on his own response to them and what gave this response the character that it had.

There is a discussion of an analogous error in a book which we know had a profound influence on Wittgenstein, Heinrich Hertz's *Principles of Mechanics* (I have abridged the passage):

One hears with a wearisome frequency that the nature of force is still a mystery, that one of the chief problems of physics is the investigation of the nature of force, and so on . . . Now, why is it that people never in this way ask what is the nature of gold . . . Is the nature of gold better known than that of force? . . . I fancy the difference must lie in this. With the term . . . 'gold' we connect a large number of relations to other terms; and between all those relations we find no *contradiction which offends us*. We are therefore satisfied and ask *no further questions*. But we have accumulated around the term 'force' . . . more relations than can be completely reconciled amongst themselves. We have an obscure feeling of this, and want to have things cleared up. Our confused wish finds expression in the confused question as *to the nature* of force . . . But the answer we want is not really an answer to this question. It is not by finding out more and fresh relations and connections that it can be answered; but by removing the contradictions existing between those already known, and thus perhaps by reducing their number. When these painful contradictions are removed, the question as to the nature of force will not have been answered; but our minds, no longer vexed, will cease to ask illegitimate questions.[1]

---

[1] Heinrich Hertz, *The Principles of Mechanics* (Macmillan, 1899), p. 8.

There is a difference between Hertz's philosopher of nature and the man who comes to feel that what he wants regarding a phenomenon is a perspicuous view of his crush of thoughts with respect to it rather than 'more and fresh relations', such as its developmental history, its historical circumstances, its remote origins, etc. For in the case of Hertz's physicist there may well be a conceptual incongruity about conjoining the notion of force with a demand for an account of its nature, such as we have in the case of gold. There is no such incongruity in the case of ritual sacrifice or dreams. So the mistake that someone might come to feel that he had made with respect to these phenomena must be of a different order. That is, in the case of the nature of force there seems no alternative direction in which to go but that of conceptual clarification of the concept of force; but in the case of phenomena investigated by Freud and Frazer there are no such conceptual obstacles to empirical enquiry.

Let us first ask what the character of this discourse is which does not depend for its successful prosecution on the gathering of more information than we already have at our disposal. A good way to begin to answer this question is by adapting what Wittgenstein says about Freud's analysis of jokes:

All we can say is that if it is presented to you, you say 'Yes, that's what happened' . . . Freud transforms the joke into a different form which is recognized by us as an expression of the chain of ideas which led us from one end of the joke to the other.[2]

If we substitute a more generic term, like 'impression', for 'joke', we get:

(The analysis) transforms (the impression) into a different form which is recognized by us as an expression of the chain of ideas which led us from one end to another of (the impression). (Or where the experience has no marked sequential structure, we can say 'which is recognized by us as an expression of the crush of thoughts which comprised the experience').

Wittgenstein's objection to Frazer, Freud and the practitioners of scientific aesthetics can then be restated: they either raise questions for which the only mode of validation is 'Yes, that's what happened', and fail to realise this, or fail to raise (or, having raised, fail to confine themselves to) questions for which the mode of valida-

---

[2] Ludwig Wittgenstein, *Lectures and Conversations* (Oxford, 1966), p. 18.

tion is 'Yes, that's what happened'. What grounds have we for saying that Frazer committed either of these errors?

Moore tells us that one of the chief points on which Wittgenstein 'seemed to wish to insist' was 'that it was a mistake to suppose that why, e.g., the account of the Beltane Festival impresses us so much is because it has "developed from a festival in which a real man was burnt". He accused Frazer of thinking that this was the reason.'[3] It is incredible that anyone should think that the impression made by a ceremony in which an effigy is burned could be explained by the fact that it is the lineal descendant of a ceremony in which a man was burned, though someone might mistakenly think that his *belief* that a man was once burned explains the impressiveness of a ritual in which an effigy is burned. Frazer's error may have been to confound the idea of the ritual burning of a man as a 'formal' term, related to the impression of the Fire-festival in making it the impression that it was, with its external relation to the Fire-festival as its original or causal antecedent.

But this is not the conceptual confusion Frazer is being accused of, which involves the unlikely assumption that someone should spend years amassing empirical evidence about a phenomenon (the Nemi priesthood say, which Frazer tells us initiated his researches) if what he explicitly wanted to know was why he felt about it as he did. Frazer's recognition of his error, unlike that of Hertz's natural philosopher, would not consist in his seeing that the amassing of all this material was a quite unsuitable way of determining 'why the Beltane Festival impresses us', or 'what makes human sacrifice sinister', but in coming to realise that it was these questions to which he really wanted an answer, and not the speculative pre-history ones which he had raised. But did Frazer even commit this error? It being the kind of error it is, Frazer alone could tell us.

There is one qualification to be made of the last remark; but it is one whose weight it is difficult to assess. Someone might produce the impression that though explicitly raising empirical questions, these were not the questions he really wished to raise, because his discourse was marked by preoccupations of a kind not to be served by advances in empirical knowledge. His discourse would manifest what I shall call 'expressive incongruity'. I will illustrate this notion from an essay on the holocaust.

[3] G. E. Moore, *Philosophical Papers* (New York, 1962), pp. 308–9.

George Steiner's essay 'Post-script to a tragedy' is a review of two books about the holocaust – Chaim Kaplan's *Warsaw Diary* and J-F. Steiner's *Treblinka*. Steiner begins his essay with two horrific anecdotes. Immediately after he has a paragraph which evokes potently the state we are left in by facts such as he has just related:

One of the things I cannot grasp, though I have often written about them, trying to get them in some kind of bearable perspective, is the time relation . . . Precisely at the same hour in which Mehring or Langner were being done to death, the overwhelming plurality of human beings, ten miles away on the Polish farms, five thousand miles away in New York, were sleeping or eating or going to a film, making love or worrying about the dentist. This is where my imagination balks. The two orders of simultaneous existence are so different . . . their existence is so hideous a paradox.[4]

In the 'hideous paradox' to which Steiner refers we can recognise a familiar ingredient in our response to facts such as he recounts, as to tragedy generally. There are moments when it is found especially troubling that 'while the mourner is burying his friend the reveller is hasting to his wine'. 'The roar on the other side of silence' was George Eliot's phrase for this paradox, and she stressed the necessity for cultivating a degree of deafness to this roar. But when Steiner goes on to raise the question of the failure of the RAF and US Airforce to bomb the gas ovens and/or rail lines leading to the death camps he has ceased to address the problems raised in his account of the state of mind induced in us by his anecdotes. The question of at how early a stage the Allies realised what was going on in the camps, and whether they might not have made more vigorous efforts at intervention, raises issues of an entirely different order from that of 'the hideous paradox', issues which require a great deal of information and assessment of evidence for their solution; whereas our recognition that Steiner in invoking 'the hideous paradox' of the collateral contemporaneity of the demonic and the quotidian had hit on a prominent component of the impression made on us by the idea of the holocaust, one of the 'crush of thoughts' this idea provokes, requires no such information or assessment. The possible culpability of the Allies in not taking preventive action, however deplorable, does not constitute a hideous paradox, and seems oddly out of place in a discussion of

[4] George Steiner, 'Postscript to a tragedy', *Encounter* 28 (February 1967), p. 33.

it. We feel we could justifiably chide Steiner in Wittgenstein's words: 'Every explanation is an hypothesis. But for someone who is troubled an explanation will not help much. It will not bring peace.' If the question is 'Did Heaven look on and would not take their part?', can the answer be 'Anyway, it seems the Allied Air Forces did'?

But an appeal to expressive incongruity can hardly be conclusive. Not only because the judgement on which it is based is an imponderable one, but because the defence could be made that the discourse was not confusing two incommensurable issues, but merely raising both.

To make a conceptual error in attempting questions like 'What makes human sacrifice deep and sinister?', 'Why does the Beltane Fire-festival impress us?', 'Why is there something especially terrible in the fact that in choosing the sacrificial victim by lots they use a cake?' would be to go in search of more information than we already have.

There is no reason to think that in these particular cases anyone has made that conceptual mistake. If the search for further information in such cases is a mistake, then it is both a more interesting and a more contentious one. It is to neglect these questions for others, for the solution of which more information is requisite. For example, how did they come to use *a cake* for casting lots?

It is one thing to object that Frazer's developmental speculations cannot untrouble us (whatever force we give to 'untrouble' (beruhigen); either, sort out our crush of thoughts with respect to a phenomenon, or, reconcile us to the incipient realisations which composed it), and quite another to object that, like Freud and the practitioner of a scientific aesthetics, Frazer first posed a question which required only that we bethink ourselves, and then went in search of irrelevant empirical data.

There is no reason to believe that Frazer thought either that discovering the origins of the Fire-festivals was the way to answer the question why they seem sinister, nor that determining why they seem sinister would settle the question of their origins. Frazer's methods did not pass his problems by; they passed *our* problems by, if, like Wittgenstein, we wish to know, 'What makes human sacrifice so sinister anyway?'

That Wittgenstein's objections to Freud's practice of dream interpretation are as much an objection to Freud's raising causal

questions at all as to his proferring conceptually inappropriate
answers to non-causal questions is suggested by his discussion of
Freud's treatment of a dream which I will refer to as the flowery
dream. (This is indexed under 'the language of flowers' in the
appendix to *The Interpretation of Dreams*.) On one occasion
Wittgenstein complained of this dream interpretation of Freud's
that in giving a causal account of the elements of the dream Freud
was doing something 'immensely wrong' and that he was 'cheating' the patient.[5] The dream in question is used by Freud as an
example of a biographical dream, uncommon outside analysis, he
says, which expressed the dreamer's joy at having passed through
life 'immaculately'. The element in the dream about Freud's treatment of which Wittgenstein particularly complains involved the
patient floating down from a height while carrying a flowering
branch in her hand, the blossoms of which looked like red camellias, and some of which had faded at the conclusion of her descent.
Freud subjects this to his standard treatment; but at this point it
doesn't seem to be Freud's tendentiousness of which Wittgenstein
is complaining, but of his assumption that his interpretation had
a content over and above the patient's endorsement of it, and so
was independent of this endorsement, i.e. was a matter of truth
and not merely of truthfulness. During this dream episode the
dreamer felt herself exalted. The branch she carried she later
likened to the lily spray carried by the Angel in pictures of the
Annunciation, and the situation in general to 'the girls in white
robes walking in the Corpus Christi processions when the streets
were decorated with green branches'. The dream 'expressed her
joy at having passed immaculately through life', i.e. without
sinning against purity. Thus far we have 'further descriptions',
characterisations of the dream which makes it the dream that it
was, characterisations which are not matters of inference. Freud
then produces his interpretation of the dream in which these
characterisations are contradicted. The branch is a phallic symbol,
the red camellias are an allusion to *La Dame aux Camelias* whose
favourite flower they were, and who wore them white for most of
the month and red when she was menstruating, and (presumably)
since she was a courtesan, the dreamer is alluding wistfully to a life
richer in sexual gratification.

---

[5] Ludwig Wittgenstein, *Lectures and Conversations* (Oxford, 1966), pp. 23–4.

But in this instance Freud was not making the mistake, which there is some reason for saying he made in his comments on jokes, of failing to see that 'the correct explanation is the one accepted'. This can't be the nature of Freud's error in the case of the Flowery Dreamer, because there is a blatant discrepancy between her own view of the dream and that of Freud, and since Freud does not on that account think he is mistaken, he has given the strongest possible reasons for concluding that he does not see himself as trafficking in further descriptions, or in the elaboration of the ideas with which the dream seemed pregnant. This must be obvious to Wittgenstein, so what is the ground of his objection? It must lie in the feeling of the irrelevance of casual questions, rather than in the incongruity of causal answers to intentionalist questions. And this would be perfectly acceptable, or at least arguable, but for the fact that the dreamer was also a patient.

The judgement in which we are involved in these discussions is not narrowly conceptual, but is rather like this:[6] 'What is intriguing about a dream is not its causal connection with events in my life, etc., but rather the impression it gives of being a fragment of a story'. The criticism of Freud, then, would be that he addresses himself to the first of these questions, that of discovering the causal connection between the dream and events in the dreamer's life rather than attempting to fill out the story of which it seems to be a fragment. So that this is a case of the thinker rather than the method by-passing the problem, and of whether he is justified in doing so.

There are reasons for saying Freud was so justified. For why should the inferences that the dream suggests or permits as to the shameful thoughts of the dreamer be eligible as interpretations of the dream only if they coincide with, or are continuous with, the nimbus of significance that a dream sometimes trails behind it? Psychoanalytic dream interpretation may well be one of the intellectual impositions of our time, but this is not a priori true, and there is no objection to be made in principle to the causal explanation of a dream, whether on Freudian lines or any others.

If it is a matter of urgency to elicit the causal relations into which a phenomenon enters as in psychopathology, then, however intrigued by the reverberations of the experience, we would

---

[6] Ludwig Wittgenstein, *Culture and Value* (Oxford, 1980), pp. 68–9.

eschew 'further descriptions' and 'similes' and 'words that sum it up' and pursue empirical investigations.

When we turn from dreams to symptoms, in spite of their miscellaneousness, in neither construal of the error does it seem one to fail to confine ourselves to 'further descriptions'; neither because they are the only conceptually appropriate response, given the nature of the question, nor because the questions to which they are answers are the ones to raise, given the nature of the occasion. Not the first, since there is no conceptual impropriety about asking for a causal explanation (in the very wide sense of 'the one agreeing with experience' as opposed to 'the one accepted'). Whether a patient felt the harsh reproof of a husband as 'like a slap in the face' is a question of whether this is 'a good simile', and this she can tell us, but the question of whether this simile played a role in the production of a trigeminal neuralgia (conversion hysteria) is something she cannot tell us. In this case the conceptual impropriety would consist rather in treating such problems as ones in which we had to give the explanation that is accepted.

A 'dream story' may well have 'a charm of its own', as Wittgenstein puts it. And causally connecting this story with fragments of the dreamer's past may well dissipate this charm, and we might justifiably find this gratuitous; but do symptoms have a charm? A delusion might have something akin to charm, it may strike us as 'an idea pregnant with possible developments', but would we not have misgivings about pursuing these (unless in the service of a diagnostic or therapeutic aim)? Neither would we think it sensible to pursue the experience of an attack of trigeminal neutralgia in the direction of 'excellent similes'.

Of course Freud had signally failed in the case of the flowery dreamer to provide 'the sort of explanation one longs for' when one wakes from a dream pregnant with significance, just as would a neurologist who responded to a patient's account of the aura of imminent revelation that preceded his epileptic fits with talk of epileptic foci and neuronal discharges. On the other hand, it seems right and proper that we should go from the rapture and the sense of imminent revelation which sometimes signals the onset of epileptic seizures, to a discussion of epileptic foci in the brain rather than in search of 'the sort of explanation one longs for' in connection with aesthetic impressions. The point is, what may be a mistake with respect to our impression of a dream (or of human sacrifice), need not be a mistake with respect to our afflictions where it is a causal investigation, either into their historical antecedents, or the neurophysiological substrate which is called for.

Though an hypothesis is an inappropriate response to a request for a further description, a request for a further description may be an inappropriate request. When we are dealing with psychopathological phenomena, the questions we want answered cannot be settled by reflection, and the questions which can be settled by reflection we ought not to be raising. If the patient complained she felt deprived because our hypotheses lacked the charm of her own elaborations of the meaning of her experience of illness, we should reconcile ourselves to this rather than capitulate to it.

But there are reservations we may need to make about this thesis. Let us first ask what it is we can be made to acknowledge we want and only then whether we ought to cease to want it.

II

One case in which it is sometimes felt that problems and method have passed one another by is that of disenchantment with biographical knowledge: the realisation that there are questions, or at any rate yearnings, provoked by our encounters with others ('the other who assaults our being' as Sartre puts it), that no amount of information about them can assuage.

Our wonder at others seems naturally to take the form of empirical speculation, of which, when pressed, we can often give no determinate account with which the wonder is commensurate. Tolstoi, on several occasions, displays his characters in this posture of wonder.

Kitty Scherbatsky wonders at her friend Varenka:

What is it in her? What gives her this power to disregard everything, to be so quietly independent of everything? How I should like to know it, and learn it from her!

Later, Kitty tells Varenka of her humiliation at being rejected by Vronsky:

'There isn't a girl who hasn't experienced the same thing. And it is all so unimportant.'

'Then what is so important?' asked Kitty . . .
'Oh, there is so much that is important', said Varanka smiling.
'What?'
'Oh there's so much that's more important', replied Varenka, not knowing what to say. Kitty held her by the hand, and with passionate curiosity and entreaty questioned Varenka with her eyes: 'What is it – what is it that is so important? What gives you such tranquillity? You know, tell me!'
But Varenka did not even understand what Kitty's eyes were asking her . . . Kissing Kitty once more, without having told her what was important, she stepped out into the twilight of the summer night, bearing away her secret of what was important, and what gave her her enviable calm and dignity.

The tendency to see the problem presented us by our wonder at the lives of others as that of a secret to be penetrated is illustrated again in a later passage where it is Levin who 'feels a longing, dissatisfied as he was with his own life, to get at the secret which gave Svisahky such clarity, definiteness and courage in life'.

Alexei Karenin, too, when 'with a sense of shame and regret he reviewed his past', asks himself:

'How have I been to blame? . . .' and as usual the question set him wondering whether all those other men – the Vronskys and Oblonskys and those gentlemen of the bed-chamber with their fine calves – felt differently, did their loving and their marrying differently. And there rose before his mind's eye a whole row of those vigorous, dashing, self-confident men who always, and everywhere, drew his inquisitive attention in spite of himself.

Suppose those gentlemen of the bed-chamber with their fine calves were disposed to indulge Karenin's inquisitiveness (as Oblonsky certainly would), what could they have told him? At most what Freud said of Goethe, and hinted of himself, that they had been 'the undisputed darlings of their mothers'. But would this have relieved Karenin's inquisitiveness?

In a biographical piece on General Marshall I read: 'Without doubt much of his command power derived from his remarkable presence which radiated superiority. It seemed never to be calculated reserve but rather the natural attitude of the full man under perfect control. We who witnessed it ever wondered how he got that way; it was a secret to be coveted.'

If the writer so impressed with Marshall's 'presence' later discovered that the General practised transcendental meditation, would this have satisfied him? Or would his curiosity have then been directed to this further nexus? I don't mean this question to be rhetorical. I only want to suggest that there are occasions on which questions of this kind would be sufficient to produce in someone the feeling that he had misunderstood himself, and that his desire for further knowledge had been a mechanical response, due perhaps to the fact that it had on other occasions proved pertinent and successul.

For there are problems presented to us by the abilities and propensities of others which the revelation of what is hidden from us does sometimes illuminate. Basil Willey tells us in his autobiography how he would attempt to overcome his dread of an interview or lecture or party by reminding himself of his ordeal in the trenches of the Western Front: 'Come on now, you fool: suppose you were going over the top tomorrow, what would you think of all these trifles then?' He says it never worked. But let us suppose that it did. We would then have a determinate answer to the question 'What is the secret of Willey's calm?'

But there are cases where our interest is directed to what might be called 'a quality of being', and these don't lend themselves to the sort of resolution achievable in the Willey case. Napoleon kept the returns of his army under his pillow at night to refer to in case he was sleepless and would set himself problems at the Opera while the overture was playing: 'I have ten thousand men at Strasbourg; fifteen thousand at Magdeburg; twenty thousand at Würzburg. By what stages must they march so as to arrive at Ratisbon on three successive days?' This explains something but not why he was Napoleonic. Is there some secret which stands to the Napoleon who 'assaulted the being' of so many generations of Frenchmen as the practice cited stands to his logistic prowess?

Sartre objected to Paul Bourget's biography of Flaubert that due to its reductionist method 'the being whom we seek . . . Flaubert, the man whom we can love or hate, blame or praise, who represents for us the *other* who assaults our being, vanishes in a dust of phenomena bound together by external connections'. In place of Bourget's 'external connections', Sartre proposes a search for 'something like a radical decision which, without ceasing to be contingent, would be the veritably psychic irreducible . . . which, when established, would produce in us an accompanying feeling of satisfaction'. No doubt it is possible through biographical enquiry and psychological speculation to resolve enigmas, plug up narrative gaps, in the case of Flaubert as in that of any other man.

But even if it were reasonable to believe that there were a set of conditions, or 'radical decisions', which when found would confer intelligibility not only on Flaubert's reclusiveness, his anti-populism, his antiquarianism, but on *Madame Bovary*; even if there were not reasons intrinsic to such a programme likely to render if futile, how would its successful consummation explain Flaubert's capacity to 'assault our being'? Among those who consider this question some may come to feel that their search for further empirical data had been misplaced, and that they stood to the quality of being which prompted this search not as Hertz's physicist stood to gold but as he stood to force. For why should Sartre's programme, any more than Bourget's, illuminate for us the Flaubert 'who is the other who assaults our being'? Would not an enquiry into the assaultability of our being by Flaubert be more pertinent? Sartre speaks of 'the being whom we seek', but how can a being whom we have not as yet found assault us, or be the object of our 'love or hate, blame or praise'?

Consider the case of someone who, impressed by the following passage, finds himself recurring to it in an attempt to fathom its expressiveness, to understand what draws him to it and others like it.

In the fifty-second year of my age, after the completion of an arduous and successful work, I now propose to employ some moments of my leisure in reviewing the simple transactions of a private and literary life . . .
I am endowed with a cheerful temper, a moderate sensibility, and a natural disposition to repose rather than activity; some mischievous appetites and habits have perhaps been corrected by philosophy or time. The love of study, a passion which derives fresh vigour from enjoyment, supplies each day, each hour, with a perpetual source of independent and rational pleasure, and I am not sensible of any decay of the mental faculties. The original soil has been highly improved by cultivation; but it may be questioned whether some flowers of fancy, some grateful errors, have not been eradicated with the weeds of prejudice. (Edward Gibbon, *Memoir of My Life and Writings*)

It is easy to imagine how an informational account of this passage might run. It would speak to us of Gibbon's temperament, and of whether the passages quoted fairly represent it; also of the development of English prose, and where Gibbon's style stands in this development; and perhaps of the influence of Gibbon's latinity on his English. But another kind of comment is possible, one whose adequacy we are competent to assess without scholarship, e.g.:

What strikes us in Gibbon's retrospect of his life is generated by our sense of the unavailability to us, those of us it does strike – for whom it wears a special aspect – of a distinctive register and cadence, a mode of self-reference which we couldn't employ without a sense of strain and affectation. The orderliness of Gibbon's progression through life (or at least his ordered sense of that progression) intensifies by contrast the phantasmagoric character of our own reminiscences, which normally yield nothing more determinate than the sense of having lurched from one exigency to another.

What this comment does is to divert our attention from the external relations of the phenomenon which impresses us to the features of our situation which confer on it the aspect which makes it the phenomenon it is – which account for our being struck.

Another instance in which the wonder provoked by another proves to be intransitive with respect to biographical knowledge is that of the diary of Samuel Pepys, the occasion of what one critic has called 'the most delightful euphoria in literature'. It is this euphoria to which our wonder is directed. Sometimes this wonder takes more determinate form as a confused desire to experience directly this quality of being ('What was it like to be Pepys?'); at others to explain it ('How did Pepys become Pepys?'). We tend to think of this quality of being, of which we crave a more intimate knowledge, as an experiential content between which and ourselves a barrier is interposed, as if there were some species of ostension to be enjoyed, as if we could pass from description to acquaintance. Sartre speaks of 'the taste which a man necessarily has for himself, the savour of his existence'. Gerard Manley Hopkins uses the same analogy; and it is a very natural one. But it is difficult to spell out the notion of ourselves feeling those states which, when evinced in speech, writing, music, painting or gesture, arrest or delight us in so distinctive a way.

Perhaps what we want with respect to Pepys and other assaults on our being, we already have, if we could look at them in the right way. Was Pepys really better placed than we to know what it was like to be Pepysian? Did Blake's tiger know that it brightly burned?

'What did Macbeth feel when he said, "Duncan is in his grave"?'[7]
What did Pepys feel when he wrote, 'Mighty merry'? Isn't knowing
what they said knowing what they felt? 'Is what is linguistic not
experience?' (*Philosophical Investigations*). Perhaps Pepys' diary
makes us Pepysian in the way that 'a walnut makes us round' (La
Fontaine).

What we might call 'the Pepys music' owes its effect in part to
his extraordinary power of absorbing himself in his circumstances. This has the effect of intensifying our own sense of what
Sartre calls 'non-immediacy', our sense of 'that solid world these
hands can never reach', of being what Heidegger calls 'a creature
of distances'. Whether this is so or not, we have in the remark
that it is, a specimen of the kind of assertion whose appraisal does
not require more knowledge than we already possess and, in fact,
precludes the use of such knowledge, since it can have played no
role in determining our relation to the being at whom we
wonder.

It sometimes happens that the intensity of our interest in the
lives of those figures whose quality of being compels our 'inquisitive attention' is parasitic on a craving for a perspicuous view of the
characterological aspirations and reforms round which our own
hopes, efforts and self-reproaches centred. And it then takes only
for this possibility to be mentioned for us to realise that it is so.
(Dilthey makes a pertinent remark in this connection. 'It is only in
comparing myself to others that I come to experience what is individual in myself.')

Another reason for feeling that 'the being whom we seek' is not
to be found through biographical investigation is that there is an
ingredient in my wonder at such beings which it shares with my
wonder at creatures who never had a being of their own, and therefore whom, of necessity, I cannot seek. It is not only Gibbon, Pepys
and Flaubert who assault my being, but Odysseus, Sir Galahad,
Falstaff, Don Juan, Figaro, Captain MacWhirr, Jeeves, Bugs Bunny
and Sergeant Bilko. And here it is clear that this assault consists of
an internal relationship between these figures and what Ortega
calls 'the programmatic personage who has to be realised'.

There are also occasions when what we want with respect to

---

[7] *Lectures and Conversations* (Oxford, 1966), p. 33. This question, from the fourth lecture
on Aesthetics, is followed by the remark, 'Can I describe his feelings better than by
describing how he said it?'

another's quality of being is less ambitious or profound, and is more akin to what Wittgenstein called 'the sort of explanation one longs for when one talks of an aesthetic impression', and which may find satisfaction if we 'find a verbal form of expression . . . the word that seems to sum it up'. John Cowper Powys, wishing to evince in communicable terms the tranquillising effect of the personality of a pious friend, invoked the Collect for the Twenty-first Sunday after Trinity, which contains the phrase 'pardon and peace'. Sartre's Roquentin may have been more astute than his creator when he satisfied his craving to know more of the life of the composer of 'Some of These Days' by inventing a presence and a milieu for him.

III

There is another area in which we tend mistakenly to think that what we require to dissipate our perplexity is a knowledge of causal relations, that of the influence of our remote past on our personal development, where we tend to confuse the role of past episodes as causal influences with their status as intentional objects of reminiscence and rumination.

In an essay on the poet John Berryman, I came across the following:

Much of Berryman's energy in later years was given over to self-analysis, a thoroughgoing process whereby he attempted to discover whether his father's suicide – which occurred when he himself was eleven years of age – did have the crippling effect on his psychological development that he thought . . . or whether he was rationalizing his subsequent neurotic conflicts, and imputing them to that cause.

There is something wrong with this. It makes Berryman's predicament in regard to his father's suicide too much like Pepys wondering why he peed so much one winter's night, and whether it was due to the unusual cold or to the oysters he had eaten. But would a straightforward answer to Berryman's question, construed as a simple counterfactual, have satisfied him? Suppose we had a highly determinate index of the neural effect of traumas, something as measurable as the piece of ass's hide in Balzac's *La Peau de Chagrin* which shrank with every wish, and we were in a position to convey this information to Berryman: his depression threshold had dropped so many notches as a consequence of his father's death: would he have seen in this the understanding for which he was seeking?

Now, of course, I can imagine a context in which the causal question was all-important, and the synoptic one frivolous: if we were conducting an epidemiological investigation of childhood traumas in the hope of devising prophylactic child-rearing regimens. But was this the basis of Berryman's interest? And, of course, the question, 'Would Berryman have committed suicide had his father not committed suicide?' is perfectly licit, and of course it demands an empirical method. But it does not follow that Berryman's own question was, or was entirely, without residue, of this kind. The predicament of someone 'bewildered at the sort of person he has turned out to be', as Rush Rhees puts it, calls for something other, or at least more, than the display of causal relations between his past and his present.

It might be asked why Berryman should desert his causal question for the more explicitly intentionalist one, 'What is it about my father's suicide which so troubles me?' Only because if that question occurred to him, or were brought to his attention, he might be willing to see in it, rather than in the causal one, the proper heir to his anguish over the manner of his father's death. This can be generalised to suggest that an entire class of questions as to the influence of our personal past on our current lives may be usurpers. If Berryman had a clearer conception of what an answer to his causal question really came to, would he have spent as much time and energy wondering about it as he did? What could a successful issue to Berryman's enquiries when construed causally have given him? At most an otiose demonstration that 'if some things were different other things would be otherwise' (as the griffin remarked to the minor canon). On the other hand, suppose Berryman's attempts at self-consolation had time and again been undermined by the reflection, 'how in a world in which such things can happen can I go on living?' And that among 'such things', lost among the crush of thoughts, and only brought to prominence by after-reflection, was the idea of his father's suicide. Might he not be willing to count this, though free of causal implication, a gain in knowledge of the significance of his father's suicide? Another example of this distinctive kind of knowledge would be Berryman's coming to an explicit realisation that a prominent theme of his rumination about his father's suicide was speculation as to whether the torments which drove him to it were like Berryman's own. What Berryman may have really wanted, which took the misleading form of a causal question, was a synoptic view of the countless reveries into which the thought of his father's suicide entered, a clearer view of what he really felt about it, of what he ought to feel about it, of what he felt he ought to feel about it.

In some other place I came across these sentences from the correspondence of Diderot: 'The more I examine myself, the more I am convinced that in our youth there comes a moment which is decisive for our character. A little girl, as pretty as a heart, bit me on the hand. When I complained to her father, he pulled up her dress before me, and that little rump stayed in my mind and will stay there as long as I live. Who knows the influence on my morals?' Is not there something to be said about this little rump without entering into causal questions, something which reflection is privileged to uncover? One wants to ask 'What is so special about that little rump?' And 'What have little rumps to do with morality?' But we know, or could make a good guess; and so it seems likely that Diderot was capable of coming to understand quite a bit about his relation to that rump without entering into difficult counter-factual questions. Having sorted out the crush of thoughts occasioned by his memory of the rump, he might have come to feel that it was not strictly causal knowledge for which he was asking. For suppose the answer was, 'No. The little rump had no influence whatever on your morals', would Diderot have straightaway lost interest in it?

Our reflections on such matters don't always find their natural consummation in the discovery of causal relations. Consider Medea's lament for Jason.

> Why lyked me thy yellow hair to see
> More than the bondes of mine honestie?

Would it have been to the point to tell her she had been imprinted? Isn't this kind of case one where, as Wittgenstein says, 'an explanatory hypothesis will not help much'?

In accounting for the development of his vocation Constable invoked 'the sound of water escaping from mill dams, willows, old rotten planks, posts and brick work. I love all such things. These scenes made me a painter, and I am grateful.' Perhaps what

Berryman wanted was to stand to the theme of his father's suicide as did Constable to the source of his impulse to paint. And if this is causal knowledge, it is so only in the sense in which Constable was manifesting causal knowledge.

Though the synoptic array may encompass factors which also stand in a causal relation to the life of the subject, they are not relations which raise evidential questions in any acute way, since they not only influence thoughts, feelings, fantasies, but participate in them.

What we want with respect to certain phenomena are not their causes, but their bearings. The lack of closure, the sense of unfinished business that we experience with respect to them is not always a matter of factual ignorance, to be relieved by the discovery of causal relations.[8]

In *Tractatus* 6.4312, Wittgenstein says of the assumption that survival after death is 'a solution to the riddle of life' that since 'this eternal life is as enigmatic as our present one this assumption will not do for us what we have always tried to make it do'. And this is what we are sometimes inclined to say of advances in knowledge, not that they are without interest or value in themselves, any more than immortality is, but that 'they will not do for us what we have always tried to make them do'. There are those for whom the argument that we sometimes ask for further knowledge when what we need are perspicuous views of what was hidden in the crush of thoughts will have no force whatever. They are never struck; they are never intrigued; they are never impressed; nothing ever seems to be saying anything; they experience no crush of thoughts. And that's that. And so it is.

But there is another objection to the preoccupation with the source of our impressions which is more worrying because less total. Though quite familiar with the experience of being intrigued and wanting to describe, of a crush of thoughts that all try to push forward and cannot get out, of phenomena that seem to be telling them something, etc., etc., those who make it do not see why these experiences should not be ignored in favour of the task of enlarging our knowledge of the phenomena which produce them. There is nothing to object to in this, once recogni-

---

[8] There is an illuminating discussion of this issue in Christopher Cherry's 'Explanation and explanation by hypothesis', *Synthese* 33 (1976).

tion has been extended to the fact that there is, nevertheless, a mode of transaction with the phenomena of our lives other than the empirical – a desire for other than a knowledge of their causes and conditions. There may be no question of convicting someone who does not acknowledge a failure of fit between his problems and his methods of error independent of his own concurrence. This thesis with regard to him may have the same character as the problems to whose distinctiveness his attention is being directed. All that can be done is to reformulate the problems which trouble him, bringing out the irrelevance of further knowledge to their solution; and either he then says 'That's what I really wanted' or he doesn't.

But in neither case is there any compulsion to acknowledge that this attempt to arrive at a clear view of the feelings and thoughts, which by virtue of their relation to certain impressions confers on them their distinctive aspect, results in a special kind of knowledge, one which is generally slighted or misunderstood. And we know that many will not say this, but will prefer to say instead that, except for a narrow range of conceptual problems whose solution is ministerial to the advance of science, when we have turned away from the search for 'more and fresh relations' we have abandoned thinking for brooding.

CHAPTER FIVE

Explanation, self-clarification and solace

I

Wittgenstein has been taxed with obscurantism for the attitude he has from time to time expressed as to the relevance and prospects of empirical explanation, whether through historical investigation or controlled enquiry. The areas in which Wittgenstein appears to see empirical discourse as an intrusion extend from dreams, jokes, and other psychoanalytic explananda to the meaning and origin of ritual practices and expressive gestures, and to our responses to music, poems, paintings, and other aesthetic products.

In the course of his apparent derogation of empirical knowledge, Wittgenstein employs two sets of contrasts. One, most generically stated, is between explaining something in the way an event is explained and attaining to a more explicit understanding of what makes it that particular something. Less generically, it is between explaining an event and coming to understand what the feelings and thoughts are which give it depth. For example, explaining how it comes about that at regular intervals a pretence is made of burning a man in a ritually prescribed way on the one hand, and understanding why this makes on us the peculiar impression it does on the other. (Sometimes the event whose explanation is contrasted with a more profound grasp of how we feel toward it is itself a feeling, and the contrast between explaining a feeling, or impression, and understanding it is all the more elusive.) The other contrast is with something less discursive than a clearer grasp of what we already know – where the impression is an aesthetic one, it is with making a gesture or drawing a face; where the impression is a troubled one, with untroubling or consoling or bringing us peace (these last three are not Wittgenstein's variant characterisations but his translators' variant renderings of *beruhigen*).[1]

When Wittgenstein says that we engage in empirical discourse when empirical discourse is not what is called for, is he saying that when we raise questions which ought properly to be resolved by reflection, by bethinking ourselves, we engage in irrelevant empirical enquiries? Or is he saying that though our discourse may be appropriate to the questions it addresses, these are the wrong questions? Freud is largely charged with one and Frazer with the other. Of these it is the second that is richest with implications for the conduct of our reflective lives.

In Wittgenstein's description of what we really want in place of empirical speculation, a key term is 'aesthetic'. When Freud does produce discourse which is pertinent to our requirements, he is said to be 'doing what aesthetics does', and Frazer in his discussion of the Beltane fires is raising an 'aesthetic question'. All he means by calling what Frazer and Freud sometimes do (and ought to have done more consistently) 'like aesthetics' is to call attention to its epistemic affinity with the problem of describing the how and why of aesthetic experience in that 'agreement is the only criterion'. In his remarks on aesthetics Wittgenstein does what, with varying degrees of explicitness, he does in the discussion of the other topics to which objection has been taken. He goes from querying the congruity between the question set and the answers given to challenging the interest, or at least the comparative interest, of the questions themselves. These considerations ought not to be confounded. 'If we want an elucidation of the impression made by our dreams, causal explanations of the images they contain won't help' raises one kind of issue; but 'we don't want causal explanations of the dream images but elucidations of the impression they make on us' raises another, very different, kind.

Charles Hanly tells us that 'Wittgenstein had to reject the idea that anything could take place in the mental life of an individual of which he was not aware at the time it was taking place which would cause him to laugh at a joke, commit a psychological error, dream,

---

[1] Ludwig Wittgenstein, 'Bemerkungen über Frazers *The Golden Bough*', *Synthese*, 17 (1967), 236. All page references are to *Synthese*. My quotations are from an unpublished translation by Anthony Manser of the University of Southampton. There are translations by John Beversluis in *Wittgenstein: Sources and Perspectives*, ed. C. G. Luckhardt (Sussex, 1971); and by A. C. Miles and Rush Rhees (but with some twenty remarks omitted) in *The Human World*, No. 3 (May 1971), pp. 18–41.

or act out a neurotic disorder.'[2] Wittgenstein does not deny that something 'in the mental life of an individual of which he was unaware at the time could cause him to laugh at a joke', etc. He denies that the discovery of such a cause could explain why he laughed at the joke in the sense in which Freud does explain why. Nor does Wittgenstein deny that the phenomena of psychopathology call for causal analysis. He says that a subclass of them call for something other than causal analysis – something which may enhance understanding but the criterion of whose correctness is that we accept it rather than that it is 'corroborated by experience'.

This is what I take Wittgenstein to be saying: Freud engages in two kinds of speculation as to our minds and the minds of his patients – hypotheses and further descriptions – and he either shows himself insufficiently aware of this, or exploits the ambiguity, treating the mode of validation appropriate to one as if it were evidence in favour of the other. It is his attitude toward this which distinguishes Wittgenstein's position from that of the scientific critics of Freud, and aligns him with the hermeneuticists. Wittgenstein doesn't advocate abandoning the patient's privileged position and adopting a method fitted to adjudicate the truth of hypotheses in its stead, as Freud's scientifically minded critics do. Rather, he attempts to confine Freud to a discourse for which the assent of the subject is an appropriate criterion. And the desirability of this raises either moral issues or issues of sensibility, depending on the questions foregone. We may be content to confine ourselves to the reasons for our laughter – while insisting on knowing the causes of our depression.

When Charles Hanly accuses Wittgenstein of obscurantism in denying the relevance of causal enquiry to Freud's interpretative activities, he cites in support some remarks on dream interpretation:

Freud does something which seems to me immensely wrong. He gives what he calls an interpretation of dreams . . . A patient, after saying that she had had a beautiful dream, described a dream in which she descended from a height, saw flowers and shrubs, broke off the branch of a tree, etc. Freud shows what he calls the 'meaning' of the dream . . . He shows relations between the dream images and certain objects of a sexual nature . . . Freud called this dream 'beautiful', putting 'beautiful'

[2] Charles Hanly, 'Wittgenstein on psychoanalysis', in *Ludwig Wittgenstein: Philosophy and Language*, ed. Alice Ambrose and Morris Lazerowitz (London, 1972), p. 93.

in inverted commas. But *wasn't* the dream beautiful? I would say to the patient: 'Do these associations make the dream not beautiful? It was beautiful. Why shouldn't it be?' I would say Freud had cheated the patient.[3]

The dream to which Wittgenstein is referring appears in the index to the *Interpretation of Dreams* as 'the language of flowers' (an account is also given in *On Dreams*). All that it is necessary to know to grasp the nature of Wittgenstein's objection is that the dreamer's favourite flower, the camellia, appears in the dream growing out of a branch she was carrying and that this image seemed to her to share the feeling tone of the angel carrying the lily spray in pictures of the Annunciation. Freud, on the other hand, thought the branch a phallus and related the camellia to the courtesan of Dumas *fils'* play, *La Dame aux Camelias*, whose favourite flower was also the camellia.

Hanly thinks that Wittgenstein's remarks warrant the inference that 'Wittgenstein felt compelled to come to the rescue of beautiful dreams and the innocence of hysterical women.' Although it is true that Wittgenstein makes remarks which depend on Freud's interpretation not being 'beautiful', as the dream itself was, this is not the main point that Wittgenstein is making. This point would hold even if it had been the dreamer who had thought her dream bawdy, and the interpretation which had been beautiful. If, for example, it had been an anagogic interpretation of the kind favoured by the disciples of Jung, in which blatantly sexual material was given a higher spiritual significance, it would still have been exposed to Wittgenstein's objections and been no less of a cheat.

The character of Wittgenstein's objection is clearer in a note of 1948. In it Wittgenstein compares dream interpretation to the unfolding of a big sheet on which a picture has been drawn and then folded in such a manner as to produce the generally puzzling and surreal juxtapositions of the manifest dream. He then asks us to imagine that, presented with the original unfolded picture, the dreamer might exclaim, '"Yes, that's the solution, that's what I dreamed, minus the gaps and distortions." This would then be the solution precisely by virtue of his acknowledging it as such.'[4] In

---

[3] Ludwig Wittgenstein, *Lectures and Conversations on Aesthetics, Psychology and Religious Belief*, ed. Cyril Barrett (Oxford, 1970), p. 23.

[4] Ludwig Wittgenstein, *Culture and Value*, ed. G. H. von Wright, tr. Peter Winch (Oxford, 1980), p. 68.

terms of this analogy, the angel holding the lily stalk which the flowery dreamer was put in mind of and which expressed her sense of exaltation at coming through life unsullied, corresponds to the unfolded sheet, the latent dream thoughts, 'precisely by virtue of her acknowledging it as such'.

Wittgenstein's remarks on dream interpretation continue:

> What is intriguing about a dream is not its *causal* connection with events in my life, etc., but rather the impression it gives of being a fragment of a story – a very *vivid* fragment to be sure – the rest of which remains obscure . . . if someone now shows me that this story is not the right one; that in reality it was based on quite a different story, so that I want to exclaim disappointedly 'Oh, *that's* how it was?', it really is as though I have been deprived of something. The original story certainly disintegrates now, as the paper is unfolded; . . . all the same the dream story has a charm of its own.
>
> . . . The dream affects us as does an idea pregnant with possible developments.[5]

These remarks make it clear that what Wittgenstein is objecting to is the discontinuity or discrepancy between the dreamer's conception of her dream and Freud's account of it – irrespective of the direction of the discrepancy. The objection this invites is: What justification can Wittgenstein give for accusing Freud of cheating the dreamer because he advances causal accounts of the generation of the dream images rather than amplifying their reverberations in a direction the dreamer can recognise as implicit in the impression it made on her? There are two possible replies to this, and it is difficult to be sure that Wittgenstein confines himself to only one of these. One is that Freud had committed himself to a conception of dream interpretation which eschews causal investigation; the other, that it is in any case an a-hypothetical, a-causal account of its meaning that a dream calls for. (This same ambiguity crops up not only in Wittgenstein's discussion of Freud's other explananda but in his discussion of Frazer as well.) Was Freud's fault merely to arouse expectations regarding his dream interpretations which he did not always fulfil, or was it rather his failure to fulfil them whether he aroused them or not?

At least it is clear what it is to have grounds for the first of these. Freud undertakes to provide 'further descriptions' of the dream and provides hypotheses instead. If this is the charge, it seems to

---

[5] Wittgenstein, *Culture and Value*, pp. 68–9.

be ill-founded, at least in this instance, for Freud shows no obvious signs of thinking of his remarks about the menstrual significance of the camellias and their relation to Alexander Dumas's *fils'* courtesan as other than hypotheses. But Wittgenstein may have had another reason for thinking Freud guilty of breeding confusion as to the status of his interpretation – a generalised expectation, bred perhaps by Freud's pronouncements as to the patient's relation to the interpretations he is proffered, that they are assimilable to back-of-minded-ness ('the patient knows the meaning of his dream, only he does not know that he knows and thinks that he does not'). A good example of the extent of this generalised expectation (and of Freud's repudiation of it) is provided by a psychiatrist informed enough about Freud's theories to travel to Vienna for some analytic sessions with him. Joseph Wortis reports that he had expressed some doubts about a dream interpretation proffered by Freud saying that he 'didn't feel that way', to which Freud replied 'impatiently': '"The trouble is that you probably don't even believe in the unconscious: you still expect to find an agreement between a dream interpretation and your conscious thoughts." . . . I replied that . . . I expected that a psychoanalytic revelation of the unconscious would be spontaneously enlightening to the patient. How was one to know if the revelation was correct or not? This last revelation was not illuminating. How could the analyst be sure that his interpretation was correct? "From the reaction of the patient", said Freud.'[6]

The 'abominable mess' which Wittgenstein charges Freud with having created is due, at least in part, to Freud's failure to realise that the statements about his dream which a patient endorses are not the same as the statements which Freud, for reasons connected with his view of the patient's past or current situation, infers or intuits. The 'ideas with which the dream was pregnant' and 'its causal connection with events in [the dreamer's] life' might coincide, thus concealing the epistemic gulf between them. Freud's anchovy-induced dreams were manifestly about thirst as well as induced by thirst, and this might mislead us into failing to notice that they would have been about thirst irrespective of how they were induced, and that they might have been induced by the eating of anchovies irrespective of what they were about.

[6] Joseph Wortis, *Fragments of an Analysis with Freud* (New York, 1963), pp. 102–3.

Often it is not Freud but our language which is equivocal. The same questions may properly preface either investigation or reflection. 'Wherefore could I not say amen?'; 'Is it perfume from a dress / Which makes me so digress?' Are these requests for hypotheses or for further descriptions? 'Had he not resembled my father as he slept I had done it.' Does this require corroboration by experience? 'The water rat was restless and he did not know why.' Is it appropriate to ask the water rat to bethink himself why? 'Márgarét, are you grieving / over Goldengrove unleafing?' Margaret mistakenly thinks so: What kind of mistake is it?

In stating that Freud's assimilation of a dream to a rebus was an excellent simile, Wittgenstein was not felicitating Freud on his discovery of dream-meaning as Hanly thinks. That dreams have meaning in Wittgenstein's sense could no more be discovered than that clouds have faces. The meaning Wittgenstein is speaking of is aspect-meaning, not inference-meaning. And what Freud is being felicitated for is an excellent simile, a good way of representing a fact. Whether or not dreams are rebuses, they are rebus-like, and we can acknowledge this without following Freud's secrets-of-Santa's-workshop conception of dream production with dream workers busily displacing, condensing, and symbolising the latent dream material until it meets acceptable standards of seemliness. Wittgenstein's view converts Freud's principles of dream production from occult processes to mnemonic accounts of the phenomenal qualities of dream images. For Wittgenstein, condensation merely describes an aspect of the dream image – just as describing the entire dream as a rebus does.

Portmanteau words are familiar examples of manifest condensation – 'insinuendo', 'intertwangled', Lewis Carroll's 'frumious' (fuming/furious) and 'slithy'. Something similar is true of some phobias. The phobic object is related to its latent meaning somewhat as a caricature to its subject (the convention in productions of *Peter Pan* of having the same actor play both Captain Hook and Mr Darling is another example of manifest condensation). Freud's dream phrase, 'a positively Norekdal style', is an instance of either manifest or occult condensation, depending on the epistemic state of the dreamer with respect to it. If the dreamer recognises the Ibsenian allusion to Nora in *A Doll's House* and Ekdal in *The Wild Duck*, then it is an instance of what Wittgenstein had in mind when he talked of Freud's account as only 'sounding like science'.

On the other hand, if the dreamer is oblivious of the Ibsenian allusion and it is inferred and then justified evidentially, 'in accordance with the order of the day as laid down by the unconscious', then to speak of condensation does more than merely sound like science. And what we then have is an hypothesis and not just a further description.

The flowery dreamer cannot know the causal origins of the dream camellia in the way that she knows the angelic significance of the flowering branch. But many of Freud's admirers would agree with this, and even insist on seeing Freud's distinctiveness in his abandonment of the causal preoccupations of traditional medicine. One commentator reminds us that Freud's book is called the *Interpretation* of Dreams and not the *Causes* of Dreams; others have argued that Freud's innovation consists precisely in that he gave neurotic patients an authority with respect to their afflictions inconsistent with a causal orientation. One adherent of the humanistic view of Freud put this by stating that Freud was the first doctor to *listen* to his patients. This is misleading. According to Freud's most explicit rationale, he was practising a psychic version of ausculation: he tapped the patient's mind and the echo gave him a hint of what was to be found there. Whatever his practice may have intermittently been, it was in this sense only that Freud claimed to listen to his patients. (And it is the sense demanded by many of his explananda.) To have listened to them in any other sense, in the sense intended by his humanist or hermeneuticist encomiasts, would have been to capitulate to 'the standpoint of the ego' as he put it in his dispute with Adler. Those who construe Freud in this fashion are inadvertently transforming him into a disciple of Carl Rogers.

Wittgenstein's thesis about Freud could be put thus: Our relation to the explananda of psychoanalysis calls not for hypotheses but for 'further descriptions' which Freud sometimes, but without sufficient consistency and with an incoherent rationale, supplies. The trouble with this thesis is that the explananda of psychoanalysis are sufficiently miscellaneous to guarantee its falsity. Getting clear about why one laughed, or why a dream makes on us the peculiar impression that it does, or why certain images occurred in it; finding out why someone stutters, or with inexplicable clumsiness pushed a friend into a river (Wittgenstein's examples) are not all to be settled in the same way. This is even more obvious if we extend the range of examples to encompass Freud's characteristic explananda – contractures, paralyses, paraesthesias, pain. Even Freud's latent contents are epistemically heterogeneous; the latent content of his dream interpretations contains idioms and advance claims as to the associative chain which culminated in certain dream images. The same is true of his accounts of the generation of hysterical symptoms. On the other hand, his joke reductions are precluded by their form from being hypotheses; his joke energetics, and humour energetics in general, by the logical character of the questions they address. Since there are so many now attempting to detach Freud from his commitment to causal explanation without sufficient awareness of how radically revisionist they are being, it is worth providing reminders that the staple of Freud's discourse is on many occasions causal explanation – and it is not less causal or hypothetical because it is so often tendentious and ill-supported.

This is Freud's explanation of hysterical migraine headaches in virgins: unconscious fantasies of being deflowered manifest themselves (through the mechanism of displacement upwards and the symbolic equation head = genitals) as migraines. This is representative and can be summed in the formula, unconscious ideation causes symptoms. Thus, symptom interpretations, unlike joke reductions, are not precluded from hypothetical status by their form. The thought of being deflowered doesn't enter Freud's explanations of hysterical migraines as the thought of how Karl Kraus would behave on the receipt of some scandalous gossip enters Freud's account of the technique of the Kraus joke. Freud's joke reductions do not tell us what was going on unconsciously when someone laughed; his symptom interpretations do just this. They claim to identify the ideational substrate of which the symptom is a manifestation.

However unconfident we may be as to the precise epistemic status of those utterances which tell us what was at the back of our minds (Wittgenstein's further descriptions), one thing is clear: the ideational content of Freud's interpretations of hysterical symptoms can't be like the pearls which can be imagined to come into existence as they emerge from the hole in the box, since the mischief Freud has them working in producing the symptoms predates their emergence from the box. When Freud introduces the expression 'like a slap in the face' into his account of a patient's trigeminal neuralgia, he intends it as a hypothesis; and it must be such if it is to account for the trigeminal neuralgia, for the patient could deny its felicity as a 'further description' of her pain and the words nevertheless have generated the pain. On the other hand, we can imagine that her attacks came on whenever she was upset and would have come on even if she had not felt 'as if she had been slapped in the face'. So it is wrong to say that Freud wasn't really proffering hypotheses to his patients, but offering further descriptions. But it is equally wrong to say that whenever he speculates as to a patient's thoughts and feelings, these speculations are such as to demand what Hanly calls 'objective methods of enquiry'.

Freud himself invokes his aesthetic explanations to elucidate the character of his psychopathological ones in the case history of the Rat Man, where he assimilates ellipsis as it occurs in obsessional thoughts with ellipsis in jokes:

An example from another one of my works, *Der Witz* . . . will recall to the reader the manner in which this elliptical technique is employed in making jokes: 'There is a witty and pugnacious journalist in Vienna, whose biting invective has repeatedly led to his being physically maltreated by the subjects of his attacks. On one occasion, when a fresh misdeed on the part of one of his habitual opponents was being discussed, somebody exclaimed: "If X hears of this, he'll get his ears boxed again." . . . The apparent absurdity of this remark disappears if between the two clauses we insert the words: "he'll write such a scathing article upon the man, that, etc."' – This elliptical joke, we may note, is similar in its content, as well as in its form, to the first example quoted in the text.

This is the first example quoted in the text:

The patient had a charming little niece of whom he was very fond. One day this idea came into his head: '*If you indulge in intercourse, something will happen to Ella*' (i.e. she will die). When the omissions have been made good, we have: 'Every time you copulate, even with a stranger, you will not be able to avoid the reflection that in your married life sexual intercourse can never bring you a child (on account of the lady's sterility). This will grieve you so much that you will become envious of your sister on account of little Ella, and you will grudge her the child. These envious impulses will inevitably lead to the child's death.'[7]

How does the thought 'When I am reminded of the infertility of my fiancée my envy of my sister's child will cause me to wish her dead' stand to the obsessive thought it is supposed to explain, 'If I

[7] Sigmund Freud, *Collected Papers*, tr. Alix and James Strachey (London, 1925), III, 362.

have intercourse with my fiancée my niece will die'? Was it at the back of the Rat Man's mind? Was it among the crush of his thoughts? Did Freud lead him from the obsessive thought to its latent meaning as he leads us from one end of the Kraus joke to the other? But even if Freud had not himself encouraged, in his footnote, the assimilation of his reconstructions of obsessional ellipses to statements such as joke reductions, of whose truth assent is constitutive, the character of these reconstructions themselves would leave us in doubt as to their status.

It is not unusual for Freud's interpretations to leave us unable to say what he himself takes their status to be. Though theoretically committed to a strict preanalytic inaccessibility, he sometimes phenomenalises the patient's latent thought processes. For example, even of the elaborate associative chain which underlay the formation of the Rat Man's 'great obsessive fear' Freud says 'vague intimations of these probably entered consciousness'. Now 'vague intimations' are precisely the kind of thing whose more precise delineation Wittgenstein thinks it a mistake to assimilate to empirical enquiry.

Wittgenstein says that we find in Freud 'a certain sort of connection' – for example, the relation of the fetal position to sleep – which appears causal but really 'does what aesthetics does': it puts two things side by side.[8] A more familiar example is Freud's assimilation of postcoital lassitude and infantile oral satiation. In a notorious passage in the *Three Essays* Freud wrote: 'No one who has seen a baby sinking back satiated from the breast and falling asleep with flushed cheeks and a blissful smile can escape the reflection that this picture persists as a prototype of sexual satisfaction in later life.'[9] What are Wittgenstein's grounds for holding that when Freud explicitly advances a genetic thesis he is surreptitiously advancing an aesthetic one? Presumably that in practice it is in the endorsement of the adult, not the behaviour of the infant, that support for the thesis consists. Freud says of the development of Dora's fellatio fantasies, 'The udder of a cow has aptly played the part of an image intermediate between a nipple and a penis.' Though there are things about the relation between nipple, thumb, udder, and penis which Dora is in a position to confirm,

[8] *Wittgenstein's Lectures 1932–35*, ed. Alice Ambrose (Oxford, 1979), p. 39.
[9] Sigmund Freud, *Three Essays on the Theory of Sexuality*, ed. and tr. James Strachey (New York, 1965), pp. 76–7.

what her current feelings about penises would have been had she not encountered udders is not among them. The udder image illustrates the two modes in which infantile experience may enter into the elucidation of adult attitudes: as a temporally remote causal antecedent and as a formal term, a simile.

There is nothing intrinsic to Freud's remark to preclude its being an empirical hypothesis (unless its unsettleability is considered intrinsic to it). What counts against its empirical status is largely the manner in which its truth is considered to have been established. If Dora finds udders nipplelike and penises udderlike or assimilates her felicity in fantasies of fellatio to the felicity she imagines, or remembers, or imagines she remembers, experiencing at her mother's breast, enquiry rests. When we recall that Freud assimilated the child's fear of being separated from his penis to his earlier separations – from his mother in being born, from her nipples in being weaned, and from his own faeces in being toilet trained – we understand better what moved Wittgenstein to say that Freud did what aesthetics does. When Freud refers to certain neurotic types as 'eternal sucklings' he may mean to call attention to their development histories, but the role such remarks play is often indistinguishable from a vernacular simile like 'he sees the world as a gigantic nipple that has run dry and blames himself for biting too hard'.

Wittgenstein's remarks are best understood as calling attention not to the formal features of Freud's genetic and developmental claims but to their spirit, to their affinities with utterances which are blatantly figurative. A noncontentious example of an allusion to infancy that blatantly, rather than surreptitiously, does what aesthetics does when putting things side by side is that of an anti-smoking poster which juxtaposes an image of a man smoking with that of an infant sucking a comforter. The antismoking poster says graphically what could be put verbally: there is in the attitude of the smoker toward his puffables something of the attitude of an infant toward the breast. Consider Gaston Bachelard's observation on claustrophilic experiences: 'Our consciousness of well-being calls for comparison with animals in their shelters.'[10] The states of affairs which figure in genetic and developmental claims are often

---

[10] Gaston Bachelard, *The Poetics of Space* (Boston, 1971), p. 91.

what our experience 'calls for' or can be made to seem to. Freud tells us that 'sucking at the mother's breast is . . . the unmatched prototype of every later satisfaction'. What comes more naturally to us, men and women both, as an image of lost felicity than the paps that gave us suck? William James cites as an example of the ubiquity of breast imagery an advertisement for a New England primer: 'Spiritual milk for Christian babes drawn from the breasts of both testaments.' For men, female breasts also figure among erotic suckables.

If men did not experience a peculiar and distinctive turbulence at the sight of women's breasts, there would then have been nothing to place side by side with the image of the infant sucking at his mother's – there would have been no formal connection for the developmental hypothesis to disguise. The erotic component in the infant's relation to its mother's breast would be just as eligible an object of scientific investigation, but speculations concerning it would have lost 'depth' (though they would probably gain in disinterestedness).

In his remarks on Frazer, Wittgenstein speaks of 'hypothetical links whose function is only to draw attention to a similarity' and illustrates with an example of the gradual transformation of a circle into an ellipse, 'not however to assert that a given ellipse in fact historically originated from a circle but only to sharpen our eyes to a formal connection' (241). Wittgenstein isn't explicit as to how these remarks apply to Frazer but it is easy to see how they might. For the historian of human culture, the Frazerian antitheses – prayer and spell, priest and sorcerer, religion and science, science and magic, godhead and kingship – are worth pondering whether he accepts Frazer's account of the order in which they succeeded each other or not. (Frazer himself sometimes speaks not of the remote prehistorical past of mankind but of 'its hidden but permanent depths' expressed in his volcano image.)

That contrasts can be instructive independently of any developmental scheme of which they form a part is illustrated when we are told by a Hegel scholar to ignore the postulated historical relation between stoic and slave and consider instead their 'dialectical interrelatedness'. The recurrent attempts to elucidate what is distinctive in modernity which we find, say, in Lukács's contrast between integrated and problematic civilisations do not require an authentic knowledge of the past but a grasp of the relation in which we stand to our ideas of that past.[11] What matters is what we feel to be characteristic, and at the same time inferior and degrading, in our current existence – and not whether the ideal, through contrast with which we attempt to define it, was realised at this or that place or stage in history. Whatever the conscious intentions of those who contrasted industrial, capitalist modernity with the classical or medieval worlds, the upshot has been that they taught us how to curse. The significance of the notion 'spontaneous totality of being' is not that the Homeric Greeks had or may have had it but that we feel that we don't. What we sometimes want is an elucidation and explication of this sense of loss, or at any rate lack, of 'spontaneous totality of being' rather than an enquiry into whether the Homeric Greeks possessed it, or if not what it was they had instead (whether by 'the Homeric Greeks' we mean those the epic stories were told by, to, or about). Paul de Man refers to Lukács's Homeric Greece as an 'idealised fiction, . . . a devise to state a theory of consciousness.'[12] When Lukács tells us 'we can't imagine one of Homer's heroes saying like Marcus Aurelius "they were like puppies fighting for a bone",' does it matter whether Homer's heroes could have said what Marcus Aurelius said if we can't imagine that they could?

Norman Rudich and Manfred Stassen charge Wittgenstein not merely with contempt for empirical enquiry but with advocating the resolution of apparently empirical questions a priori. They take him to deny that 'a given set of events or practices can be explained by uncovering their origins and causes in the earlier experiences of a society'.[13] Wittgenstein does not deny that practices can be explained by 'uncovering their origins and causes in the earlier experiences of a society'. His thesis is that practices can pose questions in addition to those of their historical origins – and it is these which this origin cannot resolve.

Lévi-Strauss described primitive ritual as 'a distorted reflection of a familiar image'.[14] And where this is so, we can properly ask of a ritual, like Nemi or Beltane, 'Of what familiar image is this a distorted reflection?' And this would not justify the imputation that

[11] Georg Lukács, *Theory of the Novel*, tr. Anna Bostock (London, 1978), pp. 29–39.
[12] Paul de Man, *Blindness and Insight* (New York, 1971), pp. 54–5.
[13] Norman Rudich and Manfred Stassen, 'Wittgenstein's implied anthropology', *History and Theory*, 10 (1971), 88.
[14] Claude Lévi-Strauss, *The Savage Mind* (Chicago, 1966), pp. 238–9.

historical questions were being resolved by an a priori method. The 'something' about the meaning of the Fire-festivals of which Wittgenstein says 'we are still sure' (when we are unsure whether Frazer's derivation of them from the prehistoric practice of burning human beings in the fires is correct) is not their origin or rationale. But Wittgenstein's objection manifests the same ambiguity as his other criticisms of empirical discourse. At a certain point it becomes unclear whether it is Frazer's answers or his questions that Wittgenstein objects to.

The impression forces itself upon us that Freud, Frazer, and others are not (or not just) being taken to task for addressing questions for which an empirical method is inadequate, but for failing to address questions for which an empirical method is inadequate. Even though determining whether the Beltane Festival originated in a rite in which a real man was burned explains neither why the ritual is still being performed nor why an account of it impresses us in the distinctive way that it does, why should it nevertheless not be an appropriate response to the natural question whether men were ever actually burned at Beltane (or the sites of other European Fire-festivals) and why? Why is the only appropriate question Wittgenstein's, 'What makes the idea of human sacrifice sinister and terrible anyway?' Isn't there something gratuitous about pitting our desire for a clearer view of the feelings and thoughts provoked in us by accounts of human sacrifice against the desire to know, for example, what of explanatory relevance happened to Aztec culture between the time they were ritually killing thirty thousand human beings at a go and an earlier period at which they were not?

I do not think that Wittgenstein is saying that the topic of human sacrifice calls only for a synoptic view of the reflections it provokes and not for speculation and investigation as to its origins, but that Frazer shows a division of purpose with respect to the topic. Rush Rhees thinks that Wittgenstein found Frazer's tone 'incongruous with the *explanation* Frazer offers: that magical beliefs are crude and mistaken forms of scientific theory.' He would not have written in the same tone if he had been giving the history of the phlogiston theory. His explanation does not help us to understand what he himself found remarkable in these practices.'[15] I

---

[15] Rush Rhees, 'Introductory note' to 'Remarks on Frazer's *Golden Bough*', *The Human World*, No. 3 (1971), 19.

have called the phenomenon Rhees comments on 'expressive incongruity'.[16] It is not necessary that the discourse itself should show tokens of expressive incongruity. It is sufficient that those who frequent it, when once the project of 'understanding the thoughts and feelings that give the picture depth' is broached, might feel that it was this 'which they really wanted'. This can happen with philosophy itself, of which Moore reports Wittgenstein said 'that though what he was doing was different from what, for example, Plato or Berkeley had done, yet people might feel that it took the place of what they had done – might be inclined to say "this is what I really wanted".'[17] But expressive incongruity is not a decisive consideration, since it could be resolved by dropping attempts at self-clarification (or any other nonempirical, nondiscursive aims) in favour of a more single-minded attempt at historical or scientific explanation. The main use of expressive incongruity is as a means of bringing us to recognise that we had misunderstood ourselves. In the last analysis, the test of whether a problem which calls for reflection on those terms, internal relations to which constitute it as the problem it is has been erroneously treated as one demanding more information, is that we would say when presented with the suggestion that this is so, or with the synoptic view itself: 'That is what I really wanted.'

II

In the remarks that follow I examine some areas where it does seem plausible to maintain that questions naturally arise which empirical enquiry is unfitted to resolve and where investigation has been permitted to usurp the prerogatives of reflection.

Wittgenstein's objections to Freudian dream interpretation have been held to assimilate him to 'a misguided person . . . wishing to protect a friend from the anxiety of having to face up to diagnosis of cancer'.[18] How persuasive we find this thesis does not depend on how compelling we find the analogy between a diagnosis of cancer based on a biopsy report and the diagnostic use of Freudian dream interpretation. Even if this were the tissue

---

[16] 'When do Empirical methods by-pass "The problems which trouble us"?' pp. 107–26.
[17] G. E. Moore, 'Wittgenstein's lectures in 1930–33', in *Philosophical Papers* (New York, 1966), p. 316.　　[18] Hanly, p. 86.

of whimsicalities a few have suspected it of being, this would not show Hanly's rebuke to have been undeserved, for Wittgenstein is rejecting the pertinence of any causal explanation and not just the plausibility of Freudian dream interpretation. If a defence is to be made, it must be in terms of two distinct demands which we make of psychological explanation – one of which a causally oriented psychoanalysis, due to its intrinsic character, cannot meet. The order we want introduced into the chaotic medley of our affective and reminiscential life is an order internal to it, however epi-phenomenal to physical or psychoanalytic processes it may ulti-mately prove. In this area utterance is as determinative of truth as the act of pointing is to the place of pain.

Behind my characteristic actions and efforts I sense an obscure teleology, a pressure to transform situations in a particular direc-tion. Whatever epistemic characterisation we may ultimately give of the attempt to arrive at a more determinate conception of this, it is clear that it is discontinuous with the procedures of psycho-analysis proper. A distinctly Freudian explanation invites us to con-sider the nonpsychoanalytically assisted recovery of the history of our failures and humiliations, and of the stratagems we evolved to avoid their recurrence or mitigate their consequences, a mere surface of which the depths pertain to an only technically recover-able order of which what we took for realities were the shadows – 'the standpoint of the ego', as Freud dismissively called it in his polemic against Adler.

Rush Rhees raises the question of the kind of discourse called for when someone is 'bewildered by the sort of person he finds himself to be'.[19] Though this might appear to be a matter of straightforward ignorance of empirical matters of fact, this is not Rhees's view, and it is easy to see why. The situation of someone 'bewildered by the sort of person he finds himself to be' isn't exhausted by ignorance as to his causal history. There is the matter of the internal, arrivable-at-by-reflection relation between the person he expected or hoped to be and the disappointing, bewil-dering person he is. Bewilderment at the sort of person we turned out to be involves an internal relation between ourselves and our hopes and anticipations, as well as the empirical problem as to why these were disappointed.

[19] Rush Rhees, 'The tree of Nebuchadnezzar', *The Human World*, no. 4 (1971), 25.

Similarly with the memory of a remote, much-brooded-on episode. This may have an enigmatic expressiveness demanding articulation as well as causal repercussions to be unravelled. Once again our interest may bifurcate: the phenomenon, whether memory or fantasy, is both an item in a causal network (and thus conceptually eligible for causal investigation into its origins and mutations) and also the vehicle of a meaning not supporting it as a noumenal substrate, but contained in it – as the ideas with which it was pregnant were contained in Wittgenstein's waking impression of his dream, or as the 'unrecovered associates' in William James's tip of the tongue case were contained in the 'tingling and trembling' which anticipated them.

Wittgenstein thinks that Goethe's attack on Newton's optics was due to a confusion on Goethe's part between a physical and a phenomenological study of colours. Something analogous to this epistemic division is at work in Wittgenstein's objections to Freud, though in this instance it is as if Newton himself had thought his optics a contribution to an a priori phenomenology. The problem in this area of discourse is recognising the distinctiveness of causal-empirical inquiry and its impertinence to many of the questions we raise and want answered, without impugning its intrinsic legitimacy and value. The question 'Why am I unhappy?' has two epistemically distinct senses: one consists in the verbal elaboration of the experience of misery and thus its clarification, the other in its causal explanation. The distinction between these isn't always as clear-cut as in the case of anomalous serotonin levels.

In his introduction to an anthology of holocaust literature, Albert H. Friedlander writes: 'Once we have mastered the facts and figures we may be able to penetrate deeper into the darkness.'[20] This is a familiar sentiment and who has not indulged it? But just how is the mastery of the facts and figures meant to facilitate deeper penetration into the darkness? That the holocaust raises many empirical problems, some of which are capable of resolution, is not in question. But will their resolution untrouble us? Will they stop the flow of thoughts? When those empirical issues raised by the holocaust have been resolved, will not the impressiveness retreat to the categories? Might not what Wittgenstein says of

[20] Albert H. Friedlander, 'Introduction', in *Out of the Whirlwind*, ed. Albert H. Friendlander (New York, 1976), p. 18.

Frazer's accounts of human sacrifice – that what we see in such
accounts is something they acquire 'even from evidence not
directly connected with them' (251) – hold for the holocaust as
well? This would explain why we feel that even after mastering the
facts and figures, the real problem would be untouched; and that
rather than helping 'penetrate the darkness', we may have been
emulating the clown Grock who searched for a key not where he
had reason to think he had lost it but where the light was clearest.

If we really don't want 'facts and figures' why do we nevertheless
ask for and frequent them? Perhaps because in spite of the horrors
they record, we turn with relief from unmediated suffering and
cruelty to the orderly world of science and scholarship. There is a
line of Donne's which, appropriately misconstrued, sheds light on
the character of our interest in these facts and figures: 'Grief
brought to numbers / cannot be so fierce.'

Chaim Kaplan recorded the following remarks after seeing a
man whipped to death in the Warsaw ghetto: 'It is hard to com-
prehend this sadistic phenomenon . . . How is it possible to attack
a stranger to me, a man of flesh and blood like myself, to wound
him and trample upon him . . . without any reason? How is it possible?'[21] Was Kaplan asking an empirical question? Kaplan was
murdered and so was given no opportunity to enlarge on what he
had in mind, but I think it likely that he was no more posing an
empirical question than was Wittgenstein's pseudocosmogenist
who – though asking as he looked about him 'where did all this
come from?' – was not 'craving' a causal explanation but 'expressing an attitude towards all explanation'.[22]

Do we have a clear enough conception of Kaplan's question to
know where we are to begin to look for an answer, or how we would
recognise one if we found it? But even if we raised no difficulties
as to the intrinsic coherence and feasibility of Kaplan's question
construed as a demand for empirical explanation, there is still
doubt as to the ability of such explanation to assuage the need that
finds expression in the demand for it. Though it is gratifying to
gain a better understanding of why the days grow shorter and the
temperature drops, it doesn't spare us the task of making a place
for winter in our lives. The contemplation of the holocaust, like

[21] George Steiner, 'Post-script to a tragedy', *Encounter*, February 1967, p. 33.
[22] Wittgenstein, *Culture and Value*, p. 85.

the contemplation of enormity in general, is not always a challenge to our explanatory capacity, and often is undertaken in the spirit in which the devout contemplate the wounds of Jesus or the worldly the motto on sun dials.

There is a danger that in our exasperation and disappointment at the failure of empirical discourse to meet one particularly urgent set of demands, we may deny its relevance to any. The correct form of the issue is not whether the holocaust demands historical, social psychological, psychopathological enquiry but whether there is in our response to it, our troubled response, something which empirical method passes by. But even this may not be a sufficient concession to an anti-epistemic orientation. Perhaps what we need with respect to the holocaust are neither the facts and figures, nor a more explicit awareness of the feelings and thoughts which give the picture depth, but adequate utterance – a mode of formulating our discoveries which, while acquitting us of the feeling of living evasively, will nevertheless not make life less bearable.

Early in the remarks on Frazer, Wittgenstein says: 'Every explanation is an hypothesis. But for someone worried by love an explanatory hypothesis will not help much – it will not bring peace' (236). But will a grasp of 'the thoughts and feelings which give the picture depth' necessarily bring peace? Why should I be any less troubled when I learn what makes human sacrifice terrible than when I have learned why and how it originated? How is the understanding which consists in seeing the connections, and which comes through arranging what we already know, related to peace and consolation? We can't call whatever brings the state of being untroubled to an end, whatever untroubles us, understanding. The love-troubled one will, as we all know, one day cease to be troubled, at least until the next time, but what will he have understood? To put it in the vocabulary of early Freud, peace may come not through understanding but through 'associative absorption' or the 'discharge of arrears of abreaction'. The rationale of contemplation in those cases in which we are troubled by the 'sinister and terrible' might be more akin to Flaubert's: 'J'ai joué avec la démence et le fantastique comme Mithridate avec les poisons ...j'ai vaincu le mal à force de l'étreindre corps à corps'[23] (I played

---

[23] Gustave Flaubert, *Correspondence, Quatrième Série (1854–1861)*, Nouvelle Édition Augmentée (Paris, 1927), IV, 181.

with madness and the fantastic like Mithridates with his poisons
. . . I overcame evil by hugging it to my breast.) (Lawrence gives
the same counsel in his introduction to the Magnus memoir
though he gratuitously gives it an ultimately epistemic justification.)[24]

Mere self-clarification may be as helpless to console us as empirical knowledge. From the fact that we may come to feel that further
information about a phenomenon is not what we really want, it
does not follow that what we do want is knowledge but of another
nonempirical kind. Coming to realise that what we really want with
respect to a phenomenon is not further information about it, but
just further contemplative transactions with it, is a discovery. But
though the discovery of what it is we really want is knowledge, that
which we discover we really want need not be. We flounder about
in search of an epistemic rationale when our preoccupation may
have quite other sources. The situation is one in which we anticipate from some future state of epistemic consummation not
merely the resolution of our perplexity as to what it is that troubles
us, but peace – whereas what keeps the thoughts flowing is not
ignorance but ambivalence, and what will put them at peace is not
a discovery but a decision. The guilt of the living toward the dead,
for example, needs to be exorcised and not merely acknowledged.
'You are allowed to forget.'

In his book *Social Being*, Rom Harré tells us that 'the basic
problem for a person in society is to be recogized as of worth', that
human beings are persistently 'seeking out occasions for acquiring
respect while risking pity or disdain', that they must live with the
perpetual possibility of 'loss of dignity, of humiliation, and expressive failure', and that their lives are punctuated by 'success and
failure in coping with occasions of hazard'. 'An occasion of
hazard', he says, 'is a social event in which persons can gain respect
by risking contempt'.[25]

What constitutes a natural resting place for the thoughts these
topics incite us to? Must it consist of empircal investigation or scientific theorising? What Wittgenstein says of human sacrifice can
equally be said of the topics broached by Harré: 'What gives the
picture depth is its connection with our own feelings and

[24] D. H. Lawrence, 'Introduction', in *Memoirs of the Foreign Legion*, by M[aurice] M[agnus] (London, 1924), pp. 89–90.
[25] Rom Harré, *Social Being* (Oxford, 1979), pp. 24, 312; hereafter cited in text.

thoughts.' And, as with human sacrifice, a need is sometimes felt to gain a clearer view of those feelings and thoughts in virtue of which the picture has 'depth'.

This is certainly the case with the 'moral careers', 'exemplary biographies', and ideal 'life trajectories' of which Harré also proposes a scientific study. For Harré, an 'exemplary biography' in accordance with which 'lives are lived' generates 'a moral career'. A moral career is the 'history of an individual person with respect to the attitudes and beliefs that others have' concerning his quality and worth (33–4, 313). But the 'moral careers' and ideal 'life trajectories', an account of which we crave, are those whose deviations from or approximations to our own lives determine our sense of failure or fulfilment. It is these which an expositor is to array if he hopes to assuage our craving for a synoptic view of the hazards of social life; and it is not to social science or to any kind of empirical discipline that he will owe his knowledge of them, but to a shared social existence. Such discourse would not address us on subjects like the aspirations to shamanism among the Bongo-bongo, nor even on the actuarial probabilities of particular turning points in our own moral careers – such as the chance of being appointed head of an Oxbridge college, or invited to give the William James lectures, or being prematurely retired, or of finding our photograph in the News of the World on the page which the week before carried the story of a clergyman who got choirboys to stand on his toes – since actuarial probabilities are not matters on which we can say, as with our reveries, 'Yes, that's what happens.' But all these 'hazards' might be appropriately invoked in an attempt to reconstruct the hopes and fears which determine our sense of malaise or well-being, which box us in, or shore us up, with respect to which we are preeminently qualified to pronounce authoritatively, 'Yes, that's what happens.'

I am saying that there are questions about social life which don't require a Harré-type empirical enquiry to resolve. But is a stronger thesis sustainable? Can we say that Harré, and those who take an interest in his program, stand to it as Wittgenstein thought Frazer and his readers stood to the historical speculation and exotic documentation of *The Golden Bough* – that is, that they are producing irrelevances?

Though it may be difficult to raise certain topics without arousing a desire for a perspicuous view of them, the fact that our

relation to social life may sometimes spontaneously take the form
of a desire for a clear view of what is involved in being a potential
object of derision or deference does not show that on every occasion on which these topics are raised this must be the manner of
treatment. What support, then, can we give for the suspicion that
the impulse which motivates much research on these topics, and
on which it is parasitic for the energy with which it is prosecuted,
supported, frequented, is not such as to be gratified by the successful consummtion of such research?

There are some suggestions in Harré of the expressive incongruity which Wittgenstein thought he saw in Frazer. In the first
chapter of *Social Being* he writes: 'The hopes of most young people
come to nothing. The disappointments of the middle years of life
are followed . . . by the ugliness, pain and despair of old age . . .
The pervasive tone of life for most people is boredom, but a
boredom made more acute by resentment' (3). It certainly seems
so often enough. The question is: What does this situation call for?
Does a program for uncovering the 'cognitive resources' that
enable me to discern that I am losing, and at how fast a rate, really
rise to the occasion?

At one point Harré speaks of the 'confusion and uncertainty' he
felt when trying to reconcile his 'experience of social life with the
representations of the processes by which that life is created that
are to be found in the writings of the social scientists'. Only in the
works of Erving Goffman and Thorstein Veblen did he 'seem to
meet [him]self and the social worlds [he] knew' (2–3). The disappointment of which Harré speaks is familiar to many of us, but
the failure of his own program to assuage it entirely prompts a suspicion that his diagnosis of its sources is not sufficiently radical.
Was it by providing him with scientific knowledge of the occult
'processes' by which social life is created that Goffman was able to
produce in him the impression that he was 'meeting himself and
the social world he knew'?

Harré refers us to Goffman's *Stigma*,[26] where the synoptic nature
of the enterprise, the extent to which it is a question of 'putting
into order what we already know', is particularly blatant. What
Goffman gives is not an empirical explanation of stigma but a clarification of what is involved in our possession of the concept of

---

[26] Erving Goffman, *Stigma* (New Jersey, 1963).

stigma (though this may be an over-intellectualised way of indicating what it is that we possess). What he provides are synoptic views of the options open to the stigmatised and the stigmatisable. Just who would I need to consult to determine that if I have an invisible or undeclared stigma, I am confronted by a choice between declaring it and learning to handle the ensuing tension, or concealing it and condemning myself to vigilance and caution? Doesn't Goffman's terminological redescription of our dilemma – 'Controlling information or managing tension', 'passing or covering', hiding 'stigma symbols', or brandishing 'disidentifiers' – stand to us not as hypotheses but as further descriptions? Doesn't he transform our ruminations into a different form 'which is recognised by us as an expression of the chain of ideas which lead us from one end' of the rumination to another?

Why do we pursue enquiries, or frequent discourse, irrelevant to our real needs? Harré inadvertently provides a clue: 'The very fact or order, when recognised by human beings, is, *in itself,* the source of a message that all is well. Orderliness of the physical environment broadcasts a kind of continuous social muzak whose message is reassurance.' On the very same page Harré gives us this: 'If we define the *Umwelt* of a human being as he or she is a person of a certain social category, we could express this in a formula: *Umwelt* = Physical Environment × Social Meanings. This formula could be taken literally as a Boolean product. Thus if someone were to be found to be using two interpretative schemata, A and B, then $U = P \times (A \lor B)$ leads to $U = (P \times A) \lor (P \times B)$; in short that person lives in two *Umwelten*' (194). Is this much more than scientistic muzak? – Harré unconsciously exploiting the ataractic potency of algebraic modes of presentation to relieve the anxiety and pain of social being? Though, as Wittgenstein says, an explanatory hypothesis may not bring peace, the decorum and psychic distancing which its presentation involves may. There is something spirit-calming in the notations which scientific expositions employ, something we respond to in Spinoza's 'I will speak of the appetites and actions of men as if it were a matter of lines, of planes and of solids.'

I am not denying the possibility or desirability of an empirical study of 'the ritual markings of contempt and respect'; I am only maintaining that there are relfective transactions with the hazards of social life that do not find their natural consummation in such activities but in Wittgenstein's synoptic views. The kind of closure or consummation that these thoughts call for is not to be achieved by acquainting us with novel discoveries as to 'the processes by which social life is created', but by something more like an updating of 'toil, envy, want, the patron and the jail'.

Of course, the demand for synoptic views or 'further descriptions' must not be made merely mechanically. Not everything 'impresses us'; not everything 'seems to be saying something'; not all facts demand to be 'perspicuously arranged'. What distinguishes those which do? What gives saliency and impressiveness to the facts subsumed under what Harré calls 'the concept pair respect and contempt' is the ambivalence of our involvement in social life. We hanker after emancipation from the demands and judgements of others but at the same time have a realistic sense of the regressive, in any case inconstant, character of such a wish. There is an ambiguity, a lack of straightforwardness in our attitude to the pursuit of esteem which is only partly attributable to our ambivalence as to the rationality of this pursuit in view of the risks it entails. It is as if we were equally ambivalent as to the absolute value of that for which the risk is undertaken, and so we had constantly to be reminded of the vicissitudes of concupiscence – the sweetness of its gratification as well as the bitterness of its disappointment – for us to be relieved of our intermittent wonder and perplexity that we live as we do.

CONCLUSION

This is what I take myself to have been saying about those occasions on which Wittgenstein either objects or appears to object to empirical discourse. When Wittgenstein objects to empirical discourse, it is because he thinks either that it is repugnant to the question addressed or that it will fail to meet the needs of the enquirer. When he thinks it is repugnant to the question addressed, it is either because the question is not empirical (this is the case when we ask for the meaning of our dreams – in the sense which Wittgenstein did when he wanted a development of the ideas with which it was pregnant – and are given instead the causal relations into which the dream images enter), or because the decision that it has been correctly answered is not based on an empirical methodology (this is the case where Freud raises straightforward

causal questions about, for example, symptoms, but then confusedly gives the patient an obscure, never clearly explained, role in
determining their truth). Sometimes Wittgenstein objects not to
the incongruity of Freud's explanatory discourse but to Freud's
mischaracterisation of it as empirical (this is the case with Freud's
joke reductions and joke taxonomies which are in order but whose
descriptions as scientific or empirical are not). Then there are
occasions when Wittgenstein is not objecting to empirical discourse at all, but only pointing out that there is an alternative to it
– that we can want to get clearer as to how we feel about something
as well as to know its causes or history (his criticism of Frazer's dealings with human sacrifices provides an example of this). Finally,
there are occasions when Wittgenstein does seem to be objecting
to empirical enquiry itself, either because it is not what we really
want or because, however misguidedly we may want it, it is not what
we need.

Wittgenstein's apparent advocacy of the clarification of intentionality as that which will meet the demand confusedly expected
of advances in empirical explanation raises the question as to
whether this self-clarification will ultimately prove any more consoling, peace-giving, or untroubling than science. Might not the
facts warrant an even more nihilistic conclusion, one which
extends Wittgenstein's doubt as to the desirability of knowledge to
nonempirical discursiveness whose pursuit might equally constitute a 'trap'?[27] Those who think otherwise can console themselves
that this is not a live option. We might just possibly break ourselves
of the habit of looking for explanations; the impulse towards self-
clarification, on the other hand, seems more spontaneous and
reflexive – not a trap into which we could avoid falling, since, if a
tiny aphorism is permissible, we are that trap.

In the end it must be admitted that after we have made all the
necessary discriminations, and explained that often when it
appears that Wittgenstein is disparaging empirical discourse he is
pointing out its conceptual inappropriateness given the character
of the question addressed, or our own ambivalence with respect to
its pertinence, an intractable residue remains. Wittgenstein does
appear to hold empirical knowledge in low esteem and to feel that

[27] Wittgenstein remarked: 'there is nothing good or desirable about scientific knowledge
and . . . mankind, in seeking it, is falling into a trap. (*Culture and Value*, p. 56)

even in those cases where we do really want it we don't really need it. To judge properly of this one would have to be clearer than I am at the moment as to in what our good and evil truly consists. What can safely be said is this: Not everything that we want to know about those facts which trouble or impress us (or safer still, not everything we want with respect to such facts) can be satisfied by the successful prosecution of empirical enquiry into their history, causes, or conditions. And on occasion we will wish to address each other as to these facts in a discourse which does not involve such enquiry, and the only test of whose adequacy is that it may extract the response 'That's what I really wanted!'

CHAPTER SIX

Wittgenstein on making homeopathic magic clear

A member of a primitive culture is engaging in behaviour which involves mimicking or otherwise deliberately calling to mind a state of affairs which is of great moment to him – rainfall, spring, the hunting of prey, the destruction of an enemy. What is Wittgenstein's thesis with respect to these 'actions that bear a peculiar character and might be called ritualistic'?

Both commentators who are favourably disposed towards it and those who reject it concur in attributing to Wittgenstein the view that, as it is put by John Cook, 'Wittgenstein was . . . offering a theory to the effect that the primitive magician, in the performance of his rites, no more intends to help his crops flourish or to harm his enemy than we intend to bring about some effect by kissing the picture of a loved one' (Cook 1983: 5). Howard Mounce too, assigns an expressive, anti-instrumental view of magic to Wittgenstein: 'The practice of destroying an effigy of one's enemy need not have a purpose in the sense of bringing something about, it is merely the expression of a wish' (Mounce 1978: 70). A. J. Ayer interprets Wittgenstein as maintaining that 'the stabbing of the picture (of an enemy) is a mere venting of the agent's spleen, a symbolic act, not seriously expected to have any practical effect' (Ayer 1980: 91). According to Brian McGuinness, Wittgenstein held that 'magical ways of thinking and acting' are not based on beliefs but are akin rather to acts 'like kissing the picture of a loved one or striking some inanimate object when angry' (McGuinness 1982: 37). M. O. C. Drury puts the same construction on Wittgenstein: 'They were not mistaken beliefs that produced the rites but the need to express something' (Drury

This essay is based on the J. R. Jones Memorial Lecture delivered at the University of Swansea in December 1984.

1974: x). Still another anti-instrumental gloss on Wittgenstein runs: 'In Frazer's view the customs he describes are based upon opinions and interpretations of nature. For Wittgenstein, those customs are instinctual responses to an inner need for release and satisfaction, unconscious and with no other purpose' (Rudich and Stassen 1971: 86).

The view that Wittgenstein straightforwardly denied the instrumental character of magic is mistaken. What creates this impression is some hyperbolic remarks, particularly the oft-quoted:

> If I am furious about something, I often strike my stick on the ground or against a tree, etc., but I don't however believe that the earth is guilty or that the blows are of any use, 'I release my rage', and all rites are of this kind (Wittgenstein 1979: 72)[1]

This is a dismally opinionated utterance and a profoundly un-Wittgensteinian one. All rites are not of 'this kind' nor of any other kind, and Wittgenstein himself knows that they are not since the statement that they are is contradicted by remarks he makes elsewhere as well as in the Frazer notes themselves.

What is most striking about Wittgenstein's attitude towards instrumental conceptions of magic is neither its penetration (Rhees, McGuinness, Drury, W. D. Hudson) nor its perversity (Rudich and Stassen, Ayer, Cook) but its incoherence. And this incoherence is striking because it is more than just a matter of Wittgenstein conceding on some occasion what he denies at others, but of himself providing the most persuasive arguments against his own anti-instrumental objections, so that what we have is more a matter of genuine ambivalence than simple inconsistency.

Now what is to be said for this exegetical thesis, since it goes against the unanimity of his commentators, both critical and laudatory, and against some of Wittgenstein's own explicit utterances?

In Moore's notes, in contradicting Frazer's view that 'when primitive people stab an effigy of a particular person, they believe that they have hurt the person in question', Wittgenstein says only that 'primitive people do not *always* entertain this false scientific

---

[1] My quotations are from an unpublished translation by Anthony Manser of the University of Southampton. Page references are to the corresponding passages in Berzelius's translation in Luckhardt (1979).

belief though in some cases they may' (Moore's emphasis – Moore 1966: 308–9). Wittgenstein is equally circumspect in Alice Ambrose's notes: 'People at one time thought it useful to kill a man, sacrifice him to the God of fertility, in order to produce good crops. But it is not true that something is always done because it is useful. At least this is not the sole reason' (Ambrose 1979: 33).

When we re-read Wittgenstein's remarks in the light of these statements their incompatibility with an unqualified anti-instrumentalist conception of magic emerges even more markedly.

Wittgenstein compromises his anti-instrumentalist thesis in those remarks in which he objects to Frazer's intellectualism and insists rather on the unratiocinated, spontaneous character of magical practices than on their lack of ulterior aims: 'Eating and drinking have their dangers . . . nothing more natural than wanting to protect oneself . . . and we could think out protective measures ourselves' (Wittgenstein 1979: 66).

In a remark that follows, Wittgenstein again concedes the correctness of the instrumental view of magic: 'In magical healing one indicates to an illness that it should leave the patient.' In his comment on this Wittgenstein implies that what is objectionable in Frazer is his ratiocinative, intellectualist view of magical practices. 'After the description of such magical cures we'd like to add: If the illness doesn't understand that, then I don't know how one ought to say it.' This is just the argument that R. R. Marett advances in attempting to enhance the plausibility and perspicuity of the instrumental conception of mimetic rites: 'How can nature refuse to follow man's lead when man points it out so clearly?' (Marett 1927: 29).

Though Wittgenstein does not explicitly generalise this argument it generalises itself. If, as Wittgenstein says, the illness can't help but understand it is not welcome and thus quit the patient, why should any other portion of reality be more obtuse? Why should not the sky understand that it is to rain; the hemp that it is to grow; the witchety grubs that they are to flourish; the prey that it is to be killed (or rather, in such cases, the power that arranges these things, that the prey is to be caught; the enemy to sicken; the woman in labour to be safely delivered etc., etc.)? As Wittgenstein himself remarks, 'we could invent the protective measures ourselves'.

Another indication of Wittgenstein's undecidedness: at one

point he distinguishes between an oversimplified notion of things and processes, ('a false picture, a picture that doesn't fit') as for example, when someone speaks of an illness as moving from one part of the body to another, and 'magical operations', by which he means the symbolic rites which Frazer mistakes for occult technology. Baptism is an example of a symbolic rite which, if it were construed as an attempt to exploit the occult consequential properties of water, would illustrate the mistaken imputation of 'a false oversimplified conception' – in this case of guilt as something which could be washed away. But having made this distinction Wittgenstein then obliterates his own contrast by taking the very example he used to make it, that of the conception of illness entertained by 'uneducated people' as something which can move from one part of the body to another, and assimilating it to the principle on which protective magical practices are based (Wittgenstein 1979: 65–6).

One way of defeating the imputation of incoherence is by reinterpreting those remarks in which Wittgenstein has been taken to express an unqualified anti-instrumentalism. For example when Wittgenstein says that 'it is not characteristic of primitive man to act from opinions', we can let the emphasis fall on the word 'characteristic' and construe Wittgenstein as only denying the preeminence of the instrumental motive in generating those practices described by Frazer. (Similarly with 'It is nonsense to say that it is a characteristic feature of ritual actions that they spring from wrong ideas about the physics of things.')

On this view when Cook says '(Wittgenstein) is suggesting that the man who makes magic over his newly planted garden is not to be thought of as taking one more technological step after preparing his tubers and testing the soil but is to be thought of, rather, as expressing something in regard to his crop, the wish that it be abundant, the hope that it has not become infested, or whatever' (Cook 1983: 4), he is overstating Wittgenstein's anti-instrumentalism. Wittgenstein may be suggesting that the man who makes magic over his garden *need* not be thought of as taking a technological step rather than that he *must* not be so thought of and that he *may* rather than *must* be thought of as expressing his hopes and fears regarding it. Wittgenstein may be enlarging the range of options rather than foreclosing them in favour of the expressive conception.

On this view Wittgenstein is protesting at the exclusivity of Frazer's instrumental conception rather than advancing an exclusivist thesis of his own. But unfortunately for this reading, Wittgenstein's anti-instrumental utterances go further than this in both letter and spirit. How, for example, is the downrightness of the remark as to all rites being akin to spontaneous, self-sufficient gestures like striking the ground in anger, to be reconciled with a qualified anti-instrumentalism? Or the incredulity Wittgenstein expresses as to a primitive who is technically sophisticated enough to construct real weapons being at the same time naive enough to think he could effect ends by ritually mimicking employment of them?

Wittgenstein, then, has two apparently inconsistent views of instrumentalist conceptions of magic – that primitives are too sophisticated to hold views so absurd and that it is the most natural thing in the world that they should do so, not requiring any elaborate ratiocinative effort or theoretical justification on their part such as Frazer attributes to them. Which of these views best captures our relation to homeopathic magic? I believe that it is when he is advocating the intuitive compellingness of magic that Wittgenstein is at his most penetrating and that his unqualified anti-instrumentalism is partly hyperbole and partly misconstrued anti-intellectualism. But whether or not Wittgenstein qualifies his anti-instrumentalism in incoherent or incomprehensible ways, he certainly advances arguments against instrumentalist conceptions of magic. What are they and what are their merits? I shall deal only with the major ones – the arguments from implausible obtuseness and non-development and from the greater eligibility of the expressive.

Wittgenstein urges against the instrumental conception that primitives were bound to discover that magic has no influence on the events that Frazer thinks it is intended to bring about; all they need notice is that these occur in any case; furthermore, we see no changes in magical practices such as might be expected of an activity whose rationale was instrumental – 'magic has no principle of development'. But a great deal of our own instrumental life is conducted in darkness, from our criminal code and penal system to our therapeutic endeavours. If it takes the systematic monitoring of outcomes – a resolute attempt to discriminate our hits from our misses – before a practice can be considered instrumental then it is not just Frazer who is wrong about magic but it is we who are wrong as to a large part of what we have hitherto regarded as belonging to epistemic life. And though this is independently arguable it is not what Wittgenstein is asking us to credit. Wittgenstein's argument would render instrumentalist conceptions of herbalism, homeopathic medicine, astrology, and any other tradition-dominated, contemporary diagnostic and therapeutic practices equally untenable.

Wittgenstein's argument that the practitioners of instrumental magic would notice that the ends the ritual is meant to attain occur 'in any case' has no generality. It may always rain in any case, and the sun rise and the spring return in any case, but an enemy doesn't suddenly sicken 'in any case'. Furthermore, Wittgenstein's argument from implausible obtuseness only works against versions of Frazer's instrumentalism which treat the homeopathic ritual as a sufficient condition of the occurrence of the desired event, but not against the belief that the representation of events, through mimicry, say, can influence rather than guarantee their occurrence. Why should not the pre-historic hunters described by Marett believe that their mimic slaying of prey influences the outcome of the hunt? The success of the hunt need not be related to the ritual in so straightforward a way as Wittgenstein's arguments demand. Its success need not be conceived as guaranteed by the performance of the ritual nor its failure by its omission. Since considerations identical to those Wittgenstein finds grossly credulous haven't kept our own contemporaries from believing that vitamin C plays a beneficent role in controlling the incidence and duration of head colds, why should it have weighed more with Frazer's primitives? And when the desired event is as indeterminate as that which Frazer often assigns his primitives – purification from evil, for example – it is hardly appropriate to speak either of the inevitability of the outcome or of its disappointment.

The problem is not why magic is retained but why it is abandoned. What counts in favour of Wittgenstein's emphasis on its non-experimental character is that when it does go it tends to go completely. There is no attempt to vary the conditions under which the practice has proved inefficacious or unreliable; no attempt to enquire, say, whether a more efficacious transaction with simulacra might not yet be discovered. People don't go from wax models to clay models or from a rite by the full moon to a rite by a gibbous moon.

But even if Wittgenstein had succeeded in establishing the implausibility of Frazer's instrumentalist view of magic, it would not serve to establish his own expressive view, for Wittgenstein systemically elides the possibility that a rite may have transcendental objectives and thus be non-empirical without being non-instrumental. Where this is so, its role in the lives of its practitioners will be quite distinct from the purely symbolic/expressive one which Wittgenstein assigns it. It matters that the priest who baptises or absolves, or the bishop who ordains, should have the transcendental authority to do so, in a way that it doesn't matter that the foreign dignitaries, receiving a twenty-one-gun salute, are Oxford undergraduates in disguise. Pontius Pilate-like ablutionary practices remain impervious to discoveries as to the properties of water for reasons different from those for which baptismal rites remain similarly impervious. The one because they have no ulterior aims, the other because they have transcendental ones.

This brings us to Wittgenstein's second and more persuasive argument against Frazer's instrumental construals. They are gratuitous. The practices described by Frazer can be accounted for without such assumptions: they do not need to be explained because they can be 'explained', i.e. 'made clear', by being brought into connection with 'an inclination of our own' to 'express feelings not connected with beliefs'.

Shortly after contrasting the explaining which involves hypotheses with 'explaining', which is brought about by 'putting together in the right way what we already know' (which Rush Rhees felicitously renders 'making clear') Wittgenstein produces the following example of making a practice clear: 'burning in effigy, kissing the picture of a loved one. This is obviously not based on a belief that it will have a definite effect on the object which the picture represents. It aims at some satisfaction and achieves it' (Wittgenstein 1979: 64).

This remark has provoked much appreciative comment. What are the commentators appreciative of? What was their original relation to effigy burning and how was it improved by the reminder that we kiss pictures of our loved ones? What do they understand by 'making clear' and why do they think that Wittgenstein has succeeded in effecting it in this instance? This is how the matter is put in a work from another tradition: 'the task of making something understandable is to make us see how it could have happened by showing how akin it is to something we can already grasp' (Sabini and Silver 1982: 87). Mounce writes of an aborigine's belief in the efficacy of a curse: 'This practice can be properly understood . . . only by comparing it with beliefs (which) rest on ideas which are absurd but which for all their absurdity, can nevertheless, in certain circumstances, affect us deeply', e.g. the belief that the loss of a wedding ring may have a baleful occult influence on a marriage. Mounce's remark suggests the general form of such issues: the question they raise is what we should have no difficulty understanding given what we already do understand.

As to the character of the satisfaction which Wittgenstein says we are seeking and which is not to be found in explanation, I think it epistemically akin to that to which Lévi-Strauss refers in *The Savage Mind*: 'When an exotic custom fascinates us . . . it is generally because it presents us with a distorted reflection of a familiar image which we confusedly recognise as such without yet managing to identify it' (Lévi-Strauss 1966: 238–9). 'Putting into order what we already know' facilitates identification of this obscurely familiar image.

Thus the most common objection to Wittgenstein's procedure, that he attempts to resolve empirical questions a priori, is misconceived; 'Making clear' is not non-empirical, intuitive explaining. 'Making clear' does not attempt to settle empirical questions a priori. It tries to take us from a state in which we find something 'difficult to understand' to a state in which we find it less so. For example: from finding it difficult to understand how people could burn effigies of enemies or of personified symbols of baleful forces just for the satisfaction it gave them, to not finding it difficult, in view of the fact that we thrash inanimate objects and kiss bits of paper for similar reasons. Or: from finding it difficult to understand that people would be sufficiently incensed about the failure to recover the bodies of their dead to take the lives of those they held responsible, as did those Athenians, who voted death for the Captains who conducted the battle of Arginousae, to not finding it difficult in view of our own multifarious manifestations of cadaveric piety.

The activity of making clear is often confounded with that of rendering an account plausible because the same considerations can be brought forward to effect either. When a practice is enigmatic, that is, when its rationale is unknown to us and we are attempting to render a conjectured rationale plausible, we adduce the same considerations as when the rationale of a practice is known to us but is found opaque and our aim is to render it more perspicuous. Cook, for example, says that John Beattie undertakes to render the primitive belief in occult connections plausible by 'suggesting how even one of us might think that his wishes had caused someone's death or injury' (Cook 1983: 6), and he quite reasonably observes that more than this is required to demonstrate the instrumental character of magic.

But the point of Beattie's invocation of our own irrational propensity to credit the occult influence of thoughts on events is not to provide additional grounds for the historicity or veridicality of his instrumental account of magic, but to facilitate its intelligibility, i.e., he is addressing the question (as Mounce poses it) 'How could they believe' in occult connections? The same is true of Wittgenstein. The point of the analogies which Wittgenstein provides is not to preclude instrumental accounts of ritual but to argue the intelligibility of ritual transactions with images without the necessity of invoking such accounts.

An argument isomorphic with Wittgenstein's on effigy-burning is G. K. Chesterton's as to the explanation of savage customs, and funerary practices in particular:

misunderstanding of the real nature of ceremonial gives rise to the most awkward and dehumanised version of the conduct of men in rude lands or ages. The man of science, not realising that ceremonial is essentially a thing which is done without a reason, has to find a reason for every sort of ceremonial, and as might be supposed, the reason is generally a very absurd one – absurd because it originates not in the simple mind of the barbarian, but in the sophisticated mind of the professor. The learned man will say, for instance, 'the natives of mumbo jumbo land believe that the dead man can eat, and will require food upon his journey to the other world. This is attested by the fact that they place food in the grave, and that any family not complying with this rite is the object of the anger of the priest of the tribe.' To anyone acquainted with humanity this way of talking is topsy-turvy. It is like saying, 'The English in the 20th century believed that a dead man could smell. This is attested by the fact that they always covered his grave with lilies, violets, or other flowers. Some priestly and tribal terrors were evidently attached to the neglect of this action, as we have records of several old ladies who were very much disturbed in mind because their wreaths had not arrived in time for the funeral'. It may be of course that savages put food with the dead man because they think that a dead man can eat, or weapons with a dead man because they think that a dead man can fight. But personally I do not believe they think anything of the kind. I believe they put food or weapons on the dead for the same reason that we put flowers, because it is an exceedingly natural and obvious thing to do. (Chesterton 1905: 144–5)

Notice that Chesterton doesn't insist on the historicity of his account but only that it is 'natural and obvious'. Similarly with Wittgenstein. What he insists can be shown a priori is the perspicuity of a non-instrumental, expressive account, of effigy burning, say, not its correctness in particular cases.

When Alasdair MacIntyre asks of the Australian aborigine's belief in an external soul: 'Does the concept of carrying one's soul about in a stick make sense?' (MacIntyre 1970: 68), he is not expressing scepticism as to accounts of aboriginal behaviour which derive them from the belief in external souls; he is asking, not for more evidence that this is indeed their reasons, but for it to be 'made clear', i.e., for the kind of thing which Wittgenstein attempts to do for effigy-burning by reminding us that we kiss the picture of loved ones and which Winch attempted to do for MacIntyre himself, when he compared the aborigine's dismay at losing his soul-stick with the feelings of a lover who lost the locket containing his loved one's hair (Winch 1972: 45). The activity of making clear which Wittgenstein recommends as the appropriate response to a certain class of perplexities is not at all peculiar to him and is indulged, when they think it is called for, by R. R. Marett, Jane Harrison, Lord Raglan, S. G. F. Brandon, Claude Lévi-Strauss, John Beattie, and Frazer himself.

The necessity for making clear arises when either we have an account of a practice which comprises the rationale of the practitioners but this is opaque to us, or we are proposing an account of an enigmatic practice and are anticipating the objection that our account lacks perspicuity. In both these cases we put forward specimens of behaviour which we are accustomed to consider non-problematic and argue their analogy to the proffered rationale. This is what Wittgenstein is doing when he urges on behalf of his expressive conception of effigy-burning that we kiss the picture of loved ones.

Howard Mounce, for example, provides a specimen of making

clear when he attempts to answer the question 'How is it possible for anyone to believe that a person's guilt can be established by administering poison to a fowl?', not by providing us with more information about those who practice perplexes us but by calling our attention to our own relation to occult phenomena. The transition from the opacity to the transparency of a practice is accomplished via analogies and reminders. It might be helpful if some examples of making clear were laid out schematically:

PRACTICE: 'Putting a curse on someone by burning him in effigy, say'.
ANALOGY: dismay at a person's blindness following piercing the eyes in a representation of him (Mounce).

PRACTICE: cave drawing of transfixed prey or miming of a successful hunt.
ANALOGY: keeping a loved one's picture or her glove (Marett).

PRACTICE: The emperor remaining immobile to preserve the tranquillity of the empire.
ANALOGY: pressing one's lips together in a way which precludes laughing or talking when we wish someone else to desist from them (Wittgenstein).

PRACTICE: sprinkling water on ground to bring about rainfall; lighting of fires in mid-winter to assist sun.
ANALOGY: tendency of 'spectators of athletic or dramatic contest to assist action by some corresponding gesture' (Brandon).

PRACTICE: bringing food and drink to the graveside.
ANALOGY: our placing flowers on the grave (Chesterton).

PRACTICE: aborigine going through a ceremony appropriate to his having died because he has lost an object which contained his external soul.
ANALOGY: apologising to loved one for having lost love token (Winch).

PRACTICE: Potlatch.
ANALOGY: extravagant expenditure on Christmas presents in Manhattan (Lévi-Strauss).

PRACTICE: administering poison to a fowl to identify evil-doer.
ANALOGY: treating loss of wedding ring as an omen (Mounce).

PRACTICE: sympathetic magic in general.
ANALOGY: occasional absurd feeling that thought and speech can have occult influence (Beattie).

Two things about this list are obvious: that more of the examples are attempts to elucidate in cognitive/instrumental terms than in expressive ones and that they vary greatly in their degree of persuasiveness. But I postpone discussion of the general problems these raise until after the discussion of Wittgenstein's case for the expressive, non-instrumental construal of ritual activities.

Wittgenstein attempts to undermine Frazer's instrumentalism by reminding us of how often our transactions with images have no ulterior aim. We also engage in non-instrumental, symbolical transactions with images, though some of these are sufficiently nuanced to be misconstruable as evincing a belief in an occult connection between the image and its object ('the RC in his blindness / bows down to wood and stone').

Nuns who cover the crucifix before undressing don't really believe they have preserved Jesus from embarrassment and would even recognise the notion as heretical. The Catholic girl in Aldous Huxley's *After Many a Summer* who covers the statue of the Blessed Mother in her room before embracing her lover, did so for her sake and not the Virgin's. Napoleon, when he turned the portrait of the Prince of Rome away from the carnage of Borodino, did not think of himself as taking prophylactic measures (nor did Lord Blandower who deals similarly with his fiancée's portrait in J. Meade Falkner's *The Nebuly Coat*). If someone were to put any of these forward as speciments of occult instrumentalism the right procedure would be to remind him of the others – 'Human life is like that.'

In rejecting the necessity for imputing false conceptions of nature to account for primitive practices involving names, Wittgenstein asks rhetorically, 'Why should a man's own name not be sacred to him?' Let us see how the proposal to relate such practices to an inclination in ourselves works in the case of the sacredness of a man's name. What stands to practices suggesting that a man's name is sacred to him as does kissing the picture of a loved one to expressive effigy-burning? Kissing the name of a loved one, of course, but this involves another person's name and not our own. Is there anything closer?

In his autobiography Goethe provides an illustration of the peculiarly intimate relation in which we stand to our names. He tells us how annoyed he was at a verse of Herder's in which Herder took liberties with the name Goethe by punning on Goth:

It was not in very good taste to take such jocular liberties with my name; for a person's name is not like a cloak which only hangs round him and may be pulled and tugged at, but a perfectly fitting garment grown over and around him like his very skin, which one cannot scrape and scratch at without hurting the man himself. (Goethe 1949: 112)

If someone knows this story and never found it odd or is told it and finds Goethe's reaction perfectly natural then calling his attention to this should do something to make clear why the name of a savage is sacred to him. Freud makes the same point as Goethe in *Totem and Taboo*: 'a man's name is one of the main constituents of his person and perhaps of his psyche'. This notion is dramatised in Athol Fugard's play *Siswe Banzi is Dead*. The eponymous hero displays a dismay at the prospect of parting with his name so that he can enjoy the amenities of someone else's pass book which is not accountable for in rational terms, and yet we are not at a loss to see why. Neither does the fact that an Algonquin Indian should, as Sapir tells us, refer to someone bearing the same name as 'another myself' strike us as particularly opaque or impenetrable.

Another area in which we seem to 'express feelings not connected with beliefs' is that of our relation to our dead. Fustel de Coulange thought the execution of the Athenian captains for failing to retrieve the bodies of the fallen at the battle of Arginousae, was only explicable in terms of the conviction of the bereaved that the dead were thereby condemned to an anguished afterlife (Fustel de Coulange 1980: chapter 1). If we were ourselves unconvinced of this and wished to bring someone round to our point of view we would produce stories like that of the distress of those parents of the Moors murder victims whose bodies have never been found and therefore never properly buried; or of Lincoln's sentiments apropos the burial of his fiancée that he could not 'bear to think of her out there alone . . . The rain and the storm shan't beat on her grave'.

Is the showing of respect for bodies of the dead where there is no distressing uptake for others unintelligible? For example, the convention observed in the dissecting rooms of American teaching hospitals of keeping the genital areas of the cadavers covered? Can such practices be exhaustively explained by invoking more and more subtle consequential considerations such as that first-year medical students are less upset if a certain decorum is observed? And what are the subtle consequential considerations in the case of the wish of lovers to be buried in a common grave? Are these not rather examples of what Wittgenstein calls attention to – 'feelings that need not be connected with a belief'?

In John Ford's *My Darling Clementine* Wyatt Earp goes to his murdered brother's graveside and fills him in on sundry matters. No one infers from this that he believes himself to have mediumistic powers nor thinks of the episode as an out-of-doors-seance. How much of what we do is an attempt to please our dead; and not just the 'passed over' Society for Psychical Research dead, nor the 'to be raised in the twinkling of an eye when the trumpet shall sound' dead, but the dead dead, the forever dead. Neither Wyatt Earp apostrophising his brother through several feet of earth nor Dr Johnson standing in the rain at Uttoxeter Market on the anniversary of some unfilial act, need be assigned a theory of the after-life for their behaviour to be understood.

How does it follow from the fact that burning an effigy can be made clear by assimilating it to our kissing the picture of a loved one that effigies are not also burned in pursuit of some ulterior objective? Or, from our understanding that a man's name can be sacred to him in a way which dispenses with the necessity of deriving this from prudence based on occult conviction, that this isn't sometimes also the case as well? From the fact that we can make non-cognitive, expressive sense of Wyatt Earp's apostrophising his dead brother it doesn't follow that all seances are really misunderstood memorial services. I think Wittgenstein's argument is meant to establish the gratuitousness rather than the erroneousness of Frazer's instrumentalism. But there are certain facts about our relation to Frazer's instrumentalist conception which make it necessary to modify even the charge that it is markedly strained or more difficult to fathom than an expressive one. (What is striking is that Wittgenstein is aware of these facts and himself calls our attention to them.)

The trouble with Wittgenstein's invocation of the potential perspicuity, the inventability, of rituals and practices in the service of an expressive construal of them is that it isn't only expressive rationales which can thus be related to inclinations of our own. Told that savages refuse to reveal their names because they fear they might come to harm we could be brought to understand why in the same way as those for whom non-instrumental effigy-burning was made clear by being reminded that they kiss pictures of loved ones.

Among the superstitious propensities which could be invoked to diminish our perplexity at the occult practices described by Frazer is the irrational dismay felt by the subjects of an ingenious *Gedanken* experiment by Howard Mounce of Swansea. He asked his students to imagine that they had pierced the eyes in a drawing of their mothers and that they then discovered that she had gone blind. Would they think themselves responsible? A certain proportion did. This argument does not get its force from how large a proportion this was but from our relation to the response of those who felt rationally unaccountable remorse. (In fact Mounce's experiment is strictly otiose and we could just ask ourselves how we would feel under the imagined circumstances.) Why don't these feelings do for effigy burning and cognate practices when instrumentally construed, what Wittgenstein's picture-kissing does for them when expressively construed?

It might be objected on behalf of the superior eligibility of the expressive construal that what Mounce's experiment illustrated was not a conviction of occult influence but a momentary reaction. But is the transition from impulsive to institutionalised expressiveness any more easy to imagine than that from impulsive to institutionalised instrumentalism? Are the instrumental analogies any more remote from the magical practices they are meant to illuminate than the expressive ones that Wittgenstein reminds us of? Even those expressive magical practices which are most like striking the ground in anger aren't completely like them. Those who practise human sacrifice (or mimic it) to celebrate the harvest can't just agree to be angry at the appropriate time nor do they just find themselves growing more irritable as the days get longer. Even in the picture-kissing case there are disanalogies not to be neglected – effigies are not burned on impulse and pictures of loved ones are not kissed at calendrically determined intervals. There is thus a gap between the institutionalised practices and the impulsive inclination which Wittgenstein brings forward to illuminate them. So in either case, instrumental or expressive, a certain imaginative leap is necessary if an analogy from our own inclinations is to make an exotic practice clear.

Boswell told Johnson that since he had been happy for moments at a time he could imagine someone else to be so continuously. If we allow a related argument to be invoked on behalf of an expressive conception of effigy burning via picture-kissing and furniture-kicking why not on behalf of instrumental effigy burning via Mounce's *Gedanken* experiment? It is not the fact of the practice which makes an exotic rite clear but the inclination it incites us to acknowledge, which we must then extrapolate to the problematic rite. We must, for example, traverse the ground from our inclination to do things analogous to pressing our lips together when we want someone to restrain himself, to the periodic immobility of the emperor as an expression of concern for the tranquillity of his empire. The distance from the inclination to the rite may be generally longer in the case of the rites instrumentally construed, than when expressively construed, but there is no difference in principle. And there are cases where the distance is not longer. It is difficult to see what expressive satisfaction could be derived from destroying the fingernails of an enemy, and in such a case thinking of our transactions with pictures of loved ones doesn't help. And it helps even less when the finger nails destroyed are one's own where the instrumental construal that it is a precautionary measure is markedly more eligible than the expressive. Does Wittgenstein pressing his lips together, or Jane Harrison making sympathetic pseudo-facilitory movements during a tennis-match, really make couvade, say, clearer than Frazer's occult homeopathic convictions make it? And in the case of the emperor's periodic immobility in connection with the tranquillity of his kingdom, Wittgenstein's expressive account is no more eligible than the instrumental one, because though we may find difficulty in crediting an instrumental rationale for the practice, we find as much difficulty in the notion that such effort would be expended in the interests of an expressive purpose alone. If someone kissed photographs of loved ones for hours at a time at fixed intervals, we would doubt the adequacy of a purely expressive account.

The real objection to Wittgenstein's pro-expressive argument from inclinations in ourselves is that it too often leaves us where we were before. Confronted by practices which are enigmatic and may be either instrumental or expressive, a more vivid sense of their connection with our own feelings and thoughts is as likely to confer perspicuity on an instrumental account as on an expressive one. I will support this claim with some instances.

Although there is no reason 'why a man's name should not be sacred to him' this does not preclude its also being a matter of occult concern to him. And there are cases where instrumentalist assumptions make as much sense as expressive ones. The assumption that a consequential rationale is required to make sense of the primitive's proscription on having a descendant named after him while he is still living, might well be felt gratuitous, but his keeping his name secret seems as intelligibly attributed to genuine apprehension as to a sense of dignity and may have as practical a rationale as an unlisted telephone number.

According to Guthrie, in the Athens of Plato and Aristotle a practice existed of writing the name of an enemy on a plate, transfixing it and then burying it in the expectation that this would injure or kill him (Guthrie 1950: 12–13). If we knew only what Wittgenstein calls 'the-external action' and not its rationale, would not rummaging among 'inclinations in ourselves' as readily provide us with an instrumental magical rationale as Wittgenstein's pro-expressive argument assumes it would an expressive one? (One of Pareto's residues is 'the mysterious linking of names and things'.)

Here is a contemporary instance of the practice described by Guthrie. It is from Nancy Mitford's *roman à clef, Love in a Cold Climate*:

It was a favourite superstition of Uncle Matthew's that if you wrote some-body's name on a piece of paper and put it in a drawer, that person would die within the year. The drawers at Alconleigh were full of little slips bearing the names of those whom my uncle wanted out of the way, private hates of his and various public figures such as Bernard Shaw, de Valera, Gandhi, Lloyd George, and the Kaiser, while every single drawer in the whole house contained the name of Labby, Linda's old dog. The spell hardly ever seemed to work, even Labby having lived far beyond the age usual in Labradors, but he went hopefully on, and if one of the charac-ters did happen to be carried off in the course of nature he would look pleased but guilty for a day or two. (Mitford 1949: 169–70)

Isn't there 'something in us too which speaks in favour' of this 'observance' of Uncle Matthew's?

When we go in search of inclinations in ourselves with which to make Frazer's examples of name magic clear (or attempt to bring to more explicit awareness those in virtue of which we already find them clear), we think of Rumpelstiltskin and are reassured that we are on the right track when we learn that Wittgenstein thought of him too. Fania Pascal tells us that Wittgenstein once read her the Grimm fairy tale about Rumpelstiltskin, the sorcerer dwarf, who agreed to relinquish his claim on the first born of the princess if she could tell him his name: 'I remember him picking up a volume of Grimm's fairy tales and reading out with awe in his voice?: "*Ach, wie gut ist dass niemand weiss / Dass ich Rumpelstilchen heiss.*" "Profound. Profound," he said. I understood that the strength of the dwarf lay in his name being unknown to humans' (Pascal 1981: 33).

Don't we find a peculiar appropriateness in the fact that it was Rumpelstiltskin's name that the princess had to divine rather than the number of hairs in his beard, say? And if the slips of paper which Uncle Matthew placed in drawers bore not the names, but the national insurance numbers of those he wished ill, would not his bizarrerie lose in intelligibility?

In the *Brown Book* Wittgenstein says: 'One could almost imagine that naming was done by a sacramental act and that this produced some magic relation between the name and the thing.' Isn't what 'one could almost imagine' one of the instruments with which making clear is accomplished? In a life of Hemingway we learn that he believed in what he called the 'spoken jinx', by which he meant the power of language to bring about misfortune merely by representing it, even inadvertently. Thus he was perturbed and angry when his publishers sent him the proofs of *Death in the Afternoon* with the identifying rubric, 'Hemingway's "Death"' at the head of each galley. Acquainting someone with facts like these might, as Wittgenstein says, make other facts like these appear 'more natural', but I don't think that this is the only, or even the main, rationale for their assemblage. I think that we are meant to feel an inwardness with the behaviour cited and this is why their historicity or veridicality is of little account. It doesn't really matter that no one may ever have kissed the name of a loved one.

Thus it is not the well-authenticated fact that men kiss pictures of loved ones which makes clear – thus depriving certain exotic practices of their opacity – but our relation to this fact. Its authenticity as custom does not guarantee its clarificatory power. Only our willingness to assimilate our expressive non-instrumental transactions with images and simulacra to that of the effigy burning and kindred activities of Frazer's primitives can do this. (Though the distinction between inwardness and mere familiarity is not one we will always be able to make with confidence and there are even instances where we will find, to our surprise, that though we do feel confident our confidence is not shared.)

It might be of no help in attempting to render perspicuous an expressive, non-Fustelian account of the execution of the victors of Arginouasae to point out that some among us have had the experience of trying to comfort cadavers for being dead and for the harm through which they came to be dead. Those to whom these facts are addressed may find them as opaque as the matters it was hoped to make clear by means of them. Someone may consider that Lincoln's response to the storm beating on Ann Rutledge's grave, rather than illuminating the vengefulness of the bereaved of Arginousae merely shows that Lincoln was momentarily deranged and thus as beyond understanding as those his behaviour was meant to elucidate. But even where there is no denying our inwardness with the practice or inclination which has been introduced to clarify an exotic ritual it may be doubted whether it succeeds because of its remoteness. We can easily imagine someone who agreed that he would experience dismay at the absurd thought that he had harmed his mother in the circumstances described by Mounce, nevertheless protesting that the gap between his momentary dismay and the routine practice of homeopathic magic was too large.

There are several instances of making clear which seem to me to fail through the remoteness of the clear practice from the opaque one it is meant to naturalise. Brandon, like Jane Harrison, thinks that homeopathic magic is a natural extension of imitative action – 'the urge on the part of a spectator to assist action by some corresponding gesture' (Brandon 1973–4, vol. IV: 100). But is the analogy between the motion of our feet when watching a footballer (or the principle it illustrates) and 'lighting fires in midwinter to strengthen the weakening sun' good enough? And isn't there a gap, if not a gulf, between the girl Jane Harrison describes leaping among the growing hemp and the motoric overspill of a sympathetic observer watching someone attempting a high jump? The hemp unlike the athlete provides no incitement to vicarious participation. Marett's invocation of our custom of mitigating the absence of loved ones by carrying their pictures to support the naturalness of the view (which he thinks lies behind pre-historic cave paintings) that 'the vivid suggestion of a desired event is a means to its realisation' (Marett 1927: 28), doesn't seem to me to draw the two practices close enough together.

On the other hand, when I think of the animated cartoon convention in which Tom or Jerry, or whoever, finding himself chased up a cul-de-sac, draws a door on a solid surface through which he then proceeds to escape, the notion that the cave paintings of speared and dying prey are examples of occult instrumentality, gains in intelligibility and plausibility. Of course in this case we can't even say that what the animated cartoon episode puts us in mind of are 'inclinations of our own'; they are more our deliria and phantasmagoria and, if Hallpike's Piagetan speculations about early childhood are right, our archaic reminiscences (Hallpike 1979). Some of us find ourselves wanting to say of the animated cartoon device in which an image becomes its object, as of Stan Laurel's transactions with his fist/pipe, what Wittgenstein said of the secret name in Rumpelstiltskin: 'Profound! Profound!' But of course we know tht there are those who will not have had the instrumental rationale for mimetic magic rendered lucid by such considerations and will be bewildered as to why we think so; what came to us as a solution is for them another mystery to be penetrated.

Closely related to name magic is the wider notion of thought/speech magic. John Beattie observes that even among ourselves it is obscurely felt that 'to say or to think something solemnly and emphatically enough is somehow to make it more likely to happen' (Beattie 1964: 204). Isn't this the self-same principle which, stylised and elaborated, has been held to rationalise much primitive ritual? Many rituals can be seen as collective wishing dramatised with whatever materials are to hand, assisted perhaps by chanted imperatives or optatives. The question is whether conceiving of this dramatised, objectified wishing as likely to influence its fulfilment can be made any less perspicuous to us, i.e., is any less intimately related to 'inclinations in ourselves', than conceiving it as expressive/symbolic merely.

Francis Cornford's account attempts to do justice to both views:

Sympathetic Magic consists in the representation of the object of passionate desire. Primarily, this representation is mimetic – in other words, the realisation of the desired end in dramatic action. The emotion is satisfied by actually doing the thing which is willed . . . In the earliest stage . . . the dramatic action and the desired effect are not distinguished. The rainmaker feels simply that he is making rain, not that he is imitating the fall of rain, in order to cause real rain to fall subsequently. When the faith in magic begins to weaken, some distinction must begin to arise between the mimetic action and the real event; some notion of causality makes its first appearance. (Cornford 1957: 139)

This account is incoherent. If the rainmaker does not distinguish between the dramatic action and the desired effect what can it mean to say that 'the faith in magic begins to weaken'? Faith in magic is only called for if magic is already conceived as a means of bringing about ends independent of, and ulterior to, the magic ritual itself. But Cornford's havering does inadvertently illustrate the ease with which the transition from an expressive to an instrumental conception of mimetic rituals is conceived.

A similar ambiguity infects the following remarks:

> To the magician knowledge is power . . . To form a representation of the structure of nature is to have control over it. To classify things is to name them, and the name of a thing, or a group of things, is its soul; to know their names is to have power over their souls. Language, that stupendous product of the collective mind, is a duplicate, a shadow soul, of the whole structure of reality; it is the most effective and comprehensive tool of human power, for nothing, whether human or superhuman, is beyond its reach. (Cornford 1957: 141)

When Cornford says that 'to form a representation of the structure of nature is to have control over it' he could mean either, that in consequence of his representation of some aspect of nature the magician thinks he can actually influence her or, that the representation of nature itself constitutes control independently of any ulterior effect it may have.

If we resolve this ambiguity in favour of an instrumental construal then we can treat Cornford, too, as testifying to the affinity between the relation in which Frazer's primitives stand to magic and we, in our metaphysical deliria, to language. Hallpike argues in his Piaget-inspired account of primitive beliefs that the mode of thought described by Cornford, which he calls nominal realism, is a phase through which all humans pass on their way to 'operatory' thought (Hallpike 1979).

When Wittgenstein spoke of 'the mythology of language' and of 'magic as metaphysics' ('bringing something higher under the sway of our words') it is probably nominal realism he had in mind. Faust's 'In the beginning was the deed' (which Wittgenstein cited in this connection) has been taken as an emendation of the first verse of John's Gospel but it may have been only an elucidation of it: 'In the beginning was the Word/deed.' Why is this (largely superseded) propensity of ours not as capable of illuminating at least a certain range of occult practices, as are Wittgenstein's instances of our expressive/symbolic inclinings?

But some of the practices described by Frazer are out of reach even of the sign/referent magic with which I have been urging our inwardness. The principle that is exemplified in many of Frazer's examples of instrumental magic is that of an occult connection between vaguely isomorphic events, one which is independent of human willing but which may be exploited by it and against which precautions must be taken, 'analogy magic' in Walter Burkert's phrase. A familiar example is the folk view that a man dying by a seashore will live until the tide goes out. Yet here too, we have something which is far from alien to us. The principle is illustrated by an incident in *Great Expectations*. The convict Magwitch, about to recount his history to Pip, takes out his pipe to fill it, and thinking that 'the tangle of tobacco in his hand . . . might perplex the thread of his narrative' puts it back again. Does this not confer a degree of intelligibility on the following custom recorded by Frazer? Among the Ainos of Sakhilin 'a pregnant woman may not spin or twist rope for two months before her delivery, because they think that if she did so the child's guts may be entangled like thread' (Frazer 1967: 17). This might seem too remote from Magwitch's behaviour to be elucidated by it but consider the following which immediately succeeds it in Frazer's text:

For a like reason in Bilaspore, a district of India, when the chief men of a village meet in council, no one present should twirl a spindle; for they think that if such a thing were to happen, the discussion, like the spindle, would move in a circle and never be wound up. (Frazer 1967: 17)

Doesn't this act as what Wittgenstein calls an 'intermediate case' thus suggesting how the impulse operative in the case of Magwitch might also underlie the Aino proscription on a pregnant woman spinning?

It is said that when Napoleon began crossing the Niemen to invade Russia his horse stumbled and someone commented, 'a bad omen; a Roman would have turned back'. Similar stories are told in connection with other ventures. If the connection between a stumbling horse and the miscarriage of an enterprise seems natural even to those who don't credit it, how much in Frazer's accounts of homeopathic magic can we find unassimilable? A clue to the depth of the homeopathic principle is provided when we reflect how different our feelings as participants in a Mounce-like *Gedanken* experiment would be if, having pierced the eyes of a picture, we were asked to imagine that the subject of it went not blind but deaf.

There was a famous Singapore towkay who was convinced that if he ever stopped building he would die. During the Japanese occupation, when he had to stop because building materials were not available, he did indeed die. This story is retold, with variations, thoughout the world, probably because it occurs, with variations, throughout the world. Don't we feel a peculiar appositeness in the relation of the compulsion to the apprehension?

I don't think that these examples work simply cumulatively, as Wittgenstein suggests. In Moore's notes he speaks of reducing our perplexity at a rite by finding similar ones since this will 'make it seem more natural'. This isn't the way it is with homeopathic magic since instances which have no weight at all as evidence of the extensiveness of a practice may nevertheless mitigate its opacity. Wittgenstein's own example of the mouse in *Alice* drying out the sodden animals by reading them 'the driest thing he knows' does this for word magic.

Something which can do this for the notion of image/object magic and yet is extravagantly incapable of acting as evidence (unlike Hemingway's 'spoken jinx') is a comic routine of Stan Laurel's. Finding himself without his pipe he makes a fist and stuffs tobacco into it. When he sets it alight – puffing on his extended thumb – smoke issues from his mouth. Isn't this a fantasy fulfilment of Frances Cornford's incoherent notion of a 'dramatic' action which is simultaneously 'its desired effect', a reversion to Freud's auto-plastic phase 'when the omnipotence of thought was a reality'?

The notion that an image may take on the property of its object (whether it is autonomous or derivable from Beattie's principle or the source of it – thought as a kind of picture) extends from myth, fantasy and fiction to folk belief; from *Galatea*, the toy figures in Hans Christian Anderson, The Commendatore's statue in *Don Giovanni, Pinocchio, The Picture of Dorian Grey*, M. R. James's 'The Mezzotint' and Anatole France's 'Le Jongleur de Notre Dame' to a multitude of weeping statues of the Blessed Mother. There is a peculiar appropriateness in the notion of an occult connection between image and object. If with every successive debauch Dorian

Grey's national insurance number became paler until it was finally illegible, the story would lack something.

What does Wittgenstein imagine our predicament to be with respect to effigy burning, and other apparently homeopathic operations, from which his picture-kissing analogy is to rescue us? He imagines us to suffer from a temporary, remediable incapacity to imagine that such activities could have other than practical objectives: and the remedy is to remind us of the strength and pervasiveness of our ceremonial, celebratory, memorialising impulses – 'Human life is like that.'

Wittgenstein's argument seems to require that whenever we have a ritual practice which Frazer construes as intended to achieve some ulterior end we can bethink ourselves of some non-instrumental practice or inclination of our own which could more economically account for it. But have not the examples just expounded illustrated the equal or greater eligibility of instrumental accounts? What grounds can be given for rejecting them?

Attempts to make clear can fail for either of two reasons: either because the practice or inclination which is appealed to is itself problematic and lacking in perspicuity, or where this is not the case, because it is found too remote from the opaque, exotic practice it was intended to clarify.

Let us examine the first requirement. In order to make anything clear we need to know something which is already clear. Now what do we know which is already clear? What is it that confers perspicuity on a practice? Why did Wittgenstein think that kissing the picture of a loved one was clear? Or beckoning to someone we wish to approach us? Or, pressing our lips together when we wish someone to be silent? Or, striking an inanimate object in anger? Familiarity?

No. Mere familiarity with similar practices is not enough. For in that case, not only could instrumental magic be rendered as perspicuous as expressive, but it would also be difficult to see how the need for elucidation of the ritual activities, recorded in *The Golden Bough*, could arise in the first place. How can 'people of the Book' have found the occult practices recorded by Frazer puzzling or his instrumental accounts of them questionable? Did not Elisha remonstrate with Joash for striking the ground with his spear thrice only, thus passing up the chance of obliterating the Syrians completely; and were not the Israelites able to defeat the hosts of

Amalek only so long as Moses's arm was upraised? Even those of us without Bible culture can't have escaped similar stories from other sources.

We are perfectly familiar with the notion of effective wishing from fairy tales (e.g. *The Three Wishes*) and from folk custom (the wishing well, wishing on a star, the fowl's wish-bone, etc., etc.). Are these fairy tales disqualified from making clear because we think them fiction whereas we know that kissing the picture of loved ones is fact? This is not the reason. Some of these stories are perfectly capable of making clear in spite of their fictional status and others are incapable of doing so even if their factual status was not in question, because they are not clear themselves. Familiarity does not guarantee perspicuity whereas it is perfectly possible for a mere fantasy to provoke an awareness of inclinations in ourselves capable of conferring perspicuity on practices hitherto opaque or only vaguely comprehensible. If being reminded of the story of Rumpelstiltskin fails to make clear the reluctance of a primitive to reveal his name, it is not because it is fiction but because it has failed to 'connect with our own feelings and thoughts'. And if kissing the picture of a loved one makes clear it is not because it is familiar but because it does.

We can't dissipate our perplexity with respect to a practice by invoking examples of superstitious practices, anecdotes, or ideas which are themselves problematic, however familiar they may be. They must first themselves be rendered clear by persuading us to see them in a certain light. This can't be done with all the omens, superstitions and stories of the supernatural we are familiar with but only with a subclass of them in which we can recognise inclinations of whose independent existence they remind us. It is not the unfamiliarity of the story of the aborigine's mislaying of the object containing his soul which makes it perplexing. Even if it had been taught in multi-cultural compulsory religious instruction classes and so was as familiar as the story of *The Three Wishes* or *Rumpelstiltskin* it could be no less in need of elucidation.

What makes an inclination to attach an occult power to names and uttered thoughts such as Hemingway displayed *our* inclination and not just *my* inclination or *his* inclination? Whether or not you agree that Harrison, Brandon, etc., have succeeded in dissipating the opacity of the notion of leaping dances, for example, you will find yourself contradicted and you won't know what to say. Should discussions of the opacity or perspicuity of exotic practices stop with success or failure at attaining the suffrage of those addressed, or are there further steps to be taken?

The following formula suggests itself – a practice has been made clear when the person to whom the parallels and reminders which are to make it clear are addressed says it has been made clear. But, can't he be wrong, not only about the pertinent others who constitute the 'we', but about himself? Not only do reminders of Stan Laurel's smoking transactions with his thumb sometimes fail in making primitive magical transactions with simulacra less opaque, but even when they do succeed, someone may, nevertheless, come to feel that he was being sequacious, and on attempting to reassure himself may find that he is unclear as to how, in a case like this, he is to distinguish non-sequaciousness from perverse contradictoriness. His grasp of what counts as 'understanding' or 'making sense' wavers.

What, finally, is the upshot of all these considerations and counter-considerations? What is the value of Wittgenstein's contrast between explaining and making clear? And why does it matter whether or not we find instrumental magic clear?

Perhaps Wittgenstein's remarks should not be read for the light they shed on ritual practices since perspicuity bears so tenuous a relation to historicity; people do act for reasons of which we can make no sense and the sense we do make of them is often not the sense they have. The extent of Wittgenstein's contribution to the explanatory enterprise is that of removing objections to non-instrumental or non-ratiocinative accounts of the score of their implausibility by relating them to inclinations on our own. But the predominant value of Wittgenstein's remarks is not their contribution to the explanatory tasks of anthropology or pre-history but for the light they shed on our relation to exotic practices – on where we might seek those 'familiar images' of which we see in these practices 'a distorted reflection', in Lévi-Strauss's formulation.

Those who attempt to address each other on questions such as these must recognise that they are questions in which many of their fellows will take no interest. The only satisfaction these seek from explanation is the satisfaction of having the phenomenon explained in the way in which only further information can explain (Ernest Gellner, Marvin Harris). But the enterprise of making clear encounters a more demoralising difficulty. It is that those who do respond with perplexity to accounts of certain practices and who are in search of the satisfaction of which Wittgenstein speaks and which can only come about by being related to an inclination of their own, will often respond diversely to the parallels and analogies which are intended to produce such satisfaction. And when they do disagree as to whether the invocation of an 'inclination of our own' has succeeded in conferring perspicuity on a hitherto opaque practice they will have no means of resolving their differences. It is on their willingness to tolerate this state of affairs that the value they place on enquiries, such as those Wittgenstein invites us to undertake with respect to magic, will depend.

REFERENCES

Ambrose, A. (1979) *Wittgenstein's Lectures 1932–5*, Oxford: Clarendon Press.
Ayer, A. J. (1980) *Wittgenstein*, London: Weidenfeld and Nicolson.
Beattie, J. (1964) *Other Cultures*, London: Routledge and Kegan Paul.
Brandon, S. G. F. (1973–4) 'Ritual in religion', *Dictionary of the History of Ideas*, New York: Scribners.
Chesterton, G. K. (1905) *Heretics*, London and New York: John Lane.
Cook, John (1983) 'Magic, witchcraft and science', *Philosophical Investigations*, vol. 6, no. 1, January.
Cornford, Francis (1957) *From Religion to Philosophy*, New York: Harper.
Drury, M. O'C. (1974) *The Danger Of Words*, London: Routledge and Kegan Paul.
Frazer, Sir J. G. (1967) *The Golden Bough* (abridged edition), London: Macmillan.
Fustel de Coulange, Numa St Denis (1980) *The Ancient City*, Baltimore and London: Johns Hopkins.
Goethe, J. W. von (1949) *Truth and Fantasy from my Life*, edited by J. M. Cohen, London: Weidenfeld and Nicolson.
Guthrie, W. K. C. (1950) *The Greek Philosophers*, London: Methuen.
Hallpike, C. K. (1979) *The Foundations of Primitive Thought*, Oxford: Clarendon Press.
Harrison, Jane (1918) *Ancient Art and Ritual*, London: Home University Library.
Hudson, W. D. (1987) 'The light Wittgenstein sheds on religion' in John Canfeild, *The Philosophy of Wittgenstein: Ethics, Aesthetics and Religion*, New York: Garland.
Lévi-Strauss, Claude (1963) *Structural Anthropology*, New York: Basic Books.
    (1966) *The Savage Mind*, London: Weidenfeld and Nicolson.

McGuinness, B. F. (1982) 'Freud and Wittgenstein' in Brian McGuinness (ed.), *Wittgenstein and his Times*, Oxford: Blackwell.

MacIntyre, Alasdair (1970) 'Is understanding religion compatible with believing?' in Bryan Wilson (ed.), *Rationality*, Oxford: Blackwell.

Marett, R. R. (1927) *Man in the Making* (revised and enlarged edition), London: Thomas Nelson and Sons Ltd.

Mitford, N. (1949) *Love in a Cold Climate*, London: Hamish Hamilton.

Moore, G. E. (1966) 'Wittgenstein's lectures in 1930–33' in *Philosophical Papers*, New York: Collier Books.

Mounce, H. (1973) 'Understanding a primitive society', *Philosophy*, October; also in R. Beehler and A. R. Drengson (1978) *The Philosophy of Society*, London: Methuen.

Pascal, Fania (1981) 'Wittgenstein: a personal memoir' in Rush Rhees (ed.), *Wittgenstein: Personal Reminiscences*, Oxford: Blackwell.

Rhees, Rush (1982) 'Wittgenstein on language and ritual' in Brian McGuiness (ed.), *Wittgenstein and his Times*, Oxford: Blackwell.

—— (1981) 'Introduction to remarks on Frazer's Golden Bough', *The Human World*, no. 3, May.

Rudich, N. and Stassen, M. (1971) 'Wittgenstein's implied anthropology', *History and Theory*.

Sabini, John and Silver, Maury (1982) *Moralities of Everyday Life*, Oxford: Oxford University Press.

Winch, Peter (1972) 'Understanding a primitive society' in Peter Winch, *Ethics and Action*, London: Routledge and Kegan Paul.

Wittgenstein, Ludwig (1967) 'Bemerkungen über Frazer's The Golden Bough', *Synthese*, translation by John Berzelius; also in C. G. Luckhardt (1979) *Wittgenstein: Sources and Perspectives*, Brighton: Harvester Press.

CHAPTER SEVEN

Wittgenstein and obscurantism

I

The thesis I want to discuss is that Wittgenstein often places gratuitous limits on the explanatory potential of empirical enquiry, allots to reflection explanatory powers it doesn't have and, when not guilty of these narrowly conceptual errors, manifests a defective epistemic sensibility in preferring to empirical enquiry and its results something he variously characterises as 'the understanding which consists in seeing the connections', 'formal relations', 'further description', 'getting clear', and, on one occasion, something as non-epistemic as 'consolation'.

I will refer to the first of these charges as limits obscurantism, the second as method obscurantism and the last as sensibility obscurantism. One of the more notorious examples of limits obscurantism is August Comte's proscription on speculation as to the chemical composition of the stars on the score of its futility. Equally familiar specimens of method obscurantism are the belief that the planets must move in circles because being supralunary bodies only an orbit which was a perfect sphere was befitting and Hegel's (apocryphal) conviction that there was no need for astronomers to search for further planets after the discovery of Uranus since for *a priori* reasons there could be no more than seven. A specimen of sensibility obscurantism, at least if you concur in deploring it, is given by Macaulay in his famous contrast between the behaviour of a follower of Bacon and that of a follower of Epictetus in their reactions to disaster. The Baconian takes practical measures to mitigate the harm. The Stoic attempts to revise the victims' conception of evil.

All three accusations have been levelled at Wittgenstein. In one of the earliest comments on Wittgenstein's 'Remarks on Frazer's

Golden Bough' Wittgenstein is accused of holding a view of explanation from which it would follow that '. . . the geocentric and heliocentric theories . . . would be equally plausible insofar as either may arouse in this breast or that a feeling of satisfaction' (Rudich and Stassen 1971: 89). Paul Ziff finds Wittgenstein's dealings with aesthetic perplexities suggestive of all three varieties of obscurantism (Ziff 1980). That Wittgenstein often displays what an empiricist admirer of science would consider normative or sensibility obscurantism is conceded by several of his admirers while dissenting, of course, from the empiricist's condemning judgement. Rush Rhees tells us that though Frazer's empirical explanations of ritual 'in one sense' explain, 'in a sense that is more important to Wittgenstein, (they) do not explain' (Rhees 1982: 99).

One defence of Freud against Wittgenstein's criticisms makes the charge that Wittgenstein prefers 'the evidence of his own introspection . . . to the results of objective methods of enquiry' (Hanly 1972: 88). The same commentator finds evidence of epistemic perversity in Wittgenstein's attitude to Freudian explanation: Wittgenstein behaves like 'a misguided person who wishing to protect a friend from the anxiety of having to face up to a diagnosis of cancer encourages a delay in the treatment until a condition that was initially operable has become terminal' (Hanly 1972: 86). Paul Redding on the other hand compares the pursuit of empirical enquiry under circumstances in which Wittgenstein thinks it inappropriate to giving someone demoralised by bereavement a copy of the coroner's report (Redding 1987: 264).

The question these differing views raise is: when may a dismissive attitude to empirical enquiry or its results be justified? When does our situation call for some sort of resolution, epistemic or otherwise, which empirical enquiry is unfitted to provide?

Let me say what conviction I believe frequentation of Wittgenstein's remarks on these topics will induce rather than what I can demonstrate in the course of this chapter. Wittgenstein does not, in general, maintain indefensible views about the limits of investigation and the epistemic powers of reflection; he has a preference for those questions to which reflection is adequate and he detects such an – unacknowledged – preference in others. And so even when he is mistaken about either the limits of empirical enquiry or its dispensability, convincing him of this would have had little effect on his judgement as to its irrelevance.

II

Wittgenstein says that a genuinely religious action (like the rite of succession at Nemi) cannot be explained and that what it calls for instead is 'putting into order what we already know'. These remarks have been held to warrant the charge that he is guilty of both method and limits obscurantism. Is an alternative construal of them possible?

Consider the limits thesis. Baker and Hacker offer a defence:

Wittgenstein does not repudiate the possibility of causal explanation in anthropology. He merely denies their ubiquitous applicability to all questions. How a ritual ceremony developed is one question. What it means is another. (Baker and Hacker 1983: 304)

But can the question of what a ritual means be entirely segregated from an account of its development? Does the Mass, for example, have a meaning independent of how it developed? Aren't there aspects of most rituals whose meaning can only be elucidated by reference to their history? Worse still for Wittgenstein's case against Frazer, isn't this particularly true of the questions Frazer raises with respect to Nemi?

In Alice Ambrose's notes Wittgenstein offers as an argument against the relevance of historical enquiry that a rite 'may have its own complex of feelings' (Ambrose 1979: 33). Why does the fact that a practice has 'its own complex of feelings' preclude the explanatory relevance of history and origins? The first passover meal no doubt expressed a complex of feelings distinct from that of a contemporary pious Jewish household but is not for that reason less explanatory of what goes on on such occasions.

I think Wittgenstein is characteristically masking an epistemic preference as a methodological thesis. It is Wittgenstein's questions and not Frazer's to which historical enquiry may be irrelevant. One of Frazer's two questions about Nemi is why a branch (the golden bough) must be broken from a tree before the combat for the succession to the priesthood can take place. (His other question is, whence this peculiar solution to the problem of tenure.) Even if there were a divergence between the contemporary rationale and the original one this would not preclude its explanatory relevance.

Moreover the Baker/Hacker paraphrase omits the more

problematic feature of Wittgenstein's argument which denies not merely the relevance of historical enquiry but of any empirical enquiry. Wittgenstein says:

the idea of trying to explain the practice is wrong . . . The religious actions of the priest-king . . . are not different in kind from any religious action today, say a confession of sins. This also can be 'explained' (made clear) and cannot be explained. (Wittgenstein 1983: 4)

By his alternative sense of explanation ('made clear') Wittgenstein means made intelligible by assimilation to a practice or inclination of our own. Why cannot a confession of sins be explained but only made clear? If it is the Catholic sacrament which Wittgenstein has in view there is not much about it that can be 'made clear' and quite a lot about it that can only be explained. If you think differently imagine trying to make clear to the Rev. Ian Paisley or a member of the 'wee free kirk' the authority of the priest to absolve by 'relating it to an inclination in themselves'. But it can be explained, even to a non-conformist bigot, though such an explanation would require an exposition of Catholic dogma – the sacrament of ordination and the historical tradition on which its validity depends; just that genre of fact on whose irrelevance Wittgenstein insists.

How then can Wittgenstein uphold a thesis so apparently perverse as that a confession of sins cannot be explained? Perhaps because the case is one where though in possession of the notions of ordination, laying on of hands etc. we are still perplexed by the underlying motive for the practice – perhaps by the piacular impulse itself – so that all that could be done would be to find a point of view from which this impulse seems less alien.

Even when we have removed the most obvious objections to Wittgenstein's thesis that genuinely religious actions can't be explained by imposing some restrictive sense on 'genuinely religious' so that it is confined to more generic features and excludes particular ones like celebrating Passover or receiving communion, it may still not be clear to everyone why the impulse to celebrate, commemorate or atone should be held unexplainable. Might not the ritual impulse be explained as well as the ritual? If not historically, as Lord Raglan insists (Raglan 1949), then perhaps phylogenetically in the way in which Walter Burkert attempts (Burkert 1980: 35–9). I am not sure. What can be safely said is that there are occasions when if we persist with our explanatory questions we lose the sense of what it is we are asking. If we are puzzled as to why the Nemi grove is off limits to horses then informing us that Virbius to whom it is sacred was believed to be an avatar of Hippolytus in whose death horses were implicated relieves our perplexity. But were we to go on to ask why this should be considered a reason for proscribing the grove to horses we would cease to be understood. The pilgrimage to Mecca is a genuinely religious action. The question 'Why Mecca?' asked in ignorance of the fact that Mahomet was born there has a clear sense. The question why a Muslim should want to make a pilgrimage to the birthplace of his prophet has not, and in this sense cannot be explained. (Though it might be 'made clear' even to those without a concept of pilgrimage if they could be brought to see a place of pilgrimage as a relic which due to its size and fixity isn't portable. And if they lack the concept of a relic, too, the practice might have to remain opaque to them.)

If this is the situation we are in with respect to the Nemi rite then the limits Wittgenstein places on the relevance of empirical enquiry may be licit. But is it? Are there aspects of the Nemi rite which, unlike the breaking of the branch, won't give up the secret of their motivation to empirical enquiry? Wittgenstein doesn't record which feature it is he had in mind but only says that like 'any genuinely religious action' it can't be explained. What is it about 'genuinely religious actions' that precludes their explanation but nevertheless permits of their being rendered intelligible?

The reason sometimes given is that this is due to their being expressive rather than instrumental. On this view Wittgenstein assumes the non-instrumental, expressive character of magical/religious rites in general and Nemi in particular. Since they are expressive rather than instrumental there is no means/end nexus to be uncovered *via* an enquiry into the occult belief system which provided the practice with its rationale; therefore if we find it opaque the only method which may relieve this opacity is that of relating their practice to our own inclinations *via* an expressive motive which they can be assumed to possess but whose operation we did not initially recognise (Redding 1987: 258).

If this was Wittgenstein's reason for denying the empirical explainability of the Nemi practice and holding it clarifiable by 'relating it to an inclination of our own' he was doubly mistaken. The contrast between the explainable and the non-explainable but nevertheless clarifiable is not a contrast between the instrumental and the expressive. Making the sign of the cross is just as much in need of and capable of explanation when it is purely expressive (thus on most occasions) as when it is apotropaic and defensive. Not all ritual is as natural and non-conventional as stamping the ground in anger. Furthermore, not all instrumentally motivated ritual is as opaque without the knowledge of its rationalising belief system as is feeding poison to a chicken, say. To take one of Wittgenstein's own examples, indicating to an illness that it should quit the patient is not. The expressive may be opaque and in need of explanation and the instrumental transparent without it (Cioffi 1990). Thus if the argument for the unexplainability of the expressive is not to succumb to a vast class of counterexamples which are blatantly expressive and nevertheless only explainable *via* further information it must be modified to exclude them. What can't or at least need not be explained are those practices which though expressive are not conventional but 'in the nature of instinct-reactions'. For example, the sign of the cross as an expression of piety can be explained (and can only be explained) by adducing historical considerations, but the impulse of which it is a manifestation – the impulse of piety (and the impulse to ritualise it – the ceremonial impulse) – cannot be thus explained. The reason, then, why Wittgenstein thinks Nemi and similar practices can't be explained is not because they are expressive but because he thinks them primal – Ur-phenomenal.

The scarecrow and the snowman. Imagine that we are explaining to someone unfamiliar with either of these phenomena what their place in our lives is. Though both are human artefacts the explanatory tasks they set us are interestingly different. The scarcrow is easy. We just give our inquisitive alien information until he tells us to stop. Maybe he hadn't understood that the field in which the scarecrow stood was under cultivation. Or maybe, though realising this, he was unaware that scarecrows frighten birds or, alternatively, that birds are bad for crops. These are all cases of information-assuagable perplexity and thus there is no occasion for invoking the fact that, as Wittgenstein puts it 'Human life is like that' (Wittgenstein 1983: 3) or that 'we do this sort of thing because this just is the sort of thing we do' (Wittgenstein 1966:

25). The case of the snowman is different. If our alien persisted in his perplexity when once his question as to what kind of creature the snowman was intended to frighten and on behalf of what crop was answered with the statement that snowmen, unlike scarecrows, are not built on behalf of any crop but 'just for the fun of it' as we say, it is hard to think what further information could assuage his perplexity. Is it the material of which the snowman is made that is the problem? Perhaps he finds snow unpleasant to handle and thus finds it difficult to believe that any but a pressing utilitarian motive could account for constructing objects from it? Or perhaps his culture lacks the plastic impulse? If so, do they draw or make designs and might not the need gratified by these activities occupy a place in their lives sufficiently akin to that which induces us to build snowmen to make it clear? ('the importance of intermediate cases').

It is plain that dissipating the perplexity induced by the snowman calls for an entirely different procedure than that called for by the scarecrow – one which is aptly described as 'bringing the practice into connection with an inclination of their own', as when the aliens' graphic impulses are invoked as an intermediate step to the comprehension of our plastic ones. But supposing all this conceded how does it absolve Wittgenstein of obscurantism in his dealings with Frazer's account of Nemi? How epistemically akin is the problem set us by the rite of succession at Nemi to that posed our alien by snowmen? On Wittgenstein's view Frazer mistakenly insists on treating Nemi like the scarecrow and speculating as to its original, instrumental function, whereas it is the expression of a primal inclination such as we can find in ourselves. But is the motive for the killing of the priest-king one which we can understand without an account of its history or of the belief system in which it is embedded?

It might be argued on Wittgenstein's behalf that though we may have no *practice* which stands to Nemi as our own expressive transactions with images to the exotics' expressive effigy burning it doesn't follow from this that there is no *inclination* in ourselves comparable to one which could give rise to the Nemi practice of killing the priest-king. But though we may all be on our thirty-third mandarin how many priest-kings have we imagined ourselves ceremonially killing?

I am not sure how such an issue is to be determined. But suppose

it settled in Wittgenstein's favour: what follows as to the unexplainability of Nemi? At this point the issue of method arises again.
Suppose we come to recognise a primal impulse in ourselves which
could account for the Nemi practice. How without empirical
enquiry are we to establish that it produced the Nemi practice?
What can it show about the veridicality of a proffered rationale that
we can relate it to an inclination of our own? Not, as Rush Rhees
seems to imply, that when we have succeeded in doing so we can
suspend attempts to discover whether we are correct (Rhees 1981:
21)[1]. 'We can make sense of the killing of the Nemi priest without
tracing it to an ancient belief that this would ensure the welfare of
the community (as Frazer implicitly denies)' may be tenable; 'and
therefore the Nemi practice did not derive from such an ancient
belief' is no good.

How can we know that there is no empirically discoverable story
which will make sense of Nemi? This problem doesn't arise for a
limits thesis when the phenomenon is epistemically unambiguous.
We can say *a priori* that Paul Dombey's craving to know 'what the
waves were always saying' was not to be assuaged by oceanographic
inquiries because we know the nature of waves and so that they
weren't saying anything. In the case of the snowman we are able to
state that it is disanalogous to the scarecrow because both practices
are our own. We know what our relation to the snowman and the
scarecrow is; we do not know what the relation of the Nemi community to the Nemi combat is; and so we cannot know that coming
to learn more about it may not confer intelligibility on it in just the
way in which learning the story of Christ's passion confers intelli-

---

[1] In his introduction to the remarks on Frazer Rhees writes: 'we need not go in search of
new facts . . . to understand how there came to be such forms of magic and ritual. All that
we need for this is in our language, in our ways of thought and feeling.' (Rhees 1981:
21). Rhees is either addressing a question other than that raised by Frazer or he is
endorsing an inadequate method for answering it.
  What Frazer's account of Nemi illustrates is not the futility of an empirical method but
the danger of an insufficiently empirical one. It seems that Frazer's ever-anxious, ever-
watchful priest is a poetic figment of Frazer's imagination (Fontenrose 1972; Gaster
1959). The Nemi combat was a festival event in which everything was prearranged except
the outcome of the combat itself (and this was a traditional component of the cult of the
dead). It could be argued on behalf of Wittgenstein's position that even if this is so there
is still something primal about the notion of honouring the dead by killing the living and
if this isn't immediately apparent 'putting into order what we already know' may make
it so. But this still leaves Wittgenstein with an unacceptable method if its aim is to reconstitute the rationale of the ritualists rather than to provide a synoptic view of our own
perspicuity-conferring inclinations.

giblity on the Mass, or being informed of the circumstances of the exodus on the Passover meal, rather than in the way that our kissing pictures of loved ones confers intelligibility on the exotics' expressive burning of effigies and their non-instrumental transactions with images in general.

There is a famous story concerning the time and motion study of an artillery team which revealed that when the piece was fired one member stood by and did nothing. It turned out that he dated from a time when the gun was pulled by horses and it was his task to hold their reigns to prevent their bolting. For Frazer, the Nemi rite is like this idle artilleryman and so only to be rendered intelligible by an enquiry into its history; for Wittgenstein, the horses are still there, only Frazer doesn't know where to look for them. On Wittgenstein's view Frazer's account of the ritual life of mankind systematically neglects the role of an autonomous ceremonial impulse which can make sense of practices like Nemi without knowledge of their historical antecedents. Although there are aspects of the Nemi rite, as of ritual in general, of which this is quite untrue and which call for Frazer's reconstructive procedure if they are to be explained, these aspects do not interest Wittgenstein, e.g., why the priest is forced to fight for this life rather than killed outright; why, that is, the wish to give expression to 'the majesty of death' found its consummation in gladiatorial combat rather than in some other way. Wittgenstein's interest is confined to those more general features of the Nemi practice which may plausibly, if not necessarily correctly, be assigned an a-historical rationale – their need to symbolically enact their relation to 'the terrible, horrible, tragic etc.' – where it is natural to feel 'Human life is like that' – rather than in the particular form their ritual takes.

If we don't make this distinction between rituality and ritual, the ceremonial impulse and particular ceremonies, or one like it, we find ourselves committing Wittgenstein to the indefensible view that, as Brian McGuinness, who appears to find it plausible, puts it, 'it is nearly always possible' to understand primitive rituals 'by bringing in inclinations we ourselves feel' (McGuinness 1982: 37). In fact it is hardly ever possible. Is McGuinness aware of any inclination in himself to determine whether someone is a witch by feeding poison to a chicken? McGuinness continues: 'We feel that we could invent primitive usages.' There is no more reason to think that McGuinness could have invented the Azande poison oracle than that the Azande could have invented the Mass. What McGuinness might have said, on fuller consideration, is that the expressive impulses which manifest themselves in the ritual behaviour of a people are not alien to us though the particular form they take has been shaped by their history and can only be understood by reconstructing that history. (Implicit in Wittgenstein's dealing with these questions is a devaluation of such knowledge when compared to an enhanced grasp of that with which we are a-historically inward – our 'instinct-reactions'.)

That we could imagine primitive practices ourselves is either false or bears a different construction than that which McGuinness places on it. The examples Wittgenstein himself gives (the manner of disposal of Schubert's scores after his death, the relation of a populace to its king) illustrate our inwardness with rituality rather than our ability to reconstitute the particular ritual life of any given portion of mankind. All that Wittgenstein's examples show is that confronted by manifestations of a non-instrumental ceremonious impulse (like the distribution of bits of Schubert's scores among his friends or their destruction by fire) we don't normally require an explanation and not that we can know without investigation why it took the particular form that it did. (Whether this question invariably makes sense is a distinct one.)

Just as we could imagine that 'if fleas had a ritual life it would pertain to the dog' so we could suppose that a people sharing our world but not our history would devise ceremonies oriented towards death and the dead, the sun and the moon, rainfall and harvest, winter and spring, the creatures on which they prey etc., etc. But how can we know without enquiry that any particular rite was actuated by an expressive motive and not, as Frazer holds, by more practical utilitarian ones? We can't. Though 'man is a ceremonious animal', as Wittgenstein says, he is also a superstitious one, and some of us will feel that if there are any rites which we could plausibly be said to invent for ourselves it is those based on the homeopathic principle – if any people at a pre-scientific stage did not feel that there was an intimate occult connection between images and names and that of which they are the images and names this, too, 'could only be an accident, as Wittgenstein puts it. We are thus left with the task of determining which of these inclinations was operative in the case of the Nemi community and only an empirical methodology can determine this. And so, though I don't think Wittgenstein gives us good enough reasons to eschew empirical enquiry if we want a resolution of Frazer's questions as to the Nemi rite, I don't think Wittgenstein himself was addressing such questions alone.

But neither do I think this disposes of the charge of obscurantism, since it arises at another level: Wittgenstein's dismissal of the hermeneutic project for that of self-understanding. 'Why ritual?' may be a more interesting question than 'Why the Nemi ritual?' And it may even be the case that people who are perplexed by accounts of ritual life really want to know the answer to the question, 'Why ritual?' rather than the 'why' of the particular ritual they happen to be reading of. The problem remains however why it should be held that even the general question 'Why ritual?' is resolvable through putting into order what we already know. Does a point arrive at which hermeneutic questions concerning ritual attain to such a level of generality that they become indistinguishable from questions of self-understanding? Where 'why ritual?' and 'Whence our inwardness with ritual?' blend? I don't know how to deal with this. But what is clear is that raising the more general question involves a change of project, one which involves dismissing clearly empirical questions and raising in their stead questions which are as epistemically discontinuous with those raised by Frazer.

III

How much interest can the notion of making clear retain when once it is conceded that its connection with historicity or veridicality is so tenuous – and furthermore, once we recognise that the unintelligibility of the rationale for an exotic practice does not preclude its correctness? Why is it necessary that exotic practices be made intelligible to us? Why does it count against an explanatory enterprise with respect to exotic practices that it may issue in accounts which we do not find perspicuous? Perhaps we should content ourselves with retrieving whatever we can of the rationales for exotic practices without insisting on the kind of understanding Wittgenstein finds desirable. For to insist on understanding in Wittgenstein's sense will often produce misunderstanding. Suppose a people who practised imitative

magic found our practice of kissing the pictures of loved ones puzzling since we obviously did not expect any beneficent effects to
ensue, and one of their number hit on the device of assimilating
it to their practice of instrumental magic by regarding it as an
aborted attempt at a magical action, thus bringing it into line with
a practice of their own. Would they not have misunderstood it in
their endeavour to 'understand' it? And so doesn't our own insistence on relating what is exotic and opaque to our own inclinations run the same risk? If Wittgenstein appears oblivious to these
considerations the reason (or perhaps the cause) is that he
attaches more importance to another enterprise which they do
not undermine.

Wittgenstein's disparagement of Frazer cannot be explained
solely in terms of his believing, either that the question 'Why the
Nemi rite?' can not be answered through empirical enquiry or that
it can be answered without empirical enquiry, but only from his
attaching greater importance to another question than 'Why the
Nemi rite?' – the question how we stand to such practices and how
our feelings about them are to be accounted for ('what makes
human sacrifice deep and sinister anyway?').

One commentator on Frazer writes, quite independently of
Wittgenstein, that 'the key image of the Golden Bough, "the priest
who slew the slayer/and shall himself be slain" corresponds to
some universal principle that we recognize in life' (Hyman 1962:
439). Whether this is so or not, the epistemic task of determining
what 'universal principle' in life it is that we recognise in a practice
is distinct from that of determining the why and wherefore of the
dramatic enactment of this 'universal principle' at any specific
time and place. It seems to be the former task that preoccupies
Wittgenstein. It is what Frazer sets himself to explain and not what
he thinks might explain it that really constitutes 'the mistake' with
which Wittgenstein charges him (Moore 1966: 309). (Just as
Wittgenstein's objection to Freud is not just that he confuses
causes with reasons [in Wittgenstein's distinctive sense of reason –
a 'further description' – something settlable by assent] but that he
prefers causes to reasons. Wittgenstein objects to Freud's explanations of dreams on occasions when Freud is no more addressing
the question what ideas the dream was 'pregnant with' than Frazer
is addressing the question what it is about the Beltane Festival
which 'impresses us'.)

What appears to be a thesis as to the lack of articulation between an empirical procedure, say, the reconstruction of the origins of a ritual, and the question what the survival itself means, is really one as to the superior interest of the question what it means, when this is construed as a question with which the historical enquiry obviously need not articulate – what it means *to us*.

That Wittgenstein is more interested in which ritual practices we could invent for ourselves than in what actually was practised at this place or that becomes blatant when he says at one point that what is 'interesting' is 'what is obvious and what we really know', e.g. 'that what a man sees year in year out all around him influences his thinking' (Wittgenstein 1983: 6); and this kind of fact leaves little scope for investigation but much for reflection, synoptic arrangement and felicitous evocation.

Consider how meagre are Wittgenstein's suggestions as to why the rituals he discusses are practised, as compared with the numerous penetrating remarks he makes as to why we respond to them as we do. He denies that the source of the impressiveness of the fire festivals lies in our conviction of the historicity of Frazer's theory that they are survivals of a rite in which a real man was burnt; he denies that it is the mere suffering of the sacrificial victim which we find 'terrible' and 'sinister' ('illness inflicts just as much suffering without impressing us'); he tells us under which conditions we would find games in which men ride men sinister and under which conditions we would not; he tells us that it is not Frazer's explanation of the Nemi practice which satisfies us but the tone in which he relates it; that practices like Beltane strike us as ancient independently of any evidence we have as to their antiquity; that hearing of such a practice is like discovering that 'on occasion a man can be frightening'; that the fact that they use a cake for lots strikes us as like 'betrayal through a kiss'; that if we credited a prosaic explanation such as that the pretended burning was sadistic horseplay it would rob the rite of its mystery; that a rite in which children burned a strawman would make us uneasy independently of any interpretation offered etc. etc.

What Bernard Williams says without reference to Wittgenstein's remarks on Frazer nevertheless has application to them: '(Wittgenstein is) concerned not so much with . . . the methodology of the social sciences, but with ways of exploring our world view . . . to make a different practice a more familiar idea to us, and

hence to make us more conscious of the practice we have'
(Williams 1972–3: 91).[2]

Wittgenstein belives us to stand to Nemi, Beltane and manifestations of ritual life generally as we do to our aesthetic experiences
(Moore 1966: 306) – like them they may leave us 'intrigued and
wanting to describe' (Wittgenstein 1966: 37). The phrase 'the
majesty of death', which describes Nemi for Wittgenstein, is like
the words for which we grope to evince our aesthetic experiences
and which sometimes succeed in 'summing them up'. It is not to
the point that some of us may find nothing majestic about murder
and particularly murder of as squalid a kind as the Nemi practice
involves (since the lack of real choice makes it more like a cock-
fight than a duel). It is the epistemic character of Wittgenstein's
solution which is at issue here. The Nemi practice, like some music
and some faces, 'seems to be saying something and it is as if we had
to discover what it is that it is saying'. There is nothing
methodologically obscurantist 'about putting into order what we
already know' to resolve this kind of problem. And Wittgenstein
himself says 'of course this is not an explanation. It puts one
symbol in place of another' (Wittgenstein 1983: 3). What some
will nevertheless find obscurantist is Wittgenstein's obtruding this
procedure into what ought to be an hermeneutic inquiry, because
for them the task of self-clarification makes no importunate rival
demand. It would be better if those of us on whom it does from
time to time make such a demand were clearer or more candid
that the connection of the phenomena with our own feelings and
thoughts was of greater moment to us than 'the inner character'
of the phenomena themselves.

IV

Another case where Wittgenstein has been held to provide
grounds for the charge of obscurantism is his dealings with

---

[2] Several commentators have proposed the study of other cultures as a means to a deeper
understanding of our own. Paul Ricoeur's formulation runs 'The central problem of
anthropology is the comprehension of the self through the detour of the comprehension
of the other'. This leaves it unexplained why, if the aim is self-understanding, it is necessary to take 'the detour of comprehension of the other'. Why would not the comparison
of our culture and practices with fabulous rather than actual ones serve as well? It is one
of the more heightened rationales for the cultivation of science-fiction. Why count on the
remote possibility of encountering Mr Spock when we can invent Mr Spock?

Frazer's account of the Beltane festival. Wittgenstein has been charged with either wantonly disparaging the activity of speculative reconstruction ('wantonly' since speculative reconstruction is held the only appropriate response to the question of how the fire festivals came into being) or of arbitrarily dismissing Frazer's question for another which he thinks more interesting – the question why accounts of the Beltane celebrations impress us as they do.

Rhees denies that Wittgenstein holds historical explanation either futile or redundant but only that it can not resolve a question concerning the festivals to which Wittgenstein attaches greater importance. One defence against the charge that it was nevertheless arbitrary for Wittgenstein to substitute his impression question for Frazer's genesis one is that it is Frazer himself who confusedly raises the impression question. 'Frazer misinterprets . . . the nature of his own question' (Redding: 261). In his analogising Frazer's speculations as to the origins of Beltane to the fanciful notion that Siegfried and Brunnhilde were acquainted before they met, Wittgenstein seems to be applying to the case of the fire festivals an idea from Part One of the remarks – 'an hypothesis of development as a disguise for a formal connection'. In invoking an ancient ritual in which human beings were burned in order to explain the Beltane and other fire festivals was Frazer disguising a formal connection? Or was Wittgenstein once again disguising his own lack of interest in empirical issues by projecting it on to the text he is discussing?

The simple coincidence of the hypothesised development connection and the formal connection does not suffice to show that the developmental hypothesis is not just what it at first seems and purports to be. The idea of ritually burning a man may occur in Frazer's accounts of fire festivals because he wants to explain why they should suggest such an idea or because he thinks that the fact that they should suggest such an idea counts in favour of its once being a reality, rather than as a disguised way of making what was immanent in the impression produced by the festivals more blatant. How can a developmental hypothesis which merely coincides with a formal relation be distinguished from a developmental hypothesis which is a disguise for one? With difficulty.

I will give some examples where it is clearer than in the case of Frazer's hypotheses as to the origin of the fire festivals that something more than developmental speculation is going on. Consider

Mario Praz's thesis that some distinctive features of Victorian fiction – in particular the preoccupation of the novels of Dickens, Thackeray, George Eliot and Trollope with domestic and quotidian matters and unheroic characters – owe their existence to the influence of the tradition of Dutch genre painting, as he expounds it in his book *The Eclipse of the Hero in Victorian Fiction*, whose rationale it constitutes. It isn't only the gross implausibility of Praz's thesis in view of the more obvious sources within British literary tradition and social life of the features he purports to explain that makes Wittgenstein's phrase 'a developmental hypothesis as a disguise for a formal connection' so apt a description of Praz's book. It is the way formal relations figure in Praz's exposition of his nominally developmental theses. When he describes the features of the novels it is his purpose to explain, or produces quotations illustrative of these features, we would expect the names of the genre painters or paintings he cites to figure as explanans but this is only rarely the case. Typically they figure as formal terms, 'further descriptions', 'good similes', i.e. as ways of elucidating the impression made on us by the passages under discussion.[3]

Thus there are cases where Wittgenstein's formula finds application. Though Praz's rationale is historical, the staple of his discourse is not, but exemplifies rather the activity Wittgenstein dubs 'putting things side by side'.

There is also a distinct class of cases in which a developmental hypothesis, though not intrinsically crypto-phenomenological, nevertheless could survive its loss of historicity because our real interest is in its formal relation to its explanandum. Consider John Crow Ransom's suggestion that Milton's 'Lycidas' was written smooth and rewritten rough. An examination of the corrections in the manuscript versions showed instead that it was written rough and rewritten rougher. In spite of which Graham Hough found the

---

[3] These are some examples: A scene from *The Mill On the Floss* 'only Peter Fendi could have painted'; 'The tavern conversations in Felix Holt make one think of Brouwer, Teniers and Jan Steen';' Fielding's moral attitude is 'in conformity with the spirit that animated Greuze's family scenes'; Partridge's wife looks exactly like the woman pouring tea in the third engraving of 'The Harlot's Progress'; 'Dickens' eye for the picturesque detail turns his pages into a series of genre pictures'; an episode in *Pendennis* in which a curate drains his glass makes Praz think of 'that scene of sprightly ecclesiastics in the act of raising their wine glasses which inspired so many nineteenth century genre paintings'; the stories of fallen women in Dickens 'find their perfect allegory in Greuze's "L'innocence enchaînée par l'amour et suivie du repentir"'; Peggotty in search of little Emily 'recalls the scenes of Waldemuller, Danhauser and Peter Fendi'.

mistaken thesis valuable: '*Lycidas* contrives to suggest an ideal of perfect formal and metrical smoothness to which it deliberately refuses to conform' (Hough 1966: 167–8). Another case is provided by Walter Pater, who says of the view that some paintings of Botticelli embodied the heretical ideas of Matteo Palmieri (that the human race was descended from those angels who remained neutral in the conflict between Jehovah and Lucifer), 'true or false the story interprets much of the peculiar sentiment with which he infuses his sacred and profane persons'. A more familiar example of the use of an hypothesis as a formal connection, though it was not intended as such, is Kenneth Clark's comment on Freud's explanation of Leonardo's use of the theme of the two mothers, as in his representations of St Anne and the Virgin. Freud thought that Leonardo's childhood contained two mother figures, thus generating 'an unconscious memory of these two beloved beings, intertwined as if in a dream'. Clark finds this 'profound' and says that 'whether true in fact (it) expresses the mood of the picture'. Wittgenstein could have said the same of Frazer's account of the sacrificial origin of the Beltane festival – 'Whether true in fact it expresses the mood of the practice.' But even though Kenneth Clark's formula can be aptly applied to the case of Frazer's account of the origins of Beltane it might still be the case that Frazer intended it to be true, as a hypothesis rather than just felicitous, as a formal relation. There is an important difference between the case where an 'hypothetical link is not meant to do anything except draw attention to a similarity' and one where it is *we* who 'can see the hypothesis as a disguise for a formal connection'. We do not stand to Frazer's invocation of the sacrificial burning of human beings as we stand to Mario Praz's invocation of genre paintings and painters but (at most) as Hough stood to John Crow Ransom's speculations as to the early drafts of 'Lycidas', Kenneth Clark to Freud's account of Leonardo's childhood and Pater to the influence of Palmieri on Botticelli.

Are we entitled to suspect that Wittgenstein's readiness to see a disguise for a formal connection in Frazer's developmental hypothesis is a manifestation of his own indifference to developmental problems and overriding preoccupation with immanent, 'formal' issues in general? Perhaps, but there is another possibility. If Wittgenstein is not being prescriptive in his dealings with Frazer's account of human sacrifice it is not because he is being text-diagnostic but because he is being topic-diagnostic. It may not be Frazer's dealings with survivals like Beltane that show him to be confused in thinking that the historicity of his conjectures is pertinent to the questions he raises but the phenomena themselves, which make epistemically complex demands on us and which we consequently feel ought not to be treated simply as explanatory puzzles.

The right thing to say about Frazer's speculations as to the origin of the Fire-festivals is that though there are no adequate grounds for thinking he was merely disguising a formal connection, the nature of our interest in such matters may induce us to overlook, misread and transform their empirical character in the service of our craving to articulate our impression and bring it to a clearer focus.

v

Does Wittgenstein's denial that aesthetic experiences can be causally explained warrant the imputation to him of an obscurantist attitude towards empirical inquiry?

Wittgenstein says that aesthetic explanations are not psychological explanations but are settled 'in an entirely different way'. Here is an illustration of what Wittgenstein means when he contrasts psychological with aesthetic explanations, or as he also puts it, hypotheses with 'further descriptions'. The fact that Doric pillars look straight because they are slightly convex and that if they really were straight they would look slightly concave belongs to the psychology of perception and not to aesthetics because the objective convexity and straightness of the column is not and is not capable of being a felt determinant of its illusory straightness and concavity respectively. This phenomenon is known as entasis. One dictionary defines entasis as 'the tapering bulge given to a column to prevent the appearance of concave tapering produced by straight sides'. It is obvious why in this sense of entasis it is incapable of figuring in an aesthetic explanation. This straightness of the sides is not capable of being what Wittgenstein calls an 'object of directed attention'. But another dictionary brings out an ambiguity in the notion of entasis in that it can also refer to a perceptible feature of a column: 'Entasis: The gently swelling convex curvature along the line of taper of classical columns. The entasis of columns gives them a sense of elasticity as though they were responding to the load of the entablature above them. Moreover entasis prevents the sense of weakness that results from the illusion of concavity in straight or regularly tapered columns'.

When Wittgenstein denies that an aesthetic explanation is a hypothesis he is so using the term that 'an illusion of concavity results when columns are straight or regularly tapered' is an hypothesis, while 'the appearance of concavity produces a sense of weakness' is not. Nor is the claim that the gently swelling convex curvature gives the column a springy organic look as if responding to the weight of the entablature an hypothesis. But this shows only that we distinguish between aesthetic and psychological explanation and not that there is no articulation at all between them.

David Pears gives an inadequate account of Wittgenstein's antipathy to the causal explanation of aesthetic impressions (Pears 1971: 79–80). Pears thinks that it springs from his belief in the irreducibility of the intentional to the causal. This leaves it unexplained why, if it is the irreducibility of the intentional to the causal that is the source of the irrelevance of empirical enquiry, Wittgenstein should emphasise so insistently the aesthetic character of the explanandum. If the redundancy of causal enquiry lies in the directedness of mind states then it is just as much the case with intentional states which do not have artworks for their objects. On the view I wish to advance the distinctiveness on which Wittgenstein insists is due to the rival demand for articulation and evocation that aesthetic phenomena sometimes make on us.

It would be surprising if as miscellaneous an activity as that of accounting for the experiences produced by art rigorously precluded causal questions from arising and I have said elsewhere why I think Wittgenstein was mistaken to exclude the relevance of causal considerations altogether (Cioffi 1986). The questions that we are in a position to demonstrate as being out of reach of an empirical methodology are not the questions which are normally addressed by those who employ one (Child). So if we are to argue for the irrelevance of such a methodology it is the questions it addresses which must be rejected and not the procedures it employs to resolve them.

Persuading Wittgenstein that he was wrong about the bearing of experiment on statements like that concerning the role of the door's height on the impression made by the facade would not convert him into an advocate of experimental aesthetics, because the unamenability of judgements of this kind to experimental assessment does not exhaust his objections to introducing causal questions into the discussion of aesthetic issues. Wittgenstein is maintaining that we have a tendency to ask for explanations of our experience when what we really want are further descriptions which may confer blatancy on what was immanent to it. The natural form of much aesthetic enquiry is 'What does this experience mean to me?' rather than 'What are its causes?'

The irrelevance of causal enquiry does not rest on its lack of articulation with questions like 'Is it the door's height which is wrong with the facade?' but with questions like 'What does this theme seem to be saying?'. When Wittgenstein says 'If we want to be exact we use a gesture or draw a face' he is evincing a conception of what is called for by an aesthetic experience which precludes causal enquiry, but not because statements which specify objects of directed attention are insulated from empirical assessment. It can't be said that the statement 'If you change this perceptible feature of the work the impression changes' fails to articulate with a question like 'Why do these bars make such a peculiar impression?' in the way that a statement of brain processes does. If Wittgenstein finds it not to the point it is for another reason – that the question it articulates with is not the kind of question that Wittgenstein thinks representative of those which aesthetic experiences naturally prompt.

As an illustration of this division consider one critic's remarks on what he describes as 'the most famous piece of art criticism in English', Walter Pater's account of the impression made by the *Mona Lisa*. After acknowledging that it contains some sentences which are aptly descriptive he continues:

> this is then abandoned for a purely lyric flight, a prose poem bearing only the most tenuous relation to its subject. The extraordinary success of the passage suggests that it manages, perhaps by means of prose cadence and imagery, to express more than a subjective impression, that is, to capture some quality inherent in the picture. One cavils only at its inclusion in the category of criticism . . .

On the view I have been assigning to Wittgenstein not only do devices like the use of 'prose cadences and imagery' to 'capture some quality inherent' in an artwork fall within the category of criticism, they are quite characteristic of it.

We can't derive Wittgenstein's more fundamental objections to Frazer, Freud, Darwin's evolutionary explanations of emotional expression and the prospects of an experimental aesthetics from his diagnosis of a conceptual mismatch between the questions they raise and empirical explanatory enterprises, but only from a devaluation of one class of epistemic enterprises as compared to another (and in some cases from a devaluation of epistemic enterprises altogether (Cioffi 1987)). What sometimes makes empirical enquiry inappropriate is not the failure of articulation between our questions and the answers it can provide but the failure of our questions to express adequately the cravings which prompt them. Though it may not be possible to establish general claims of the form 'Whenever such and such a topic is broached – dreams, exotic rituals, human sacrifice, aesthetic experience, laughter – we must take the discussion in the direction of assent-decidable, overview-assuagable discourse', what we can sometimes show is that empirical investigation does not exhaust what we wish to understand with respect to certain phenomena, and further that on particular occasions we failed to realise this, pursuing investigations irrelevant to our real needs.

We are thus left with the diagnostic thesis: there are occasions when we raise empirical questions whose resolution we can be made to realise is not what we really want, whatever independent grounds there may be for welcoming such resolution; and that we suffer in general from a deep-seated tendency to anticipate from advances in knowledge what can only come from a reconstitution of our problematic perplexities clearly displaying their sources or, when this is insufficient, from some mode of adaptation to them. The problem is that there are cases where this activity of self-clarification seems genuinely to compete for our attention with empirical knowledge of causes and we can't escape decisions as to when an occasion calls for the kind of explanation that makes things clear (and may bring peace) and when for the kind which keeps bridges from falling down.

Perhaps the most we can hope for is greater clarity as to which of these enquiries we are pursuing. Though for some of us the consequences of this clearheadedness will be that certain enquiries will be pursued less vigorously, if at all. In 1930 Wittgenstein wrote:

'If the place I want to get to could only be reached by a ladder I would give up trying to get there. For the place I really have to get to, is the place I am already at now' (Wittgenstein 1980: 7). It is for each of us to determine for ourselves when and to what extent it is the place we are already at which is the place we really have to get to.

REFERENCES

Ambrose, A. (1979) *Wittgenstein's Lectures 1932–5*, Oxford: Clarendon.
Baker, G. P. and Hacker, P. M. S. (1983) *Wittgenstein: Meaning and Understanding*, Blackwell: Oxford.
Burkert, Walter (1980) *Structure and History in Greek Mythology and Ritual*, University of California Press.
Child, Irwin. 'Esthetics' in *Handbook of Social Psychology*, vol. 3 Gardner Lindzey and Elliott Aronson (eds.), Addison-Wesley: London.
Cioffi, F. (1986) 'Aesthetic explanation and aesthetic perplexity' in *The Philosophy of Wittgenstein: Aesthetics, Ethics and Religion*, John Canfield (ed.), Garland: 1986; *From Theology to Sociology*, S. Schanker (ed.), London: Croom Helm.
 (1987–8) 'Explanation, understanding and solace', *New Literary History*, vol. 19.
 (1990) 'Wittgenstein on making homeopathic magic clear' in *Value and Understanding*, R. Gaita (ed.), Routledge: London.
Danforth, Loring (1982) *Death Rituals in Rural Greece*, Princeton, New Jersey.
Fontenrose, J. (1971) *The Ritual Theory of Myth*, University of California: Berkeley.
Gaster, Theodore (1959) Editor's foreword to *The New Golden Bough*, New American Library.
Hanly, Charles (1972) 'Wittgenstein on psychoanalysis' in *Ludwig Wittgenstein: Philosophy and Language*, A. Ambrose and M. Lazerowitz (eds.), London.
Hough, Graham (1966) *An Essay on Criticism*, Duckworth.
Hyman, S. E. (1962) *The Tangled Bank*, Athenaeum: New York.
Lévi-Strauss (1968) *Structural Anthropology*, Allan Lane.
McGuinness, B. F. (1982) 'Freud and Wittgenstein' in *Wittgenstein and his Times*, Oxford: Blackwell.
Moore, G. E. (1966) 'Wittgenstein's lectures in 1930–33', *Philosophical Papers*, Colliers: New York.
Pears, David (1971) *Ludwig Wittgenstein*, Fontana: London.
Mario Praz (1965) *The Eclipse of the Hero in Victorian Fiction*, Oxford University Press.
Raglan, Lord (1940) *The Origins of Religion*, Thinker's Library.

Redding, P. (1987) 'Anthropology and ritual: Wittgenstein's reading of Frazer's *The Golden Bough*', *Metaphilosophy*, vol. 18, nos. 3 and 4, July.

Rhees, R. (1981) Introduction to 'Remarks on Frazer's *Golden Bough*', *The Human World*, no. 3 May.

   (1982) 'Language and ritual' in *Wittgenstein and his Times*, Bryan McGuinness (ed.), Oxford: Blackwell.

Ruidich, N. and Stassen, M. (1971) 'Wittgenstein's implied anthropology', *History and Theory*.

Williams, B. (1972–3) 'Wittgenstein and idealism' in *Understanding Wittgenstein*, Godfrey Vesey (ed.), Royal Institute of Philosophy Lectures, vol. 7.

Wittgenstein, L. (1980) *Culture and Value*, Oxford.

   (1958) *The Blue and Brown Books*: Blackwell.

   (1983) *Remarks on Frazer's Golden Bough*, The Brynmill Press Limited.

   (1966) *Lectures and Conversations*, Oxford: Blackwell.

Ziff, Paul (1980) 'Quote: Judgements from our brain', *Perspectives on the Philosophy of Wittgenstein*, Irving Book (ed.), Blackwell: Oxford.

CHAPTER EIGHT

Wittgenstein on Freud's 'abominable mess'

The 'abominable mess' of which Wittgenstein complains is that of confounding reasons and causes. What does Wittgenstein mean to call attention to by this contrast and why does he think himself entitled to hold that Freud confounded them? Sometimes by reasons he means just what someone says on being asked why he did what he did or reacted as he reacted, and sometimes what an experience meant to a subject on further reflection upon it – its 'further description'.

There is certainly a confusion, in Freud and about him, over the status of explanations invoking unconscious wishes, motives, thoughts, fantasies; but calling it a confusion between reasons and causes is not felicitous and perhaps no brief characterisation could be. Wittgenstein thinks that Freud sometimes falls into confusion (or summons it to his rescue) through denying patients their say on matters on which their say is authoritative and sometimes through according them a say to which they were not entitled. Freud is doing the first when he tells his patients what they really thought or dreamt since this is 'not a matter of discovery but of persuasion' (*Lectures and Conversations* 27) and the second when he treats his patients' acceptance of his empirical explanations as criteria of their validity 'What the patient agrees to can't be a hypothesis' (Moore 1966: 310).

Wittgenstein's formula 'Freud confuses reasons and causes' masks a variety of related but distinct antitheses and this complicates the task of assessing its justice.[1] What Freud is accused of con-

---

[1] For example, in the following remarks a different antithesis is in view. '"Because" and "why" can refer to either a reason or a cause. If a traffic signal acts on you in a manner analogous to a drug, then your explanation of your action is giving a cause. If, on the other hand, you see the red light and act as if someone had said "The red light means stop" then your explanation would be giving a reason'. Here the drug-cause of the stopping isn't even capable of being a reason. Furthermore it is not clear whether when Wittgenstein says 'Freud had genius and could therefore sometimes give someone the reason for his dream' (Moore 1966: 310), the genius in question is the fertility in felicitious further descriptions kind, or of the kind which enabled Poe's Dupin to infer the location of the purloined letter.

founding are, variously, hypotheses with 'further descriptions'; the cause of an impression with 'getting clear about' it, e.g. getting clear about why you laughed; an empirical explanation of a mental state with an account of what was 'at the back of our minds'; science with 'sounding like science' or a 'good way or representing a fact' and 'discovery' with 'persuasion'. Even if I am right in thinking that there is one core antithesis inhabiting most of these expressions – that between that of which we can bethink ourselves and that which we can only learn through empirical inquiry – it is one so problematic that to confound them might seem beyond even Freud's obfuscatory powers. Nevertheless there are specimens which allow us to make the distinction with some confidence and which Freud does confound.

I

This is one of Wittgenstein's accounts of his 'further description' alternative to psychoanalytic dream interpretation construed as a scientific decoding of the dream: 'It's like searching for a word when you are writing and then saying, "That's it, that expresses what I intended!" Your acceptance certifies the word as having been found and hence as being the one you were looking for . . .' (*Culture and Value* 68). We can recognise Wittgenstein's 'further descriptions' in these remarks of Carl Rogers (though Rogers calls them 'inner hypotheses'):

Any datum of experiencing – any aspect of it – can be symbolised further and further on the basis of continuing inward attention to it. (Rogers 1964: 127). Any one who has experienced psychotherapy will have lived through this way of contradicting or sharpening previously held inner hypotheses. Often an example of it in psychotherapy is the way in which the client searches and searches for a word that will more accurately describe what he is experiencing, feeling or perceiving. There is a sense of real relief when he discovers a term which 'matches' his experiencing, which provides a more sharply differentiated meaning for the vague knowing which had been present. (ibid. 111)

This is Wolfgang Koehler making the distinction (in a work that Wittgenstein had read by the time he gave the lectures on aesthetics and psychology):

We ought to distinguish between two things: in some cases the Freudian may be right, while in others people merely fail to recognize their inner states. I am inclined to believe the many observations which the Freudians interpret in their fashion are actually instances in which recognition does not occur. (Koehler 1947: 196)

This is Gustave Ichheiser describing the same phenomenon in a paper in which, like Koehler, he accuses Freud of misrepresenting it:

Our feelings are often peculiarly vague and elusive (so) we have considerable difficulty in describing them correctly . . . We are aware of the innumerable symbolic meanings which permeate our perceptual experience . . . and we must react to them . . . in a peculiarly implicit way . . . What we call insight consists in the ability to make these implicit meanings explicit. (Ichheiser 1970: 141–2)

On Freud's conception of the unconscious, when, for example, Dora spoke of Frau K's 'adorable white body', there was some substrate occurrence in a realm discovered by him which made it true that her remark expressed an homoerotic infatuation rather than an aesthetic appreciation; whereas on Wittgenstein's view there need only have been the manifest character of the utterance and the less manifest features which nevertheless made it the utterance it was and of which the subject was capable of coming to a more explicit cognition. This contrast can also be illustrated in the case of associations. The associations to a dream are epistemically heterogenous. Or, as Wittgenstein puts it, 'Interpretations are not all of one kind. Some still belong to the dream.' In the Wolf Man's nightmare the tree on which the immobile wolves sat was later identified by the dreamer himself as a Christmas tree (Freud 1924: 505). It is natural to mark this distinction by saying that he was indicating a feature of his dream image that was internally related to it, that made the image the image that it was rather than identifying a causal antecedent of it. But it is a distinction that Freud often confounds or ignores.

Here is an example of the confusion which also brings out its affinity to what Wittgenstein objects to in Russell's behaviouristic account of wishing and desiring. One of Freud's paradigms of a manifestly wish-fulfilling dream is his water-quaffing dream. He tells us that he has this dream on nights on which he has eaten anchovies and consequently wakes thirsty during the night, though only after the dream has enabled him to prolong his sleep by providing him with an hallucinatory gratification of his thirst. But it is not the concomitance of thirst-inducing circumstances and water-quaffing dreams that makes these dreams wish-fulfilling; their wish-fulfilling character is intrinsic to them however they came about and whatever their effects are. Freud goes on to say that his water-quaffing dream could not satisfy his need for water as his need for revenge against his friends and colleagues was satisfied by the Irma dream. But we have no more reason to say that Freud's thirst for revenge was assuaged by the Irma dream than his need for water by the water-quaffing dream. Otto's negligence and Dr M's glibness are internal to the manifest content of the dream of Irma's injection just as Freud's water-quaffing was and we have no more reason to think that Freud was any less prone to critical reflections on his two unappreciative colleagues after the Irma dream than that Freud was less thirsty after he dreamt of drinking water. Freud fails to see this because his vocabulary allows him to conflate desire and need, motive and function. The dream which provides him with an hallucinatory satisfaction is wish-fulfilling in quite a different sense from that in which the same dream permits him to prolong his sleep before attending to his wants. The sleeping was not hallucinated.

I will try to convey the feel of this contrast between hypotheses and 'further descriptions' by comparing some specimens of each.

Jung tells the following story to illustrate how the unconscious may influence perception. A poet on a Sunday country walk once expressed unaccountable irritation at some pealing church bells which, though famous for their beauty, he described as ugly and unpleasant. Jung's explanation was that the pastor from whose church the offending sounds came was also a poet but unlike the listener a successful and appreciated one; thus the sound of the bells had activated the listener's 'rivalry complex' and so caused him to perceive the bells as ugly. Contrast the epistemic status of Jung's explanation in terms of an unconscious 'rivalry complex' with the following case. Two English friends were trying to work out why the sound of some church bells at Winchester had so distinctive an effect on their spirits. One remarked that it was because 'their sound was unchanging from age to age' and Chaucer and Shakespeare and Dr Johnson had heard those very same peals. 'One's own tastes's take different forms from age to age but church bells are always the same.' His friend agreed and added, 'And so they recall the transitory expectations of the past and being unchanging themselves promise something that does not pass away.'

Of the plethora of hermeneutic issues that this exchange raises I want to confine myself as far as possible to one. Were the friends advancing causal conjectures? These are my reasons for saying that they were not but that Jung was. It is not just that Jung was entitled to insist on the correctness of his account irrespective of the endorsement of the irate poet, but that we can readily imagine other reasons why the same experience of disagreeableness might have been produced. The reason the bells sounded cacophanous might have been due to rivalry in love rather than poetry, or the displeasing impression might have been due to a complex other than rivalry. By contrast, in the case of the impression made on the two Englishmen the characterisations of the peals proffered were what made the impression the impression it was. We might even prefer to call their remarks elucidations or analyses rather than explanations. Wittgenstein marks this distinction by saying that further descriptions are internally related to the impression they explain whereas hypotheses are externally related to them.

There are instances which are more epistemically ambiguous and where we enjoy a considerable degree of discretion as to which epistemic direction discussion of such remarks is to be taken, though we may be unaware of this until our account of an impression is challenged or our attention called to its ambiguity.

D. W. Harding once suggested that the striking impression made on us by atrocity stories was due to our harbouring, unconsciously, the same impulses, which led to their commission:

People . . . feel what they can only describe – if they are honest with themselves – as the magnetic quality of atrocity stories . . . they find themselves in a state of horrified fascination. This quality of feeling is at its strongest when the atrocities have an admixture of the obscene or sexual. The conscious effect of the story is to arouse pity, indignation or disgust. Unconsciously, however, it has brought up the possibility of committing or suffering such an atrocity ourselves. Any submerged sadistic or masochistic impulses which we may harbour are immediately stimulated. It is this which gives our feelings a special quality. We may find that other crimes – for instance – the conviction of Dreyfus by forged evidence – give rise to equally strong or stronger indignation or pity. But many people find that such crimes claim less compulsive attention than a story of torture and brutal flogging, and a view that is due to some unconscious fascination seems the most plausible that psychology can offer. (Harding 1941: 143)

Harding presents his analysis as a conjecture and in his last sentences appeals to external, empirical considerations. But, though we may have no difficulty in imagining the issue being discussed in empirical terms, reflection also convinces us that as natural a direction for the discussion to take is one in which the linking of our state of 'horrified fascination' with morbid or perverse sexual feelings provokes us to recognise a quality of which we were already peripherally aware so that the case seems more felicitously described as a 'focusing utterance' – one which puts 'into unambiguous words something which has been vaguely "known", suspected or "felt" . . . just outside the focus range of consciousness' (Jones 1968: 95), and so results in our recognising, and not just in our inferring, the sexual quality of our experience.

Our ordinary discourse is often ambiguous with respect to this distinction. 'Meaning is mainly potential', as Frank Ramsey said a long time ago, and it is often for us to decide in which direction to take the discussion. And so, when presented with questions or conjectures as to our feelings or impressions, we may decide rather than determine their epistemic status. It is not possible to say whether, when Eliot's Prufrock asks, 'Is it perfume from a dress which makes me so digress?', it is appropriate to proffer him an hypothesis rather than to help him to get clearer about the relation between the perfume and his digression. And one reason for this ambiguity might be the restriction on our ability to make in practice the distinction it obscures. Though it is clear enough when we are proceeding independently of the say-so of the subject, it is often far from clear, when we decide to consult him, what the epistemic character of his authority to resolve our perplexities with respect to his actions or reactions is. To take a familiar example, when Proust's Marcel asks on the famous occasion of his tasting the tisane-soaked madeleine, what it was about the experience that made him so happy, we are clear what it would be to give an account in a Pavlovian or Skinnerian spirit; but when we restrict ourselves to his own self-deliverances we are not clear at what points, and to what extent, these are based on evidence only adventitiously unavailable to us.

Nevertheless there are also cases where the distinction is clear, and in the lecture in which he accuses Freud of malpractice Wittgenstein presents what he takes to be some. How good are his grounds for saying that Freud confounds them?

In the third of the lectures on aesthetics, Wittgenstein gives two
examples of explanation in terms of unconscious thoughts and
wishes, one in which someone is pushed into a river with unconscious intent, the other in which a woman who has a 'pretty
dream', 'which expressed her joy at having succeeded in passing
through life immaculately', is said to have 'quite lost her liking for
this pretty dream after it had been interpreted' (Freud). This is
what Wittgenstein says about it:

Freud does something which seems to me immensely wrong. He gives
what he calls an interpretation of dreams . . . A patient, after saying that
she had had a beautiful dream, described a dream in which she
descended from a height, saw flowers and shrubs, broke off the branch
of a tree, etc. Freud shows what he calls the 'meaning' of the dream . . .
The coarsest sexual stuff, bawdy of the worst kind . . . Freud says the
dream is bawdy. Is it bawdy? He shows relations between dream images
and certain objects of a sexual nature. The relation he established is
roughly this. By a chain of associations which comes naturally under
certain circumstances, this leads to that etc. Does this prove that the
dream is what is called bawdy? Obviously not . . . Freud calls this dream
'beautiful' putting 'beautiful' in quotation marks. But wasn't the dream
beautiful? I would say to the patient: 'Do these associations make the
dream not beautiful? It was beautiful. Why shouldn't it be?' I would say
Freud cheated this patient. Cf. scents made of things having intolerable
smells . . . You don't say that a person talks bawdy when his intention is
innocent. (*Lectures and Conversations* 23–4)

This is from Freud's account of the flowering branch episode:

The dreamer saw herself climbing down over some palisades holding a
blossoming branch in her hand. In connection with this image she
thought of the angel holding a spray of lilies in pictures of the
Annunciation – her own name was Maria – and of girls in white robes
walking in Corpus Christi processions when the streets are decorated
with green branches. Thus the blossoming branch in the dream without
any doubt alluded to sexual innocence . . . However, the branch was
covered with red flowers each of which was like a camellia . . . Accordingly
the same branch which was carried like a lilly and as though by an innocent girl was at the same time an allusion to La Dame Aux Camelias who,
as we know, usually wore a white camellia except during her periods when
she wore a red one (Freud 1954: 354)

What is it which Freud does which is 'immensely wrong'?
Though Wittgenstein felt that it was wrong of Freud to imply the

incompatibility of the dreamer's sense of the beauty of this episode with its unconscious meaning, this is unlikely to be all that he objected to, since not all dreams are beautiful and the objection would not have the generality which it obviously is intended to have. What does have generality is the assumption that the associative connections which explain the appearance of the dream image also constitute its meaning and thus undermine the dreamer's own account of this meaning.

David Pears takes Wittgenstein's thesis to be that though the 'path through the complicated maze of the dreamer's associations may lead him to an interpretation of his dream this does not prove that this is what his dream must have meant or even that it had any meaning at all' (Pears 1970: 195). This formulation leaves open several possibilities (as do Wittgenstein's own remarks). I think the pertinent one is that dream images, utterances, episodes may have a sense which is not the sense that the psychoanalytic procedure, conceived as an objective method of inquiry, uncovers and that it is in failing to assist in the elucidation of this sense of the dream and even undermining it by persuading the dreamer that it was Freud's psychoanalytically inferred one that was its real meaning, that Freud cheated.

Wittgenstein holds that a causal connection between the flowering branch and repressed ideation involving the phallus, say, is not enough to make the phallus the meaning of the branch or what the branch 'really' stood for. What is 'immensely wrong' then is not that the connections uncovered by Freud's methods are 'fanciful pseudo-explanations', as Wittgenstein puts it elsewhere, but rather that Freud has adopted a convention according to which, when certain evidential conditions are fulfilled, it is to be said of the patient that in dreaming her dream she was having such and such thoughts; but the patient is not informed of this convention, she is only informed as to what she was 'really' thinking, dreaming etc. (Freud did something similar with the term memory in the early expositions of the infantile aetiology of the neuroses. Only after repeated attempts at paraphrase does it become clear that when Freud says that his patients had such and such memories of remote infantile events, often he only means that he is convinced of the historicity of certain images which the patient 'produces' in the course of the analysis so that even when the patients deny any recall of the events in question they are to be described as having remembered them.)

Freud writes: 'The ugliest and most intimate details of sexual life may be thought and dreamt of in seemingly innocent allusions' (Freud 1949a: 382). It is Wittgenstein's view that whatever the role of these ugly and intimate details in the production of the dream through which they were detected, it did not constitute either the thinking or the dreaming them. ('The dream is not bawdy; it is something else.') Hanly (1972: 93) says, 'Wittgenstein had to reject the idea that anything could be taking place in the mental life of the individual of which he was not aware at the time.' This is not Wittgenstein's view. What is correct to say is that Wittgenstein rejects the idea that anything 'taking place in the mental life of the individual of which he was not aware at the time' could be the meaning of that of which he was aware. Consider for example Freud's treatment of the theme of masturbation. Freud says of the flowery dreamer's request to 'take one too', of some branches which had been cut down and to which people were helping themselves, that she was asking whether she might masturbate. I think that Wittgenstein's objection here is that whatever the causal influence of the German idiomatic expression for masturbation on the wording of her request she cannot be described as asking for permission to masturbate. The dream narrator's sentences cannot be given a meaning other than the meaning she gives them.

Consider the sentence, 'Father I am burning', from the dream of the burning child. Freud invokes a rule according to which sentences heard in dreams must be based on sentences heard while waking and advances a plausible conjecture as to when this sentence was addressed by the child to its father. Now, the question what this sentence meant on such occasions and whether these were indeed a *sine qua non* of its occurrence in the dream are distinct from the question what it meant to the dreamer or dream narrator. We can imagine that the dream utterance has quite another significance for the dreaming, or dream-telling, father attempting to fathom his child's words. Reflection on this significance would take us in a different direction from that of Freud's conjectural causal origins.

But Wittgenstein's other example of the cause/reason distinction does not serve him as well as that of the flowery dream. He asks us to consider the following case. While walking along the river with his friend, Taylor, Taylor extends his arm and pushes Wittgenstein into the river. Taylor believes it to have been an accident, his intention in extending his arm was to point out a church spire. The psychoanalyst says it was due to unconscious hostility seizing on the occasion as a pretext for pushing Wittgenstein in the river. How are these two accounts related to each other and what would confusing them amount to? This is Wittgenstein's view: 'Both explanations may be correct. Here there are two motives – conscious and unconscious. The games played with the two motives are entirely different. The explanations could in a sense be entirely contradictory and yet both be correct' (*Lectures and Conversations* 23).

Though the expression 'in a sense' weakens Wittgenstein's compatibility thesis it does not weaken it sufficiently. The games played with the two motives are not 'entirely different' since both are used to answer the question why Wittgenstein was pushed into the river and one denies that he was. Though there may be occasions when Freud treats his explanations as undermining the correctness of the subject's own account of matters where he has not the authority to do so and so might be thought to confuse two 'games' this is not one of them. How can we distinguish between these occasions?

Unlike the image of the flowering branch, the experience of pushing Wittgenstein into the river had no interest such as invites further description. If Taylor had been asked not why he pushed Wittgenstein into the river but what his feelings toward Wittgenstein were, we would once again be addressing issues for which an eligible course might be reflection and its elaboration rather than hypothesis and empirical inquiry. Earlier in the lecture Wittgenstein had argued that if someone finds a facade displeasing and wonders why, then the statement 'if the height of the door were altered you would no longer find it displeasing' is an inappropriate answer because what the enquirer wants is to get clearer as to what was at the back of his mind when he found the facade (or the door) displeasing. Even if this is right, can we say anything analagous of the question why Taylor extended his arm, thus pushing Wittgenstein into the river? As it stands the pointing/pushing example is not suited to bringing out the rival interest that the non-causal 'further description' question might have. Taylor did not stand to it as the flowery dreamer to the image of the flowering branch. Suppose that Taylor stood to the point-ing/pushing episode in an epistemic relation like that in which the flowery dreamer stood to the camellia sprouting branch – it seemed to be saying something and it was as if he had to discover what it was that it was saying and this finally precipitated out as a reminder of the precariousness of life, the abrupt transformation of an idyllic riverside walk with a church spire on the horizon into a companion's drenching with the risk of worse. Then we would have something of which we could say 'an entirely different game' was being played.

Thus far I have argued that, though Wittgenstein was mistaken as to how the action of the pointer/pusher is to be described in the light of its psychoanalytic explanation, he has some ground for his objection to Freud's comments on the flowery dream. On the psychoanalytic view, Freud, in uncovering the nocturnal transac-tions between the unconscious ideas and images of phalluses, menstruation, courtesanship, masturbation and the dream image of the camelia-sprouting branch, is not confusedly by-passing the subject's question as to the meaning of her dream for one about its causal conditions – he is answering it: his knowledge of the mechanism of dream-formation permits him to explain the dream while simultaneously informing the dreamer what she 'really' had dreamt, what thoughts she was expressing, what states of affairs she was unconsciously entertaining, though this is not what we nor-mally mean by expressing thoughts or entertaining images.

In his 1933–4 lectures Wittgenstein said that though Freud had really discovered 'phenomena and connections not previously known' he talked as if he had found 'unconscious hatreds, voli-tions, etc., and this is very misleading because we tend to think of the difference between a conscious and unconscious hatred as like that between a seen and unseen chair' (Moore 1966: 304). And in the 1938 lecture Wittgenstein says the flowery dreamer did not 'really' have the thoughts imputed to her by Freud though he got her to believe that she had. What, short of being aware of them, would constitute 'really' having them? Wittgenstein is more toler-ant of such innovation in the *Blue Book* where he says of the state-ment that someone has unconscious toothache, when used to refer to the fact that he suffers from tooth decay without accom-panying pain, that 'there is nothing wrong about it' but 'that it is only a new convention' (*Blue Book* 23).

One reason Wittgenstein may have objected to Freud's thinking that he had discovered a new class of happenings – unconscious thoughts, feelings, etc. – is that those who did not explicitly recognise the conventional component in this discovery will forget its status and think there is some other way in which someone can have toothache than either his feeling it or having a decayed tooth. They will think that with the help of psychoanalysis he can eventually come to stand to his unconscious toothache – the toothache he does not feel at the moment – in the same relation in which he stands to his conscious toothache – that he can come to remember having had it, after all – thus enabling them to dispense with evidence that his tooth was in a state of decay, and even with clarifying the sense in which someone who does not feel toothache and does not have a decayed tooth may nevertheless have toothache. ('The new expression misleads us by calling up pictures and analogies which make it difficult for us to go through with our convention' (*Blue Book* 23).)

But Wittgenstein seems to have a more absolute, less pragmatic, objection to the idioms in which Freud communicates his discoveries as to his patients' unconscious ('This ugly explanation makes you say you really had these thoughts whereas in any ordinary sense you really did not.') What has the dreamer been cheated into accepting about her thoughts when she agrees that she really had them though she was not aware of having them? We get a better grasp of the character of Wittgenstein's misgivings on this point if we ask ourselves how we are to imagine an unconscious thought. Suppose we begin with a conscious fantasy, what must we think away for it to be an unconscious fantasy? What can we subtract from our conception of it as conscious which, while rendering it unconscious, still leaves it thought or fantasy? We qualify our thoughts in all sorts of ways in which it makes no sense to qualify something of which we are not conscious. But to preclude any talk at all of unconscious thoughts would, in view of the extraordinary scope of the term 'thought', be peremptory as well as inconsistent with the permissiveness of the Blue Book: 'Should we say that there are cases where a man despises another man and does not know it; or should we describe such cases by saying that he does not despise him but unintentionally behaves towards him in a way, speaks to him in a tone of voice, etc. etc. which in general would go together with despising him? Either form of expression is correct . . .' (*Blue Book* 30).

Perhaps Wittgenstein felt that what he conceded of attitudes like
despising does not apply to dream interpretations because we can
imagine someone who was unaware of despising another nevertheless behaving 'in a way . . . which in general would go together
with despising him' (*Blue Book* 30). We do not know what it would
mean to say of one of Freud's dream interpretations (much more
elaborate than the dream itself) that the person whose dream it
was behaved in a way which generally went along with dreaming
dreams with that particular latent content. But suppose we simplify
matters by restricting the interpretation to one dream image – that
of the flowering branch. There is a famous case which is representative of a class of cases in which a literal mode of expression
seems justified – Morton Prince's patient with a phobia for church
bells of which she could give no account: 'While she was narrating
some irrelevant memories of her mother the hand wrote rapidly
as follows . . . "I prayed and cried that (my mother) would live and
the church bells were always ringing and I hated them." This last
sentence was accompanied by anguish and tears quite incongruous with her oral narration' (Prince 1913: 40). Do not we want to
say of this kind of case that here the picture Freud encourages of
unconscious thoughts as behind or alongside the conscious ones
finds application? But can we transfer the natural implications of
Prince's account to cases like that of the flowery dreamer and so
say that while she dreamt that she was holding a flowering branch
she was really grasping an erect phallus just as Agave was really
holding her son's head? I am not sure.

In Prince's bell-phobia case there was accompanying 'expression–behaviour' appropriate to the unconscious thought – not so
with the flowering branch. If we decide to forego such 'expression–behaviour', it may involve us in commitments which, when
we became aware of them, would cause us to backtrack and
concede that we ought not to have said that, in those circumstances, someone had thoughts but did not know it, or believed
they were thinking about one thing when they were really thinking about another, or thinking one thing about it when they were
really thinking another thing about it. We are not clear as to when
a new fact about a psychological state authorises us to redescribe
its intentionality. If I have understood Wittgenstein's objection
then, 'An unconscious wish to have sexual intercourse caused you
to dream of watering a garden', is unobjectionable ('connections

not previously known'). Whereas 'Your dream of watering a garden was really about making love' amounts to cheating. But need it? 'Someone only thought that he was pointing out something to a companion but really was pushing him' is not, as Wittgenstein implies, cheating. We need not confine ourselves, as he would have us ('two entirely different games'), to 'His wish to push his companion into the water caused him to extend his arm at the first plausible pretext thus pushing him into the river but it is nevertheless true, as he himself believed, that he was pointing.' Can we assimilate the dream image to the pointing and hold that Wittgenstein was wrong about this too?

We see why it would be misleading to say that since the perfume was 'made from things having intolerable smells' it really stank, but the issues raised by Wittgenstein with respect to the flowery dream are much less clear. Suppose the dreamer was addressed as 'Violetta' (the name La Dame aux Camelias bears in Verdi's opera), would not that entitle us to something stronger than just a causal connection between the camellia-sprouting branch and 'La Dame aux Camelias'? Is not the stench breaking through? There are closely related issues here, one as to what, if anything, would entitle us to speak of someone having unconscious thoughts, feelings, etc., and the other what this implies about the experience of which the analytically uncovered one was the unconscious substrate. When can I say not only that at some stage she had the unconscious thoughts of an erect phallus but that in entertaining the image of the flowering branch she was unconsciously entertaining a state of affairs involving an erect phallus – i.e. that the branch was really a phallus?

The latter issue may be like that which leads people to object to the statement 'Water is H_2O' (D. H. Lawrence, Michael Oakeshott and Wittgenstein himself). And the solution may be the same as that suggested by Lawrence in the case of water. Just as Lawrence concedes that 'alert science' is not reductionist and does not intend 'Water is H_2O' to be a denial of the reality of the phenomenal qualities of water, neither need an 'alert' psychoanalysis be reductionist. This still leaves the problem of the precise content of an imputation of unconscious thoughts stripped of reductionist implications. The presuppositions of Freud's theory of dreams is that in the course of the night the dreamer had such and such thoughts of which she was unaware and which when subjected to certain translations of which she was also unaware became the manifest dream which she relates on waking.

Suppose we get rid of the special epistemic difficulties attaching to the imputation of thoughts to a dreamer (*Zettel* 71–2) and apply Freud's interpretation to the dreamer's associations instead. Let us suppose that, as often happens, the flowery dreamer had a vague sense of the significance of the blossoming branch but only after some hesitation and effort was able to formulate it in the words, 'It is as if I were the angel Gabriel in pictures of the Annunciation', or – in a way which is characteristic of dream-talk – 'as if I were both the angel transmitting God's message to the Virgin and the Virgin receiving it as well as one of the white-clad little girls walking in the Corpus Christi procession'. This was the 'development of the ideas' with which the episode of the blossoming branch was 'pregnant' as Wittgenstein puts it in the 1948 entry on dream interpretation (Culture and value, 68). Now let us replace Freud's causal story as to how the flowering branch image arose during the night and substitute a causal story as to why the association to the Annunciation scene arose during the dream narration – so: flowering branch (conscious) – erect phallus (unconscious) – lily stalk held by the Angel of the Annunication and thus sexual purity (conscious). Though the sequence I have described may not warrant the strong conclusion that in thinking of the lily stalk she was thinking of a phallus, surely it warrants the claim that at some stage she thought of a phallus?

How much of what we mean when we speak of someone having thoughts carries over into our talk of unconscious thoughts may be an issue too ambiguous or nuancé for resolution. It may be like that which arises when one Catholic feels from some turns of phrase used by another, together with his general attitude, that he is badly instructed and entertains misconceptions as to the sense in which the consecrated host is simultaneously the body and blood of Christ. Or like that between realists and idealists as to how best to speak of the furniture in deserted rooms.[2]

---

[2] There are remarks in Freud which Wittgenstein might have found conciliatory had he known of them. In *New Introductory Lectures* Freud says of the unconscious processes which bring about symptom formation that he 'dare hardly call them thoughts' (Freud 1933: 29). And in the *Outline* he says that the occurrence of unconscious thoughts is something of which 'we are totally unable to form a conception' (Freud 1949b: 66). On the other hand, he does intermittently phenomenalise the unconscious, implying that

III

Even if Wittgenstein were wrong in thinking that it is necessarily mistaken for Freud to describe himself as having literally discovered the existence of unconscious thoughts, feelings, volitions, etc., there is still a distinctive feature of Freud's account of the unconscious which warrants the charge of confusion. This is Freud's view that the agent's original account is to be superseded by the psychoanalytic account through some species of introspection in spite of the fact that complete subjective ignorance intervenes between the original occurrence of the unconscious thought and its recognition.

In the sixth of the Introductory Lectures Freud assimilates the anamnesis of an hypnotic subject for his experiences during the trance state to the dreamer coming to understand the meaning of her dream ('exactly similar'). But of course these cases are not even roughly similar. Those who come to accept a psychoanalytic interpretation of their dreams do not do so because they come to remember transforming the latent dream content into the manifest dream. And though they may recollect wishes corresponding to the latent dream thoughts, they do not locate them in the night during which they dreamt their dream but in their waking life.

The problem this raises is not that of reconciling explanations invoking unconscious motives with those in which we normally privilege the subject's own account of matters, but of explaining how their unconscious antecedents can be out of reach of introspection at the time of their occurrence and yet, thanks to psychoanalytic technique, later recalled along with their causal role in the episode they explain. Freud cites in support of this possibility the phenomenon of post-hypnotic compliance. The fact that someone who has responded to a cue by obeying an hypnotically implanted suggestion and denies he knows why, or gives a spurious reason for his action, can nevertheless later realise why, is said to be proof that someone may know something without knowing that he knows it (Freud 1949: 84–5). But what is it that the post-hypnotic subject can

what we now see through a glass darkly, we may under favourable conditions see face to face. In *New Introductory Lectures* he also writes: 'certain practices of mystics may succeed in upsetting the normal relation between the different regions of the mind so that the perceptual system becomes able to grasp the relations in the deeper layers of the ego and the id which would otherwise be inaccessible to it' (Freud 1933: 106).

be said to know? We have no subject protocols of what this knowing is like, i.e., on what the subject's conviction of understanding the behaviour which was formerly misunderstood or opaque to him is based. So let us ask instead what Freud thought was going on and whether we can make sense of it. Why did Freud think the subject was later entitled to say that he knew why he had earlier taken off his shoe, or whatever the hypnotically implanted order was? What Freud's argument in favour of the validating role of belated avowal requires is that the subject finally recalls taking his shoe off in compliance with an order. But what sense can we make of someone now remembering something he truthfully denied being aware of at the time? What we can conceive the subject finally remembering is the occasion of the hypnotic order itself, thus enabling him to make sense of his formerly opaque or implausibly accounted for action, by *inferring* that it was due to the hypnotist's command and his expressing this by saying he 'now knew' why he did it.

This avoids the incoherence involved in remembering the never experienced – but at a cost – since Freud assimilates the production of dreams and symptoms to compliance with a post-hypnotic order. For even if there was some phenomenological equivalent to the recall of the post-hypnotic order in the case of dreams or symptoms, something essential would be lacking for them to be relevantly analogous. Our grounds for crediting the veridicality of the patients' anamnesis would be missing. In the case of the post-hypnotic order, we were there: we saw and heard. Nothing like this is available in the case of the dream work or the symptom work. Thus the justice of Wittgenstein's remark, 'We are likely to think of a person's admitting in analysis that he thought so-and-so as a kind of discovery which is independent of his having been persuaded by an analyst . . . this is not the case'. (*Lectures and Conversations* 27).

Freud's incoherent invocation of the 'ultimate' say-so of the subject is not a mere excrescence which could be removed by simply adopting a version of psychoanalysis which restricts the use of the subject's endorsement as a method of validation. The content of many of his most distinctive and characteristic imputations and explanations, e.g. the full statement of the latent dream thoughts, is too elaborate to be linked to behavioural criteria while at the same time being too elaborate to have lurked unnoticed at the back of our minds. They demand anamnesis and are yet incapable of it.

Consider Freud's surmise that though, at the time Dora slapped Herr K when sexually importuned by him, she thought it was from outraged propriety, it was really from affronted vanity and jealousy at her recognising in Herr K's words, 'I get nothing from my wife', the same formula he had used when attempting to seduce their governess ('what, thought you, dare he treat me like a servant'). The reason that we can credit the confirmation of Freud's reconstruction by Dora's belated acknowledgement is that, in this case, at the time of the slap Dora had no opportunity to deny that these were her feelings. This is not the case with 'the scornful doubt and denial' of the bedtime ritual girl of Introductory Lectures 17, say, and it is this kind of case which is more representative of Freud's procedure (and which the concept of resistance was introduced to rationlise.)

In his unpublished University of Virginia lectures, John Wisdom deals with the shock produced by the notion that an explicit denial might intervene between the subject's recognition of a mental state of affairs and his initial obliviousness to it by arguing that Freud has merely shifted the subject's authority, in a way familiar to us from folk psychology, to a further point along what Wisdom calls the 'corrigibility scale'. But even if this were conceded it would not resolve the problem which many of Freud's instances of patient-avowal as a criterion of validation present – hatred such as the Rat Man was held to have felt for his father, for example. Should he ever have come to recall it after such persistent denial we would speak not of ignorance but of hypocrisy and, if precluded from speaking of hypocrisy, we would deny his admission any probative value at all. Sartre is among those who have pointed out the incoherence which results from combining Freud's objectivism with the validating role of the patient's acknowledgment: 'Though the testimony of the subject is precious for the psychoanalyst . . . the sign that he has reached his goal . . . nothing in his principles . . . permits him to understand or to utilize this testimony' (Sartre 1962: 56–7).

The question of the limits of corrigibility raises issues too particular for demonstration. There are no simple conceptual truths to be appealed to. We cannot issue a general proscription on the imputation of mind-states on the basis of the patient's later acceptance where these were earlier denied. We can only say that belated recognition is incompatible with a certain kind of denial, or with a certain kind of content, or with a certain kind of denial coupled with a certain kind of content. These distinctions are rooted in our practices which place unformalisable limits on what we can intelligibly say. We can only discover that we are being over-restrictive by denying it and seeing what others have to say for it. Thus I say that we can imagine Dora coming to realise that the big book she was reading in the dream was an encyclopaedia (as Freud maintains) but not that, though she dreamt that she read it calmly, she now remembers that she read it agitatedly (as Freud also maintains).

There is an additional limit on the appropriateness of self-validation and one which is stronger than the ignorance which is incoherently superseded by knowledge. It has to do with the nature of the explanandum rather than the subject's epistemic state with respect to it. Freud says of one patient:

I was curious to discover whether [her facial neuralgia] would turn out to have a physical cause. When I began to call up the traumatic scene the patient . . . described a conversation with her husband and a remark of his which she had felt as a bitter insult. Suddenly she put her hand to her cheek, gave a loud cry of pain and said: 'It was like a slap in the face . . .' There is no doubt that what happened was a symbolization. She had felt as though she had really been given a slap in the face . . . the sensation of a slap in the face came to take on the outward form of a trigeminal neuralgia . . . afterwards it could be set going by associative reverberations from her mental life. (Freud 1895: 178–9)

Here we have Freud addressing a question which calls for an hypothesis by advancing an hypothesis. Where then is the confusion? It does not lie in any incongruity between the question and the answer but only follows from Freud's commitment to self-intimation as a mode of validation. If Freud thinks that the causal relation of the simile '. . . like a slap in the face' to the hysterical symptom it explains can be determined as its felicity as a 'further description' of the state of mind which prompted it can be determined then he *was* confusing reasons and causes. Those philosophers who have seen no anomaly in Freud's commitment to belated introspection as a mode of validation were momentarily amnesic for the fact that the concept of the unconscious grew out of attempts to explain non-intentionalist phenomena like pains, paraesthesias, contractures, paralyses and convulsions (Cioffi 1974: 344–5).

The epistemic predicament of the flowery dreamer can be used to illustrate the contrast which Freud is accused of obscuring between hypothesis and further descriptions, between problems which require investigation and those which will yield to reflection. Consider the concluding portion of the dream in which the dreamer rebukes a young man for embracing her and he assures her that it is permissible. Might not an image from the sphere of sexual life stand to this episode in a more epistemically direct way than as the outcome of an inferred nocturnal transformation of the ideas of a courtesan and a phallus into that of a flowering branch? Might not the relation be rather the same as that in which the flowering branch stood to the Angel of the Annunciation – as an idea with which the dream was pregnant 'precisely in virtue of acknowledging it as such' (68e).

Even that portion of the dream which the dreamer associated with the Annunciation may well have been concerned with sexuality without its being the case that it was the causal connection between either the flowering branch and unconscious ideation pertaining to phalluses, or between the red camellias and the courtesan/heroine of Dumas fils' play which entitled us to say so, but a quite different consideration, one which locates the theme of sexual deprivation and temptation among the ideas with which the dream episode of the flowering branch was pregnant. For how could the dream 'express her joy at having passed through life immaculately' (Freud 1954: 319) – loosely speaking, presumably she consummated her marriage – without simultaneously containing the theme of sexual dissoluteness or at least of a grand passion like that of La Dame aux Camelias? On this view Freud's fault would then have not been that he produced an ugly interpretation of a beautiful dream (which some have taken Wittgenstein's central objection to be), but that (at least with respect to the general theme of sexuality) he behaves like a dishonest taxi driver who takes one by a gratuitously long route to a destination which was round the corner. In general what Freud does which is 'immensely wrong' is to ignore the themes implicit in the manifest content of the patient's communications and to insist that the meaning of the dream is only to be found with the help of his theory of dream formation.

There is, thus, much this woman's dream would have taught her about herself and her relation to her sexuality without embarking on a causal investigation of the images it contained – 'the whole thing could have been treated differently'. Psychoanalytic dream interpretation loses much of its interest if the preoccupations or wishes in whose service the dream is said to have been enlisted are accessible without these interpretations. (The empirical case for the dispensability of Freud's 'deep' interpretations is made in Fisher and Greenberg (1977: 63–74).)

Of course such a procedure ignores the theme of guilt over infantile masturbation in which Freud finds the true meaning of the dream, but in doing so it ignores just that component in dream interpretation which Freud both asserts and denies is accessible to the dreamer, and whose veridicality we have no way of determining; that is, it evades the 'abominable mess'.

IV

Wittgenstein has a further reason for his charge of confusion. Freud was mistaken to proffer hypotheses at all and not just to misconstrue them as revelations as to what the patient was 'really' doing, thinking or saying. And if this encounters the objection that, when we are dealing with the kind of matters which brings people to analysts, hypotheses are precisely what we want, then a reply is possible along the following lines: the matters which bring people to analysts are epistemically miscellaneous and many of them, including many broached by Freud, are appropriately addressed by reflection. If we replace joke-laughter or dream-impression, for which Wittgenstein holds empirical explanation inappropriate, by the states of mental distress that neurotics typically give accounts of – feelings of helplessness, worthlessness, abandonment, isolation, rage – does Wittgenstein's notion that to advance hypotheses with respect to them is a sign of confusion necessarily lose its plausibility?

An ambiguity dogs the concept of self-understanding as it figures in enterprises such as attempting to understand the sources of our unhappiness, the nature of our aspirations, the precise content of our regrets, disappointments, apprehensions, remorse, self-felicitations, anger. These expressions can be understood in such a way that empirical enquiry bears on them, or so that it does not. In which of these senses is Freud deploying the notion? It is the diversity of answers that have been given to this question which suggests that we are dealing with a mess.[3]

Joseph Wortis was an American psychiatrist who had a short training analysis with Freud in 1933 and has left a record of the experience. One episode in particular is instructive for what it reveals about the epistemic character of the expectations aroused by Freud and his intermittent repudiation of these expectations. On one occasion Wortis had a dream in which he asks of someone who had had a psychotic breakdown whether they had manifested their latent homosexuality during it. Freud propounded an interpretation of this dream which Wortis found unconvincing and which moved him to offer his own: 'Why not say that it showed an anxiety that I would show homosexual traits if I ever became psychotic?' 'That is your idea,' said Freud. 'It would be nothing new. You knew that before. I was telling you something you did not know before because it was unconscious. You still have not learned the meaning of the term "unconscious".' On another occasion Freud remonstrates with Wortis for doubting an interpretation on the grounds that he 'did not in the least feel that way': 'The trouble is that you probably do not believe in the unconscious; you still expect to find an agreement between a dream interpretation and your conscious thoughts.' (Wortis 1954: 103). The conception of his task Freud evinces in this anecdote is remote from that which he expresses at other times and which is assigned him by his hermeneutic and humanist admirers and is unlike what Allen Bergin calls 'accurate empathy': 'responding to client affect just below the surface and labelling, identifying or emphasizing it' as contrasted with 'making connections between past and present, being diagnostic or theoretical, or telling the patient about feelings he 'really has' when he is not experiencing them.' And yet Bergin goes on to say that 'it is very difficult to distinguish between the technique of "accurate empathy" and what some analysts call "good interpretation"' (Bergin 1966: 24). To the extent that this is so, 'good interpretation' is not properly psychoanalytic and is not even appropriate where the problem the patient presents calls for explanation rather than clarification.

---

[3] Freud himself invokes his aesthetic explanations as elucidatory of the character of his psychopathological ones. In the case history of the Rat Man he assimilates ellipsis as it occurs in obsessional thoughts to ellipsis in jokes.

To see how Wittgenstein's confusion thesis sets limits to psychoanalytic explanatory pretensions, while at the same time setting
limits on the appropriateness of a procedure in which such pretensions were candidly abandoned, consider his remarks on dream
interpretation in a notebook entry for 1948:

We might think [of Freudian dream interpretation] in the following way:
a picture is drawn on a big sheet of paper which is then so folded that
pieces which do not belong together at all in the original picture now
appear side by side to form a new picture . . . (This would correspond to
the manifest dream, the original picture to the latent dream thought).
Now I could imagine that someone seeing the unfolded picture might
explain 'Yes, that's the solution, that is what I dreamt, minus the gaps and
distortions.' This would then be the solution, precisely in virtue of his
acknowledging it as such. What is intriguing about a dream is not its
causal connection with events in my life but rather the impression it gives
of being a fragment in a story . . . What's more if someone shows me that
this story is not the right one: that in reality it was based on quite a different story, so that I want to exclaim disappointedly 'Oh! So that's how it
was!' it is really as though I have been deprived of something. The original story certainly disintegrates now as the paper is unfolded . . . but all
the same the dream story has a charm of its own like a painting that
attracts and inspires us. The dream affects us as does an idea pregnant
with possible developments. (*Culture and Value* 68)

Let us assume, as Freud enjoins us to, that it is a matter of great
importance what is on this unfolded sheet because folded up in a
different way, under different conditions, it results not in the surrealistically juxtaposed images and episodes of the manifest
dream, but in an affliction – vaginismus, say, or anorexia, or hysterical migraines. For example, Dora, who Freud thinks limped
because of an unconscious fantasy of bearing a child out of
wedlock, might have dreamt of limping as well, in which case the
successful deciphering of her dream would have yielded the secret
of her limp. Would we not say that, in these circumstances, psychoanalysis had done Dora a service much more valuable than that of
helping her to formulate the ideas with which her dream had been
pregnant? There are occasions when, though an hypothesis is an
inappropriate response to a desire for a further description, a
desire for a further description may not be an appropriate desire.

Over forty years ago John Whitehorn, in an influential paper,
'Meaning and cause in psycho-dynamics' (Whitehorn 1947),
remonstrated with psychoanalysts for indulging in aetiological

speculation and urged them to concentrate on 'the meaning implied in the patient's experiences' instead. Perhaps because his preoccupations were predominantly therapeutic, the epistemic character of this enterprise was left unclear. Were hypotheses relating past to present to be abandoned for hypotheses pertaining to the patient's current psychic state or, as Whitehorn's language suggests but does not entail, was he going further and recommending what Bergin called 'accurate empathy' and forgoing causal inquiry altogether?

A quarter of a century on we find comparable ambiguities in Roy Schafer's *Language and Insight* – the Sigmund Freud Memorial Lectures for 1975–6. Schafer tells us that he proposes to emancipate the practice of psychoanalysis from the mechanistic implications of Freud's metapsychology by replacing it with an 'action' language. But this turns out to perpetuate the traditional equivocations. On the one hand an attempt is made to distance the new approach, not merely from mechanism, but from causal categories altogether ('one is under no obligation to use a grammar that commits one to causal questions and answers'). For example, instead of saying 'the reason an analysand skipped an hour was to avoid a hostile confrontation with the analyst', we ought to say that 'the analysand avoided that hostile confrontation by skipping an hour', so that we 'will be speaking of one event not two and so will not be implying causal relations between reasons and actions . . .' (Schafer 1978: 191). Yet in the same lecture we are told that among the 'actions' that the analysand comes to acknowledge are 'entering into the breast, explosively expelling bad objects, hiding a secret penis', etc., etc. But is it likely that the analysand's epistemic relation to these is that in which he stood to his reason for missing the analytic hour, as the use of the term 'recognition' implies? Are they internally and a-hypothetically related to their manifestations in the way that the source of the poignancy of the pealing church bells was?

Or consider the introduction to a book of essays commemorating the twenty-fifth anniversary of the William Alanson White Institute. We are told that, by 1970, patients were presenting with complaints different from those they presented with in the early days of psychoanalysis. Instead of the hysterical symptoms which were then so common, there were 'character problems, feelings of ennui, alienation, meaninglessness. Difficulties in living had

supplanted paralyses and blindness.' (Witenberg 1973: 5). It is
plausible to construe this shift from blindness and paralyses to feelings of ennui and alienation as involving a radical change in the
epistemic character of the understanding sought. But when the
exposition combines a full-fledged dissociative conception of the
unconscious in which 'the analyst's knowledge of the unconscious
determinants is taken for granted', and the patient is asked 'to view
himself as an object', with one in which he is asked to engage in 'a
careful inquiry into his feelings and attitudes' and to 'relive his
experience, attending to nuances previously ignored' (ibid.) we
are entitled to suspect, as in the case of Schafer, that 'the abominable mess' was well and thriving.

What is it, then, that patients feel they have learned as to their
propensities, susceptibilities and misconceptions in the course of
the analysis? What grounds do they believe themselves to possess
for their new-found understanding? Is the process like what John
Wisdom described as 'coming to see more clearly the things they
had felt creeping in the shadows', or rather like what he described
as being enabled to read the invisible writing to which a re-agent
has been applied (Wisdom 1973: 90–103)? Until we are clearer as
to what it is analysts claim to know in consequence of their
patients' corroboration and what it is they feel entitled to impute
to them without their concurrence, we will not be in a position to
decide when they are being gullible (or overbearing), and when
they have expedited illumination of a kind which can licitly dispense with extra-reflective support (or have quite properly over-
ruled the patient on matters beyond his jurisdiction.)[4] In the same

---

[4] More recent specimens of the confusion are to be found in those peer group comments
on Grünbaum's *The Foundations of Psychoanalysis* (1984) which defend the relevance of
the subjects' ultimate recognition of their motives or meaning, and in Grünbaum's
denial of it (*Behavioural and Brain Research*, June 1986). Those who attempt to justify the
patients' 'privileged cognitive status' claim too much and Grünbaum concedes too little.
How can we be unqualified to judge whether episodes from our past which figure in our
self-elucidations as 'psychological fixed stars' have not also exerted a causal influence
over us? How can I come to realise that throughout my life I have felt like an unprepared
schoolboy praying that the period would end before he was called upon, while not at the
same time having come into possession of the answer to many questions that present
themselves to an outside narrator as explanatory puzzles? Of course there are truths
reflection alone could not bring to light – facts 'beyond the truth of immanence' in
Merleau-Ponty's phrase. But is our epistemic relation to 'the expectant libidinal impulses
we bring to each new person' (Freud 1924: 313), or to the hidden teleology behind the
repeated self-frustrating relationships that Freud describes, like that in which we stand
to an undiagnosed cancer (Hanly)? As for the issue that Grünbaum poses of avoiding

paper John Wisdom describes the task of the analyst as that of 'bringing to light those (unconscious) models from the past which powerfully influence our lives in the present' (ibid. 96). There are both therapeutic and epistemic purposes for which it is not necessary to construe these models as occult causes waiting for the analyst to summon them from beyond the veil of appearances.

The past can figure in psychoanalytic discourse in a way other than that of a speculative causal antecedent of a current proclivity. It may stand to the present not just as a putative influence determining or conditioning it, but as that which confers on our current anticipations, apprehensions and demands that which makes them what they are. We may call attention to the relation between past and present with the same aim with which in Wittgenstein's analogy, attention is drawn to the relation between an ellipse and a circle – not to speculate that this particular circle evolved from that ellipse but 'to sharpen our eyes to a formal connection'.

An evocative account of the subjective side of this enterprise has been given by William James:

Whenever we seek to recall something forgotten, or to state the reason for a judgement which we have made intuitively (the) desire strains and presses in a direction which it feels to be right but towards a point which it is unable to see . . . What we are aware of in advance seems to be its relations with the items we already know . . . we know what we want to find out beforehand in a certain sense . . . and we do not know it in another sense. (James 1950: vol. 1, 585, 588)

When Rush Rhees says that a man 'bewildered at the sort of person he finds himself to be' may feel a need to talk to someone 'who could help formulate what was in [his] mind', the need he refers to is not to be appeased by properly psychoanalytic accounts whether they were like the stale cigarette smoke to which Rhees unkindly compares them or not (Rhees 1971: 23–6). As a recent account of Wittgenstein's views puts it, 'Freud seeks to offer

the *post hoc propter hoc* error when imputing a patient's improvement to the therapeutic sessions, his way of putting the matter homogenises the phenomena excessively. Precisely what improvements? Why is it reasonable for a man who takes to weight lifting to attribute his expanding pectorals to his work on them, or for someone to attribute his increasing proficiency in a foreign language to his exercises in it, or the improvement in his game to the coaching of a golf or tennis pro, but not reasonable for a patient to attribute his improved mental state to the therapeutic sessions? The answer to this question will depend on the particular character of the changes explained. The problem cannot be resolved in the abstract terms in which Grünbaum poses it.

explanations where . . . what is required is not explanation but clarification' (Johnston 1989: 50).[5]

In conceiving of his inquiry as one into the causes of his patients'
condition Freud may sometimes have misconstrued his own questions and not merely theirs (Habermas's 'scientistic self-misunderstanding'). Consider the epistemic character of the hidden
teleology Freud imputes in the following passage:

We have come across people all of whose relationships have the same
outcome; the benefactor who is abandoned in anger after a time by each
of his proteges . . . the man whose friendships all end in betrayal by his
friend; the man who time after time in the course of his life raises
someone else to a position of great authority . . . and then, after a certain
interval, himself upsets that authority and replaces him; the lover each of
whose amorous relationships passes through the same stages and reaches
the same conclusion. (Freud 1959: 44)

Does Freud mean us to assimilate these to the predicament,
poignantly described by Dr Johnson, of the epileptic who 'tumbles
and revives and tumbles again and all the while he knows not why'?
Must we accept this assimilation?

Despite Freud's occasional equivocations and tergiversations,
fundamental to psychoanalysis is a conception of lived life as epi-
phenomenal to processes which must be laboriously excavated and
could have been otherwise, just as the cause of pain of a certain
locale, quality, duration and periodicity is only laboriously to be
determined and could have been otherwise (referred pain). But
life-pain need not be entirely like that. Its complete understanding
may require two distinct enterprises, one employing reflection and
the other investigation. What we have instead is, for the most part,
the Freud-inspired hodgepodge with one hitching a ride on the
back of the other and which is doing the epistemic and therapeutic work only to be guessed at – 'an abominable mess'.

REFERENCES

Bergin, Allen (1966) 'Some implications of psychotherapy research for
    therapeutic practice' *Journal of Abnormal Psychology*, 71.

[5] Van den Berg, a phenomenological therapist, describes the Freudian unconscious as 'a
second reality behind the phantoms of healthy and neurotic life' (and holds it to be the
mistaken result of 'the premature cessation of psychological analysis') (Van den Berg:
1960: 83).

Cioffi, F. (1974) 'Symptoms, wishes and actions', Aristotelian Society, *Proc.*, vol. 48.

Engleman, P. (1967) *Letters from Ludwig Wittgenstein, with a Memoir* (Oxford: Blackwell).

Fisher, S. and Greenberg, R. (1977) *The Scientific Credibility of Freud's Theory* (Sussex: Harvester).

Freud, S. (1895) *Standard Edition, vol. 2* (London: Hogarth Press, 1953–74).

Freud, S. (1924) *Collected Papers, vol. 2* (London: Hogarth Press).

Freud, S. (1933) *New Introductory Lectures on Psychoanalysis* (London: Allen and Unwin).

Freud, S. (1949a) *Introductory Lectures on Psychoanalysis* (London: Allen and Unwin).

Freud, S. (1949b) *Outline of Psychoanalysis* (London: Hogarth Press).

Freud, S. (1954) *The Interpretation of Dreams* (London: Allen and Unwin).

Freud, S. (1959) *Beyond the Pleasure Principle* (New York: Bantam).

Grünbaum, A. (1984) *The Foundations of Psycho-Analysis* (Berkeley: California University Press).

Hanly, C. (1972) 'Wittgenstein on psychoanalysis', in *Ludwig Wittgenstein: Philosophy and Language* (ed. Ambrose, A. and Lazerowitz, M. (London: Allen and Unwin).

Harding, D. (1941) *The Impulse to Dominate* (London: Allen and Unwin).

Hertz, H. (1954) *The Principles of Mechanics* (New York: Dover Press).

Ichheiser, G. (1970) *Appearances and Realities* (San Francisco: Jossey-Bass).

James, W. (1950) *The Principles of Psychology* (New York: Dover).

Johnston, P. (1989) *Wittgenstein and Moral Philosophy* (London: Routledge).

Jones, S. (1968) *Treatment or Torture* (London: Tavistock Press).

Koehler, W. (1947) *Gestalt Psychology* (New York: Liveright).

Malcolm, N. (1958) *Ludwig Wittgenstein: A Memoir* (London: Oxford University Press).

McGuinness, B. (ed.) (1967) *Wittgenstein und der Wiener Kreis, Shorthand Notes recorded by F. Waismann* (Oxford: Blackwell).

McGuinness, B. (ed.) (1982) *Wittgenstein and his Times* (Oxford: Blackwell).

McGuinness, B. (1988) *Wittgenstein: A Life, Young Ludwig (1889–1921)* (London: Duckworth).

Moore, G. (1966) *Philosophical Papers* (New York: Collier Books).

Nisbett, R. and Wilson, R. (1977) 'Telling more than we know,' *Psychological Review*, 84.

Pears, D. (1970) *Wittgenstein* (London: Fontana).

Prince, M. (1913) 'The psychopathology of a case of phobia – a clinical study', *Journal of Abnormal Psychology*.

Rhees, R. (1970) *Discussions of Wittgenstein* (London: Routledge and Kegan Paul).

Rhees, R. (1971) 'The tree of Nebuchadnezzar', *The Human World*, no. 4.

Rhees, R. (ed.) (1981) *Ludwig Wittgenstein: Personal Recollections* (Oxford: Blackwell).

Rogers, C. (1964) 'Towards a science of the person', in *Behaviourism and Phenomenology*, ed. Wann, T. (Chicago: Chicago University Press).

Sartre, J.-P. (1962) *Existential Psychoanalysis*, ed. May, R. (Chicago: Chicago University Press).

Schafer, R. (1978) *Language and Insight* (New Haven and London: Yale University Press).

Tyler, E. B. (1920) *Primitive Culture* (London: Murray).

Weil, S. (1957) *Intimations of Christianity among the Ancient Greeks* (London: Routledge and Kegan Paul).

Whitehorn, J. (1947) 'The concept of "Meaning" and "Cause" in psychodynamics', *American Journal of Psychiatry*.

Wisdom, J. (1973) 'Philosophy, metaphysics and psychoanalysis: extract' in *Freud: Modern Judgements*, ed. Cioffi, F. (London: Macmillan).

Witenberg, E. (1973) *Interpersonal Explorations in Psychoanalysis: New Directions in Theory and Practice* (New York: Basic Books).

Wortis, J. (1954) *Fragments of an Analysis with Freud* (New York: Charter Books).

CHAPTER NINE

Congenital transcendentalism and 'the loneliness which is the truth about things'

I take the phrase 'congenital transcendentalism' from Santayana who defined it as 'the spontaneous feeling that life is a dream'. 'The loneliness which is the truth about things' is a phrase of Virginia Woolf's. The thesis I will advance is that many expressions of doubt or denial of the shareable world are self-misunderstood manifestations of the state indicated by Woolf's expression. But the loneliness of which Woolf speaks must not be construed as the kind of loneliness which can be assuaged by family, friends, lovers or company. Nor is it the loneliness which a convinced solipsist might experience. It is rather the loneliness of 'that "I" and that "life of mine"' which is 'untouched whichever way the issue is decided whether the world is or is not' (Husserl 1970: 9).

The earliest manifestation of congenital transcendentalism known to me is the familiar story from Chuang-tse (*c.* 300 BC) of the sage who has increasingly vivid and long-drawn-out dreams of life as a butterfly until he reaches a point when he can no longer be sure whether he is a man dreaming that he is a butterfly or a butterfly dreaming that he is a man. There is an episode with the structure of the Chuang-tse anecdote in Lewis Carroll's *Sylvie and Bruno* (a favourite of Wittgenstein's) where at one point the narrator says, 'Either I have been dreaming about Sylvie and this is the reality, or else I have been with Sylvie and this is the dream.' I do not think that fancies like these are the product of philosophical tradition but rather of that ubiquitous feature of our lives known as the 'egocentric predicament'.

Here is one account of the egocentric predicament. It is Samuel Taylor Coleridge's. Coleridge calls the belief 'that there exist things without us' a 'prejudice at once indemonstrable and irresistible', whereas 'the other position . . . namely I AM, cannot so properly be entitled a prejudice (since) the existence of things without us, from its nature, cannot be as immediately certain . . . and as independently of all grounds as the existence of our own being' (Richards 1950). This apparent asymmetry naturally leads to the impugning of our supposed knowledge of the external world. Philosophical scepticism as to the knowability of the external world must be distinguished from another less theoretical question with which it is often intertwined. This might be described as conspiratorial or Potemkin village scepticism, after the minister of Catherine the Great who (apocryphally) arranged that on her progresses through her kingdom the misery of the populace was concealed by lining the village streets with well-fed peasants, and doing up the fronts of the houses. William James called the fact that at any given moment things are going on which are out of the perceptive range of any one person 'collateral contemporaneity'. It is the 'meanwhile, back at the ranch' order of fact, 'the simultaneous existence of objects not simultaneously perceived' as Strawson puts it. It is a prominent component of what Husserl dubs 'the natural attitude'.

Here is a vernacular expression of the natural attitude from one of the most familiar verses of the North American Continent: 'somewhere in this favoured land / the sun is shining bright / the band is playing somewhere / and somewhere hearts are light / and somewhere men are laughing / and somewhere children shout / but there is no joy in Mudville / mighty Casey has struck out'. A playful expression of the antithesis to the 'natural attitude' is found in a poem of Housman's: 'Good creatures, do you love your lives? / and have you ears for sense? / Here is a knife like other knives, / that cost me eighteenpence. / I need but stick it in my heart / and down will come the sky. / And earth's foundations will depart / and all you folk will die' (*More Poems*, no. 26). The ubiquity of the natural attitude is unquestionable but isn't there something natural in the idea that Housman plays with, too? Isn't this idea of the dependence of worldhood on selfhood both bizarre and familiar?

'Let us imagine', said the philosopher Ortega to his audience once 'that on leaving this hall when my lecture is over we find that there was nothing beyond, that is, that the rest of the world was not around it, that its doors gave not on the city but on nothing. Such a discovery will shock us with surprise and terror' (Ortega y Gasset 1963: 64). Ortega does not mention a by no means unimaginable response to the contingency he mentions – that of the congenital transcendentalist – 'I knew it! I knew it!'

There are occasions which seem to involve a departure from what Husserl calls the natural attitude and yet are as natural as the natural attitude itself. This fact has been thought to demonstrate the irrefutability of solipsism but I think it means something different.

Here are some examples apparently illustrative of the ubiquity of sceptical doubt: At the end of Mark Twain's *The Mysterious Stranger*, the stranger addresses the narrator:

'Life itself is only a vision, a dream.'
It was electrical. By God! I had that very thought a thousand times in my musings!
'Nothing exists: all is a dream. God – man – the world – the sun, the moon, the wilderness of stars – a dream, all a dream; they have no existence. *Nothing exists save empty space – and you! . . . And you are not you – you have no body, no blood, no bones, you are but a thought.* I myself have no existence; I am but a dream – your dream, creature of your imagination. In a moment you will have realized this, then you will banish me from your visions and I shall dissolve into the nothingness out of which you made me . . . It is all a dream'
He vanished and left me appalled; for I knew, and realized, that all he said was true.

Here is the same sentiment from a work by someone as different from Twain as is conceivable, Walter Pater: '. . . what pure reason affirmed as the beginning of wisdom was that the world is but a thought . . . the product of his own lonely thinking power . . . as being zero without him'. The same view is expounded by the narrator of Tolstoi's semi-fictional memoir, *Boyhood*, who reminisces: 'By none of my philosophical tendencies was I so carried away as by scepticism . . . I imagined that beside myself nobody and nothing existed in the universe. There were moments when under the influence of this *idée fixe* I reached such a state of insanity that I sometimes looked rapidly round to one side, hoping to catch emptiness unawares where I was not.'

The extent to which these men were drawing on their own reflections which they then imputed to imagined characters is unclear, and even so might suggest that such fancies are confined to febrile men of letters. Here then is a specimen indistinguishable from those cited from the autobiographical memoir of a distinguished physicist:

An event that stands out in my mind must have happened in my early teens. I was paddling a canoe on a clear night and letting my thoughts roam. Suddenly it came over me, and with something of a shock, that maybe everything that I considered most real was pure imagination. The lake, the canoe, the paddle, the stars, the night, the trees, even the feeling of water on my hand, might merely be sensations. Indeed, it might be that I was the only person who existed in the world, that my father and mother, my brother and sister and friends were all just figments of my imagination – that the feeling of the solid earth when I walked on it was only a feeling. There seemed to be nothing to disprove the hypothesis. On the other hand, what would be the sense of such a thing? It occurred to me that possibly this was all a matter of education. Perhaps really I was not a young boy alive here in the world, but one of a group of other kinds of beings, perhaps a God or supernatural being of some sort who is merely going through a course of training; prepared for him by other supernatural beings. At the time, no-one seemed particularly interested in this form of nonsense, but when I studied philosophy in college it was somewhat of a thrill to realize that I was by no means the first to have considered the possibility. (Bitter 1960: 20–1)

Wordsworth was also prone to sceptical doubts similar to those that afflicted Tolstoi. When a child he would grasp at a wall or tree to assure himself of the existence of the external world. In old age he reminisced, 'There was a time in my life when I had to push against something that resisted to be sure that there was anything that was outside me. I was sure of my own mind; everything else fell away, and vanished into thought.' Is it an adequate response to my patchwork to discuss the cogency of the views expressed? That is, whether Wordsworth and Tolstoi were not making Dr Johnson's mistake when he kicked the headstone in Harwich Churchyard to refute Berkeley? Bitter does not tell us why he concluded his conspiratorial intuitions were mistaken, nor does Tolstoi tell us why he came to regard his sceptical doubts as insane. But we can assume that it was not because of repeated failures to catch nothing at it. And when Cardinal Newman tells us of a time in childhood when 'I thought life might be a dream, or I an angel, and all this world a deception, my fellow angels by a playful device concealing themselves from me and deceiving me with the semblance of a material world,' he may not, as it appears, just be presenting us with a supernatural version of Freud's family romance; his case may be no different from that of the physicist Bitter. What I believe we have in these cases is what John Wisdom described as 'the interpenetration of issues'. It is worldhood itself which these men were, confusedly, calling in question when entertaining such fancies and not just whether the consensual world is the real one. If Tolstoi cannot trust what he sees when his back is not turned to things, why trust what he sees when he sees nothing? Similarly with the metaphysical family romances of Newman and Bitter – what guarantee is there that these supernatural beings who are suspected of producing a simulacrum of reality will not themselves prove ultimately illusory (and thus immediately questionable). What we have in these instances is an incoherent mingling of doubt as to whether things really are what they seem with the more radical doubt whether the way things seem can ever warrant how they really are.

Yet I feel that we would be doing Bitter, Pater, Tolstoi, *et al.* an injustice if we contented ourselves with exposing the incoherence of their solipsism. This is not the way to deal with these utterances because what their authors have stumbled on, in however confused a manner, is Husserl's 'greatest and most magnificent of all facts, that of transcendental subjectivity'. But though the problem explicitly posed by Husserl is, 'How is it possible to derive the intersubjectivity of the world from the intentionalities of my own conscious life' and again, 'How can the world as a world for everyone and the existence of others, be established', this problem masks another – that of the incongruity of our existence as beings both isolated and accompanied, as simultaneously just 'one other among others' and yet the hub around which everything revolves – of our perplexity that, as Wittgenstein puts it, though 'what solipsism means is true . . . it cannot be said'.

The thesis I wish to advance is that the utterances in which the problem of solipsism finds expression are precipitates of something else, more cloudy and indeterminate – the feeling of having stumbled on a momentous but deeply hidden significance, involving the epistemic relation of our being in the world to that of the being of others. The solipsism I want to direct attention towards is not just an apparently counter-intuitive implication of a verificationist semantics. This would only lead to an effort to see how the implication might nevertheless be suspended, or to an acknowledgement that it constitutes a *reductio* of the semantics in question. The solipsism I am talking about requires oxymoron for its expression – it might be called universal solipsism. The feeling of a profound and irremediable solitude which finds expression in solipsistic fantasies transcends scepticism and is unaffected by its

refutation. When Ortega tells us that 'human life is radical solitude', he immediately issues an assurance that 'in no sense would
I suggest that I am the only thing that exists'. Life is not 'a tena-
cious and exuberant dream, an infinite phantasmagoria secreted
by my mind . . . The radical solitude of human life does not consist
in their really being nothing else. There is an infinity of things but
. . . (each one of us) is alone with them' (Ortega y Gasset 1964:
47). This suggests that when this distinctive, unutterable loneliness is expressed as solipsism what is problematic has been distorted *en route* to articulation. What then is this residual
problematicality involving the unreachableness of the otherness of
others, and thus reciprocally of one's own, which fails to dissipate
when the sceptical problem in its various formulations is resolved?
Its main feature is a feeling of incongruity between our special
epistemic relation to ourselves and the assumptions of our worka-
day lives.

This is what Wittgenstein has to say about solipsism in the
Tractatus: 'What solipsism means is true only it cannot be said'
(Wittgenstein 1949: 5. 62). I want to argue for a more intimate
relation between this remark and what Wittgenstein calls 'the
riddle of life' in *Tractatus* 6. 52 than may initially seem plausible.
In *Notebooks 1914–16* he says: 'What do I know about God and the
purpose of life? I know that this world exists. That I am placed in
it like my eye in its visual field. That something about it is problematic which we call its meaning' (Wittgenstein 1969, 11/6/16,
72–3). What did Wittgenstein mean by 'the purpose' of life, in this
remark? And how is it related to our being placed in the world like
the eye in its visual field?

If his remarks on the problem of life are not overdetermined on
each or most occasions they certainly meant different things at
different times. The problem which involves 'God and the purpose
of life' is remote from the problem in *Tractatus* 6, 52 whose solution discovered 'after long doubting' is unutterable by those who
have discovered it. If in spite of having arrived at the meaning of
life they nevertheless, 'cannot then say in what this meaning consists' it cannot be with them, as with others, because they were persuaded that 'there shall be no more death; neither sorrow nor
crying', since this would result not in silence but in proselytisation.
So we are not dealing with common or garden theodicy as the
expression 'God and the purpose of life' suggests.

The question of theodicy can only arise within the natural attitude. The question which Wittgenstein broaches in the *Tractatus* lies outside it or concerning it. It involves the relation between what in the *Notebooks* he called 'the two godheads' – 'the world and my independent I' (Wittgenstein 1969, 8/7/16, 74). But neither is Wittgenstein's problem, as this phrase can suggest and, as J. N. Findlay thought, the problem of solipsism as ordinarily conceived. Doubt or denial of the everyday world are not involved. In his memoir of Wittgenstein Findlay imputes to him

a deep personal solipsism which is probably among the persistent, secret, and necessarily inexpressible sources of many of Wittgenstein's positions ... He believed what ordinary metaphysical men would express by saying that he alone was conscious of anything and alone had true feelings and that others were only conscious and had feelings in a different utterly behavioural sense. (Findlay 1973: 180)

Wittgenstein, says Findlay, 'is one of the few genuine solipsists who ever existed but he suffered the great personal agony that it made no sense to him to avow his solipsism either to himself or anyone else'. We have here the paradox of something which is deemed inexpressible but of which we have a sufficiently clear conception to impute to someone and even to give a role, if an unconscious one, in his ratiocinations. I do not think there was anything particular to him in Wittgenstein's dilemma as Findlay himself concedes in another remark: 'Wittgenstein's secret metaphysical belief – and I am sure many others have entertained the same – was in some egocentric predicament in which each man necessarily treated his own conscious ego as the unmentionable pivot and limit of the world.' Findlay thinks this is merely a conceptual confusion: 'Plainly our understanding and knowledge of the existence of foreign experience and its distinction from and independence of the criteria in virtue of which we establish it is something infinitely better founded than any semantic theory, however ingenious, and the confusion of one with the other, which certain semantic theories entail, is plainly a flat denial of the understanding and knowledge in question' (Findlay 1973: 180). I doubt that Wittgenstein needed to be told that. In the sense of solipsism which implies doubt or denial of the reality of others it is not a view which there is any reason to think Wittgenstein ever held. And Findlay's view of the issues leaves unexplained why it should cause 'great personal agony'.

Wittgenstein says of the notion of wondering at the existence of the world that it is nonsensical because we cannot imagine it not existing, and a similar problem arises in connection with the experience I have described as the finding of something anomalous about one's own existence. The question naturally arises; with respect to what is it anomalous? T. S. Eliot objected to the use I. A. Richards made of the idea of 'Man's loneliness (the isolation of the human situation)' in the much mocked 'sincerity ritual' expounded in *Practical Criticism* (Richards 1953: 290). Eliot professed not to understand 'an isolation which is not an isolation from anything in particular'. 'In what sense' he asked 'is man in general isolated and from what?' (Eliot 1933: 132). In his reply Richards reduced the ambiguity of the expression 'Man's loneliness' by quoting Eliot himself ('thinking of the key each confirms a prison'), thus making it clear that the isolation he was referring to was that of each man rather than of mankind, and that the isolation in question was that of the egocentric predicament (Richards 1953: 291). This still leaves Eliot's objection of incomprehensibility through lack of contrast unanswered. There is an aphorism of F. H. Bradley's. 'Wherever you are puzzled you have made an assumption and it is your duty to discover what that assumption is', which has sometimes served me well but is difficult to apply to the case at issue. What could the puzzle-generating assumption be in the case of our wonder, and perhaps dismay, at our being placed in the world 'like the eye in its visual field'?

One way of conveying the character of this wonder is to say that it is as if I were capable of imagining a mode of being less personal than that which I have. But how can this be? Here is an analogy which may be helpful. In answer to an interviewer's question as to when he first became conscious 'of his own individual self' Carl Jung replied that it was in his eleventh year. On his way to school he 'stepped out of a mist . . . and I knew "I am". And then I thought "What have I been before?" And then I found I had been in a mist not knowing how to differentiate myself from other things. I was just one thing among other things' (McGuire and Hull 1980: 381). The mist I am thinking of is analogous to Jung's but it is one which we return to and spend most of our lives in, emerging only fitfully to wonder plaintively what had woken us.

This is Anthony Powell's account of the same dawning of self-awareness:

One afternoon – I was about five or six – we had returned from Kensington Gardens and were waiting outside the door of the flat to be let in. After the park and the street the interior of the building seemed very silent. A long beam of sunlight, in which small particles of dust swam about, all at once slanted through an upper window on the staircase and struck the opaque glass panels of the door. On several occasions recently I had been conscious of approaching the brink of some discovery, an awareness that nearly became manifest and suddenly withdrew. Now the truth came flooding in with the dust-infected sunlight; the revelation of self-identity was inescapable. There was no doubt about it – I was me!

'I was me!' – a statement which makes no sense and which everyone understands. Isn't Powell's 'revelation of self-identity' recognisably akin to the phenomenon to which Husserl is referring when he writes: 'I was a transcendental ego even while living in the natural attitude, but I knew nothing about it' (Husserl 1970: 15). This is how sense may be given to the obscure conviction that there is something enigmatic and anomalous about our positioning in the world as just a self among selves and yet not just unique but uniquely accessible.

It might seem that the proper response to Wittgenstein's oft-quoted remark is that what solipsism means is not true and that the silence which Wittgenstein enjoins could be appropriately broken by showing that this is so. Certainly there is no dearth of philosophical discourses of the highest order which do, or purport to do, just that; not least Wittgenstein's own. But such discourses are beside the point of that particular remark which addresses a problem which arises just as much for Heidegger, who does not deny worldhood, as for Husserl who suspends it. James Thurber once wrote: 'It occurred to me today that the world exists only in my own consciousness; whether as reality or illusion the evening papers do not say.' If a day comes when the evening papers do say, the problem addressed by Wittgenstein's remark will not have been resolved. This problem persists even after we have allowed Heidegger to persuade us that worldhood and selfhood are given together, or Wittgenstein that 'when the solipsist retreats into his private world the ability to make discriminating references to individuals is something which he is unable to take with him' (Pears 1988: 230).

In connection with Wittgenstein's later arguments against solipsism David Pears quotes a remark from 1916: 'The I, the I, is what

is deeply mysterious' (5 August 1916) and asks 'What has happened to his original feeling for the mystery of the ego?' (Pears
1988: 226). One possibility is that in Wittgenstein's later dealings
with the incoherence of solipsism he is not addressing the question of the mystery of the ego as he originally understood it – the
unaccommodatability of the 'I' to the natural attitude; an
unaccommodatability which is nevertheless not solipsistic doubt
or conviction.

To make the state I am trying to gesture towards more discernible let us imagine the epistemic problems addressed by Husserl
and others as arising through our being called on to give an
account of how the members of a community of intersubjectively
related monads are able, each, to assure himself that they do
indeed share a common world; we would then have the setting for
a debate as to whether it is Heidegger or Husserl who had given a
more correct account of their situation. But the problem I wish to
address (or the symptom I want to present for diagnosis) does not
arise until I remind myself that I am myself a member of such a
community. It also distinguishes the problem I want to call your
attention to, that it is blurred when we speak of it as the question
why there is something rather than nothing, since I am quite
happy to respond, 'Why not?' to that question. But if the question
is phrased 'Why is it me in particular who is called on to bear
witness that there is something rather than nothing', the response
'Why not?' sticks in my throat.

The difficulty of conveying the experience of being struck by
one's own existence constrains us to violate normal standards of
intelligibility. One issue raised by Wittgenstein's remark that what
solipsism means cannot be said is whether 'saying' is so clearcut a
notion that we can be confident that it cannot be done? I have
myself gone from thinking Wittgenstein's remark on solipsism
nonsense, and quoting with approval Frank Ramsey's 'If you can't
say it you can't say it and you can't whistle it either', to finding it
extraordinarily penetrating without being able to say why in any
sense that I would have previously found acceptable. So perhaps
you can whistle it after all. Wittgenstein's later remarks do something to characterise more particularly this meaning which can
and cannot be said. In his 1932 lecture on ethics he said, in
connection with the experience of wonder at the existence of the
world, that this astonishment cannot be expressed in a question

and that it was a misunderstanding to think that any formulation we arrive at could correspond to what we meant, but that nevertheless 'the tendency, the thrust, points to something' (Wittgenstein 1965: 8).

The distinctiveness of this pointing is also stressed by Heidegger. In the *History of the Concept of Time* he writes: 'It is not a question of deducing propositions or propositional sequences from each other but of working out the access to the matters from which propositions are to be drawn in the first place . . .' (Heidegger 1985: 146). But Heidegger's assertion of the distinctiveness of the issue and its exemption from normal criteria of intelligibility and cogency has been found unpersuasive by those in the analytic tradition. The passage on 'Nothingness' from Heidegger's 'What is Metaphysics?' which Carnap demonstrated to be meaningless if literally construed might better have been criticised as rhetorically inept. Similarly Heidegger's attempt to convey the situation for which he adapted the term Dasein (being-there) – 'the unique ontologic structure which is being in the world' – may require utterances like – 'Dasein is the entity which I myself am in each instance' (Heidegger 1985: 195) and 'It is a matter of an entity to which we have this distinctive relationship, we are it itself – an entity which is only insofar as I am it' (Heidegger 1985: 149–50).

These remarks are as vulnerable to unsympathetic, literal paraphrase as those on 'nothing' and yet this does not preclude their efficacy in 'working out access to the matters from which propositions are to be drawn'. The trouble is that the tradition insists that we take Heidegger's formulations to other of his formulations, or to the formulations of others, rather than to the 'primordial experiences' which generated them in the first place. Elsewhere in the *History of the Concept of Time* Heidegger speaks of the analysis of being as 'the discovery of the very possibility of doing research in philosophy'. To the state I want to convey, it is as much an *a priori* restriction on the appropriate response to the revelatory experience of 'being there' that it should take the form of research as are 'the latently operative and spurious bonds of the tradition' to which Heidegger scornfully refers. Why must we assume that the disclosure of being would leave us anything much more to say? Why must there be a structure of being to be arduously excavated, taxonomised and architectonically displayed? Moreover do not we sometimes have the feeling that Heidegger himself often expresses his deepest philosophical convictions in a format and in accordance with conventions that contradict them? Might not there be a gross incongruity in passing from the illumination of being to the historical exegesis of Parmenides, Descartes or Kant? Is not it as if one were to announce that Jesus died for our sins and then try to arouse interest in the minutiae of daily life in ancient Palestine?

Certain philosophical illuminations may be like suicide in that once successfully communicated they leave their authors hard pressed for an encore. The revelation of being may be an enterprise of a distinctive, comparatively unratiocinative kind – a matter of finding ways to convey the illumination rather than pseudo-ratiocinative demonstrations; and the gifts required for this task closer to those displayed by Tortelier in his master classes than in ratiocinative philosophy. The right considerations to bring to bear on discourse of this kind may be rhetorical. Wittgenstein's remarks are often too austere, e.g. 'There is indeed the inexpressible. This shows itself; it is the mystical.' In general Wittgenstein's ladder has too few rungs, Heidegger's too many. Whatever the justice of this judgment perhaps it is in these terms that the discussion ought to be carried on rather than in those of logical impropriety.

When I gave the talk on which this paper is based Professor Griffiths asked me his standard question, of which I had been forewarned, what problem had I raised of whose resolution I was uncertain. I answered then that it was to what degree the questions I was raising belonged to psychology or psychopathology rather than philosophy. Though I would give the same answer if I were asked it now, it is for different reasons. Whereas at the time I was thinking predominantly of the kind of doubt as to the common world avowed by Bitter, Wordsworth, Tolstoi, etc., and described by the last as insane, in which we have a mixture of philosophical and non-philosophical, conspiratorial Potemkin-village scepticism, my grounds would now be my uncertainty as to whether dismay at the fact 'of a prior, primordial, transcendental sphere of peculiar owness' (Husserl) or, as Ortega puts it, that 'each "I" is in its very essence solitude,' is idiosyncratic or demanded by the nature of the relevation. Not only may the problem as I have described it be too idiosyncratic to be generally communicable, but it manifests a puzzling intermittent inertness for the very persons who are troubled by it. Those who address such questions must therefore reconcile themselves to the minuteness of their constituency at any given time and to its inconstancy and fluctuating membership – this kind of problematicality waxes and wanes. The moments of revelation or lucidity are succeeded by judgments as to the banality of the content of the revelation. And yet every once in a while we are struck by our peculiar and distinctive accessibility to ourselves and for some of us this thought has a disquieting hinterland – something distinct from the epistemic conundrums it sets.

In his *Self-Consciousness: Memoirs*, in a paragraph which begins with the single word 'Dasein', John Updike writes: 'Billions of consciousnesses silt history full and every one of them the center of the universe. What can we do in the face of this unthinkable truth but scream or take refuge in God' (Updike 1986: 36–8). What was there in the notion that 'billions of consciousnesses silt history full and each of then the center of the universe' to make Updike want to scream? It does not make everyone want to scream. It did not make even Husserl want to scream and he cannot be accused of simple obliviousness. Nor do the numerous professional philosophers who discuss the topic of transcendental intersubjectivity show any such inclination – unless from exasperation. Being says 'Boo!' to some of us; but we cannot help but notice that scarcely anyone else is frightened. There is a problem here. Heidegger has suggested one solution: 'Whenever a phenomenological concept is drawn from primordial sources, there is a possibility that it may degenerate if communicated in the form of an assertion. It gets understood in an empty way and is thus passed on, losing its indigenous character . . .' (Heidegger 1962: 60–1). Thus the jibe, 'Death, to a Heideggerian, is what he lectures on in the Spring term.'

The verbal formulae in which we express these intuitions 'have their dead and vital seasons', in Robert Musil's metaphor, and so not only may they be deployed by those who have never fully realised them, but even those who once have may lose touch with the primordial experience from which they are drawn. Even those who have not lost touch find it difficult to communicate the experience in its fullness by bare statement. At best this is like handing someone a photographic negative and leaving to him the task of developing it.

What more can be done in the way of 'primordial pointing out' than assemble hopefully apposite quotations? 'What has history to

do with me? Mine is the one and only world' (Wittgenstein). 'The
who of Dasein is not at all the "I myself"' (Heidegger). 'I am not
the ego of an individual man. I am the ego in whose stream of
consciousness the world itself – including myself as an object in it
. . . first acquires meaning and reality' (Husserl). 'There is no such
thing as the subject that thinks or entertains ideas. If I wrote a book
called the world as I found it . . . it alone could not be mentioned
in that book' (Wittgenstein). 'Each "I" is in its very essence solitude' (Ortega). These can only function as reminders for those for
whom there are reminiscences to be evoked.

If it were necessary to attempt to convey the dismaying aspects
of the experience I am speaking of I would start with an exchange
from D. H. Lawrence's story 'The Captain's Doll', in which the
eponymous captain compares his dead wife to a caged bird he
once owned who seemed to think of the bars of his cage as inside
him. 'He thought it was part of his own nature to be shut in. And
she thought it was part of her nature. And so they both died.' But
when his interlocutor interposes 'What I can't see is what she could
have done outside her cage. What other life could she have except
her bibelots and her furniture and her talk?' the Captain back-
slides (whether with or without Lawrence's knowledge I am not
sure):

> 'Why none. There is no life outside for human beings.'
> 'Then there's nothing?'
> 'That's true. In large measure, there is nothing.'
>
> (D. H. Lawrence, 'The Captain's Doll')

But though this captures one aspect of the revelation it is not particular enough. It veers towards the same ambiguity as the first
item in I. A. Richards' sincerity ritual – 'Man's loneliness' – which
he eliminated in his reply to Eliot. It is not a question of 'we
humans' and nothing, but of you, whoever you are, and nothing;
and yet not in the sense intended by solipsism. It might help to
further specify this sense if I add that broaching to an audience a
sense of their own ultimate solitude in its concreteness might be
felt as a betrayal because those who assembled did so on an unspo-
ken understanding that they would not be driven back on themselves in this particular fashion. It is unlikely that Fichte's students
were at all disturbed when asked to 'think the wall' and then to
think of themselves 'thinking the wall', but the kind of reflexivity

I have in mind can, if developed, be deeply disturbing. It may help further to characterise this version of the transcendental revelation that, even were its recipients too robustly constituted to experience dismay, its content is such that feeling it too vividly in company would constitute a breach of decorum akin to erotic fantasising so intense that we erect or lubricate. Perhaps there is a kind of philosophical rumination which should only be engaged in privately. Husserl's suggestion that we could undertake the epoché in the company of others always struck me as strangely improper. (It is pertinent that Ortega connects this ontological revelation with a sense of shame: 'Is shame the form in which the "I" discovers itself?' (1964: 179.) Perhaps an ingredient in the satisfaction taken in praying for the souls of all the living and the dead may be mitigation of our guilt at our irrepressible claim to uniqueness and privileged ontological status.

It may further help to characterise the fact I am trying to gesture towards that it was inevitable that I should have been oblivious to it during the bulk of the period during which this paper was written and even during the writing of much of it. But why should an idea of which I am oblivious for most of my life seem so momentous on those rare occasions when it presents itself? Why does it seem so impossible to accommodate it within the assumptions on which my daily life is lived? Might it not be some kind of aberration?

In Edmund Wilson's essay on Paul Valéry he passes on an idea of Valéry's which was prompted by Pascal's reaction of terror before the silence of the infinite spaces. Valéry believed that in the future 'our increasing knowledge of the universe will have come to change not merely our ideas but certain of our immediate reactions' and 'what one might call Pascal's reaction will be a rarity and a curiosity to psychologists' (Wilson 1971: 78). Cannot we imagine something comparable happening to Wittgenstein's feeling that 'the "I" is deeply mysterious'? Professional philosophers do not find it so. Why should what is true of many now not become universally true at some future date so that though Husserl's arguments, say, might remain graspable, the centrality he attached to them or better, the peculiar sacramental tone which he, Ortega, Heidegger and others sometimes adopt would have become inexplicable. This is how Ortega for example introduces the topic of the primacy of the self: 'we are to descend boldly below what each one customarily thinks his life to be and which really is merely its crust; piercing the crust we will enter into subterranean zones of our own living, zones which hold for us the most intimate secrets of being, secrets of our deepest selves, of the pure being of our being' (Ortega y Gasset 1964: 18). Even more striking because of his normal desiccation are the places in Husserl where our necessary egocentricity is expounded in the rhetoric of salvation ('the greatest of all discoveries', 'the greatest and most magnificent of all facts', 'my true self'). It is as if through the phenomenological epoche we become twice born.

   Yet this falls short of the dismay I suggested belongs to the revelation. There is no way to demonstrate that those who take up a clinical attitude towards what they would regard as our problematising compulsion with respect to selfhood are mistaken, nor even to reassure ourselves, in those moments when our relation to the natural attitude seems unproblematic, that we have not succumbed to a delusion; that what we have been saying is not merely gabble but morbid gabble. In attempting to respond appropriately to that unsayable truth which solipsism means – which though it can be indicated by words is not a saying by them – we may be dealing with a phenomenon akin to the delusions of reference which psychiatrists have studied (and which Wittgenstein tells us sometimes afflicted him). Wittgenstein speaks in *The Blue Book* of this 'strange illusion' in connection with a musical theme and describes it as the impression that the music seems to be saying something and it is as if we had to discover what it says. He does, however, place one restriction on the delusory character of this sense of imminent revelation – we may licitly look forward to its belated elucidation by analogy or felicitous description – 'the word that seems to sum it up' (Wittgenstein 1958: 166–7). I have said that for me what sums up the experience of 'the unique ontological structure of being' is Virginia Woolf's: 'The loneliness which is the truth about things.' But of course I know that there are many for whom it does not and for still others it is not even a question of evocative summing up but of a more intellectual, examinable enterprise. Those of us who think otherwise need the courage of our parochialism and to cultivate a more intense awareness of the message-in-a-bottle character of our efforts at communication. There are some lines by Philip Larkin which have a peculiar pertinence to the transcendental loneliness which is the truth about

things: – 'Saying so to some/means nothing; others it leaves/
nothing to be said.'

REFERENCES

Bitter, F. (1960) *Magnets; The Education of a Physicist*, London Heinemann.

Carnap, R. (1954) 'The elimination of metaphysics', in *Logical Positivism*, ed. A. J. Ayer, New York: Free Press.

Eliot T. S. (1933) *The Use of Poetry and the Use of Criticism*, London: Faber.

Findlay, J. N. (1973) 'My encounters with Wittgenstein'. Philosophical Forum.

Heidegger, M. (1985) *History of the Concept of Time*, Bloomington: Indiana.

Husserl, Edmond (1970) *The Paris Lectures*, The Hague: Martinus Nijhoff.

Housman, A. E. (1945) *The Selected Poems*, Armed Forces Edition New York.

McGuire, W. and Hull, R. F. C. (1980) *C. G. Jung*, London: Pan Books.

Ortega, Y. Gasset (1963) *Man and People*, New York: Norton.

(1964) *What is Philosophy?* New York: Norton.

Pears, David (1988) *The False Prison*, Oxford: University Press.

Richards, I. A. (1950) *Practical Criticism*, London: Routledge.

(1953) *Coleridge on Imagination*, London: Routledge.

Tolstoi, Leo (1964) *Childhood, Boyhood and Youth*, Harmondsworth: Penguin.

Updike, John (1986) *Self-Consciousness: Memoirs*, London: Penguin.

Wilson, Edmund (1971) *Axel's Castle*, London: Fontana Collins.

Wittgenstein, L. (1949) *Tractatus Logico-Philosophicus*, Routledge and Kegan Paul.

(1958) *The Blue and Brown Books*, Oxford: Blackwell.

(1965) 'A lecture on ethics', *Philosophical Review*, 74, January.

(1969) *Notebooks 1914–1916*, Oxford: Blackwell.

Afterword

CHAPTER TEN

Explanation and self-clarification in Frazer

Wittgenstein has two conceptual arguments against Frazer's introduction of empirical conjectures into his discussion of Nemi and the other practices he discusses. One is that they are out of reach of empirical explanation and the other that they can be made perspicuous without it. Neither of these arguments succeeds. This leaves the most novel of his arguments, that in human sacrifice (or ritual in general) we are confronted with a phenomenon which demands of us other than an empirical explanation even if such explanation is possible.

WITTGENSTEIN'S LIMIT THESIS: IS NEMI EXPLAINABLE?

Wittgenstein's thesis that the Nemi rite cannot be explained has won some acceptance but as it stands it is fallacious even if we accept the notion of unexplainability.

One argument for unexplainability is the idea of a phenomenon so basic and fundamental that we would be unable to say what it would be to explain it. What, for example, would explain our kissing the pictures of loved ones? Our puzzlement as to why someone is kissing a bit of paper is dissipated when we learn that it is a photograph of his children. It isn't clear what would answer the further question why he is kissing a picture of his children: people kiss images of those they love and the question why they do doesn't normally arise. Such practices owe their perspicuity – and their power to confer perspicuity on any practice which can be assimilated to them – to the fact that we don't have to ask why and not to the fact that asking why would make no sense. Wittgenstein seems to acknowledge this when he observes of the making of a connection between a puzzling practice and our own inclinations which resolves a 'particular difficulty', not that further enquiry is senseless but only that it would take us 'in a different direction'. (*Sources and Perspectives*, C. G. Luckhardt, Sussex: The Harvester Press 1979, p. 72.)

What makes the argument fallacious, irrespective of whether we accept the notion of unexplainability, is that the practice, like those at Nemi to which it is applied, is not ours and so we do not know what its rationale is, and so cannot say that the rationale is so transparent that we have no idea what more might be required to explain it. Even if we concede that a genuinely religious action can't be explained, how do we know, *a priori*, that the Nemi rite is a genuinely religious action? Furthermore, if it is conceivable that there may be practices of our own, calling attention to which would render the Nemi practice clear – i.e., perspicuous or unproblematic as Wittgenstein maintains – would not the discovery that this was, or had at one time been, the very same rationale of the practitioners of the exotic, problematic rite themselves, explain it? In general, if it can be 'made clear' it can be explained. Once again we have an instance where Wittgenstein impugns the relevance of empirical enquiry on inadequate grounds. And we suspect that the unstated premise from which its irrelevance follows is that another question to which it is irrelevant ought to have been raised instead; one which demands clarification and not explanation.

WHAT IS THE RELATION BETWEEN THE ORIGIN OF A PRACTICE AND ITS MEANING?

The argument which imposes a limit not on explainability in general but on explainability by origins has more merit but not as much as Hacker and others impute to it. There is one use of genetic considerations which Wittgenstein reminds us is illicit and that is the attempt to settle what a rite means to its practitioners by invoking its origins, since it may have 'its own complex of feelings'. This thesis of Wittgenstein's has been pithily expressed by Peter Hacker as the 'no action at a distance' principle. But there are a number of practices to which this rule does not apply. Hacker argues (Peter Hacker, 'Developmental hypotheses and perspicuous representations', *IYYUN, The Jerusalem Philosophical Quarterly*, July 1992, p. 287) that if the practitioners of a rite 'are ignorant of the genesis of the ancestry of their ritual, then the bare fact of its genesis can contrib-

ute nothing to explaining its significance. The remote and long forgotten origins may well be irrelevant to its current significance.' In
spite of Hacker's cautious transition from 'can contribute nothing'
to 'may well be irrelevant' this is not his main equivocation which
consists rather in the equation of significance with 'current significance'. Is the significance of a practice exhausted in what it means
to its current practitioners? Isn't Hacker nourishing his imagination
on only one kind of example? Hacker overlooks, or ignores Tyler's
distinction between 'form and meaning' on the one hand and 'signification' on the other and the problem set us by 'time honoured
religious customs whose form has been faithfully and even servilely
kept up while their nature has often undergone transformation'.
Consider Tyler's rationale for the enquiry into origins: 'some religious ceremonies are marvels of permanence holding substantially
the same form and meaning through age after age far beyond the
range of historic record. On the other hand the signification of ceremonies is not to be rashly decided on by mere inspection. The
ethnographer who brings together examples of a ceremony from
different stages of a culture can often give a more rational account
of it than the priest, to whom a special signification, sometimes very
unlike the original one, has become a matter of orthodoxy.'
(Edward Tyler, *Primitive Culture*, London: John Murray, 1920, p.
363.) What fallacy has Tyler committed?

Consider the kind of case represented by the superstitious practice of knocking on wood. A genetic account of the practice of
knocking on wood to prolong good fortune or avert bad runs as
follows: people once believed that knocking on wood summoned
the protective, benevolent intervention of the dryad who lived in
the tree from which the wood knocked on came. Would not this
confer intelligibility on the practice in spite of its remoteness from
its current significance in Hacker's sense? Don't we now understand something which previous to the discovery of its origins we
did not understand? Not only is it arbitrary to exclude the only
genetically explicable features of a practice from its meaning, to
reduce significance to significance for the current practitioners of
the rite, but it is particularly arbitrary with respect to those practices which excited Frazer's particular interest and of which he
took Nemi to be one: survivals.

Consider the case of the exorbitant penalties exacted in recent
times for bigamy. These are accounted for by the fact that bigamy

was once considered a profanation of the sacrament of marriage and therefore a species of blasphemy which was once thought to risk horrendous consequences for the community at large. This illustrates the common case where a practice appears inadequately motivated and can only be rendered intelligible through an account of its origins.

That the custom of letting the best man be the first to kiss the bride is an attenuated survival of an ancient practice based on the belief that it was dangerous for the husband to deflower his own wife, and so the task was delegated, tells us nothing of the current practice and can only provide raw material for jokes and wise-cracks, but can it be said not to explain it? Our custom has its own complex of feelings and saving the bridegroom from danger is not among them (though Ernest Jones thought it present and active in the unconscious). Nevertheless, belief in its putative origin would confer intelligibility on the practice.

Is there no illumination to be found in the kind of development compressed in the Monty Python *Life of Brian* sketch – a deaf man on the fringes of the crowd hears 'Blessed are the peace makers' as 'Blessed are the cheese-makers', thus prompting the question, 'Why cheese-makers in particular?' Whether 'Blessed are the cheese-makers' had 'its own complex of feelings' or not, it is only to be explained genetically.

Is Frazer imputing a rationale to the later practitioners of a rite that properly characterises only its origins and ignoring the possibility that it has 'its own complex of feelings'? This is hardly compatible with the the following remark about the burning of effigies, 'That the true character of the effigy as representative of the beneficent spirit of vegetation should sometimes be forgotten is natural. The custom of burning a beneficent god is too foreign to later modes of thought to escape misinterpretation. Naturally enough the people who continued to burn his image came in time to identify it with persons, whom, on various grounds, they regard with aversion, such as Judas Iscariot, Luther, and a witch.' (J. G. Frazer, *The Golden Bough*, abridged edition, London: Macmillan, 1967, p. 853.) This may be excessively speculative but why does Hacker think it illustrates the supposed fallacy of 'action at a distance'? In stating his 'no action at a distance' principle Hacker takes a more restrictive view of the relevance of genetic facts than Wittgenstein himself does. Isn't Wittgenstein himself indulging in genetic explanation when he explains certain idioms suggestive of outlandish beliefs, such as that men can be descended from snakes, by suggesting that what happened was that a figure of speech 'exuberated' into a misunderstanding? (quoted by Rush Rhees 'Language and ritual' in McGuinness, *Wittgenstein and his Times*, London: Blackwell, 1982, p. 97).

SYNOPTICALITY MAY CLARIFY BUT CANNOT EXPLAIN

The synoptic method which Wittgenstein recommends ('putting into order that we already know') cannot resolve the hermeneutic problem which Frazer explicitly addresses. Some commentators like Bell acknowledge this but defend it on the grounds that it is the appropriate response to an issue more fundamental than the hermeneutic one. But others, like Peter Hacker, insist that it can accomplish the hermeneutic aim which Wittgenstein sets it. Hacker writes: 'Frazer's data are relevant to an elucidatory enterprise – an arrangement which will display the specific, ceremonial, ritual physiognomy of a given savage practice against the backcloth of a whole family of analogous rituals.' (Peter Hacker, 'Developmental hypotheses and perspicuous representations', *IYYUN, The Jerusalem Philosophical Quarterly*, July 1992, p. 295.) (But this is question begging. We do not know which rituals are analogous to which until we know the rationales the arrangement is intended to elucidate. Fontenrose denies that the Nemi figure who engages in ritual combat with an interloper is symbolic of the community. (J. Fontenrose, *The Ritual Theory of Myth*, University of California: Berkeley, 1971, pp. 36–49.) If Fontenrose is right how would Hacker's procedure detect the fact? We could be seeking for analogies to a practice which does not exist – at least not at Nemi.

Paul Redding takes the same view as Hacker

Instead of bringing the facts of the festival into contact with the postulated facts of its historical origins, one charts the formal relations between the expressive character of the festival and those forms of life of the community which provide a background and whose spirit the festival expresses. (Paul Redding, 'Anthropology and ritual: Wittgenstein's reading of Frazer's *The Golden Bough*', *Metaphilosophy* vol. 18, nos. 3 and 4, July 1987, p. 260.)

But even if we had independent knowledge of 'the forms of life of the community' how would our ability to see the festival as a manifestation of these assure us that it was in fact so? This sounds like the discredited principle of *Geistesgeschichte*. In any case, what aroused Frazer's interest in Nemi is precisely that it was apparently not expressive of the life of its community but a barbarous anomaly, human sacrifice having been long discarded.

Johnston seems to me to commit the same error as Hacker:

In his essay 'Wittgenstein and the fire festivals' Frank Cioffi accuses Wittgenstein of failing to make a clear distinction between issues concerning the inner nature of the practice and those concerning its relation to ourselves. The two themes however are necessarily closely linked, for the inner nature of the practice is only accessible to us in so far as the practice relates directly or indirectly to our own experience. (Johnston, *Wittgenstein and Moral Philosophy*, London: Routledge 1989, p. 221)

But how can its accessibility 'to us' determine its inner character? Are we never to leave others to their otherness? It is one thing to express dissatisfaction with an account that does not leave us feeling that we understand it and quite another to insist that an account can only be true if we do understand it. We should adapt to such occasions a remark of G. K. Chesterton's Father Brown, 'We have discovered the truth – and the truth makes no sense.'

Redding quotes Dilthey's gnomic 'Understanding is a rediscovery of the I in the Thou.' The problem that this naturally poses is how the discovery of 'the I in the thou' is to be distinguished from its delusive projection there.

Similar considerations apply to 'making clear'. Making clear cannot resolve hermeneutic puzzles. The fact that we kiss the pictures of loved ones can be employed to make apparently pointless transactions with images clear; but making clear confers eligibility not veridicality. It is not self evident to an outsider, given an account of a Passover meal, why the matzoh forms part of it, or the bitter herbs, or the salt water in which the vegetables are immersed. If he doesn't know, no amount of putting into order what he already knows will help. Only telling him what he doesn't know will.

One explanation of Wittgenstein's dismissal of Frazer's explanatory efforts is that what interests Wittgenstein is rituality rather than ritual. What I mean by rituality is that though we may have a natural expectation that when people go from a profane to a sacred precinct they will adopt some change in demeanour or adornment, that Christians remove their hats and Moslems their shoes, or that Jews cover their heads while Christians uncover theirs, needs to be explained. So with Nemi. Even if we are right in thinking that what is being done at Nemi is being done because, as Wittgenstein says, it is terrible, this still leaves unexplained why these *particular* terrible things were done.

Wittgenstein is unlikely to have thought that we could have invented the idea that the tenure of a priest should depend on his ability to survive combat with a runaway slave. What he may have felt we could have invented is the notion that some surrogate for the community should die violently. And even if we agreed that this was an apt way of expressing the way we feel about things so that we could say, 'Human life is like that' this would not preclude the sacrifice nevertheless having a magical instrumental aim. Human life is like that too.

Of course we don't have to derive prayer from spell via the demoralising discovery that spells don't work and the hope that prayer might (as Frazer does); we can just put prayer and spell side by side, perhaps adding scientific experiment as well, thus composing an *Übersicht* of the diverse means men may resort to in coping with danger and uncertainty. But to what end? It involves deserting the problems posed by particular hermeneutic puzzles. Man may be a ceremonious animal but he is not a crossing-himself animal, nor facing-east-when-he-prays animal, nor a Passover-celebrating animal. *Übersicht* – what I have called synopticality – is not an appropriate response to a genuinely hermeneutic puzzle because if we know why the ritualists do what they do then there is no need to put into order what we already know and, if we don't know, putting into order what we already know is a precarious ground for the inference that motives that have been made perspicuous to *us* also activated *them*. And this procedure is rendered particularly futile, in the case of magic, by a fact to which Wittgenstein intermittently calls our attention. We are as inward with the occult, instrumental, ulterior, benefit-seeking rationale for ritual as with self-sufficient expressive ones.

What is it we understand better about human sacrifice, magic and ritual, not as concepts but as exotic anthropological phenomena, after taking in what Wittgenstein has to say about them? Not much. It is the ambiguities and limits of our modes of understanding which profit from the attempt to clarify. We become aware that we number among our explanatory paradigms several with which we are nevertheless not inward, which enable us to explain but not understand, and thus that there are respects in which our own non-exotic fellows are alien to us and, on the other hand, that several of our paradigms of understanding have a reach we had not previously accorded them.

WHEN IS IT A MISTAKE TO EXPLAIN?

I have attempted to show that the raising of empirical questions as to the practices described by Frazer involves no conceptual confusions and that it is doubtful that Frazer shows any signs of division of purpose such as can be found in Freud. But Wittgenstein has another objection to Frazer. Having remarked that every explanation is an hypothesis, Wittgenstein does not go on to say, as one might expect, that therefore an hypothesis is conceptually ineligible for explaining Nemi. What he goes on to say is that a person troubled by love will not be comforted by an hypothesis – i.e., not that an hypothesis won't explain Nemi but that the Nemi-troubled don't want it explained; they want the impression it makes on them clarified.

Paul Redding writes:

Wittgenstein draws attention to the fact that not all 'why' questions are requests for causal explanations. Someone bereaved might exclaim, 'Why did she die?' Such a question, uttered in a particular tone and under particular circumstances, would only be taken by the most obtuse as requests for an explanation – as being satisfied by the sort of response appropriate to the question in the context, say, of a coronial enquiry. (Paul Redding, 'Anthropology and ritual: Wittgenstein's reading of Frazer's *The Golden Bough*', *Metaphilosophy* vol. 18, nos. 3 and 4, July 1987, p. 264.)

What entitles us to assimilate Frazer's attempts at an empirical resolution of the hermeneutic question 'Why human sacrifice?' to a tactlessly proffered coroner's report? Although some of us will recognise an obscure and troubling awareness of the relation of human sacrifice to our own feelings and thoughts, and a craving to have these clarified, it must also be acknowledged that not everyone will experience this craving, and so the coercive tone adopted by those who feel as Wittgenstein does is not appropriate. Johnston speaks of 'irritation at the crassness of Frazer's confusions'. (*Wittgenstein and*

Moral Philosophy, London Routledge 1989, p. 221) and Redding refers to Frazer's 'self-deception' (p. 266).

Must the desire for a perspicuous view of the feelings and thoughts provoked in us by accounts of human sacrifice necessarily take precedence over the desire to know, for example, what of explanatory relevance happened to Aztec culture between the time they were ritually killing thousands of human beings in the course of a morning, and an earlier period in which they were not? A synoptic view will not tell us whether animal sacrifice preceded human or replaced it, nor whether it is characteristic of the more rather than the less technologically advanced cultures. Why should we not wish to know this?

In his assumption that the account of Nemi calls for clarification and not explanation Wittgenstein is producing a specimen of the discourse Simmel attempted to elucidate by talking of a 'third something' whose response to experience is neither that of our individual subjectivity nor logically compelling. Simmel called it 'the typical mentality'. When Wittgenstein speaks of 'we', 'us' and 'our', it is this 'typical mentality' for which he assumes himself to be speaking. And unless we can find a way of circumscribing the 'we' spoken for so as to exclude the bulk of Frazer's commentators his assumption is false.

It is in reminding us that there is an alternative direction of interest to that of explanation, and not in demonstrating its intrinsic priority, that the value of Wittgenstein's objections to Frazer's empirical procedure lies. Though there are topics which may incite us to produce accounts of them which will banish their power to trouble us it does not follow that attempts at empirical explanation of them is mistaken. What we *can* say is that among those who asked for explanation some can be brought to realise that what they really wanted was a discourse which would introduce order into the turmoil of their thoughts and feelings. However those of us in whom Wittgenstein's remarks on the desirability of an *Übersicht* of our feelings and thoughts with respect to human sacrifice, produces the realisation that this is what we 'really wanted', must not fall into the error of erecting our receptiveness into a standard. It should not be our aim to transform explainers into clarifiers.

CHAPTER ELEVEN

Explanation and self-clarification in Freud[1]

HYPOTHESES AND FURTHER DESCRIPTIONS[2]

The instruments of self-clarification are 'further descriptions'. Wittgenstein's examples are varied but the contrast with that which we can only know through investigation is maintained. All these are dubbed hypotheses. The notion of identifying, elaborating, correcting, refining on an earlier mindstate is familiar. William James has several felicitous evocations of the incitements to this activity. He speaks of '. . . relations and objects but dimly perceived'; of the 'halo or penumbra that surrounds' an image; of

[1] There is a comprehensive treatment of Wittgenstein's criticism of Freud in Bouveresse's *Wittgenstein Reads Freud* (Princeton: Princeton University Press, 1996). My own account is circumscribed by the centrality I give to the contrast between explanation and clarification and the attendant antitheses: hypothesis/further description; causal/formal; external/internal, etc. I stated a few reservations in a review in the *London Review of Books*, 25 January 1996.

[2] Wittgenstein sometimes uses the expression 'formal relation' when he wants to characterise that which is knowable without hypothesis, when, for example, in the remarks on *The Golden Bough* he speaks of an hypothesis as cloaking or disguising a formal relation. I have preferred to avoid the term 'formal' where possible because it is not felicitous, given what Wittgenstein needs to mean by it. A formal relation (sometimes referred to as an 'internal' relation) is one, lacking which the object would not be that which we meant to speak of, i.e. it is an identifying characteristic of the object. Wittgenstein seems to have transposed the term from his logico-mathematical interests. What makes the expression infelicitous is that a term can be formal in the logico-mathematical sense without being formal in the phenomenological, back-of-mind, tip of tongue sense that Wittgenstein intends. This can be illustrated with his own earth–girth puzzle which Norman Malcolm says he used to illustrate the nature of philosophy. The puzzle: if a belt were tied snugly round the earth at the equator and then a one-yard length was inserted and the belt stretched to its fullest extent how high above the surface would the belt now be? The answer is easily attained by anyone philistine enough to know the circumference of the earth and to apply the $2r$ formula, but for the rest of us the intuitive answer is that the relation of the belt to the surface would be altered to a minuscule degree. It thus comes as a surprise to us that the answer is 'nearly six inches'. The answer 'nearly six inches' is formally but not phenomenologically related to the question, which is phenomenologically but not formally related to the misleading picture of a minute difference.

'being aware in a penumbral nascent way of a fringe of unarticulated affinities'; of 'vast premonitory glimpses of schemes of relations between terms'; of a 'halo of felt relations'; of 'the vague sense of a plus ultra' etc. (William James, *The Principles of Psychology*, New York: Dover, 1950, 254–9).

A psychotherapist calls the statements in which we attempt to articulate the 'unarticulated affinities', of which James speaks, 'focusing utterances', 'the putting into unambiguous words of something (which) is just outside the 'focus range' of consciousness'. He illustrates: 'let us suppose that a disinterested friend say to a man who has for a long time been suffering from a vague malaise,

If you were honest with yourself you would admit that you are bored with your job and unhappy with your wife and that you stick in the rut out of habit and fear of change. This remark comes at a time when it is sufficient to make his dissatisfaction specific and fully conscious. In one sense of 'know' he had known for a long time what his friend had put into words. (G. Seaborn Jones, *Treatment or Torture*, London: Tavistock Press, 1968, p. 95)

This is Gaston Bachelard making the same point:

In the field of psychoanalysis the naming of things is often sufficient to cause a precipitate. Before the name there was often only an amorphous, troubled disturbed solution. After the name crystals are seen at the bottom of the liquid. (Gaston Bachelard, *The Psychoanalysis of Fire*, London: Routledge 1964, pp. 39–40)

There is a nice example of this kind of linguistic transaction in Stephen Mulhall's book on Heidegger and Wittgenstein:

... a human being in a state of deep despair may come across Marlowe's lines in Dr Faustus ('a perpetual cloud descends') and acknowledge it as a uniquely appropriate articulation of the state of mind in which he finds himself; it may even be a means of allowing him to understand more clearly the precise nature of his own moods and feelings by permitting him to put that fact of his inner world to words for the first time.[3] (Stephen Mulhall, *Being in the World*, London and New York: Routledge, pp. 109–10)

In the dream discussed by Wittgenstein – the flowery dream – this is the further description:

[3] It is unlikely to be a coincidence that Mulhall's example is the same one used by Wittgenstein ('care as the descent of a permanent cloud') in a remark in which he expresses regret that he had not stressed the importance of this kind of paraphrase sufficiently (Ludwig Wittgenstein, *Zettel*, Oxford: Blackwell, 1967, no. 517, p. 91).

In connection with this image (the flowering branch), she thought of the angel holding a spray of lilies in pictures of the Annunciation.'

And this is the hypothesis: 'The same branch which was carried like a lily and as though by an innocent girl was at the same time an allusion to La Dame aux Camelias who, as we know, usually wore a white camelia, except during her periods, when she wore a red one. (Sigmund Freud, *On Dreams*, London: Hogarth, 1952, p. 27).

What makes the allusion to La Dame aux Camelias an hypothesis is that it was inferred by Freud and not produced or recognised by the dreamer as the development of the idea with which her dream image was pregnant. But when the interpretations are not explicitly reported as the patient's own elaboration of her original statement it can be unclear whether they are hypotheses or further descriptions.

Are Freud's interpretations explanatory or self-clarificatory? Any monolithic characterisation of Freud's imputations of unconscious mental contents to a subject are bound to be false for these are not epistemically homogenous. And even if we take Freud's interpretations singly they may defeat us, for they are often individually ambiguous. Furthermore their miscellaneousness is not much mitigated by sticking to one class of explicanda, symptoms say, or dreams, for there will be epistemic variety within the class. To complicate matters still more the meaning of Wittgenstein's own expression 'further descriptions' has to be gathered from his examples which are not homogenous. Some are similes, some reminiscences, some vague thoughts 'at the back of one's mind', some just 'objects of directed attention'. They are only united by what they are contrasted with – hypotheses – imputations of mind states for which we feel it natural to produce or demand evidence beyond the say so of the subject. Wittgenstein's fullest account of the antithesis to hypothesis-propounding is his account of what Freud is doing when he is explaining how jokes work. In the second Lecture on Aesthetics Wittgenstein says

All we can say is that if it is presented to you, you say 'Yes, that's what happened' . . . Freud transforms the joke into a different form which is recognized by us as an expression of the chain of ideas which led us from one end to another of the joke. (*Lectures and Conversations*, p. 17)

It was a mistake for Wittgenstein to suggest that Freud's joke paraphrases are paradigmatic of his interpretations in general. There are too many instances where being 'led from one end to another' doesn't fit the interpretation Freud proffers, e.g., a patient being told that a pain in her forehead was due to her having been the recipient of 'a piercing glance'. But even where the analogy with joke-paraphrases is not ruled out by the non-intentionalist character of the explicanda, it can be unclear whether it is an hypothesis which is being advanced. This is Freud's account of an obsessive bedtime ritual in an adolescent girl:

One day she divined the central idea of her ritual when she suddenly understood her rule not to let the bolster touch the back of the bed. The bolster had always seemed a woman to her, she said, and the upright back of the bedstead a man. She wished therefore by a magic ceremony, as it were, to keep man and woman apart; that is to say, to separate the parents and prevent intercourse from occurring.

That she thought of the bolster as a woman and the bedstead as a man is clearly 'further description'. It is likely, too, that in preventing contact between them she was preventing an act of intercourse, was also a further description – 'she suddenly understood'. But was the conclusion that the act of intercourse in question was one between her parents, Freud's or the patient's? It is impossible to say. And of course even if it was the patient's this would not show conclusively that it was a further description; this would depend on what her grounds for this were. But there is more wrong with Freud than mere ambiguity.

Freud's assimilation of the dream work to the joke work proof of confusion

In *The Interpretation of Dreams* Freud relates the following dream for the purpose of illustrating the mechanism of condensation:

On one occasion a medical colleague had sent me a paper he had written in which the importance of a physiological discovery was in my opinion overestimated and in which, above all, the subject was treated in too emotional a manner. The next night I dreamt a sentence which clearly referred to this paper: 'It's written in a positively norekdal style.' The analysis of the word caused me some difficulty at first . . . At last I saw that the monstrosity was composed of two names Nora and Ekdal – characters in two well known plays of Ibsen's (*A Doll's House* and *The Wild Duck*). (*The Interpretation of Dreams*, New York: Avon, 1967, p. 331).

Compare this with Freud's account of the operation of the mechanism of condensation in jokes which he illustrates with a joke that plays on the French expression '*tête-à-tête*' (head to head i.e. a cosy

intimate chat) by rendering it *tête-à-bête* (head to beast). The joke
runs 'I spoke with X *tête-à-bête*.' Freud's paraphrase runs: 'I talked
with X and X is an ass.' This is patently what Wittgenstein calls a
'further description'. The term condensation when it occurs in a
dream interpretation does not refer to a feature of the dream
which can be determined by simple inspection but to a hidden
process which it took Freud's genius for decipherment, and not
just for reformulation, to discover. Notice the epistemic difference
between the relation of Freud to the solution of his puzzling
dream utterance 'nor-ek-dal' and that of the reader to Freud's
account of the paraphrase of the *tête-à-bête* joke. In the case of the
joke the reader is being offered a, hopefully, recognisable paraphrase of the joke for which he will acknowledge the felicity of the
expression 'condensation'. But condensation as it occurs in
Freud's interpretation of his dream is an inference not a description, however well-founded it might be. To make the contrast even
clearer imagine that Freud had made the Norekdal comment, not
in a dream but in waking life, as a sardonic commentary on the
style of which he disapproved. It would still be an example of
condensation but this time not a matter of inference and thus
amenable to Wittgenstein's 'assent is the only criterion' account.

When should we eschew clarification of our dreams for explanation of them?

Since there were no conceptual objections to advancing hypotheses to account for the image of the flowering branch what then are
the appropriate considerations for determining whether Freud
should have advanced further descriptions of the image, or sought
to explain it? Freud does engage from time to time in helping his
patients to formulate what was in their minds – to draw on Rush
Rhees's expression. And when Wittgenstein says that Freud had
genius and therefore could sometimes find the reason for your
dreams it is this talent for reformulation that he probably has in
mind. The fact that most counts in favour of the argument that
Wittgenstein was mistaken to condemn Freud for advancing a
causal hypothesis about the camellia sprouting branch in the
flowery dream rather than a further description of the dreamer's
waking relation to it is that she was a patient and not a confidante.
This being the case, of the two alternative modes of dream inter-

pretation that Wittgenstein describes in the 1947 remark (*Culture and Value*, Oxford: Blackwell, 1980, p. 68) – that of the sheet which when unfolded reveals a picture which we recognise as an elaboration of our sense of the hidden significance of the dream and that which attempts to relate it causally to our mental life, though at the cost of destroying our sense of its incipient meaning – isn't it the latter which Freud was under an obligation to provide?

Let us assume, as Freud enjoins us to, that it is a matter of great importance what is on this unfolded sheet because folded up in a different way, under different conditions it results not in the surrealistically juxtaposed images and episodes of the manifest dream but in an affliction – vaginismus, say, or dysmenorrhoea or hysterical migraine. For example, Dora, who developed a limp which Freud held due to an unconscious fantasy of bearing a child out of wedlock, might just as readily have *dreamt* of limping in which case the successful deciphering of her dream would have yielded the secret of her limp. Suppose that contemporaneous with her unaccountable, puzzling limp Dora had the following dream: 'I met Herr K (the man she unconsciously desired to have a child by) in a bustling street. He tried to embrace me but I repelled him. A while later I notice I am limping.' The analyst tries reversal on the bustling street and gets a secluded glade, the repelled embrace becomes a sexual consummation, Freud's wordplay applied to the dream limp yields the out-of-wedlock childbearing (just as it did when applied by Freud to Dora's real limp). Would we not say that in these circumstances Freud had done Dora a service much more valuable than that of helping her to formulate 'the ideas with which her dream had been pregnant'?

The flowery dreamer may be making an ambiguous demand and only she can tell us whether clarification or explanation was the appropriate response to it. Just as only Nicolson can tell us whether he already had a sufficient grasp of his sexuality and its aims and that his desire for a knowledge of its physical conditions was clear-headed and not a self-misunderstood displacement of a need for self-clarification. Charles Hanly is scathing about Wittgenstein's charge that Freud cheated the flowery dreamer of her pleasure in her dream, warning that 'the sentiment and aura of beauty that invests certain dreams may be a cover up for an unhealthy sexuality . . . to cooperate with it is to deny the individual any prospect of achieving a healthy sexuality and the authentic beauty of person that is its concomitant' (Charles Hanly, 'Wittgenstein on psychoanalysis', in *Ludwig Wittgenstein: Philosophy and Language* (ed. Ambrose, A. and Lazerowitz, M. (London: Allen and Unwin, 1972, p. 86). We must not allow the sanctimoniousness of this to distract us from the fact that a cogent objection is being raised. The flowery dreamer was a patient and a causal orientation towards her problems could have been perfectly in order, though it need not have been. It would not have been, if what she brought to Freud was not an hysterical symptom but an unfocused unhappiness. It could then have been appropriate to help her formulate what was in her mind, to solicit further descriptions of her misery, to put things 'side by side' – scenes from her childhood, say, and those of her current life – and to ask her whether she found the juxtaposition illuminating and why – all this would be clarification and not out of place. But now suppose that her major problem was disabling menstrual periods; that it had been diagnosed as hysterical and Freud felt (as he did) that her dreams contained the clue as to what repressed ideational material was being converted into the presenting symptoms. This could be challenged on grounds of the feebleness of its empirical basis (Freud's 'colossal prejudice') but not for its conceptual or moral inappropriateness.

One of the constructions that could be put on the thesis that clarification rather than explanation is the appropriate response to dreams is not that there is any conceptual anomaly in attempting an explanation of the dream, nor that this is not what is called for by the problems Freud addresses, but that clarification of our thoughts and feelings is what we expect of Freud in particular, in view of his practice and pronouncements. However, it is often maintained, not least by Freud himself, that this is a misunderstanding of the sense in which Freud holds meanings to be unconscious.

Consider Wittgenstein's remark that dreams or at least some sequence of dream images are rebus-like. Meaning, in the sense in which Wittgenstein says dreams have it, is a communal intersubjective aspect of dreams, not something which had to wait for Freud to discover. It is helpful when discussing these matters to distinguish and bear in mind the distinction between aspect-meaning and inference-meaning. Aspect-meaning is not a matter of evidence, and may profit from attempts at self-clarification; inferred meaning requires empirical inductions and investigations. Whether the architect of St Basil's Cathedral in Moscow actually intended to convey something by the distinctive way in which each of the five spires that so impressed Wittgenstein were convoluted could only be discovered by art-historical enquiry, but Wittgenstein's impression of a secret significance would be untouched by the outcome of such enquiry. It is in this sense that Wittgenstein holds dreams to be rebus-like. That dreams have meaning in Wittgenstein's sense is no more a matter of discovery than the man in the moon. Wittgenstein commended Freud for hitting on the term rebus to particularise one aspect of this impression of significance. The smoking cigar in the last panel of every instalment of the Popeye comic strip is a rebus in the inference sense. It strikes us as significant and is, in that it was chosen by the cartoonist Segar, the creator of Popeye, to represent his name. On the other hand the recurrent 'nov shmov kapop' in the Smokey Stover strip is certainly language-like, and even Slavonic or Yiddish-like, but whether it means anything we shall have to wait for some learned historian of the comic strip to tell us. What Freud claimed to have discovered is not that dreams have meaning in Wittgenstein's sense but that he could decipher them. It is on Freud's unacknowledged oscillation between clarification of aspect meaning and the inference to repressed meaning that Wittgenstein's charge of confusion is partly based.

Does Freud equivocate as to the sense in which mental contents are unconscious?

There is something to be said for the thesis that Freud led his patients to believe that the enterprise in which they were mutually engaged was clarification. Though Freud does say that 'all the acts and manifestations which I notice in myself and do not know how to link up with the rest of my mental life must be judged as if they belonged to someone else' (Sigmund Freud, 'The Unconscious', *Collected Papers*, vol. IV, London: Hogarth, 1925, p. 102), he also intermittently advances a different account of the sense in which mental contents are unconscious. Here is a striking example. In *Studies on Hysteria* Freud tells a patient that she is in love with her employer and she agrees. He asks her why she did not tell him earlier and she replies, 'I didn't know or didn't want to know. I wanted to drive it out of my head and not think of it . . .' It is the relation to 'repressed' mental states evinced by such remarks which imply that what is called for by the disturbance they cause is clarification via further description rather than explanation via hypotheses. Freud then makes an extraordinary comment: 'I have never managed to give a better description of the strange state of mind in which one knows and does not know a thing at the same time.' He then relates a comparable experience of his own of which he says, 'I was afflicted with the blindness of the seeing eye which is so astonishing in the attitude of mothers to their daughters, husbands to their wives and rulers to their favourites.' (*Studies on Hysteria*, London: Penguin, 1991, p. 181.) This expression of a conception of the unconscious which he so often repudiated is not a matter of development from one view to the other, for in the same work he speaks of the analysis uncovering thoughts which 'the patient will never recognise as his own' and 'which he never remembers', but are nevertheless imputed to him (*Studies on Hysteria*, p. 388). Here we have both conceptions of the unconscious – the clarificatory/assent-decidable and the explanatory/hypothetical – side by side. Each of those two notions of what an analyst is doing when he acquaints a patient with the contents of his unconscious is a feasible one. Why then is the hypothetical one deemed ineligible and only the clarificatory one demanded by the context?

Since Freud did, on many occasions, expound a notion of unconscious contents as only arrivable at by inference he would have felt himself quite justified when he accused Joseph Wortis of not believing in the unconscious because he had rejected an interpretation which awoke no resonances in him. Freud was thus entitled to offer non-clarificatory explanation – explanations which did not strike the patient as developments of ideas with which their thoughts and feelings were pregnant and so were not back-of-mind-like, but this still leaves open the question of whether he needed to. There are intuitive reasons for feeling that Freud's insistence that only specially qualified decoders like himself could arrive at a correct conception of a subject's unconscious was often gratuitous.

Whenever I have detected in myself something I would have preferred to be otherwise – more rancour, or envy, or vanity, or sexual perversity than I had previously acknowledged – I have almost always had the feeling that it was something of whose presence I was obscurely aware for a long period preceding its explicit recognition; and I have some grounds for thinking that this is the way it is with others as well. This has led me to suspect accounts like that implicit in Tolstoi's account of Anna's discovery of her love for Vronsky.

At first Anna sincerely believed that she was displeased with (Vronsky) for daring to pursue her; but soon after her return from Moscow, having gone to a party where she expected to meet him but to which he did not come she distinctly realised by the disappointment that overcame her, that she had been deceiving herself and that his pursuit was not only not distasteful to her, but was the whole interest of her life. (L. Tolstoi, *Anna Karenina*, London: Penguin, 1954, p. 143)

Can we really credit that Anna's disappointment at Vronsky's absence was the sole ground for her realisation that his attentions were not unwelcome to her? Don't we feel that Tolstoi's way of putting it was just a *façon de parler* and find it natural to eke out this account with her recognition of past occasions on which a more candid inspection of her feelings would have exposed the true state of affairs? Wouldn't that be more in accord with our feelings as to how things go?

   Consider an Anna Karenina-like example in a paper of 1920. Freud writes of a patient: 'She is only slightly aware of the sensations of intense love until a certain disappointment is followed by an absolutely excessive reaction which shows everyone concerned that they have to do with a consuming passion of elemental strength.' Freud makes the following comment,

I will not miss this opportunity for expressing at once my astonishment that human beings could go through such great and momentous phases of their love life without heeding them, sometimes indeed without having the faintest suspicions of them. (S. Freud, *Collected Papers*, vol. 2, 1924, p. 225).

Freud here concedes that it is only sometimes that the subject of the states in question is 'without the faintest suspicion of them'. This would seem to allow a certain scope to a method which confined itself to soliciting clarificatory 'further descriptions'. Why can't it be argued on Freud's behalf that he was practising both genres of interpretation – the clarificatory, further description

kind and the inferential, hypothesis-propounding kind. Because –
and Wittgenstein is comparatively clear about this – Freud uses his
patients' acquiescence to further descriptions as criteria for the
correctness of hypotheses at the same time as he imputes to them
mind states – such as that they thought of this or that, meant this
or that, represented this by that – which only their acquiescence
and not the 'inexorable context' could validate – 'conscious
thoughts which were somehow unconscious'. This is the 'abominable mess'.

Hypotheses as disguises for further descriptions

The general bearing of this topic on our central question of when
it is inappropriate to engage in empirical enquiry is that one of the
things which causes us to overestimate the pertinence of investigation is that often, when we feel enlightened as a consequence of
the frequentation of ostensibly empirical discourse, though the
enlightenment may not be illusory, its dependence on the veridicality of the hypotheses which occasioned it, is. This is best illustrated by Freud's treatment of jokes and kindred phenomena.
Though Freud gives a causal cast to his questions about jokes, his
joke analyses do not answer to a causal account, and his joke
energetics, when illuminating are crypto-phenomenological, that
is, they are redescriptions of our experience disguised as hypotheses as to their causes.

This is Freud's tripartite division of humour with its accompanying explanation. The pleasure of wit (jokes) originates from an
economy of expenditure in inhibition; of the comic, in thought;
of humour, in feeling. Wittgenstein thinks Freud is confused as to
where the 'economies' of which he speaks are to be observed.
Sometimes Freud is straightforwardly untheoretical:

the release of distressing affects is the greatest obstacle to the emergence
of the comic. As soon as the aimless movement does damage, or the
stupidity leads to mischief, or the disappointment causes pain, the
possibility of a comic effect is at an end. (S. Freud, *Jokes and Their Relation
to the Unconscious*, London: Routledge, 1960, p. 228)

For example, 'The way he rolled about was hilarious until I realised that he was really having a fit.' But this is precisely the kind of
thing which Wittgenstein thinks Freud confused with an hypothesis and which answers to the same account as that he gave of joke

analyses. 'All we can say is that if it is presented to you, you say "Yes, that's what happened"' (*Lectures and Conversations*, p. 18).

Similarly with Freud's account of humour. Unlike jokes where the effect arises from an economy in expenditure on inhibition, the pleasure of humour comes about 'at the cost of a release of affect that does not occur; it arises from an economy in the expenditure of affect.' A case of economy in the expenditure on affect can be illustrated by the conundrum 'What do men do standing up, women sitting down and dogs on three legs?' The solution – 'shake hands' – effects a circumvention of the anticipated embarrassment at having to refer to bodily functions, thus releasing the energy prepared for this purpose, which energy makes itself felt as humorous amusement. But note that we don't *infer* the correctness of the Freudian account since the anticipated embarrassment and its avoidance are introspectible states whereas Freud's energic speculations pertain to a hidden, noumenal process.

Similarly with Freud's answer to the question, 'Why are a clown's movements funny?' This is due to 'an innervatory expenditure which has become an unusable surplus when a comparison is made with a movement of one's own.' This can be read as a restatement in Freud's 'sounding-like-science' language of energic economies and expenditures of what he had previously said without it; that in laughing at a comical movement we compare, in our imaginations, our movements with those of the clown, and the discrepancy between the effort it would take us and the effort it took him, amuses us. That this is not a question of the effect of hidden goings on in the psychic apparatus is also shown by the fact that we can see, without any such knowledge of hidden processes, that Freud's explanation of our laughter at the clown is mistaken or elliptical. It is not the mental processes of the clown, e.g., of the man who invented and performed Grock, Adrien Wettach, that we are contrasting with our own but that of a projected image. That our laughter in such cases differs from that at a genuinely awkward action, as in Freud's example of the child protruding her tongue as she makes her first attempts to write the letters of the alphabet, is revealed by introspective reflection not investigation.

Consider Freud's observations that the source of comicality of physiognomies is our assimilation of, for example, the clown's bulbous nose, or outsize ears to his clumsy movements. 'Bodily shapes and facial features are comic because regarded as though the outcome of exaggerated or pointless movement' (S. Freud, *Jokes and the Unconscious*, London: Routledge and Kegan Paul, 1962, p. 190). For example, outsize ears are funny because we think of their possessor as sticking them out as he might stick out his tongue. We think of a man with a comical cast of countenance as of someone who is making a face, e.g. as walling his eyes or crossing them. These are not hypotheses. Freud's assimilation of the comic of physiognomy to the comic of movement is not an inference as to the similarity or identity of the processes underlying them, but is constituted by analogies between the phenomena themselves as they are experienced. The statements in which Freud invokes differences in energy expenditure are crypto-phenomenological – 'hypotheses as disguises for formal connections'. They are 'good ways of representing' familiar facts and not speculations as to occult ones. They illustrate what Wittgenstein wanted to call attention to when he says of Freud's theorising about why we laugh at jokes that Freud 'encouraged a confusion between getting to know the cause of your laughter and getting to know the reason why you laugh', and that 'he was constantly unclear as to when he was advancing a hypothesis' because 'what he says sounds as if it were science when in fact it is only a wonderful representation'.

In general, when theorising, Freud confuses his production of descriptions which refer to shared manifest features of different kinds of laughables, for speculation as to the hidden processes which produced them. Heine's Hirsch-Hyacinth says that the wealthy Salamon Rothschild treated him as an equal – 'quite famillionairely'. Freud asks, 'What is it that makes Hirsch–Hyacinth's remark into a joke?' That is, what differentiates the way jokes produce amusement from the way in which other humorous phenomena do? Could investigation of the energy distribution in the psychic apparatus answer Freud's question? Is it akin to 'What makes an aspirin analgesic?' Freud illustrates the technique of 'condensation with modification' by citing a witticism provoked by the girth of a famous diva called 'Wilt' – 'Around the Wilt in 80 days' – here the condensation is a manifest feature of the joke. If you noticed that the joke hinges on the similarity between the sounds 'Wilt' and 'Welt' would you have to wait on the outcome of an experiment in which it was told in another language, French, say, to see whether it raised a laugh?

Imagine a world in which, like ours, people laughed at jokes, but unlike ours did not know what they were laughing at until they discovered the unconscious energic processes hypothesised by Freud – only after peering through the psychoanalytoscope were they able to pronounce – 'Just as we thought: a classic case of condensation with slight modification.' You would then have a picture of the world Freud intermittently beguiled himself (and us) into believing he was living in and which prompts Wittgenstein's attempts to wake us by reminding us of its unreality – 'a powerful mythology'. We can't escape the conclusion that Freud's theoretical pronouncements are only redescriptions of the phenomena they purport to explain. What makes them 'good representations of the facts', as Wittgenstein puts it, are Freud's perceptiveness and expressive powers.

(The same Janus-like character can be discerned in I. A. Richards' *Principles of Literary Criticism* where his invocation of a balance or harmony between competing or antagonistic impulses to account for the value of a poem is sometimes felt to be apposite, although we have no idea what it would be to identify these harmoniously reconciled impulses independently of our experience of the poem). Even if we could look forward to a time when a libido-meter would enable us to determine, of someone listening to a joke, what processes of cathexis and counter-cathexis were taking place in his mind, we would still need to have recourse to old-fashioned methods of paraphrase to make clear to ourselves just what it was that he found amusing.

Further descriptions that sound like science: sexuality

The feature of Freud's theorising which induced Wittgenstein to compare it to the putting of things side by side in an aesthetic discussion is not confined to his book on jokes. For example, when Freud characterises an activity as sexual it is sometimes unclear whether he intends to advance a thesis as to the processes of which it is an epiphenomenon, or to convey something as to its experiential quality, either for the subject himself or for an observer. How, for example, are the following descriptions of obsessive thinking to be taken?:

The thought process itself becomes sexualised, for the sexual pleasure which is normally attached to the content of thought becomes shifted on to the act of thinking itself, and the gratification derived from reaching the conclusion of a line of thought is experienced as a sexual gratification. (*Collected Papers*, vol. III, p. 380)

The suppressed sexual activities return in the form of brooding sufficiently powerful to sexualise thinking itself and to colour intellectual operations with the pleasure and anxiety that belong to sexual processes proper; investigation becomes a sexual activity . . . the feeling that comes from settling things in one's mind and explaining them replaces sexual satisfaction. (*Leonardo Da Vinci and a Memory of his Childhood*, London: Penguin, 1985, p. 170)

The status of the 'suppressed sexual activities' invoked in this passage is rather that of a qualitative colouring of the experience putatively explained than a substrate process which scientific advance may one day render inspectable.

This is Freud's account of 'the difference between ordinary object-cathexis and the state of being in love'. In the latter, 'more cathexis passes over into the object – the ego emptying itself into the object, as it were'. Since this image is more evocative of the climax of lovemaking than of love it is easy to imagine that it was the manifest properties of the phenomena of lovemaking that determined the account given of the hidden causal substrate of which it was an ostensible product. Similarly with Freud's explanation of the mood swings in cyclothymia as due to a 'dynamic alternation in the quantity of energic cathexis'. Once again it seems as if the appearances have been jargonised and projected behind the phenomena as processes of which these are the ostensible manifestations. These examples do not have the compensating merit of Freud's joke energetics because the aspects to which they call attention are already sufficiently blatant to deprive us of any sense of something dimly perceived being brought into focus.

'It is all excellent similes': maternal breasts as hypotheses and as further descriptions

When Wittgenstein says that Freud does 'what aesthetic does', he is referring to the putting of things 'side by side' with the aim of effecting some mutual illumination as was achieved for Wittgenstein by his placing certain themes of Brahms alongside certain features of Gottfried Keller's prose. He illustrates this putting things side by side in Freud with Freud's assertion of a connection between the posture of the foetus and that of a sleeping adult. Wittgenstein denies that this is an hypothesis. I believe the same point is being made as when, in the notes on Frazer, he speaks of an 'hypothesis of development as a disguise for a formal connection'. In other words, as a disguise for something which is internal to the impression made by a phenomenon, is constitutive of it, as the burning of a man is internal to the impression made by the Beltane Fire Festival, and yet which is confusedly presented as explanatory of it. Or, as it might also be put, clarification is disguised as explanation. In Freud's aetiologies we have hypothesised infantile episodes in place of prehistoric rituals. Once again it is important not to put the emphasis on conceptual matters even if there are conceptual anomalies in Freud's verbal formulations. It is not merely the 'form of words' but the 'use made of the form of words' to which Wittgenstein is calling attention, when he calls Freud's infantile aetiologies 'myths', for example. In the remarks on Frazer he asks us to imagine the case of an ellipse being transformed before our eyes into a circle but only as a means of 'sharpening our eyes' to the relation between them, and not in order to assert an actual temporal sequence from one to the other, though there would be nothing conceptually confused about doing so. When Wittgenstein was illustrating his remark that Freud's claims as to the influence of infantile 'primal' scenes were myths, the example he gave was the birth trauma theory which is the most readily epidemiologically assessable of all the infantile aetiologies, since records are kept of the length of labour. Freud himself invoked this fact when he reproached Rank for not supplying statistical evidence of the influence of birth conditions on the disposition to neuroses and demonstrating the comparative freedom from neuroses of those who were, like Caesar and Macbeth, from their mother's womb 'untimely ripped' and thus spared the usual parturitional mauling.

Here is an example of putting things side by side where the reproach of confusion between clarification and explanation would be unjustified. Imagine an anti-smoking poster that consisted of two faces side by side, that of a baby sucking on his comforter/dummy and that of a businessman smoking a cigar. Though this doesn't say that there is a causal relation between the baby's sucking and the adult's smoking something is nevertheless being said as to the relation between them. What is implied is rather that the satisfaction taken in smoking is as infantile as that of the baby's sucking. This cannot be said to constitute a *disguise* for a further description since it is overtly 'formal' and a-causal. If those who found the juxtaposition felicitous took this as evidence of a causal relation we would then have what Wittgenstein complains of in Freud.

Freud writes

No one who has seen a baby sinking back satiated from the breast and falling asleep with flushed cheeks and a blissful smile can escape the reflection that this picture persists as a prototype of sexual satisfaction. ('Three essays on sexuality', in *On Sexuality*, Penguin, 1977, p. 98)

Freud here places two things side by side – a post-prandial baby and a post-coital adult. We are being asked to see affinities between our sexually satiated somnolence and the baby's, but some indeterminate developmental claim is being simultaneously advanced. The relation of the post-sumptuary somnolence of the infant to the post-coital lassitude of the adult is ostensibly external-hypothetical; the picture which Freud asserts to persist is the infant's, not the onlooker's. But the ambiguity is instructive. Do post-prandial babies just make us think of post-coital adults or is our post-coital lassitude really an unconscious revival of our infantile oral bliss? The same ambiguity is found in another remark: 'sucking at the mother's breast is . . . the unmatched prototype of every later satisfaction' (*Three Essays on Sexuality*, p. 145). This could be taken as a statement of what we naturally compare our later satisfactions to, or as an hypothesis as to the source of this sensed affinity. When Freud writes 'the sight of a child nursing revives the prehistoric impression of sucking at the mothers breast' isn't the nursing child redundant? Isn't the exposed breast alone sufficient? It is spontaneously numbered among suckables whether it is being sucked at by a baby or not. The hypothesis is parasitic for its plausibility on the appositeness of the further description. The natural affinity some of us may feel between a baby nursing and our own erotic transactions with breasts does not entail a causal relation between these. Cats are strokable and dogs pattable to those who have not spent any appreciable time of their infancies doing either. What reason are we given for thinking it otherwise with the suckability of breasts? What grounds are we given for imputing a causal influence on our adult oral transactions to our infantile mammary ones? Consider Richard Wollheim's thesis that phallic fantasies are 'later reworkings' of fantasies about the nipple. How does Wollheim imagine this transition to have been effected? Does he conceive of it as like going from soft drugs to hard via processes which, if they were conscious, would have been of the order, 'If nipples were nice penises would be even nicer'? He doesn't say. And it is this reticence, rather than any formal defects in Freud's developmental explanations, which provokes Wittgenstein to the hyperbole of Freud 'does what aesthetics does', puts things side by side.

That there is nothing inherent in developmental speculations to prevent them from being treated as genuinely empirical is indicated by Richard Brinsley Sheridan's rebuttal of the Prince Regent's suggestion that 'the feeling men entertain towards women's breasts is due to their having derived from that source the first pleasurable sensation of infancy' by pointing out that though 'some men have been raised by hand no man has ever felt any intense emotion of amatory delight on beholding a pap spoon'. An earlier champion of the unconscious, Eduard von Hartmann explained 'the powerful charm which a voluptuous female bosom exerts on a man' as due to 'the unconscious idea of the abundant nutrition it would provide a newborn child' (Eduard von Hartmann, *Philosophy of the Unconscious*, London: Kegan Paul, 1931, p. 236).

The distinction between an hypothesis and a further description becomes clearer if we contrast this gratifyingly disinterested account of the appeal of woman's breasts with one which invoked the 'unconscious idea' of the tactile and buccal pleasure they would provide (what G. F. Stout called the 'forefeel' of an image). If von Hartmann is right all the while that frequenters of the girlie magazines with their mammary freaks have been derided as lubricious idiots they have been manifesting their unconscious concern for the wellbeing of the race. But von Hartmann's conjecture, unlike several of Freud's, cannot serve as a clarification – as bringing an unarticulated hinterland into focus. Only for someone very hungry or very thirsty could von Hartmann's conjecture 'sharpen one's eyes to a formal connection'; and so unless it is a genuine hypothesis it forfeits our interest. When we trans-

fer Browning's line about 'the breasts' superb abundance' from a
woman to a cow we become aware of a component in its application to a woman that is missing in the naturally hypothesis-like
Hartmannian sense it takes on when applied to bovine udders. No
'forefeel' is involved in the dairy farmers speculations as to the
cow's milk yield. In the *Three Essays on Sexuality* Freud cites the case
of a grown up girl who had never given up thumbsucking 'and
who represents the satisfaction to be gained from sucking as
something completely analogous to sexual satisfaction, particularly when this is obtained from a lover's kiss'. Here we have the
formal relation, i.e. the clarificatory function, undisguised – the
erotic sucking explicitly assimilated to the ostensibly non-erotic –
a further description without the developmental disguise. In the
remarks on Frazer Wittgenstein suggests that 'the feeling that we
chose our own standpoint in the world is the basis of the belief
that we chose our body before birth'. Similarly the feeling we have
for breasts is the basis of the belief that the infant's pleasure in
sucking them is erotic.

Putting things side by side: nipples and penises

In the *New Introductory Lectures* Freud writes that 'interest in the
penis has a powerful root in oral erotism; for after weaning, the
penis inherits something from the nipple of the mother's breast'
(London: Hogarth, 1949, p. 131). How is this doing what aesthetic
does? Freud puts infantile sucking side by side with 'perverse
kissing', fellatio, smoking and other adult oral activities, and this
may enable those who engage in such activities, or find them
appealing to better grasp, or to better convey, the character of the
satisfaction they take in them; and those who do not, but wish to
understand or describe these, to diminish their oddity, to domes-
ticate them, as it were. Though it was traditionally maintained that
in assimilating the satisfaction of the baby in sucking the breast to
the fellator's in sucking the penis Freud was maligning the infant,
he can just as easily be seen as rehabilitating the fellator. The
analogy, rather than making the infant look less innocent makes
the fellator look less depraved. Freud's speculations as to our
infantile transactions with nipples do not explain adult oral transactions with penises though they may clarify them; at least for
those who have such transactions and want them articulated or

evoked. To adapt Wittgenstein's remark about laughter, 'being clear about fellatio is not being clear about a cause'.

WHEN SHOULD WE SEEK EXPLANATION AND WHEN CLARIFICATION?

In an account of Wittgenstein's objections to Freud P. Johnston writes, 'Freud seeks to offer explanation where . . . what is required is not explanation but clarification' (P. Johnston, *Wittgenstein and Moral Philosophy*, London: Routledge, 1989, p. 50). The least interesting feature of this statement is that it is blatantly false. What is of much greater moment is the problem it raises as to the concepts of clarification and explanation themselves – what they are meant to call our attention to, and how the line between them is to be drawn in those cases where its falsity is not blatant. And most momentous issue of all, when we have decided where the line is to be drawn, how we are to decide which – clarification or explanation – we should pursue. The following imagined exchange may convey the nature of this last issue:

'Should a man who, like Kirilov in Dostoievski's *The Possessed*, has rhapsodic "moments of harmony" which may be signs of epilepsy, be given clarification or explanation?'

'Explanation.'

'Should someone moved by Mozart's *Requiem* and unsure as to why, be given explanation or clarification?'

'Clarification'

'Should a young man who is disconcerted to find himself sexually indifferent to the bodies of women be given explanation or clarification?'

'mmmmmmmm'.

As to its blatant falsity, consider this sampler, from Freud's own account of the variety of problems his patients brought to him.

She is a pianist but her fingers are overcome by cramp and refuse to serve her. When she thinks of going to a party she promptly becomes aware of a call of nature the satisfaction of which would be incompatible with a social gathering. She is overcome by violent headaches, or other painful sensations at times when they are most inconvenient. She may even be unable to keep down any meal she eats . . . ('The question of lay analysis', in *Two Short Accounts of Psychoanalysis*, London: Penguin, 1962, p. 94)

How can it be said of these conditions that what they require is clarification and that it was remiss of Freud to proffer explanations instead? What can be said is that there are other conditions about which patients may be troubled – painful and disabling affective states, or disadvantageous attitudes, for example, and that, though with respect to these, too, empirical hypotheses are in order, they do invite an alternative mode of enquiry. They do not, in themselves, demand 'clarification' and preclude explanation, any more than human sacrifice does, but as with human sacrifice, we may feel a more pressing need for clarification than for explanation; or may come to realise that though we asked for explanation we really wanted clarification.

The explicanda of psychoanalysis are epistemically various. In the inventory of conditions from which the neurotic suffers, from which I have just quoted, Freud also lists 'fluctuations of his moods which he cannot control, a sense of despondency by which his energy feels paralysed, a nervous embarrassment among strangers'. These are conditions which can be imagined to have content of a kind which would lend itself to clarification. But not only is it not clear when the attempt at clarification should be made, it *is* clear that it would be perfectly in order to ignore the clarification of content and proceed to explanation of the affliction of which it is symptomatic. In his autobiography Mikhail Zoshchenko gives an account of how he went from believing that his lifelong misery was a justifiable response to the nature of existence to deciding that it was the result of an 'unfortunate accident in early life' (M. Zoshchenko, 'Beyond Sunrise' in *Nervous People and other Satires*, London: Gollancz, 1963, p. 343). He went from an intentionalist conception of his predicament in which it had objects which he names at length to a causal one which moves him to conclude 'I am unhappy and do not know why'. In rejecting self-clarification for causal explanation what mistake is he supposed to have made?

Here is an example of the kind of problem raised by Freud where clarification has something to be said for it: 'Every human being has acquired . . . a special individuality in the exercise of his capacity to love . . . Expectant libidinal impulses will be aroused by . . . each new person coming upon the scene . . .' ('Dynamics of the transference', 1912, *Collected Papers*, vol. 2, London: Hogarth 1924, p. 313). It is with respect to the anticipated gratification of our amorous and affiliative needs 'by each new person coming upon the scene' that clarification is appropriate. When Virginia Woolf speaks, in connection with her love for Vita Sackville-West, of 'the maternal protection which, for some reason, is what I have almost always most wished from everyone' (*The Diaries of Virginia Woolf*, vol. 2, 1925–30, ed. Ann Olivier Bell, London: Penguin, 1982, p. 52) she raises two distinct epistemic issues. In the phrase 'for some reason' she may be referring to those 'buried and forgotten love emotions' (Freud, 1924, p. 322) that Freud claims an authoritative relation to, whereas when she speaks of 'the maternal protection' she 'wished for from everyone', (implying that Vita Sackville-West provided it), she seems to be referring to 'the expectant libidinal impulses aroused by . . . each new person coming upon the scene', something as to which we have no grounds for impugning her authority. Nevertheless, Freud insists that the 'invaluable service of making the patient's buried and forgotten love emotions actual and manifest' is the task of the analyst in his role as authoritative translator of the patient's 'transference' behaviour. So the mistake of thinking that Freud gave explanations when clarifications were called for is twofold. It overlooks the non-intentionalist phenomena Freud was attempting to account for and it overlooks that even where the phenomena are intentionalist, causal questions, both distal and proximate, may be appropriately raised with respect to them.

Suppose we impute an adult's morbid fear of fire to a forgotten episode of having been burnt as a child. Why ought we to have proffered clarification instead? Can we say, as with the ellipse/circle analogy Wittgenstein uses in connection with the Beltane fire festival, that what is of interest is the formal relation between the childhood trauma and the adult disorder – that what matters is his realisation that there is something preterite and infantile in his fear of fire – and not whether one was in fact causally related to the other? Surely not.

ON DRAWING THE LINE BETWEEN EXPLANATION AND CLARIFICATION

What makes an example of enhanced self-understanding clarificatory rather than explanatory? Wittgenstein seems to have two distinct grounds for impugning the pertinence of empirical explanation and thus of empirical enquiry. One is that the problem posed does not require additional information for its solution. The solution lies entirely in what we can call to mind 'without adding anything'. The other, more restrictive view, is that the solution is internally related to the state of perplexity we want assuaged – as the ellipse is to the circle. These two may coincide but need not. But in the second word-at-the-tip-of-tongue sense the thesis is false even with respect to intentionalist states. I can't believe that Johnston thought that all the answers to the questions Freud addressed as to his patients' past must have been 'at the back of their minds' at the time. That which resolves a perplexity may qualify as something I already knew without having been at the back of my mind in the way the word on the tip of my tongue is. Consider the perplexities posed by ritual practices. It is enough to remind me of my own expressive inclinations vis-a-vis images, e.g., that I am familiar with the phenomenon of kissing pictures of loved ones to make non-instrumental effigy burning perspicuous; it is not necessary that it should have been at the back of my mind while I wondered what the effigy burners were up to.

I shall be using clarification in the extended sense in which the contrast with explanations is that, unlike explanation (as it figures in the contrast), it confines itself to what we already know – what we can call to mind. But even in this extended sense Johnston's thesis is false, though it calls attention to something of great interest and importance: that there is an alternative enterprise to explanation by more information and that it is often confused with it, particularly by Freud, to the detriment of both.

When is seeking explanations a mistake?

One of the most common grounds for disparaging empirical explanation, or for expressing disappointment at its results is its frequent failure to confer perspicuity on the phenomena explained. The perspicuity requirement may seem gratuitous when we are dealing with afflictions where the priority ought to be instrumental power and not understanding. The spirochaete which reached the brain of Ibsen's Oswald explains his derangement but not why he asked to be given the sun rather than the moon. Why should that be a black mark against Noguchi? But many cases in which explanatory questions arise are not so clear cut.

Harold Nicolson is said to have contemplated the possibility that his homosexuality was due to his blood calcium levels. Supposing the story is not apocryphal. Nicolson's interest in his calcium levels strikes us as odd because we expect someone with an interest in something as intimate as his sexual feelings to be in search of an account which will confer perspicuity on them, i.e., which stands to them as the burning of the child to the pyrophobia of the adult or as a punctiform surface to a punctiform sensation, and don't see how blood chemistry can supply this. The same opacity objection has been lodged against psychoanalytic explanations by phenomenologists. But is this enough to preclude their relevance or desirability?

'My homosexuality comes from my calcium levels' is clearly a hypothesis and not 'formally' related to my sexual feelings, i.e., not elucidatory of them. How about 'My homosexual feelings are rooted in my infantile relation to my brother?' Difficult to say; this might carry an implication as to the colouring of my feelings as well as their causes; but with two terms as amorphous as homosexuality and brother love it is always possible that at this or that angle or, in this or that light, some kind of mutual illumination might occur. But that my homosexuality is due to my reaction against my incestuous desire for my mother is so remote from my homo-erotic feelings themselves as to be incapable of conferring intelligibility on them, and so is an explanatory hypothesis which belongs epistemically with the blood calcium levels. But this precludes neither it nor the blood calcium one from being conceptually eligible, nor from being 'what the context calls for'. It is true that what a physical condition cannot do is confer perspicuity on the particular content of someone's feelings; for example, that Nicolson was only attracted by younger intellectual men of his own class and that the idea of sleeping with a guardsman was repugnant to him. If you doubt the *a priori* implausibility of discovering perspicuity-conferring physical conditions imagine the following absurd exchange.

Medical researcher: 'We now know, Sir Harold, that your homosexuality is due to the potassium levels in your blood.'

Nicolson – in astonishment – 'Potassium levels!'

Researcher: 'Did I say potassium levels? I am so sorry. I meant calcium levels.'

Nicolson: 'Ah! that's more like it.'

But all that the absurdity of this exchange demonstrates is that it would be a mistake for Nicolson to have anticipated from a knowledge of the influence of his blood chemistry a clarification of the nature of his erotic feelings. It does not show that it was a mistake for him to suspend his demand for clarification and seek explanation instead.

What may make explanation inappropriate is not the failure of articulation between it and the question addressed but the failure of the question itself to express adequately the craving which prompted it. Nicolson may not have been making the conceptual mistake of thinking his blood calcium level could shed light on why his homo-erotic feelings were confined to men of his own class. His mistake may have been rather one of self-misunderstanding – the failure of his curiosity about the physical conditions of his homosexuality to express adequately the craving for clarification of the homo-erotic feelings which – confusedly – gave rise to it. *If* what Nicolson really wanted to know about his homosexual infatuations was just what it was he was being suscep-tible to, and, of his homosexual love affairs, what he expected to get out of them, *then* his interest in his calcium levels was a mistake. But no doubt we could imagine that what he wanted to know about his homosexuality his calcium levels could tell him.

There is, moreover, a reason other than their intrinsic interest for seeking non-perspicuity conferring explanatory hypotheses, like blood calcium levels. It is that a physical explanation will exclude a certain class of hermeneutic possibilities. Though it might be of no interest to Nicolson whether it was potassium or calcium levels that determined his homo-erotic feelings, the knowledge that it was one or the other, and that his homo-erotic feelings had no intimate, hidden significance – that e.g., they were not stratagems to enable him to avoid a full realisation of his incestuous craving for his mother – might come as a relief to him. Just as a bedwetter who was given a non-psychodynamic explanation of his condition that excluded the possibility that it was only one of the less repellent manifestions of his general need to soil whatever he came into contact with would welcome the 'external' causal account. (An ado-lescent bedwetter on being given an impersonal account of his condition smiled with relief and said 'Then it has nothing to do with me!') Of course this implies, what we all know, that such exter-nal/causal accounts may be seductive without being cogent.

Memories as further descriptions and as hypotheses

What kind of enterprise is it to determine 'how from what we once were . . . we developed and became what we are' (Dilthey). Why should it not call for explanation rather than clarification? It can. Consider what Dilthey calls 'the roundabout way of understanding': 'What we once were, how we developed and became what we are, we learn from the way in which we acted, the plans we once adopted, the way in which we made ourselves felt in our vocation, from old dead letters, from judgments on us, spoken long ago' (Wilhelm Dilthey, *Meaning and Pattern in History*, ed. Rickman New York: Harper Torchbook, 1962, p. 71). But as well as explanatory narratives which can be compelling, whether within the subject's ability to confirm or not, there is also explanation via a particular subclass of self-clarifications – those which are retrospective and pertain to multitudinous occasions. In 'Freud's abominable mess' I asked, rhetorically I hoped, how someone could come to realise that he has all his life felt like an unprepared schoolboy praying that the period would end before he was called upon, without at the same time discovering the answer to many explanatory puzzles his life presents. This was an imaginary example. Here is a real one. The analyst Paul Schilder discriminated a special form of neurosis which he designated a 'social neurosis', because it was 'dominated by suffering in social contacts'. Schilder held it to be the 'result of impossible expectations of attention' derived from excessive parental appreciation. (Paul Schilder, 'The social neurosis', *Psychoanalytic Review*, 25, 1938, p. 1). The epistemic character of the patient's conviction that his adult disappointment at the amount of attention he receives was due to his infantile treatment by his parents is unclear. But if we imagine it to be without mediating anamnestic content it is natural to take it as an hypothesis which exceeds his ability to confirm; whereas that his uneasiness in social interaction was a function of his own 'impossible expectations of attention' gravitates towards Wittgenstein's 'further description'. And yet if this further description is felt to be as true of his past interactions as his current ones doesn't 'impossible expectations of attention' have considerable explanatory potency which, nevertheless, does not exceed the epistemic warrant that the subject's assent is capable of providing? In cases like these it is as if I was myself the circle that got squashed into elliptical deformity and so can bridge the gap between formal and causal-hypothetical uses of the past via my memories.

The narrator of Proust's 'Remembrance of Things Past' speaks of 'things half felt by me, half-incomprehensible, the full understanding of which was the vague but permanent object of my thoughts'. There are cases where the half-incomprehensible not only sets the problem but contains the solution as well. What was comprehensible lay behind the 'half-incomprehensible' as the face in the picture puzzle. So that when Proust goes on to speak of 'the most permanent and intimate part of me, the lever whose incessant movements controlled all the rest' we do not conceive this 'lever' as a hidden mechanism which will startle us by the novelty of its operation, as do Freud's laws of unconscious distortion of the repressed via the primary process. The account we want and expect of that most 'permanent and intimate part' of us is one in which the movements of the lever will have, nevertheless, been continuously in view but unremarked. If I had a continuous view of all my past ruminations, their sequence and thematic transmutations what would the character of any residual ignorance as to the source of my current proclivities and aversions be? What Freud calls the repeating 'clichés or stereotypes inside us, which perpetually repeat themselves as life goes on' and the 'expectant libidinal impulses' which are 'aroused by . . . each new person coming upon the scene' are just the kind of thing of which we can expect to gain a better understanding without transcending our own anamnestic resources. Their epistemic status is akin to that of Wittgenstein's back-of-mindedness. Although it can be objected that this better understanding cannot encompass the processes according to which the stereotypes were generated in the first place, there is little reason to believe that psychoanalysis is in a position to supply these either. So though explanation via hypotheses is an eligible mode of conferring perspicuity the explanatory possibilities of clarification have been systematically underestimated.

Explanation without hypothesis: anamnesis

What is the probative value of veridical anamnesis? Can a reconstitution of ancient internal soliloquies confirm certain explanatory conjectures, or come as a solution to certain behavioural conundrums? Why shouldn't successful attempts at self-clarification result in causal knowledge? Consider the case of a morbidly bereaved man who realised one day that his reluctance to be comforted and his incessant recurrence to his loss had an ulterior motive – an attempt to distance himself from his own worldly failure – 'All is but toys.' Had he not attained causal knowledge? He had come to recognise the influence of a motive for the prolongation of his grief, but in an intimate way which the expression 'causal hypothesis' doesn't do justice to and is better captured by 'self-clarification', or even 'a-hypothetical explanation', i.e., of explanation which does not transcend that of which the subject may with effort, bethink himself.

The question is whether someone can pass from a state of ignorance to a state of knowledge with respect to causal relations between his past and later states on the basis of anamnesis alone, not only without nomothetic support but even without support from a circumstantially dense narrative that draws on material unknown to him. I remember seeing it suggested that Ernest Shackleton, the polar explorer, owed his determination to excel in physically taxing and dangerous enterprises to a minor organ inferiority – his small hands. I understood that I was not being presented with a generalisation and asked to qualify it appropriately but with the outlines of a story that I was expected to fill in appropriately. And though I might picture witnessable surroundings, such as public school humiliations on the rugger field, the really pertinent bits of filler would consist of recurrent pieces of Shackleton's interior monologue pertaining to resentments, consolatory fantasies and resolves. It would be on getting this right that the truth of the conjecture would depend, and not on the bare counterfactual 'If Shackleton had had bigger hands we would never have heard of him.' Similarly with the conjecture that Prosper Mérimée's 'harsh, curt exterior' was 'created uniquely by the fear of appearing ridiculous', which was in turn due to an occasion in childhood, when, having been scolded, 'he heard his parents laugh at the blubbering face he made'. What would we call being proved right about this but an internal soliloquy consonant with it?

Can our success in retrieving the thoughts which at one time returned repeatedly – like the tunes of a barrel-organ, as Hazlitt puts it – be without explanatory bearings? How can a synoptic view of the images that once dominated and haunted consciousness be bereft of explanatory power? How much would total anamnesis of our past subliminal mumblings and grumblings leave for psycho-analysis to explain? Suppose it were the case that a person's diffi-dence was due to his having, during his formative period, encountered too many significant others 'whose contempt for him was so strong that it became infectious and he caught it' (as Pip says of the effect on him of Estella's disdain). Would we not expect this explanatory formula to stand in some recognisable relation to his habitual broodings and self-communings?

Somerset Maugham supplies an example of someone who while acknowledging the influence on him of certain features of his early circumstances, nevertheless professes dissatisfaction with their per-spicuity-conferring power, i.e., with the lack of what William James called 'inward belonging together of the sequent terms':

My soul would have been different if I had not stammered or if I had been four or five inches taller: I am slightly prognathous; in my childhood they did not know that this could be remedied by a gold band worn while the jaw was still malleable; if they had, my countenance would have borne a different cast, the reaction towards me of my fellows would have been different and therefore my disposition, my attitude to them, would have been different too. But what sort of thing is this soul that can be modified by a dental apparatus?' (Somerset Maugham, *A Writer's Notebook*, London: Pan Books, 1978, p. 327)

(The issue raised by Maugham is raised by Wittgenstein in a note of 1950 (*Culture and Value* 84) 'There is nothing outrageous in saying that a man's character can be influenced by the world outside him.' This provokes Wittgenstein to ask 'but how can what is ethical in a man be coerced by his environment', and to make some suggestions as to how the paradox might be resolved which unfortunately seem to depend on substituting for the initial ques-tion concerning a man's character one as to his actions. (*Culture and Value*, p. 84.)

The speciousness of Maugham's complaint as to the gap left between the vicissitudes of his life course and his soul by empirical explanation is apparent in the tendentiousness with which his puzzle is recharacterised, so that the question as to the relation between his fellows' reactions to him and his current dispositions and attitudes becomes one as to that between a soul and a dental apparatus. The explanatory gap between life history and selfhood seems less unbridgable if the original terms of the question are borne in mind. What else could his soul – conceived of as his attitude towards his fellows and towards himself – be, but the sort of thing that is generated and modified by their reactions to him? It is precisely that sort of thing – a social being. Maugham's complaint of a bewildering gap could more justifiably have been levelled at the relation between Nicolson's blood calcium levels and whatever in the line of male prepossessingness made his heart go thumpity-thump. What lies behind Maugham's complaint, if it is not entirely assimilable to Wittgenstein's rejection of explanation simply because it is explanation, may be a failure in his command of his past and it is doubtful whether he would have made it had his past been perspicuously before him. If Maugham's complaint was due to the apparently non-perspicuous relation between things like a dental apparatus and his self-feeling then there is a certain subclass of self-clarifications – those which are retrospective and pertain to recurrent situations – whose power to fill the gap of which he complained cannot be, *a priori* impugned. The influence of Maugham's stammer, his lack of inches and his distinctive cast of face on the formation of what he refers to as his soul need not be imputed to some subterranean, only psychoanalytically retrievable processes, but may have done their work, if not in full view, at least not hidden from him the way in which the processes that determined the shape of his jaw and his height were hidden from him. Getting retrospectively clear about how one felt about being continually referred to as 'titch' or 'shorty', and of the stratagems one adopted to cope with this situation is the most promising way of bridging whatever perceived gaps generate puzzles as to what Rhees describes as 'the bewildering person one finds oneself to be'. Freud himself once wrote 'self-regard arises in part out of such omnipotence as experience corroborates'. (S. Freud, 'On Narcissism', *Collected Papers*, vol. IV, London: Hogarth, 1956, p. 58.) This portion of self-regard at least should yield its secret to an adequate anamnesis. Robert Hogan, a personality theorist, describes 'the principle end products of personality development' as 'a set of self-images that serve to guide self-presentation during social interaction . . . reflecting the expectations of the significant others in one's life', and goes on to speak of 'a set of self-presentational behaviour's and stylised role performances acquired over the years' (Robert Hogan, 'A socioanalytic theory of personality', *Nebraska Symposium on Motivation 1982: Personality Current Theory and Research*, Nebraska University Press, 1982, p. 78). The story of how these self-images, perceived expectations and stylised role performances were acquired would seem to be eminently eligible for a self-clarificatory anamnestic overview. A procedure analogous to that which Wittgenstein recommends in semantic enquiries may have application in such cases: 'When formulating a rule we always have the feeling: that is something you have known all along. We can do only one thing – clearly articulate the rule we have been applying unawares.' (*Ludwig Wittgenstein and the Vienna Circle; Conversation Recorded by Friedrich Waissman*, Oxford: Blackwell, 1979, p. 77). Can't this be extended to our lives? May we not have been following unawares rules which need only be clearly articulated for some of the perplexities which beset us to be resolved? Would not this be a licit extension of Wittgenstein's famous formula 'the problems are solved, not by giving new information but by arranging what we have always known'? (L. Wittgenstein, *Philosophical Investigations* Oxford: Blackwell 1953, 109).

Doubts and limitations

Of course the transparency of the causal relations between earlier and later phases of a life such as we found in Shackleton *et al.* is not to be found in all reconstitutions of the history of the subject's interior life. Though we may become inward with the 'special individuality in the capacity to love' of which Freud speaks, without discovering its causal conditions – historical or hereditary, unconscious or physiological – there is a point at which what we need to know must transcend what we already know, even in a generous sense of 'already know'. The subject himself may express doubt as to how much his successful anamnesis enables him to explain. Freud's Wolf Man, Sergei Pankieev, said of his seduction by his sister:

the story about the sister is something I remembered. She played with my penis. But must that necessarily have such consequences or is it already a sign of sickness that something like that has consequences? Perhaps it also happened to other boys and had no effect. I don't know . . . It is no reason for someone to turn neurotic (Karin Obholzer, *The Wolf-man: Conversation with Freud's patient – Sixty Years Later*, New York: Continuum, 1982, p. 37).

We need not insist – though it is possible – that more resolute attempts at anamnesis would turn up narrative sequences initiated by his sister's seduction as transparent as those between a felt inferiority and a determination to excel. We may well have arrived at an explanatory gap not to be filled by lived life and which can only be filled by facts which transcend it.

The epidemiological evidence that the early death of a parent predisposes to depression in later life would count as explanatory whether the episode formed the topic of reminiscential further descriptions on the part of a patient or not ('I am terrified that I will lose my husband as I did my father'). There are thus occasions where we must content ourselves with causal relations unmediated by internal soliloquies – and these causal relations could be of the unconsciously mediated kind that Freudians claim to supply. We must thus concede that we may be mistaken in our assumption that the persistent themes of our ruminations played a causal role in producing the character structure we want explained. It may not stand to them as occupational deformations of musculature and posture stood to the daily grind of the coal hauler or cobbler. There may be nothing pathogenic to be recalled and it could be to the noumenal processes of psychoanalysis (or of neurophysiology) that we must look for the secret of our character deformities. The right analogy for some of the puzzles presented by our developmental history may be that presented by the disturbing sexual stirrings of pubescence where a search among the antecedent childhood experiences turns up nothing which would make its salient features perspicuous – like the Gaderene swine. I will only say on behalf of the epistemic powers of anamnesis that what it cannot tell us we are unlikely to learn elsewhere – psychoanalysis notwithstanding.

Why properly psychoanalytic accounts are necessarily non-clarificatory

Stuart Hampshire thinks that psychoanalysis can lead to the 'the discovery that a memory of something in the past has been continuously the reason for inclination and conduct unknown to the subject and without his having been aware of the memory as a memory' (Stuart Hampshire, 'Disposition and memory', *Philosophical Essays on Freud*, edited by R. Wollheim and J. Hopkins, Cambridge: Cambridge University Press, 1982, p. 83). This sounds as if it might appropriately be described as 'clarification', if it is the right kind of discovery. What kind of discovery is it? What kind of evidence does it require or dispense with? Hampshire thinks it has the same dispensation from epidemiological support as have convictions based on conscious memories. This seems to assimilate it to Wittgenstein's 'further descriptions' and other utterances for which the criterion is assent. He writes: 'the now consciously remembered experience explains his inclination in the same sense that an observed feature of his present situation might explain his inclination' (ibid., p. 85), i.e., my formerly unconscious-now-made-conscious infantile fear of my father will explain my phobia for some innocuous situation on to which it has been displaced just as my conscious memory of my father's mistreatment of me explains my resentment of him. 'When the memory is revived there is an instant recognition of the continuity and unbrokenness of the memory discernible in consistent misreading of situations . . .' (ibid., p. 86). This sounds very like Wittgenstein's own example of losing one's way because of the likeness between the topography of a current neighbourhood and that of an old familiar one and then coming to realise the source of one's disorientation by recognition of the misleading similarity. Hampshire's application of this account to psychoanalytic explanation would obliterate the difference between it and Wittgensteinian clarification. But the assimilability is an illusion. If we apply Hampshire's explanatory schema to the genuinely psychoanalytic instances that presumably inspired it, it will be seen to be a false account of them. This is most expeditiously demonstrated by examining Freud's case of the fetishist who went from being an English-speaking child with a fetish for women's noses to a German-speaking adult with a fetish for women's *shiny* noses. Could he superimpose on his current fetish a memory of his ancient one and so understand, in the sense Hampshire advances, how the transition was affected by the fact that the English word glance is a homophone of the German word for shiny ('Glanz'), so that he went from the requirement that he *glance* at women's noses to 'Glanz auf der Nase' ('shine on the nose') (S. Freud, *Collected Papers*, vol. 5, London: Hogarth, 1950, p. 198). The implausibility of Hampshire's account, when construed as a rationale for the validation of psychoanalytic explanatory reconstructions, is not due to the content of this particular instance of Freud's reconstructive achievements but to a much more general feature of psycho-analytic accounts: the manner in which the repressed past is subject to transformations via the primary process, thus making the route from past to present, reconstructible, perhaps, but not recognisable. Freud's infantile aetiological solutions to his patients' manifold disabling susceptibilities are thus often hypotheses – explanations proper, not clarifications – and so not susceptible to the kind of validation described by Hampshire; but humanistic non-psychoanalytic aetiologies like those we have imagined for Mérimée and Shackleton are.

We may have ulterior motives for deciding that our 'bewilder-ment at the sort of person we find ourselves to be' lies beyond our own epistemic resources. Consider the epistemic ambiguity of Diderot's self-questioning as to the influence on his morals of his early glimpse of a little girl's bottom (p. 125). Need it take us in the direction of psychoanalytic causal speculation? Is it not much more likely that the question he was raising was one which anamnestic effort could resolve, if anything could? Since the revelations within reach of clarification are so often discreditable there is every interest in the subject's colluding in the Freudian fiction that they are unconscious and thus sparing themselves the discomfort of remembering in all their dismal detail, the paltry, depraved and vicious impulses and reveries they have repeatedly entertained. Whenever there is a danger of genuine self-revelation the Freudian unconscious comes to the rescue.

Whether on any occasion explanation or clarification is called for only those addressed can say. Whether their perplexities as to their sexuality (or any other topic) are out of reach of empirical discourse is not a matter to be resolved by conceptual analysis of the question posed. How, for example, could it be shown that the dismissive attitude towards empirical explanation that Rush Rhees manifests in the remarks quoted in my introduction is mis-taken? He has no conceptual objections to the appropriateness of explanation and shows that he has not overlooked the problems concerning our sexuality toward which more knowledge could make contributions. But his conclusion, 'What bewilders me about sex is not like that' will exasperate the empirically minded who will ask irritably what else there is to be bewildered about after knowledge of the conditions of the phenomena have been achieved? Self-clarification, an enhanced grasp of the relation in which we stand to our sexuality, and why it perturbs us, provides an answer.

Of course, that there are *any* specimens of explanatory, yet a-hypothetical, anamnesis may only persuade those who have made resolute attempts at autobiographical solutions to the conundrums they present themselves and are convinced they have sometimes succeeded on the basis of anamnesis of the kind Hampshire describes. Among the grounds for the conviction that the motivating rationales for certain behaviours were continuously present, but merely unobtrusive, is that it sometimes happens that when people attain to 'hours of backward clearness' they are struck, in the light of it, by how sensibly, unknown to themselves, they have managed their lives. Decisions that at the time they thought happenstance or impulsive, present themselves to a searching anamnesis as elaborately ratiocinated. For example, how right they were to marry or not to marry; to have no children or to have many; to eschew conventional ambitions or to seek their main satisfaction in professional rather than private life. The bearing of all this on the question whether explanation has been proffered where clarification was called for, is that this will depend on whether it was clarification in the sense explained above which was sought, and not on explanation being conceptually disqualified, or being precluded, by what the situation, independently of our demands, 'required'.

While Wittgenstein's objection to Freud's preference for a non-imminent, causal interpretation of an hysterical neurotic patient's dreams fails, a distinct and stronger case can be made against psychoanalytic accounts which treat the subject's experience as without explanatory power of their own, but just as springboards for inferences as to the real unconscious determinants. This is because, where it is 'bewilderment at the person we find ourselves to be' which drives some to scrutinise their life histories for clues, we do not encounter the overwhelmingly compelling normative demand for causal understanding that serious affliction implies and that Hanly invokes against Wittgenstein.

Whereas there may be a gulf between the demands aroused by the 'significant and enigmatic whole' formed by a 'medley of recollections', L. Wittgenstein, *Culture and Value*, Oxford: Blackwell, 1980, p. 83) and the task of explaining my actions; my actions in their contingency, adventitiousness and overdetermination, may have explanations remote from the self-knowledge I am seeking. Not why

I did what I happened to have done, but the stories I once told myself about things, the topics of recurrent hopes, broodings and exaltations, may be the proper aim of my anamnestic efforts. What I habitually thought about, is closer to what I was, than what I happened to do. But this interest does not have the universal, thereness-for-everyone character implicitly claimed for it in some of Wittgenstein's remarks and in Johnston's gloss, since it is explanation that is sometimes demanded, as Nicolson's curiosity as to the influence of his blood calcium levels, if we do not second guess him, shows.[4]

Explanation is to be forgone, then, not because it is conceptually ineligible nor because clarification is always called for by the problems we set ourselves but because in specific cases we can be brought to acknowledge that what explanation is capable of doing is not what we want done.[5]

Clarification for its own sake

Life may be seen as marriage to an internal soliloquy, revolving endlessly round the same hopes and fears, self-reproaches and self-felicitations, or to a succession of them. An obsessive concern with certain ancient scenes may be due not just to curiosity as to their causes or consequences but to the need to arrive at a consistent and stable view of the matters they raise. The success of our anamnestic exertions need not result in any marked character changes or even enhanced prudence, for us to feel the effort invested in their retrieval justified. The attainment of a perspicuous view of the themes on which our mind played its variations, a discursive equivalent of time lapse photography, can be an end in itself. (Although what Wittgenstein says of exotic rituals is just as true of our own character traits, to assemble their varied manifestation makes them seem more natural and is consequently, in a

[4] Avishai Margalit stresses the subjective nature of the demands made in such cases when, though observing that '... someone who is suffering the pains of love is more likely to find satisfaction in understanding his situation through reading about the sorrows of Werther than through an explanation about the endogenous opiates that mediates his addictive dependence on his beloved' he nevertheless adds, 'Perhaps a compulsive gambler might find more satisfaction in reading about the opiates mediating his addiction to gambling than in reading Dostoievski's *The Gambler*' ('Sense and sensibility: Wittgenstein on the *Golden Bough*', *Iyyun, The Jerusalem Philosophical Quarterly*, 41, July 1992, p. 301).
[5] I discussed a related matter, the possibility of a non-explanatory rationale for literary biography, with David Ellis, a literary critic and biographer of D. H. Lawrence in 'Explanation and biography' in *Imitating Art* ed. David Ellis, London: Pluto Press, 1993.

broad sense, explanatory.) A vivid retrieval of the person I, at various stages, was, spares me surprise at the person I became.

The memory of a remote but much brooded on episode may have an enigmatic expressiveness to be fathomed as well as causal repercussions to be investigated. Once again our interest bifurcates: the phenomenon, whether event or fantasy, is both an item in a causal chain, and thus conceptually eligible for causal investigation into its origins and secret mutations, but also the bearer of a meaning *contained in it*, as the face is contained in a picture puzzle, and not sustaining it as a hidden substrate. This would seem to constitute the apposite epistemic consummation of the perplexities expressed in the childhood reminiscences in which Henry James records the manner in which other children and their diverse 'gifts' shaped his sense of himself: 'They were so other, that was what I felt; and to be other . . . seemed as good as the probable taste of the bright compounds wistfully watched in the confectioner's window' (*Henry James: Autobiography* ed. Frederick Dupee, London W. H. Allen, 1956, p. 101). The problems raised by the phase of James's life which is the subject of this reminiscence are not confined to determining either its causes or its causal repercussions, but could appropriately take the form of providing an *Übersicht*, a synoptic array, of 'the probable tastes' he had been denied and of the 'gifts' not his. It is sometimes these visions of enviable otherness that we want synoptically reviewed. Nevertheless, there are naturally arising questions which do not call for, and will not yield to, this kind of putting-into-order-what-we-already-know procedure. The relation in which Tolstoi's Pierre Bolkonsky stood to Prince Andrew would seem to have been clear enough already.

All the projects Pierre had attempted on his estates – continually switching from one thing to another, and had never carried through – had been brought to fruition by Prince Andrew without display and without noticeable exertion. He possessed in the highest degree a quality Pierre lacked, that practical tenacity which without fuss or undue effort on his part gave impetus to any enterprise.

What this seems to call for is not clarification but explanation of a kind which requires greater knowledge than we possess or are ever likely to possess.

CHAPTER 12

Conclusion: two cheers for the coroner's report

How do we stand to the rival projects of clarification and explanation in general? We must avoid two complementary errors, that of
seeking to resolve by reflection what can only be resolved by
investigation and that of seeking explanation when even its
successful consummation could not give us what we anticipate
from it. Though we can produce specimens of both errors we have
little means of knowing which is most prevalent. The habit of mind
which produced the coroner's report is to be encouraged, even if
it sometimes leads to breaches of decorum, such as proffering it
under circumstances which called rather for theodicy. Here is an
example of someone assigning to scientific explanation powers
that many will feel it does not possess. Richard Dawkins writes, '. . .
the deep and universal questions of existence and the meaning of
life are scientific matters which should properly be dealt with in
science classes'. Among these 'deep and universal questions' he
instances 'Who am I? Where did I come from? What am I for?' (*The
Independent*, September 1993). This is pretty overweening stuff but
it's no matter. This is not why I have withheld the third cheer.

Schiller is reported to have observed that whereas to some
people science is a goddess, to others she is the cow that gives milk.
For many men of our time science is the goddess that gives milk;
and if we stop treating her like a goddess she may stop giving
milk, so let's go on treating her like a goddess. It is not the
coroner's lapse that should concern us. It is when the bereaved
themselves take a fuddled interest in coroner's reports, as with the
holocaust, that we should ask them to reconsider.

What is important to note is not that there are those who will
insist on scratching us where we don't itch but our own tendency
to scratch ourselves where we don't itch. And this is shown not by
logical demonstration but by soliciting responses to questions like

the one Wittgenstein asked, apropos immortality as a solution to
'the problem of the meaning of life', – 'Is not this infinitely pro-
longed existence as enigmatic as our present one?' But we can
imagine that there are those who are unmoved by this question;
who find existence itself non-problematic but only the notion that
it should have a term mysterious and unsettling. A similar tempera-
mental gulf may account for Dawkins' incapacity to imagine a
mysteriousness which is not susceptible to scientific resolution,
and for his boast concerning the capacity of science to resolve the
problem of life's meaning; an issue that some will feel Wittgenstein
disposed of in *The Tractatus* – 'It is not the problems of science
which have to be solved' (L. Wittgenstein, *Tractatus Logico-
Philosophicus*, London: Routledge and Kegan Paul, 1922, 6.53.)

A philosopher has recently written an ingenious paper, 'Qualia
and materialism', on the old, presumably intractable, problem of
rendering it perspicuous why our colour experiences should have
the causal conditions they do and not others, – i.e., of demonstrating what William James called 'the inward belonging together of
the sequent terms', where the sequent terms are the apparently
incommensurable ones of the experience of redness and its causal
conditions. The paper was subtitled 'Closing the explanatory gap'.
So we have the prospect of one of the standard examples of an issue
said to be beyond the powers of science to resolve being reopened.
Are we then to look forward to one day being able to close the gap
between questions like, 'Who am I?' and advances in science, so
that we may be able to say 'The big bang and me: closing the
explanatory gap', or 'Natural selection and me: closing the
explanatory gap'? There are those who would not find my question
rhetorical and I see no way of forcing on them the conviction that
to seek from science a solution to the meaning of life is to fail to
have thought precisely enough on how the articulation between
scientific discovery and the questions of life's meaning is to be
effected. But can the issue be genuinely conceptual when we
cannot neutrally state what the question is with which *any* scientific
answer would fail to articulate? There are those who, like
Wittgenstein, would reject any explanation simply because it was an
explanation, and those who would not. And though it may be due
to fatigue rather than philosophic penetration it is there that I
think this matter must be left, along with other intractabilities, such
as that between those who attach terror to the notion of absolute

solitude and those who can hardly attain to the notion of absolute solitude. It is only if those who conceive of the problem of the meaning of life as resolvable by further information generalise this response that we can speak of error. They would then be as wrong as to the bearing of scientific explanation on the felt perplexity of existence as Wittgenstein was as to the irrelevance of empirical explanation to the problem presented by human sacrifice.

The reason I withheld the third cheer is that the prestige of science produces an inclination to misunderstand ourselves, and to cast all our perplexities into an inappropriately explanatory mode. It must be acknowledged, however, that there is also a tendency, in reaction against this distortion, to place obscurantist limits on the relevance of empirical knowledge. An example of this is that instead of restricting objections to Freud to his confusions and equivocations he is reproached for addressing the questions he raises in an explanatory spirit at all. Drury wrote that 'personality is a matter which the notion of explanation is not applicable to' (M. Drury, *The Danger of Words*, London: Routledge, 1972, p. 92). This is wrong. This genre of objection to an explanatory psychology ought to be treated as Wittgenstein treats Goethe's objections to Newton's optics. The project of explanation is not intrinsically incoherent but fails to meet a particular demand.

What ought to be said is that our lives, when contemplated in a certain spirit, have an expressive character as well as a causal history; they 'seem to be saying something', and it is as if we had to discover what it is they are saying. On such occasions the 'self' we are attempting to fathom does not figure as merely a datum, the causal history or condition of which we must ascertain, but as an obscure object of apprehension whose various and inconstant aspects we are striving to fix and discriminate, and towards which we are trying to clarify our feelings. But this does not preclude an alternative enterprise, a properly explanatory one, which will strip us of any special authority to adjudicate its findings. The fact that extravagant claims have been made as to the success of this project must not blind us to its feasibility, at least with respect to our more determinate afflictions. More importantly, we must acknowledge that even if explanation is not feasible, our existential predicament is not merely one of bewilderment but of genuine ignorance and that it is vulgar knowledge that some of the perplexities presented by the person we find ourselves to be call for. It is this common or garden ignorance which we must reconcile ourselves to. John Berryman may have pondered whether the suicide of his father influenced his own propensity to self-destructive behaviour by delaying it, through a determination not to emulate him, or expedited it, by producing in him a sense of the fatefulness of his inheritance. An *Übersicht* of his 'medley of recollections' on this topic, however tranquillising, would have left his question unanswered. Wittgenstein reminds us that 'one can learn the truth by thinking as one learns to know a face better by drawing it' (L. Wittgenstein, *Zettel*, Oxford: Blackwell, 1967, p. 48, no. 255). But however rewarding we find this activity we must resist the temptation of thinking that it can tell us why the nose is strong or the chin weak. This mode of exploration of my condition may leave me clearer as to who or what I blame and yet no wiser as to who or what is really to blame.

We have therefore not only to live with limits on our power to satisfy our need for revelatory synoptic presentations of the scenes through which we have passed and to articulate our 'half felt, half incomprehensible' thoughts and feelings concerning them, but with simple ignorance of the forces which constrain our existence.

Index